This book is due on the last date stamped below. Failure to return books on the date due may result in assessment of overdue fees.

OCT 1 2 2009
OCT 0 7 REC'D

D0037158

	FINES	.50 per day	

W
wh
pl
of
fea
No
dir
Be
To
Si
A
Br
pl
Be
C
Pa

M.F.A. from Mason Gross School of the Arts is a 1989 recipient of the New Jersey Governor's Walt Whitman Award for Writing, and 1989 recipient of an Honorary Doctorate of Humane Letters from Rider College.

American River College Library
4700 College Oak Drive
Sacramento, CA 95841

AMERICAN RIVER COLLEGE
3 3204 01422 7838

Smith and Kraus *Books For Actors*

THE MONOLOGUE SERIES
The Best Men's/Women's Stage Monologues of 1993
The Best Men's/Women's Stage Monologues of 1992
The Best Men's/Women's Stage Monologues of 1991
The Best Men's/Women's Stage Monologues of 1990
One Hundred Men's/Women's Stage Monologues from the 1980's
Street Talk: Character Monologues for Actors
Uptown: Character Monologues for Actors
2 Minutes & Under: Character Monologues for Actors
Monologues from Contemporary Literature: Volume I
Monologues from Classic Plays

FESTIVAL MONOLOGUE SERIES
The Great Monologues from the Humana Festival
The Great Monologues from the EST Marathon
The Great Monologues from the Women's Project
The Great Monologues from the Mark Taper Forum

YOUNG ACTORS SERIES
Great Scenes and Monologues for Children
New Plays from A.C.T.'s Young Conservatory Volume I
Great Scenes for Young Actors from the Stage
Great Monologues for Young Actors

SCENE STUDY SERIES
The Best Stage Scenes of 1993
The Best Stage Scenes of 1992
The Best Stage Scenes for Men/Women from the 1980's
Scenes From Classic Plays 468 B.C. to 1970 A.D.

CONTEMPORARY PLAYWRIGHT SERIES
Romulus Linney: 17 Short Plays
Eric Overmyer: Collected Plays
Lanford Wilson: 21 Short Plays
Horton Foote: 4 New Plays
Israel Horovitz: Collected Plays

GREAT TRANSLATION FOR ACTORS SERIES
The Wood Demon by Anton Chekhov

OTHER BOOKS IN OUR COLLECTION
Humana Festival '93: The Complete Plays
The Actor's Chekhov
Women Playwrights: The Best Plays of 1992
Kiss and Tell: Restoration Scenes, Monologues, & History
Cold Readings: Some Do's and Don'ts For Actors At Auditions

If you require pre-publication information about upcoming Smith and Kraus monologues collections, scene collections, play anthologies, advanced acting books, and books for young actors, you may receive our semi-annual catalogue, free of charge, by sending your name and address to *Smith and Kraus Catalogue, P.O. Box 10, Newbury, VT 05051.* (800) 862 5423 FAX (802) 866 5346

WILLIAM MASTROSIMONE *Collected Plays*

Contemporary Playwrights Series

SK
A Smith and Kraus Book

A Smith and Kraus Book
Published by Smith and Kraus, Inc.

Copyright © 1993 by William Mastrosimone.
All rights reserved

COVER AND TEXT DESIGN BY JULIA HILL
Manufactured in the United States of America

First Edition: February 1993
10 9 8 7 6 5 4 3 2 1

Library of Congress Cataloging–in–Publication Data
Mastrosimone, William
    [Plays]
    William Mastrosimone: collected plays. --1st ed.
      p. cm. --(Plays for actors series)
    Contents: Sunshine -- Tamer of horses -- A stone carver --
    Extremities -- Nanawatai! -- The woolgatherer -- Shivaree.
      ISBN 1-880399-32-6 : $14.95
      I. Title. II. Series: Plays for actors.
    [PS3563.A8352A19   1993]
    812'.54--dc20   93-40471
                                     CIP

Dedicated to George P. Lane

CONTENTS

written/produced

INTRODUCTION

William Mastrosimone's plays are audacious. This is not all they are of course, but they challenge us, sometimes to make us recoil in shock or at least become unsettled. Who else dares to give the rapist the funny lines as Mastrosimone does in *Extremities*. Nor is this audacity limited to social or political issues. Who else confronts the driver-owner of a transcontinental semi with a reclusive dime store clerk, as in *The Woolgatherer*, or a belly dancer who has the soul of Isis with a shut-in hemophiliac as in *Shivaree*. In these plays Mastrosimone has found vastly dissimilar characters who are drawn to each other, and he probes until he enables us to see past our stereotypical expectations. Fresh insights enrich us and we are reminded of that endless human diversity – indeed human potential – that we so often never recognize on our own.

Mastrosimone's audacity is never calculated, never an end in itself. It is simply the way he sees the world – the world of his imagination. For most of us, with our feet firmly planted on the ground, what seems improbable or implausible is rarely examined. We know a glass that's half empty when we see one. Mastrosimone always sees that glass half full. His imagination isn't conditioned, isn't fettered, indeed is drawn to what most of us dismiss. And far from being cynical, Mastrosimone is non-judgmental and non-despairing. When he does write cynical characters, he pulls no punches. In *Tamer Of Horses* he presents Hector, a street raised teenage thief with a wicked tongue. When confronted by some good and vulnerable people, and by the Hector of Troy, this modern Hector is compelled to define himself by taking action, instead of copping an attitude or hiding in his words.

Mastrosimone's plays have "the common touch." There is no

ix

judgment which separates a cultural and intellectual elite from the great unwashed. Although his characters are usually articulate and often surprisingly well read, they are not erudite and they rarely engage in intellectual debate. The stakes in Mastrosimone's plays are always personally felt and can be understood by all.

The realism of Mastrosimone's plays is deceptive. Because his dramatic structure and his dialogue seem to take their form from "real life," we often overlook the "adventures in wonderland" which his plays often are. The opening scene of *Nanawatai!* is of Afghan women beating a lost Russian tank with sticks. In *Sunshine* a glass booth porno queen has a live lobster for a pet. She talks to it through the glass of her aquarium. These scenes are far from kitchen sink realism. It is the very theatrical cast of his imagination, rather than a reach for non-realistic forms, which elevates his plays and makes them engage our imaginations. Mastrosimone trusts the truth of the imagination as a judge trusts the truth of facts, and that unconditional trust brings theatrical life and intuitive conviction to his works on the stage.

Mastrosimone's plays always make us laugh though only a few would be classified as comedies. It is the wit of his characters that we enjoy. They are quick; they remember what's been said and can turn it into fresh, outrageous directions or to absurdities. A monologue such as Shivaree's when she speaks of her dancing, speaks of Nefertiti, Solomon, Caesar and Tutenkamen but also of the sheiks who look like a sheet sale and the desert that has no biscuits and gravy. It is the sweep, the scope of her imagination that wins us to laughter and applause.

But it is Agostino in *The Stone Carver* who is Mastrosimone's triumphant character. This play could be said to take place wherever the powerful, in the name of progress, are tearing down buildings or bulldozing new roads. The old Italian stone carver strides through this play like a Colussus. He is in his last extremity, has no monologues, indeed a very limited vocabulary in English, but he brings one to laughter and tears and outrage all at once.

Mastrosimone is midway in his career as a dramatist. He is also in constant demand as an established screen writer. This collection is the work of a prolific playwright, especially for one who is barely middle-aged. So we can look forward to new plays which will follow these, and new characters to go on challenging and delighting actors and audiences. His grasp of the potential of the stage is clear and masterful, and he has an open-eyed and open-hearted vision of humanity. It is splendid to know that these volumes are just the beginning.

M.E. Comtois
Founding head of the Playwriting Program
at Rutgers University

A STONE CARVER

*Dedicated to my mother and father
and Betty Comtois*

A STONE CARVER was first produced in 1987 at Seattle Repertory Theatre as THE UNDERSTANDING. The play was directed by Douglas Hughes with the following cast:

AUGOSTINO .... John Aylward
RAFF .... Scott MacDonald
JANICE .... Sarah Brooke

Characters

AGOSTINO MALATESTA
RAFF
JANICE

Setting

I would prefer that the set designer engage the audience's imagination by rendering the set in a minimalist way.

SET: A kitchen. A table, chair, barrels of various sizes. The dimensions of the room should be at least that of a boxing ring.
A kitchen door leads to a backyard (unseen) and alleyway (between this house and the next) which is blocked by a wrought-iron gate.
A cellar door (or entrance way).
An archway that leads to the rest of the house (unseen).
On a dolly rests a block of stone from which the crude outline of a feminine angel begins to emerge by the sculptor's chisel. The face is more developed than the rest. Stone carver's tools are strewn all about.
A Victrola.
SOUND: From time to time we hear distant bulldozers knocking down houses.

A STONE CARVER

Lights up. October light. AGOSTINO sits chipping at the stone. An old phonograph plays a loud, scratchy Caruso singing, "Siciliana," from Cavalieria Rusticana. *Agostino works with the music. He stops.*

AGOSTINO: Brutta bestia! (*Over his shoulder.*) Wha? (*Beat. To the air.*) What the hella you talkin' about? The eyes too big! It's finish now! The whole thing, throw it away. Wha? (*Beat. To the air.*) Look, Emma! The stone's got a como si chiama. Sonomabitcha bast. The stone break, you see? Heh? (*Beat. To the air.*) Make the other eye big? Then I have two mistakes! Porco Dio! Wha? (*Beat.*) Maybe. Maybe not. (*Knocking on the front door. AGOSTINO turns off the music. Beat. More knocking. To himself.*) Brutta bestia. (*He gets a single barrel shotgun, opens the kitchen door, aims the shotgun in the air, fires.*) Who's there?

RAFF: It's me.

AGOSTINO: I said who's there?

RAFF: It's me!

AGOSTINO: Heh?

RAFF: Raff.

AGOSTINO: Who?

RAFF: Open up.

AGOSTINO: Lupo? You come here, I kill you, Lupo!

RAFF: Da!

AGOSTINO: Wha? (*He reloads.*)

RAFF: It's "Mensamens." (*Beat.*)

AGOSTINO: (*To himself.*) Manage a madone! Why you don't say so!

RAFF: Open up!

AGOSTINO: Wait a minute.

RAFF: What?

AGOSTINO: I said wait a minute!

RAFF: You okay?

AGOSTINO: Wha?

RAFF: Open up!

AGOSTINO: Come in the back door!

RAFF: What's wrong with the front door?

AGOSTINO: Shut the hell up and come down the alley! Slow! (*AGOSTINO sees them.*) Who's that?

RAFF: What's the gun for?

AGOSTINO: What the hella you think? They try to take my house. You don't know?

RAFF: Yeah.

AGOSTINO: Who's she?

RAFF: My fiancee. Janice, this is my father.

JANICE: How do you do?

AGOSTINO: Putan a diavolo! What the hell you bring a girl here for?

RAFF: Can we come in?

AGOSTINO: You see cops out there?

RAFF: No.

AGOSTINO: You sure?

RAFF: Yeah.

AGOSTINO: Look.

RAFF: Nobody's there.

AGOSTINO: Heh?

RAFF: It's just us.

AGOSTINO: What the hella you want?

RAFF: I came to see you.

AGOSTINO: Wha you bring the girl for?

RAFF: Can we come in?

AGOSTINO: Porco diavolo.

RAFF: Open the gate. It's locked.

AGOSTINO: Aspet. (*AGOSTINO gets the key hanging around his neck on a string. He stops when he hears RAFF and JANICE talking.*)

JANICE: What's it mean?

RAFF: Mensamens? "Half 'n half." He called me that since I was a kid.

AGOSTINO: Wha?

RAFF: I was talking to Janice.

AGOSTINO: T'who?

RAFF: The girl.

AGOSTINO: How many goddamn girls you got out there?

RAFF: It's the same girl! — Da, will you open the gate? (*AGOSTINO hands him the key.*)

AGOSTINO: Don't break the key in the lock!

RAFF: I don't know why you have to lock the gate.

AGOSTINO: Shut the hell up and lock it again!

RAFF: What for?

AGOSTINO: I said lock it again!

RAFF: All right.

AGOSTINO: Let me see. Shake the lock.

RAFF: See? It's locked. (*AGOSTINO opens the back door, keeping the chain lock fastened. We see RAFF and JANICE through the crack between the door and the jamb. Beat.*)

AGOSTINO: You no see no cops?

RAFF: I told you no.

AGOSTINO: They park down the end.

RAFF: We walked past the barricade, didn't see any cops.

AGOSTINO: No, eh?

RAFF: Can we come in?

AGOSTINO: Wha for?

RAFF: Talk.

AGOSTINO: Talk, eh? (*JANICE hand AGOSTINO a bottle of wine through the crack.*)

JANICE: Hello.

AGOSTINO: Wha's this?

RAFF: For you.

AGOSTINO: What for?

RAFF: I missed your birthday.

AGOSTINO: Hmmm. You miss you ass. (*AGOSTINO closes the door. Beat. He listens. He undoes the chain lock and opens the door. RAFF steps inside.*)

RAFF: What the hell happened here?

AGOSTINO: I don't like no strangers in this house. (*JANICE stops.*)

RAFF: Come in. It's all right.

JANICE: Maybe I'll wait in the car.

RAFF: Janice, will you please come in?

AGOSTINO: Please? You have to tell her please?

JANICE: It's okay, really, Raff.

AGOSTINO: Wha's she want? In or out? (*RAFF takes JANICE by the hand and pulls her inside. AGOSTINO slams and locks the door. Beat.*)

RAFF: This is my father. (*JANICE proffers a handshake. AGOSTINO doesn't reciprocate. Beat.*)

JANICE: How do you do, Mr. Malatesta.

AGOSTINO: Manage a madone. You beg her please come in my house?

RAFF: All right, Da.

AGOSTINO: Please.

RAFF: All right, Da, all right.

AGOSTINO: Please. What's she got down there, diamonds?

RAFF: All right, watch your mouth.

AGOSTINO: You don't like how I talk, get the hell out.

RAFF: Can't you be civil here?

AGOSTINO: I don't know why you bring her here.

RAFF: You want us to go?

AGOSTINO: Wha the hella my care?

RAFF: Give me the key to the gate. (*Beat.*)

AGOSTINO: You wanna glass wine first?

RAFF: Do I want a glass of wine. (*To JANICE.*) See what I'm talkin' about?

AGOSTINO: Make up you goddamn mind!

RAFF: Yeah, Da. How'd the house get like this?

AGOSTINO: Stazit.

RAFF: Where's all the furniture?

AGOSTINO: I burn it.

RAFF: Why's the window boarded up?

AGOSTINO: Kids throw stones, break all the window up and down the street.

RAFF: They broke the stained glass?

AGOSTINO: No. I take it down.

RAFF: There was a huge stained glass window here. Big purple grapes this big; green leaves against a blue sky.

JANICE: Was it antique?

AGOSTINO: Eh?

JANICE: I was answering Raff.

AGOSTINO: Eh?

JANICE: About the stained glass.

AGOSTINO: Wha glass? There's no glass.

JANICE: I know—

AGOSTINO: You see glass?

RAFF: Da—

AGOSTINO: I said I take it down.

RAFF: Da, okay. (*RAFF picks up a mistreated sewing basket.*) What the hell? Look what you did to Mom's sewing basket.

AGOSTINO: Oh, he care about the thing, but he never come see his mother.

RAFF: Jesus Christ. (*RAFF discovers a box of boxing trophies, plaques, hockey sticks. He pulls out a pair of boxing gloves, very old, battered, cracked, and dusty. He looks at AGOSTINO, drops the gloves back in the box.*) Why's all my stuff down here?

AGOSTINO: Take.

JANICE: You won those, Raff?

RAFF: What're all these rat traps for? (*Beat.*) We never had rats before.

AGOSTINO: The bulldozer break all the house on the street, the rats look for food, come here.

RAFF: Jesus.

AGOSTINO: Sit down and shut the hell up! (*They sit at the kitchen table. AGOSTINO puts a short barrel by the table. JANICE stands up by the only chair. AGOSTINO begins dusting it off with his hat.*)

JANICE: Thank you.

AGOSTINO: Wha?

JANICE: Thank you.

AGOSTINO: For wha?

JANICE: For . . . dusting off the chair.

AGOSTINO: It's not for you.

JANICE: Oh.

AGOSTINO: You keep the hell out of this chair.

JANICE: I'm sorry.

AGOSTINO: My chair. (*JANICE sits on a short barrel at the end of the table. RAFF sits on a trash can. AGOSTINO tosses a corkscrew on the table and looks for glasses in a cupboard. He puts down two large glasses, and a tiny glass in front of JANICE. RAFF pulls the cork. AGOSTINO looks at the wine label.*) What the hell's this?

JANICE: Medoc.

AGOSTINO: Eh?

JANICE: Medoc. It's French.

AGOSTINO: French?

RAFF: Don't make a big deal, okay? It's good wine.

AGOSTINO: How it can be good? It's French. (*AGOSTINO pours for all.*)

JANICE: Thank you.

RAFF: Salute.

AGOSTINO: Salute.

JANICE: Cheers. (*Beat.*)

AGOSTINO: Where 'ja get this girl?

JANICE: Salute. (*They drink. The sound of a bulldozer in the distance. Everyone looks up. Beat. The sound of a wall crashing down, and then the bulldozer backing up, fading. Beat. They drink.*)

AGOSTINO: How much you pay for this?

RAFF: Just enjoy it.

AGOSTINO: How much?

RAFF: Don't worry about it.

AGOSTINO: I just wanna know.

JANICE: A lot.

AGOSTINO: What's a lot?

JANICE: About thirty dollars.

AGOSTINO: For that I make a barrel of wine! Where's the taste? I don't taste la terra in this wine. I don't taste no amore in this wine.

JANICE: This is a vintage wine.

AGOSTINO: Wha?

JANICE: It's a hundred percent Medoc grapes from the same year.

AGOSTINO: It's a hundred percent bullshit. (*He tosses his wine down the sink, gets an empty bottle.*) Now I show you what wine is . . . Real wine . . . Thirty dollars . . . (*Exit AGOSTINO down the cellar, laughing.*)

JANICE: Why's he upset?

RAFF: He's not upset. That's him. Watch.

JANICE: Where'd he go?

RAFF: Wine cellar. (*RAFF breaks the shotgun open, pockets the shell, puts the gun back exactly as it was. They both look around the kitchen.*)

JANICE: Is this it?

RAFF: No. It's a box of shotgun shells this big.

JANICE: How do you know he's got more?

RAFF: Lupo saw 'em.

JANICE: Why'd you never visit your mother?

RAFF: Because he was here. (*He finds an old wooden spoon.*) You know how many times my mother shook this at me? (*Beat.*) "Have some pasta." I'm not hungry, ma. "Half a dish." Ma, I'm not hungry. "Two bites." Ma, please. "What am I gonna do? I made a whole potful, for you." All right. "How is it?" Beautiful. "Have more." No. "You don't like it." I love it. "Then have more. Make me happy." All right, ma. (*Enter AGOSTINO with a bottle of* *wine.*)

AGOSTINO: Wha the hella you do? (*RAFF holds the spoon, puts it back. AGOSTINO puts the wine on the table.*)

JANICE: You make wine from scratch?

AGOSTINO: No, from grape.

RAFF: He buys California grape and presses it.

JANICE: Must be a lot of work.

RAFF: It's a killer.

AGOSTINO: How the hella you know?

RAFF: I remember.

AGOSTINO: Remember what?

RAFF: How we made the wine.

AGOSTINO: We?

RAFF: I used to help.

AGOSTINO: Help who?

RAFF: You.

AGOSTINO: When?

RAFF: Lots of times.

AGOSTINO: Name one time.

RAFF: The year you fell off the scaffold, I made the wine myself.

AGOSTINO: That was the year it turned to vinegar.

RAFF: Your memory's starting to go.

AGOSTINO: Oh, yeah? When do you put the yeast?

RAFF: I don't know.

AGOSTINO: What's the diff between aligante, moscato, and zinfandel?

RAFF: Don't know.

AGOSTINO: How long you keep the skins in the wine?

RAFF: Don't know.

AGOSTINO: How much—

RAFF: All right! I don't know!

AGOSTINO: You don't know nothing! When I go, all I know goes in the grave, too. But you like to drink it, eh? And talk about it, eh? But make it. No. You buy that dirty water they sell in the store. This wine. Look. Bella. (*AGOSTINO pours JANICE's glass half full.*) Don't touch! It's too strong for a girl. I cut it with water. Aspet.

JANICE: If you don't mind, Mr. Malatesta, I'll drink it straight.

AGOSTINO: Tell her I cut it with water.

JANICE: I've drunk stronger things than this.

AGOSTINO: Where 'ja get this girl?

RAFF: This wine's over twenty percent alcohol.

JANICE: What's normal?

RAFF: Twelve.

JANICE: It's good.

AGOSTINO: Wha she say?

JANICE: The wine.

AGOSTINO: What about the wine?

JANICE: It's good.

AGOSTINO: How the hella you know?

JANICE: I . . . tasted it.

AGOSTINO: And you know good wine from bad wine?

JANICE: It tastes good to me.

AGOSTINO: It does, eh?

JANICE: Yes.

AGOSTINO: This is the worst goddamn wine I ever make. (*Beat.*)

JANICE: It has more body than the French wine.

AGOSTINO: You Italian?

JANICE: No.

AGOSTINO: It's all right. Don't be ashamed. (*Beat.*)

RAFF: What are you looking at?

AGOSTINO: You make you hair to the side now, eh?

RAFF: I always did.

AGOSTINO: No.

RAFF: It's the same.

AGOSTINO: You comb it back before. Back.

RAFF: No.

AGOSTINO: Don't tell me! Back! Back!

RAFF: Whatever you say, Da. You're never wrong.

AGOSTINO: I don't forget niente. Sono Siciliano.

RAFF: I'm an American.

AGOSTINO: Where you learn to talk like this? Don't say in this house. This is not you. (*Beat. JANICE picks up a trophy.*)

JANICE: (*To RAFF.*) You never said you were a boxer.

AGOSTINO: Golden glove champ. Seventeen. He fight an animale. Everybody say Raffe lose. Bell ring. Raffe run from his corner to animale. One, two, three punch, animale down. K.O. Best day of his life. After that, niente. (*A rat trap goes off somewhere in the house.*) Shhh!

RAFF: Rats?

AGOSTINO: Shh! Brutta bestia. (*Beat.*)

RAFF: So what kind of wine you make this year?

AGOSTINO: No wine.

RAFF: No wine.

AGOSTINO: You know what no wine means? No wine.

RAFF: You make wine every October.

AGOSTINO: I crank the wine press every ottobre since I'm a baby. A baby like this. But this year, no wine. E la luna e perfetta. Lupo don't tell you nothing?

RAFF: I don't see Lupo.

AGOSTINO: No, eh?

RAFF: No.

AGOSTINO: The truck come with the grape. I pay. He put the grape on the sidewalk. Lupo and the cops they wait for me to get the grape. How many times he sit here and talk and eat and drink and laugh?

RAFF: He's almost an uncle.

AGOSTINO: No uncle! Nemico! He wait for me all day, all night, but I don't go out. I let the grape rot. I let the rats eat the grape. That's why no wine this year. My last barrel. (*JANICE looks at AGOSTINO's record collection by the Victrola.*)

JANICE: What do you have besides Caruso?

AGOSTINO: There's nobody else. What the hella you know about opera?

JANICE: I drag Raff to an opera every once in a while. Raff falls asleep.

RAFF: I was resting my eyes.

JANICE: We saw Pavarotti in *Il Trovatore*.

AGOSTINO: You like that?

JANICE: Well, yes . . . very much.

AGOSTINO: Pavarotti, Pavarotti. Don't make me laugh, Pavarotti. When Pavarotti sing, I think a dog got hit by a car, Pavarotti. God whisper in the ear of Caruso, and Caruso sing like un angelo. There was one Caruso. No more. Pavarotti.

JANICE: Caruso, Pavarotti—when they sing "Pagiliacci" I still lose it. Raff took me around and showed your stone carvings. You're really quite wonderful.

AGOSTINO: I made a living. (*RAFF picks up a phone that's unplugged and wrapped in the cord on a shelf.*) Don't touch.

RAFF: Why don't you answer your phone?

AGOSTINO: Who I talk to?

RAFF: Plug it in.

AGOSTINO: Wha for? Put it back. I said put it back.

JANICE: Uncle Lou and Uncle Frank want to talk to you.

AGOSTINO: Why you call them uncle? They no your uncle.

JANICE: They will be in June.

AGOSTINO: Oh, you go there? Why you go there?

RAFF: Eat.

AGOSTINO: Talk?

RAFF: Yeah.

AGOSTINO: Talk about me, eh?

RAFF: A little.

AGOSTINO: The crazy old man, eh? And wha' you say when my brothers talk bad to me?

RAFF: They don't talk bad about you.

AGOSTINO: Bullshit.

RAFF: We went to the cemetery . . . The ground was a little caved in . . . So we smoothed it over and planted some flowers.

AGOSTINO: How nice to think of your mother . . . Too bad you never think of her when she was alive.

RAFF: Hey, look, I don't want to hear this bullshit. (*AGOSTINO rises to answer in kind.*)

JANICE: We planted daffodils.

AGOSTINO: Wha?

JANICE: Daffodils from my parents' garden.

AGOSTINO: Wha color?

JANICE: Yellow.

AGOSTINO: She hate yellow. (*Beat. They drink.*) So what you do now?

RAFF: Construction.

AGOSTINO: Who you work for?

RAFF: Myself.

AGOSTINO: Heh?

RAFF: I own the company.

AGOSTINO: Do wha? Stone carve?

RAFF: No. Just masonry.

AGOSTINO: You do stonework?

RAFF: I run it.

AGOSTINO: Oh, big boss.

RAFF: Not big boss, my own boss.

AGOSTINO: Big shot. Big shit.

RAFF: All right, all right.

AGOSTINO: You use what I teach you?

RAFF: You taught me how to be a good donkey. I taught myself how to make it.

AGOSTINO: But what do you make?

RAFF: Money.

AGOSTINO: From wha?

RAFF: My brains.

AGOSTINO: If you don't sweat, you don't work.

RAFF: Them days are gone.

AGOSTINO: You hire scabs?

RAFF: I hire masons and bricklayers.

AGOSTINO: Sloppy work.

RAFF: Never had a complaint yet.

AGOSTINO: In ten years when the house fall down, you have a complaint! The house I build forty years ago, still no problem! So what you call this company?

RAFF: Malatesta Construction.

AGOSTINO: So people think it's me, eh?

RAFF: Would you be happier if I changed my name?

JANICE: We're building a house in the township.

AGOSTINO: How much the foundation?

RAFF: Sixteen inches.

AGOSTINO: Too small! The house fall down!

RAFF: We'll take a chance. They just put the roof up. We're ready for stonework now.

AGOSTINO: Who do it?

RAFF: We're looking for somebody good. (*Long pause. RAFF and AGOSTINO stare at each other.*)

JANICE: Raff.

RAFF: What?

JANICE: Well?

RAFF: Forget it.

JANICE: What about our stonework?

RAFF: Just forget it.

JANICE: Raff and I would be very happy if you would do the stonework on the house. (*Beat.*)

AGOSTINO: I'm retired.

JANICE: Oh.

RAFF: We'll use one of my guys.

JANICE: But we wanted your father's hands to build it.

RAFF: But he doesn't want to.

JANICE: It would mean an awful lot to us.

RAFF: Janice.

JANICE: Every time we go out, Raff points out your stone carving.

AGOSTINO: Where?

JANICE: The angels on St. Hedwig's. St. Catherine's.

AGOSTINO: Eh.

JANICE: Raff showed me the gargoyles, and the one you made of him . . . And the fountain at the governor's mansion . . . The amphora spilling into the pool, and the amorini playing in the water.

AGOSTINO: The wha?

JANICE: Cupids.

AGOSTINO: Heh?

JANICE: Statues of the naked children.

AGOSTINO: Ah, them little bastards. You like that, eh?

JANICE: A lot. We don't want you because you're Raff's father. We want you because you're the best. You build things to last forever. That's what we want. (*Beat. AGOSTINO turns away. JANICE sees she's making headway.*) Even if we have to wait months, or years, it's worth it to us. (*Beat.*) Even if you just supervise the stonework. You wouldn't have to get your hands dirty.

AGOSTINO: Wha the hella you know? You have to pick up the stone, feel it, turn it, talk to it, find where to break it to make it fit, and drop it and fit perfetto and then you satisfatto, eh?

JANICE: Satisfied?

AGOSTINO: (*To RAFF.*) What make you satisfatto? When they send the money? (*Beat.*)

JANICE: So you will?

AGOSTINO: You don't understand. After I fall from the scaffold, I don't work no more.

JANICE: But you're stone-carving an angel for the church.

RAFF: Janice.

AGOSTINO: How you know?

JANICE: Father Albert said.

AGOSTINO: You know everybody.

JANICE: He's marrying us. So you're coming out of retirement?

AGOSTINO: It's my last job. I do it for God.

RAFF: Insurance policy, eh?

AGOSTINO: Stazit! I spend half my life in the catedrale. Why I should go on Sunday? (*Beat.*) So what kind of stone you use on the house?

RAFF: Fieldstone.

AGOSTINO: Wha?

RAFF: You heard me.

JANICE: Fieldstone.

AGOSTINO: The worst!

RAFF: What's wrong with fieldstone? Give me one reason. One.

AGOSTINO: It breaks easy. It's ugly. I don't like it. It's no good and it's ugly. And I don't work with fieldstone.

RAFF: You hear this guy?

JANICE: Mr. Malatesta, please let me explain. The land we bought is covered with fieldstone. It means we don't have to buy stone.

AGOSTINO: So if the land covered with bullshit, you make the house with bullshit?

RAFF: We don't have money for stone.

AGOSTINO: Then wait until you have money! How you think I make this house? Stone by stone! When I build a house, the earthquake don't break it!

RAFF: We don't have earthquakes.

AGOSTINO: Maybe we get one! Then what? Eh?

RAFF: Then everybody's house falls down.

AGOSTINO: Not my house! It's no fieldstone. I don't work with fieldstone.

RAFF: That's why the architect designed.

AGOSTINO: Ba fungoul architect! You let me talk to him! I put a two-by-four on his head! Fieldstone. (*He looks at JANICE.*) Pavarotti.

RAFF: Da, the guy knows what he's doing.

AGOSTINO: I don't?

RAFF: I didn't say that.

AGOSTINO: But you think it.

RAFF: Forget it.

AGOSTINO: You see this kid? That's his answer to everything. Forget it.

RAFF: That's right. Forget it.

JANICE: Raff, maybe he's right.

RAFF: He's not right.

JANICE: It's for the rest of our lives. Maybe we've been a bit hasty.

RAFF: Okay. What kind of stone would you use?

AGOSTINO: Something beautiful.

RAFF: Like what?

AGOSTINO: Knock you goddamn eye out.

RAFF: Yeah, like what?

AGOSTINO: The best!

RAFF: Like what?

AGOSTINO: Limestone.

RAFF: Limestone? He wants to use limestone. This is a house, not a mausoleum.

AGOSTINO: You gonna tell me about stone? You gonna tell me about stone now?

RAFF: Da, forget it.

AGOSTINO: Forget it.

JANICE: Raff?

RAFF: What? What?

JANICE: Let's think about it.

RAFF: No! The house is fieldstone! That's all!

JANICE: What's the stone on this house?

RAFF: What do you think? Limestone.

AGOSTINO: What's wrong with my house?

RAFF: It's not for me.

AGOSTINO: She like it.

JANICE: It's perfect for you but I'm not sure about us.

AGOSTINO: Stazit! When the fieldstone house fall down, don't call me to fix.

RAFF: Don't worry about it.

AGOSTINO: And don't invite me there.

RAFF: Don't worry about that either.

JANICE: You're welcome anytime, Mister—

AGOSTINO: I don't take a chance in a fieldstone house.

RAFF: Everything he builds has to be a medieval fortress.

AGOSTINO: House fall down, everybody die.

RAFF: (*To JANICE.*) Now you see what I'm talkin' about?

AGOSTINO: You never sell that house with fieldstone—

RAFF: All right, da! You had the last word! (*Beat. They drink. AGOSTINO downs his wine, grabs two pairs of boxing gloves out of the box, dangles them in RAFF's face.*)

16 / *William Mastrosimone*

AGOSTINO: Put the gloves, me and you.

RAFF: Forget it.

AGOSTINO: Hai paura, eh?

RAFF: I don't do that anymore.

AGOSTINO: Oh, big shot no sweat, eh?

JANICE: Father Albert would like to know when he can pick up the angel with a crew.

AGOSTINO: A crew, eh?

JANICE: To pick up the angel.

AGOSTINO: What crew? Cops to trick me?

JANICE: Father Albert wouldn't do that.

AGOSTINO: He's a sneaky sonamabitch. (*He crosses himself.*) He try and take my shotgun.

RAFF: Maybe he was just trying to make sure nobody got hurt over here.

AGOSTINO: He's on their side.

RAFF: Da, look outside. Bulldozers just leveled four city blocks on every side of you. You think the road's gonna go around you? What're you, the exception? The road's an ugly fact. You have to accept it.

AGOSTINO: Basta.

RAFF: The city's expanding. More people, more cars, more roads.

AGOSTINO: Basta!

JANICE: If you two would like to speak privately, I don't mind.

RAFF: Janice, stay, please. (*JANICE steps on a rat trap. It clamps onto the front of her shoe.*)

JANICE: Somebody please take this filthy thing off my foot. (*AGOSTINO removes the trap from her foot, removes the shoe from her foot, looks at her instep, puts the shoe in his back pocket.*)

RAFF: You okay?

JANICE: Yes, thank you. Pardon me.

AGOSTINO: Heh?

JANICE: My shoe?

AGOSTINO: Wha?

JANICE: You have my shoe.

AGOSTINO: Heh?

JANICE: May I have my shoe, please?

AGOSTINO: Forget about it.

RAFF: Da, what're you doing?

AGOSTINO: Heh?

RAFF: Give her the shoe.

AGOSTINO: Wha shoe?

RAFF: What shoe.

JANICE: The shoe in your back pocket.

AGOSTINO: Peccata.

RAFF: Da, what the hell's wrong with you? Give her the goddamn shoe.

JANICE: Take your time, I'll be outside.

RAFF: Janice, hang on a second.

AGOSTINO: Say please, puppydog, and maybe she let you stay.

RAFF: You win. (*They start to go.*)

AGOSTINO: Heh. (*They stop, turn to AGOSTINO.*) One glass of wine and I give the shoe.

RAFF: Pour.

JANICE: No. I want my shoe first.

AGOSTINO: Che bocca.

RAFF: Let's do it his way, okay? (*Beat.*) Pour. (*AGOSTINO pours one for RAFF, one for himself, goes to pour for JANICE but she covers her glass with the flat of her hand.*)

AGOSTINO: No wine, pasta ajuta?

JANICE: No, thank you.

AGOSTINO: You said you like. (*RAFF downs the wine.*)

RAFF: Give me the shoe.

AGOSTINO: No shoe. Pasta ajuta don't drink.

JANICE: Excuse me—what's he calling me?

RAFF: Pasta ajuta . . . Dry pasta.

JANICE: In other words—?

AGOSTINO: Who the hell wants it?

JANICE: Charming.

AGOSTINO: Heh?

JANICE: Mr. Malatesta, I'm a very understanding person—to a point. We've just reached that point. Now please, my shoe.

AGOSTINO: Why?

JANICE: Why?

AGOSTINO: Why?

JANICE: You don't take peoples' shoes!

AGOSTINO: Why?

JANICE: It's mine!

AGOSTINO: So's my house. (*He hands her the shoe. Beat. She takes it, goes to put it on. He holds her arm to give her balance. A rat trap goes* *off somewhere in the house.*) Shh! (*Silence.*)

RAFF: What?

AGOSTINO: Shh! Brutezza! Rat this big. Three legs. I catch one time but Brutezza eat off his leg and run away! (*Exit AGOSTINO with a baseball bat. RAFF continues to look for shotgun shells.*)

RAFF: I shouldn't've taken you here. Lupo didn't say he was this mental.

JANICE: Raff, you can't say he's non-comp because he doesn't understand eminent domain. He's confused. He's frightened.

RAFF: He also gives names to three legged rats. (*Sound of a baseball bat hitting something many times.*)

AGOSTINO: (*Offstage.*) Die, you ugly sonamabitch! Die!

RAFF: Okay? (*RAFF continues to look for shells.*)

JANICE: Raff, you're the only one he can trust now, and, forgive me, but you don't give him the courtesy you'd give to a tenant you're evicting. He's your father. I've seen you in town council meetings with crude, rude, irate people voicing the most illogical arguments, and you sit in the hot seat behind the mic with a patience not to be believed. Why is it all your virtues are lost in your father's house? (*AGOSTINO laughs from a farther room; more sounds of the baseball bat.*) What will we say to our kids? "You have a grandfather but we don't talk to him." I don't want us to start off with a broken family. You have a chance to start over with him. Why can't you just put your arms around the guy and say, "Dad, it's not so bad; you have family; we'll take care of you."

RAFF: We'll take care of you? This is not your folks where we all make a cocktail and pull up a chair and let it fly. This is another country over here. We'll take care of you.

JANICE: Let me try. I've got nothing to lose. I'm dry pasta.

RAFF: Hey, he wouldn't say that if he wasn't crazy about you. Now, look, sweetheart, for me to say, "We'll take care of you," I've gotta get a lobotomy. Let me do what I came to do.

JANICE: But not guff. Be nice. Explain the legal process to him. In a nice way.

RAFF: Nice.

JANICE: Yes.

RAFF: "Da, you don't move out some nice cops are gonna put you in a nice cell."

JANICE: Raff, please. Just say, "Dad, you don't deserve to live this way—" (*Enter AGOSTINO laughing.*)

RAFF: Da, you know something? You live like an animal.

AGOSTINO: Heh?

RAFF: You want to live with rats?

AGOSTINO: Yeah.

RAFF: Yeah, he says.

AGOSTINO: I like rats.

RAFF: He likes rats. He likes rats.

AGOSTINO: Yeah. Rats more onesto than people. Onesto. What I say? Onesto.

RAFF: Honest.

AGOSTINO: The rat say, "Hey, Malatesta, we take you house." But not Lupo. Lupo come to take my house, but he don't say that. He say, "Hey, Augi, open the door, we drink you wine and talk, eh?" But c'mer, you see this. I shoot the wall and he run and drop the papers.

RAFF: What papers?

AGOSTINO: The papers.

RAFF: What papers?

AGOSTINO: From the state.—Then Lupo send Father Albert. He say, "Good morning, Mr. Malatesta, I come for you to make confession." I say, "Here's my confession, Father," and I shoot the wall and he run like hell.

RAFF: I know. Then Uncle Frank and Lou came and you shot the wall again. Your own brothers.

AGOSTINO: Don't tell me about brothers. All you life you eat, sleep, play, work together. Go to school together. When we was small, big boys beat up Lou and Frank. I go fight for them. We stick together. Now? They should be here with me! They should help me fight now!

RAFF: What do the papers say?

AGOSTINO: What the hella my know?

RAFF: Didn't you read them?

AGOSTINO: No.

RAFF: Da, you have to read 'em.

AGOSTINO: Shut the hell up and drink you wine.

RAFF: Why don't you read 'em?

AGOSTINO: I start to, but the first word it piss me off, so I don't finish the rest.

JANICE: What word?

AGOSTINO: What the hella my know?

RAFF: Let me see the papers.

AGOSTINO: I don't know where I put.

RAFF: Look for 'em.

AGOSTINO: What for?

RAFF: So I can see the word.

AGOSTINO: What for?

RAFF: So I can read it.

AGOSTINO: Never mind you own goddamn business.

RAFF: I want to help.

AGOSTINO: Help me?

RAFF: Yeah, that's right.

AGOSTINO: Quando sono morto nella terra.

RAFF: C'mon. Where are they?

AGOSTINO: Wha?

RAFF: The papers.

AGOSTINO: Wha papers?

RAFF: From the state!

AGOSTINO: Wha state?

RAFF: What state. How many states do you live in? This state!

AGOSTINO: Can't remember nothing.

RAFF: C'mon, get 'em. (*AGOSTINO produces a wad of soiled and ragged papers from somewhere which shows his utter contempt for authority. RAFF carefully unfolds them. Reading the first page.*) "Whereas . . . "

AGOSTINO: That's the sonamabitch!

JANICE: What's the word?

AGOSTINO: What the hella you care?

RAFF: Whereas.

AGOSTINO: That's the one!

RAFF: Why didn't you just skip over it?

AGOSTINO: Skip you ass! Them goddamn lawyers they make up that word!

RAFF: Da, no they didn't.

AGOSTINO: They make it up to confuse me.

RAFF: Da, that's a real word.

AGOSTINO: So you on their side?

RAFF: I'm not on their side! It's a real word.

AGOSTINO: All my life I never hear this word.

RAFF: It's a word.

AGOSTINO: What language?

RAFF: English.

AGOSTINO: Lawyer English?

RAFF: Yeah.

AGOSTINO: Ba fungoul lawyer English. Che vuol dire? What's it mean?

RAFF: Whereas?

AGOSTINO: Yeah.

RAFF: It means . . . ahhhhh . . . whereas, you know.

AGOSTINO: If I know, you think I ask you?

RAFF: Janice, what's it mean?

AGOSTINO: Porco diavolo.

JANICE: Whereas means . . .

AGOSTINO: Heh?

JANICE: It's like a traditional thing?

AGOSTINO: Wha?

JANICE: It's . . . a preamble to a document.

AGOSTINO: (*To air.*) You see what the hell I'm talkin'? You ask what one word means, and they give you another word that's a more hard!

JANICE: No, it's simple. A preamble is something that "goes before."

AGOSTINO: Before what?

JANICE: Before the rest of the document.

AGOSTINO: Heh?

JANICE: The papers!

AGOSTINO: Don't talk bullshit to me! You tell me what the hell's a whereas or shut the hell up!

RAFF: Da, it's not important what it means.

AGOSTINO: If they use it to take my house, it's important! Whereas, whereas. I know what "where" means. Like where you goin', eh?

RAFF: Right.

AGOSTINO: And I know what "as" means. Like, pasta ajuta is dumb as Raffe. But when you put the where with the as, ba fungoul! I can't figure out the sonamabitch.

JANICE: In place of whereas, you could say "because of."

AGOSTINO: Because of?

JANICE: Yes.

AGOSTINO: Because of what?

JANICE: Because of—whatever.

AGOSTINO: Eh?

JANICE: Because of whatever the papers say.

AGOSTINO: Wha they say?

JANICE: I don't know. Why don't we sit down and read them together?

AGOSTINO: You read 'em.

JANICE: Maybe we can figure a way out of this.

AGOSTINO: The Mafia come to my father in Sicilia. "Give us money." He give. They come every week. He give. He tell me, "Go America. Nobody take what's yours." I come, work, pay the land, pay the stone, make the house. The state come. "Give us the house." Not for sale. They take. Mafia, state, che e la differenza? Basta. (*AGOSTINO laughs and pours wine for all, picks up the boxing gloves.*) C'mon, Mensamens.

RAFF: No.

AGOSTINO: How many times we box in the kitch?

RAFF: A lot.

AGOSTINO: His mother say, "Don't break the kitch, go fight outside."

RAFF: If I didn't go five rounds with the old man before supper, I didn't eat.

AGOSTINO: I make him tough.

JANICE: I noticed.

AGOSTINO: Sometimes I make believe he knock me out.

RAFF: After I decked him for real.

AGOSTINO: Fantasia! Andiamo!

RAFF: No.

AGOSTINO: Perche no? 'Cause you mother no here to stop the fight? Eh?

RAFF: Forget it.

AGOSTINO: His mother stop the fight when Raffe cry like a baby.

RAFF: This guy's a real dreamer. I never cried.

AGOSTINO: Never?

RAFF: He used to hit me in the face 'cause he knew that made me crazy.

AGOSTINO: Then he fight good, like an animale. Me and you. One round!

RAFF: I think we should talk about the papers first.

AGOSTINO: No papers! Put the gloves!

RAFF: No gloves.

AGOSTINO: Chicken, eh?

RAFF: Yeah.

AGOSTINO: Chicken.

RAFF: That's right.

AGOSTINO: You not the man you was.

RAFF: Who is?

AGOSTINO: Me. Me. More than before. (*AGOSTINO throws a pair of boxing gloves at RAFF.*) Put the gloves!

RAFF: Da, the papers are important!

AGOSTINO: Okay, let's talk about the papers.

RAFF: Good.

AGOSTINO: What's whereas mean?

RAFF: I don't know.

AGOSTINO: No more papers! Put the gloves!

RAFF: Da, will you listen?

AGOSTINO: No whereas, no talk! Put the gloves!

RAFF: This is a Summons and Complaint.

AGOSTINO: More words.

RAFF: You were summoned to appear in court, but you just didn't go.

AGOSTINO: Nope.

RAFF: Da, when you get a Summons, you have to appear.

AGOSTINO: If the court want something from me, tell the court come to me.

RAFF: That's not how it works.

AGOSTINO: I don't leave the house for nothing. Niente.

RAFF: And how long do you think you could hold out?

AGOSTINO: Who knows?

RAFF: It's a matter of time, isn't it?

AGOSTINO: Sure. They break down sometime.

RAFF: Da, the state doesn't break down.

AGOSTINO: Me, too.

RAFF: They're strong.

AGOSTINO: Me, too.

RAFF: How will you make it through the winter?

AGOSTINO: The rats teach me.

RAFF: And eat what?

AGOSTINO: Fresh meat everyday. (*Beat.*)

RAFF: They'll put in the state hospital.

AGOSTINO: They don't put me nowhere.

RAFF: They'll come and break down the door.

AGOSTINO: And the next day they dig a lot of graves. I don't shoot the wall next time. (*AGOSTINO puts a box of shotgun shells on the table. Beat. RAFF opens the box, takes one out, looks at it.*)

RAFF: You got it all figured out, don't you?

AGOSTINO: No. Not you. I don't figure you out. I don't know where you stand.

RAFF: See this? It's called a Writ of Possession. That means the state condemned and appropriated the property.

JANICE: They took it.

RAFF: They gave you fair market value and put it all in escrow.

JANICE: Put it in the bank in your name.

RAFF: Move out today and you get it all.

AGOSTINO: If no.

JANICE: You lose it all.

RAFF: You forfeit everything.

AGOSTINO: Who make the law? Lawyers, eh? Why they don't put the road in their house?

RAFF: Da, don't be ridiculous.

JANICE: Raff—

RAFF: I pulled every string I could for you. I had 'em keep the lights on and the water running. Don't say thanks. You might get a hernia. Half of my day is wasted on the phone about you. To hold up a road for you. I don't have any more time for this. I owe favors on top of favors. You're breaking the law. You have to obey the law. Your neighbors loved their houses, too.

AGOSTINO: But not too much.

RAFF: Awww, stop it, will ya? They took the cash and ran 'cause most of 'em wanted out, and they got a good deal, too. With state money I could get you a nice condo on a golf course. No maintenance. Not just a home. An investment. Think about it. You could meet people your age. Live decent. You don't even use all the rooms here. Get smart, da. (*AGOSTINO dumps the shotgun shells on the table in such a way that they slide across and fall into RAFF's lap.*)

AGOSTINO: See how they fall? That's how many people fall for this house. (*He flings the papers in RAFF's face. Beat.*) Condo. . . . Golf course. (*Pause.*)

JANICE: Well, you're asking him to give up his home, but what're you offering him?

RAFF: How 'bout this? There's a goddamn bulldozer gonna come through that wall tomorrow about 8 a.m. That a good reason?

AGOSTINO: How you know that?

JANICE: You know what I mean, Raff? Where can he go? With whom? For how long? (*Beat.*)

RAFF: We'll take care of him.

AGOSTINO: Wha?

RAFF: Your brothers and myself, we'll take care of you.

AGOSTINO: Wha?

RAFF: We'll take care of you. (*AGOSTINO slaps RAFF in the face. RAFF impulsively raises a hand to strike back. AGOSTINO reels back. Beat.*)

AGOSTINO: Hit me. What's amatter? Why you don't hit me? Hai paura, eh? Afraid, eh? Eh? Eh? Wha? Wha? Now get the hell out. Go obey the law. (*AGOSTINO throws RAFF the gate key. RAFF and JANICE begin to go. RAFF opens the gate.*) Wha kind of flowers you put the grave?

JANICE: Daffodils.

AGOSTINO: Wha?

JANICE: Daffodils.

AGOSTINO: What's this, something new?

JANICE: No, no, they've been around awhile.

AGOSTINO: Around awhile? You put old flowers?

JANICE: No, no, new flowers.

AGOSTINO: Manage a madone!

JANICE: Fresh flowers! Fresh flowers!

AGOSTINO: Eh . . . How long they last?

JANICE: Oh, I don't know . . . Years . . . We planted them.

AGOSTINO: You know how to plant?

JANICE: Yes.

AGOSTINO: How?

JANICE: We dig a hole and put the plant—

AGOSTINO: No! No! No! First you make the hole, then you put the water, to make is soft. Then you put the—wha?

JANICE: Daffodils.

AGOSTINO: Manage a madone. If them flowers die, you pull them!

RAFF: All right.

AGOSTINO: I don't want no dead weeds on her grave.

JANICE: We'll make sure.

AGOSTINO: You fix the grass?

RAFF: Yeah.

AGOSTINO: Don't let it get ugly.

RAFF: We keep it up.

AGOSTINO: Don't forget.

RAFF: We won't.

AGOSTINO: 'Cause I don't go there.

RAFF: I know.

AGOSTINO: 'Cause she's still here, not there. (*Beat.*) You mother and father alive?

JANICE: Yes.

AGOSTINO: In good health?

JANICE: Yes, thank you.

AGOSTINO: God bless them. What's he do, you father?

JANICE: Self-employed.

AGOSTINO: But what's he do?

JANICE: Business.

AGOSTINO: Business.

JANICE: Un-huh.

AGOSTINO: What kind of business?

JANICE: Partnership.

AGOSTINO: But what does he sell?

JANICE: His services.

AGOSTINO: Wha service, manage a madone!

JANICE: He's a lawyer.

AGOSTINO: Don't be ashamed you father.

JANICE: I'm not.

AGOSTINO: He can't help he's a sonomabitch lawyer.

JANICE: Excuse me. My father is an honest man. You don't know him. How can you say that?

AGOSTINO: I'm sorry. You right. It's nice you don't let nobody speak bad to him. Some people go eat and drink with the enemies of the father, and when the enemies talk bad, they sit and shake the head like a dope. (*Beat.*) Ho fame?

RAFF: No.

AGOSTINO: I can tell you hungry.

RAFF: He can tell.

AGOSTINO: Blackbirds.

RAFF: You got any?

AGOSTINO: No, I get 'em.

RAFF: Where?

AGOSTINO: Manage a patat! Where do blackbirds come from, dope? We catch with the trap. Let's eat.

RAFF: It's too much trouble.

AGOSTINO: Trouble? Wha trouble?

RAFF: Some other time.

JANICE: You eat blackbirds?

RAFF: It's an old country thing. They're delicious.

AGOSTINO: Then stay! Where you have to go?

RAFF: I have a meeting.

AGOSTINO: Wha meeting?

RAFF: Town Council.

JANICE: Very important meeting. Today they're voting on whether to paint more yellow curbs downtown.

AGOSTINO: Ho leguemi del giardino.

RAFF: Nah.

AGOSTINO: Arugula.

RAFF: You got arugula?

AGOSTINO: Wha the hella you think?

RAFF: You don't have arugula.

AGOSTINO: How much you want? I bring in the wheelbarrel. Eh?

RAFF: Nah.

AGOSTINO: Nah? Wha nah? Slice tomato con basilico e olio dei oliva.

RAFF: Nah.

AGOSTINO: Listen to this guy. His mouth make water but he say nah.

JANICE: Raff.

AGOSTINO: C'mon, you love blackbirds and arugula. Don't tell me no!

RAFF: You don't have any bread. I can't eat blackbirds without bread.

AGOSTINO: Listen to this guy.

JANICE: Well, go buy some.

AGOSTINO: That's right. You go for bread, I catch the birds.

JANICE: And get some canoli.

AGOSTINO: And hurry up.

RAFF: I can't, I can't.

JANICE: Oh, Raff, c'mon.

AGOSTINO: Aspet! (*Exit AGOSTINO. RAFF picks up the shells on the floor, puts them in the coffee pot.*)

RAFF: Help me.

JANICE: Raff, you'll lose him. You'll lose him.

RAFF: Help me.

JANICE: You'll lose him if you do it this way.

RAFF: I don't have a choice.

JANICE: Just talk to him. Man to man. That's all he wants.

RAFF: Did you see how he is? You don't talk with this guy. You listen. I never could talk with him. Never.

JANICE: If you bend a little, maybe he will, too.

RAFF: I did all the bending I'm ever gonna bend. Janice, there's too much unfinished business between me and him. Don't open it up now or you'll see things you wish you didn't see. You understand that?

JANICE: This'll be the last time you have with him in this house.

RAFF: What do you want from me?

JANICE: Just stay for a meal?

RAFF: I don't know. (*He's about to pour wine into the coffee pot to ruin the shells. Janice stops his hand.*)

JANICE: I thought you'd be some kind of hero and negotiate him out of the house. This is just sneaky. He's your father. (*RAFF pours the wine into the coffee pot. Beat.*)

JANICE: Oh God.

RAFF: Don't give me that. Don't give me that. Last time I stood in this kitchen and told him I quit stone carving, he threw a punch. I ducked, caught him with a left hook then sent him ass over heels. At the funeral we didn't say one word to each other. Not a word for two years. My uncles had to stand between us the whole time. If you weren't here, we'd be slugging it out right now. That's just the way it is. He looks at me and wants to knock me down. And I feel the same way. You'll never understand that. That's why I never took you here.

JANICE: Why'd you take me here today? To hide behind? (*RAFF puts down the wine as AGOSTINO enters with a homemade jar of tomato sauce.*)

AGOSTINO: Pasta putanesca with sauce your mother make with her hands. Last two jars. Eh? How you say no to your mother? (*Beat.*)

RAFF: Blackbirds and pasta and we go.

AGOSTINO: First go take down the spauracchio.

RAFF: The what?

A Stone Carver / 29

AGOSTINO: Spauracchio.

RAFF: Talk English.

AGOSTINO: C'mer so I can smack you, dope. Spauracchio. What's this? (*He poses like a scarecrow.*)

RAFF: Crucifixion?

AGOSTINO: Scarecrow! Manage a madone! You knew that when you was five! Go take down the spauracchio whereas I break your face. (*Exit RAFF.*) Pasta ajuta, go pick lettuce and tomato. Pasta ajuta.

JANICE: Yes?

AGOSTINO: C'mer.

JANICE: Yes?

AGOSTINO: You know how, eh?

JANICE: To pick a tomato?

AGOSTINO: Si.

JANICE: Of course.

AGOSTINO: Tell me how.

JANICE: I know how to pick a tomato.

AGOSTINO: If you so smart, tell me how.

JANICE: You . . . just pick it.

AGOSTINO: No. No.

JANICE: What?

AGOSTINO: You think you know everything. You don't know nothing. I teach. Come here. First, you take the tomato in la mano, eh? Like this. (*Taking her hand with tenderness, folding her fingers into a fist, treating it like a tomato on the vine.*) Then you make a little twist, eh? Like this. Little. Not big. And if it's ripe and it's ready, it falls off, eh? If not, it stays.

JANICE: I understand.

AGOSTINO: Don't force it! (*Grabbing her hand again.*) Little. Not big.

JANICE: I know how!

AGOSTINO: Show me, manage a madone! (*She attempts it.*) Too big! (*She tries again.*) Too hard! Easy! Little. (*Trying again.*)

JANICE: Little.

AGOSTINO: Molto bene. Little.

JANICE: Little. (*Enter RAFF carrying a scarecrow made with cross sticks, RAFF's old hockey shirt, goalie mask for the face, holding a hockey stick in one hand, a cap pistol in the other. He sees AGOSTINO and JANICE holding hands.*)

RAFF: You ruined my hockey stuff.

AGOSTINO: Pick peppers, too. Red and green. Then get in the kitchen and chop garlic and hurry up. (*Exit JANICE.*)

JANET: Excuse me ...

AGOSTINO: Don't say nothing. This is marriage.

RAFF: What else you need at the store?

AGOSTINO: Bread. Semolina. Thick crust. You know what I like.

RAFF: How many?

AGOSTINO: All you can carry.

RAFF: I need the gate key. (*AGOSTINO throws the gate key to RAFF, moves a barrel to the center of the room.*) So what do you think?

AGOSTINO: If she's for you, don't ask nobody. Help me here. If you not sure, don't marry.

RAFF: I'm very sure.

AGOSTINO: Then don't ask me.

RAFF: Forget it. (*He starts to go.*)

AGOSTINO: Before I marry, I go to my father first. I ask his opinion. That's rispetto. You know that word, rispetto?

RAFF: Respect.

AGOSTINO: I hear that word, I get a cold up my spine. Rispetto. Sonamabitch.

RAFF: What?

AGOSTINO: This is a beautiful goddamn barrel. (*AGOSTINO takes a hammer and knocks the hoops off the barrel.*)

RAFF: What're you doing?

AGOSTINO: This barrel older than you . . . Look at that wood . . . LoBianco made this . . . When he make a barrel, it last a hundred years . . .

RAFF: Why do you have to burn it? It's a good barrel.

AGOSTINO: We make a fire, cook the blackbirds. Smell that wood. C'mer, smell. What you smell?

RAFF: I don't know.

AGOSTINO: Manage a madone. Smell the sonamabitch. Smell like muffa. What's the word? Dewmil.

RAFF: Mildew.

AGOSTINO: C'mere. What you smell. Smell this barrel. What you smell?

RAFF: Vinegar.

AGOSTINO: That smell's good. You smell vinegar, you put the new wine. But you smell muffa . . . Ahh, I talk to myself. You don't make no wine. You might get your hands dirty, eh?

A Stone Carver / **31**

RAFF: Who has time?

AGOSTINO: Everything my father teach me, it all stop in this house. (*AGOSTINO bundles up the staves and takes the legal papers for the fire.*)

RAFF: Hey, I'm out there making a living. Who has time?

AGOSTINO: Where I get time? Make time. Stone carve in the Malatesta family seven generation. Seven. Number eight throw it away. You, number eight.

RAFF: You can't make a living stone-carving today.

AGOSTINO: I do.

RAFF: Did.

AGOSTINO: I made a good living.

RAFF: So who wants to make a living? A garbage man makes a living. And the guy who owns the company, he lives.

AGOSTINO: Freddo, freddo. Cold.

RAFF: What can I say?

AGOSTINO: It's in the Malatesta blood to make beautiful things.

RAFF: So you drive by the church and look up and say, "I carved that angel." Big deal. You have security? Nobody knows who did it. Two hundred years from now, if there's still a world, the angel will still be up there. And where'll you be? So you made a lot of beautiful things. And you forget about the times you had to do masonry to get by.

AGOSTINO: You have good years, you have bad years.

RAFF: Don't you get it, Da? Classical's out. Today you build to meet the code. There's no angels in the code.

AGOSTINO: Freddo, freddo.

RAFF: I didn't invent that. That's the world.

AGOSTINO: Maybe I go back to Sicilia.

RAFF: You're crazy.

AGOSTINO: Maybe I work there.

RAFF: There's a classical job on the courthouse. They're looking for a carver.

AGOSTINO: Yeah?

RAFF: They want a statue.

AGOSTINO: What kind?

RAFF: Statue of justice.

AGOSTINO: With the things?

RAFF: What things?

AGOSTINO: In the hand, the things.

RAFF: Scales, yeah.

AGOSTINO: What is it?

RAFF: Scales of justice.

AGOSTINO: I make one like that in Philadelphia. Three hundred feet up.

RAFF: I remember.

AGOSTINO: What remember? You don't help me with that job.

RAFF: I was right next to you on the scaffold.

AGOSTINO: No, no, don't say me this. You afraid to go up the scaffold. I go alone.

RAFF: No, no, no, no, no. You made me go up.

AGOSTINO: I don't do that.

RAFF: No, not you. You interested in the job?

AGOSTINO: You work with me?

RAFF: I'm not in that line of work anymore.

AGOSTINO: You afraid to go up the scaffold?

RAFF: Afraid? Why should I be afraid of a shaky scaffold on a shaky ladder 300 feet up with a half-nuts guy with wine on his breath? Why should I not want to carry your tools and walk three steps behind you and be in dirty pants all the time and work in the rain, work when I'm sick, work in the cold, and work when other people take the day off? Why shouldn't I want to taste grit in my sandwich and go home with splinters in my arm from heaving planks? Why shouldn't I want that life anymore? Afraid? Or smart?

AGOSTINO: I try to make a man of you!

RAFF: I was born a man. I don't need your help.

AGOSTINO: I go up the scaffold, wind, rain, snow, what the hella my care?

RAFF: Yeah, but you're nuts.

AGOSTINO: Maybe.

RAFF: If you're interested in the job, let me know.

AGOSTINO: They tell you hire me?

RAFF: A guy on the search committee owes me a favor. (*Beat.*) I'm gonna go.

AGOSTINO: Hurry up.

RAFF: Da.

AGOSTINO: Wha?

RAFF: So what do you think of her?

AGOSTINO: Don't have a big wedding.

RAFF: Why do you say that?

AGOSTINO: She want kids?

RAFF: Yeah.

AGOSTINO: You?

RAFF: In a few years.

AGOSTINO: Don't wait. Do it now.

RAFF: All the money's tied up in the new house.

AGOSTINO: Don't worry, when you hear the baby cry, you find the money on the trees. (*To JANICE in the garden.*) Hey, you wait for tomatoes to grow? Hurry up!

RAFF: Don't talk like that to her.

AGOSTINO: Look at the faults now. They get more worser later. Don't marry for a pretty face. It change. Everything change. If you lose the legs, she stay with you? If you lose the eyes? Lose the house, the car, no money? She want you? Or something else? You know the answer here?

RAFF: No.

AGOSTINO: Then don't marry.

RAFF: You can't know those things until they happen.

AGOSTINO: If she the right woman, you know. If you don't know, tell her, "I change my mind. Maybe you make better wife to somebody else. Goodbye." Finuto. Can you say that to her?

RAFF: What the hell are you talkin' about? We're engaged. You understand? We're engaged.

AGOSTINO: But you can say it?

RAFF: I don't have to.

AGOSTINO: Me and you, we go to my village, Villaba in Sicilia, and we find you a beauty, eh? A woman like a stone. She don't move for nothing but you, eh?

RAFF: You outta your mind?

AGOSTINO: I tell her for you.

RAFF: No.

AGOSTINO: I tell her one, two, three, finuto.

RAFF: Da. No.

AGOSTINO: One, two, three.

RAFF: No. (*JANICE enters.*)

JANICE: Where's the canoli and bread?

RAFF: I didn't leave yet. We were just talking.

AGOSTINO: What took you so long?

JANICE: Why's that tree all wrapped up?

AGOSTINO: Fig tree.

JANICE: Why's it wrapped in a blanket?

RAFF: He buries it before the frost.

JANICE: Buries what?

RAFF: The tree. Digs it up by the roots, buries the whole thing in a hole. At Easter, he replants it.

AGOSTINO: Santa Maria, the kid remembers something. Raff wants to tell you something, one, two, three.

RAFF: Don't listen to this guy.

JANICE: What?

RAFF: Be right back. See ya. (*RAFF kisses JANICE goodbye. AGOSTINO locks the gate behind RAFF.*)

AGOSTINO: How nice.

RAFF: (*Offstage.*) Shut up!

AGOSTINO: And don't buy no creampuffs! His mother make him creampuffs when he's this big. I never know he grow up to be a creampuff. Get the thing.

JANICE: What thing?

AGOSTINO: Bird trap. Open the trap door. Put the stick. Tie the string. (*Exit JANICE.*)

JANICE: (*Offstage.*) To what?

AGOSTINO: Your nose! The stick! To what. You have a degree, eh? (*Throwing her a stale loaf.*) Shut the hell up and break in the cage. Too small! If it's small, the bird can fly away. If big, it has to stay and eat, eh? Bring the string in the house. Hurry up. (*Enter JANICE.*) Get two chairs. Get the wine. Get two glasses. Pour. Sit down and shut the hell up. Hold the string.

JANICE: How long do we have to wait?

AGOSTINO: What the hella I know?

JANICE: When do I pull the string?

AGOSTINO: I tell you . . . Why you don't pour wine for you?

JANICE: I don't want any.

AGOSTINO: C'mon, take a little wine, pasta ajuta.

JANICE: It's very kind of you to offer. But thank you anyway.

AGOSTINO: You see this wine? If you drink this wine for a hundred years, you live to be very old.

JANICE: Is that a fact?

AGOSTINO: But you don't drink before. You wise guy. You cover glass with hand like this. Have some wine.

JANICE: I'm really not thirsty.

AGOSTINO: Why not?

JANICE: I'm just not.

AGOSTINO: You nɔt mad?

JANICE: No.

AGOSTINO: You mean you this way all the time? (*AGOSTINO takes a pepper from the basket of vegetables.*) Have a pepper.

JANICE: No, thank you.

AGOSTINO: C'mon.

JANICE: No, thanks.

AGOSTINO: Have a pepper.

JANICE: I don't want one.

AGOSTINO: They good.

JANICE: I'm sure.

AGOSTINO: Ever eat one like this?

JANICE: No.

AGOSTINO: Then how could you be sure? Have a pepper.

JANICE: I don't like hot food.

AGOSTINO: This kind is sweet.

JANICE: It looks hot.

AGOSTINO: You never go by looks.

JANICE: It's sweet?

AGOSTINO: Like honey.

JANICE: It looks hot.

AGOSTINO: I don't care what it looks. I teach. You see this kind with the— (*He whistles to indicate the curved tip of the pepper.*)

JANICE: Yes.

AGOSTINO: When the pepper has the—(*He whistles.*) —It's sweet like candy. But watch out for the straight ones. They burn like fire. Have a pepper.

JANICE: Why do I have to eat something?

AGOSTINO: It's the way I am. You in my house. I don't have much, but what I have, it's yours. (*JANICE nibbles the end of the pepper. The unbearable hotness registers on her face. She spits it out. AGOSTINO laughs. She grabs for the wine bottle, but AGOSTINO holds it at arm's length.*) What's a matter, pasta ajuta? You wanna a little wine now? (*JANICE yanks the wine from his hands and guzzles from the bottle.*) Manage a madone! You like wine, eh? I thought you was no thirsty. (*Offering a pepper.*) This make you feel better.

JANICE: You sonofabitch!

36 / *William Mastrosimone*

AGOSTINO: Bella, bella, I'm sorry . . . Here, take my chair . . . Listen . . . C'mon. (*AGOSTINO puts on a Caruso aria. JANICE sits. They listen.*) You hear that? Listen. You hear that?

JANICE: Yes.

AGOSTINO: He's a beautiful sonofabitch.

JANICE: You like Puccini? (*AGOSTINO kisses his fingers in answer.*) Toscanini?

AGOSTINO: Magnifico.

JANICE: Verdi?

AGOSTINO: Un genio.

JANICE: Mozart?

AGOSTINO: Heh?

JANICE: Mozart.

AGOSTINO: Wha?

JANICE: Wolfgang Amadeus Mozart.

AGOSTINO: Wha country?

JANICE: Austria.

AGOSTINO: No Italiano, no can make opera.

JANICE: What about "Cose Fan Tutte"?

AGOSTINO: He make that opera?

JANICE: Yes.

AGOSTINO: His mother was Italiana.

JANICE: I don't think so.

AGOSTINO: Then he stole it from Puccini.

JANICE: Mozart was a hundred years before Puccini.

AGOSTINO: No, no, no.

JANICE: Yeah, yeah, yeah.

AGOSTINO: Stazit! You make the birds go away! Shh! (*He points to unseen birds alighting near the bird cage.*)

JANICE: Pull the string?

AGOSTINO: Wha I say? I tell you when. Aspet! (*Beat.*) So he show you my work on the churches, eh?

JANICE: Yes.

AGOSTINO: He tell you I'm stone carver, eh?

JANICE: The best around.

AGOSTINO: He said that?

JANICE: Yes.

AGOSTINO: How he said it?

JANICE: He said— "My father's a stone carver—the best around."

AGOSTINO: Sometimes that kid's not so dumb. I want to teach him, but he don't want to learn it.

JANICE: Was he a good stone carver?

AGOSTINO: The worst. When he make the anglo, it look like a diavolo.

JANICE: Isn't that proof that he shouldn't do it?

AGOSTINO: No! It takes twenty years to make a stone carver.

JANICE: Maybe he doesn't have your gift. Maybe he has other gifts.

AGOSTINO: Wha gift? I break my ass for this gift.

JANICE: Pull the string?

AGOSTINO: When I tell, manage . . . (*JANICE picks up a picture from the base of the statue.*) Is this—? Was this your wife? (*Beat.*) She's beautiful.

AGOSTINO: She's ugly in the picture. She's more bella than the picture.

JANICE: Raff looks just like her.

AGOSTINO: Eh?

JANICE: The eyes.

AGOSTINO: Eh.

JANICE: Where'd you meet?

AGOSTINO: Sicilia. My father know her father. My father say, "I got a son." Her father say, "I got a daughter." Boom.

JANICE: Boom?

AGOSTINO: Boom.

JANICE: Did you love her?

AGOSTINO: Wha love? You learn to love. You no start with love. You end with love. You want a family, he want a family, poco a poco, love, eh? (*Pause.*) Never find her no more. Just one like that. If she was starve, she don't say nothing. Eyes, big. And when she laugh, she fall on me, like this. Lose the babies all the time. I should have six kids. Just one live. Don't love somebody too much. Then when they go, Dio cane . . . Eat. Sleep. Work. Niente. (*Beat.*) So where you meet Raff, in a bar, eh?

JANICE: I don't go in bars, eh. He called me about property I had listed. We met, he took me to dinner, boom.

AGOSTINO: Raffe asked you to marry?

JANICE: Yes. (*AGOSTINO laughs.*) What's so funny?

AGOSTINO: Tell me how he said it.

JANICE: Don't you think that's personal?

AGOSTINO: C'mon, just whisper it to me.

JANICE: I'm sorry.

AGOSTINO: C'mon, I don't say nothing.

JANICE: No.

AGOSTINO: You say yes?

JANICE: Of course.

AGOSTINO: You crazy.

JANICE: Why?

AGOSTINO: You should think about it.

JANICE: Why?

AGOSTINO: He's got a lot of faults.

JANICE: Like what?

AGOSTINO: Bad temper.

JANICE: Temper?

AGOSTINO: Bad.

JANICE: I never saw a temper.

AGOSTINO: The worst. Like my father.

JANICE: He's so sweet.

AGOSTINO: Sweet? Tell him put the gloves on and you see sweet. Animale. And tell you the truth, I don't know if one woman enough for him.

JANICE: I'm enough.

AGOSTINO: How you know?

JANICE: We live together.

AGOSTINO: Heh?

JANICE: Raff and I live together.

AGOSTINO: Sleep the same bed?

JANICE: Of course.

AGOSTINO: So you have the canoli before the pasta, eh?

JANICE: I just wanted to be careful not to make another mistake. I'm divorced.

AGOSTINO: So wha. Raffe, too.

JANICE: Pardon?

AGOSTINO: Wha? He don't tell you?

JANICE: No.

AGOSTINO: Three kids. He don't tell you nothing?

JANICE: No.

AGOSTINO: That sonamabitch. He do this all the time. Bring the girls, don't tell 'em nothing. But I tell you one thing . . . I miss them kids. He beg her to take him back, but I don't blame her for to go. He stay out all night, gamble, drink, who knows what else, eh? Beautiful girl, too. I show you her picture.

JANICE: No! . . . Show me. (*AGOSTINO laughs.*) You rat!

AGOSTINO: What's amatter? You feel gelosia, eh?

JANICE: I felt like killing him!

AGOSTINO: Look at you face! All red!

JANICE: You come to our wedding?

AGOSTINO: No.

JANICE: Why not?

AGOSTINO: No pants.

JANICE: I'm sorry?

AGOSTINO: No pants. Rats ate all my pants.

JANICE: We'll get you a tux.

AGOSTINO: Wha?

JANICE: Tuxedo.

AGOSTINO: Get the hell away from me! I don't wear that. Like this or nothing. Maybe you have a fight and divorce again, eh? That's the way it is today.

JANICE: No. I want this one to work.

AGOSTINO: Before you sleep, you make peace, every night, capice? You fight, lay in bed, he no talk, you no talk, eh? You the woman, so you give in first.

JANICE: Wait a second.

AGOSTINO: Stazit. I tell you how. You turn in bed, eh? Make you foot bump his, eh? And you say, "Excuse me," and he say, "Don't worry about it," and you say, "Goodnight," and he say, "Goodnight," then maybe a kiss, finuto. But think bout it, because you marry a lazy dope.

JANICE: You're wrong.

AGOSTINO: I'm not wrong. He's a dope. I never see such a dope.

JANICE: Some day your kid's going to be Mayor of this town.

AGOSTINO: Him? Mayor of ugotts!

JANICE: Careful! You might have to eat a lot of words later.

AGOSTINO: I have a big appetito.

JANICE: You better have a big appetito, because that kid of yours is going to run for Mayor next year, and he's going to win.

AGOSTINO: Raffe? He's just a kid. Wha's he know? Niente.

JANICE: You should hear him speak at the town council meetings. He moves people.

AGOSTINO: He move you, eh? C'mon, tell me how he said it— "Please marry me, my sweet baby?"

JANICE: That's between us.

AGOSTINO: So when you marry?

JANICE: Sometime next summer.

AGOSTINO: You don't love nobody. If you love, you can't wait, you marry now.

JANICE: We can't now. We want to travel first.

AGOSTINO: Travel, what travel? When you make babies?

JANICE: Eventually.

AGOSTINO: Wha?

JANICE: In the future.

AGOSTINO: Wha future?

JANICE: After we're married awhile.

AGOSTINO: Of course after while! You think babies happen overnight?

JANICE: No.

AGOSTINO: It takes months and months!

JANICE: I know.

AGOSTINO: Manage! Somebody better talk to you! A girl you age, she should have three kids hang on the legs and one in the oven, and the only travel is in the backyard to hang the clothes.

JANICE: Blackbirds.

AGOSTINO: Aspet.

JANICE: Pull the string?

AGOSTINO: Aspet, aspet.

JANICE: What's that mean, aspet?

AGOSTINO: Shut the hell up. See that big sonomabitch?

JANICE: Yes.

AGOSTINO: I try to catch him for a year but he too smart.

JANICE: Really?

AGOSTINO: He beautiful, eh?

JANICE: Yes.

AGOSTINO: I want to eat him for supper. When he go in the trap, pull the string.

JANICE: This is mean.

AGOSTINO: Raffe's mother hold the string, too. I turn around, she let 'em go. (*JANICE picks up the picture again, studies it, looks up at the statue, holds the picture up to the face of the angel.*)

JANICE: That's her.

AGOSTINO: Emma.

JANICE: You carved her face in stone.

AGOSTINO: Go back to all the church. All the angeli are Emma.

JANICE: Really?

AGOSTINO: Go look.

JANICE: Raff never told me that.

AGOSTINO: Because he don't see, capice?

JANICE: Nobody ever noticed that before?

AGOSTINO: Just you.

JANICE: That smile tells me everything about her.

AGOSTINO: Sometimes I make the smile one, two, three and Dio touch me and say, "Augi, piano, piano. This stay here sempre. Forever. Sempre." And the monsignor say, "Malatesta, you take all day to make the smile. Hurry up. Finish next week the whole job." So I hurry up and Dio make me fall from the scaffold and he say, "Who the boss, eh? Piano, piano." So now I listen to the boss. He's a stone carver, too, eh? First one. Ten Commandments, eh? And the monsignor say, "Malatesta, hurry up!" I say, "God is my boss." And monsignor say, "Malatesta, who pay you?" (*He looks at the vacant air.*)

JANICE: What?

AGOSTINO: Shh.

JANICE: Blackbirds?

AGOSTINO: Shhhh.

JANICE: Pull the string?

AGOSTINO: Stazit. Emma? Sta qui?

JANICE: What is it?

AGOSTINO: She's here.

JANICE: Who?

AGOSTINO: Emma.

JANICE: What?

AGOSTINO: Emma . . . Dov'e? . . . (*He laughs.*)

JANICE: What?

AGOSTINO: She like you.

JANICE: How do you know?

AGOSTINO: (*To Emma.*) What? She's a little skinny but its the best Raffe can do. (*Beat.*) Che fa? Che fa?

JANICE: What's the matter?

AGOSTINO: No, Emma, no sta qui Raffe . . . See her face? . . . She worry for Raffe . . . Emma, che importa? . . . He went to the store . . . Bread . . . We eat now . . . She don't believe.

JANICE: Why not?

AGOSTINO: Perche? . . . She go look for Raffe from the window . . .

42 / *William Mastrosimone*

She always wait for him to come home . . . She sit by the window upstairs . . . (*Beat.*) Why Raffe come here? Don't tell me stonework. I don't say anything.

JANICE: To visit you.

AGOSTINO: I know him thirty years. I wipe his nose. He cry in the night, I go see in his room. I know how his brain work. Raffe don't visit nobody. I see in his eye. Tell me. I don't say nothing. Why Raffe come here?

JANICE: Talk about the papers.

AGOSTINO: Who send him here? Lupo?

JANICE: This is between you and him.

AGOSTINO: You marry him, you marry me, too. We family now. Tell me.

JANICE: You want me to speak against the man I'm about to marry? Is that the sort of wife you want me to be? (*Beat.*)

AGOSTINO: No.

JANICE: Then stazit.

AGOSTINO: Okay. Now I know everything.

JANICE: The big sonamabitch's in the trap.

AGOSTINO: Pull the goddamn string. (*She pulls the string. AGOSTINO exits.*)

AGOSTINO: (*Offstage.*) Hello, my little friends! I'm so happy you come for supper. Hey, big sonomabitch! (*Enter RAFF.*)

RAFF: Hey, open the gate!

JANICE: Raff's back! Give me the key!

AGOSTINO: Aspet! Look how many!

RAFF: Janice!

JANICE: Wait a second! (*AGOSTINO opens the gate. RAFF comes in with bakery box and a loaf of bread.*)

AGOSTINO: Just one! I eat one myself.

RAFF: They didn't have any more.

AGOSTINO: What're you talkin' about? They make bread all day there.

RAFF: That's all they had.

AGOSTINO: You see cops?

RAFF: No. You okay?

JANICE: Yes, sure.

AGOSTINO: Raffe, kill the birds. Hurry up.

JANICE: How do you kill them?

AGOSTINO: Raffe! C'mon! I make the fire and boil water. Make pasta ajuta pull the feathers.

JANICE: I'm not doing that!

AGOSTINO: Then you don't eat.

JANICE: Then let go all the birds I would've eaten.

AGOSTINO: I let go nothing.

JANICE: How do you kill the birds?

AGOSTINO: Twist the neck.

JANICE: That's cruel.

AGOSTINO: If birds was bigger than us, they twist our neck. Shut up and kill the birds. You remember how?

RAFF: Yeah.

AGOSTINO: How?

RAFF: Twist the neck one way and then the other way quick.

JANICE: C'mon, really? Raff, you can't do that!

AGOSTINO: Ask pasta ajuta please to kill the birds.

RAFF: You kill the birds.

AGOSTINO: Oh, how nice! She don't let you!

RAFF: I don't want to get dirty.

AGOSTINO: I know who the boss in that house! Maybe she make you have the baby! I go make the fire, puppy dog! You, chop garlic.

JANICE: Please. (*JANICE pours herself a water glass of wine.*)

AGOSTINO: And hurry up. Tell her chop garlic.

RAFF: You tell her.

JANICE: Ask me nice.

AGOSTINO: Straighten 'em out in the beginning or later on—oh boy. Who drank all the wine?

JANICE: It's the best. (*She pours the last few drops in her glass.*) Let's have some more.

RAFF: That's enough.

AGOSTINO: Stazit. Wine make her face rosy.

RAFF: Be careful. That stuff'll put you to bed.

AGOSTINO: Put the gloves. Before we eat, five minutes.

RAFF: No.

AGOSTINO: Pasta ajuta, pour wine for everybody.

JANICE: Please.

AGOSTINO: And hurry up.

JANICE: Teach me Italiano.

AGOSTINO: Wha for?

JANICE: So I capice when you talk. How do you say—to

understand?

AGOSTINO: Capire.

JANICE: Capire. How do you say, I understand, you understand, he understands?

AGOSTINO: I don't understand, you don't know what the hell you talkin' about, and he's a dope. (*AGOSTINO throws the gloves at RAFF.*) Put the gloves.

RAFF: I don't want to get all sweaty.

AGOSTINO: Pasta ajuta, tell Raffaele put the gloves.

JANICE: What'd you call him?

AGOSTINO: His name.

JANICE: Say again?

AGOSTINO: My father's name—Raffaele.

JANICE: Raffaele—I didn't know that. That's nice—Raffaele.

RAFF: Don't ever call me that.

AGOSTINO: He's ashamed!

JANICE: He's ashamed of me, too. On the way here, he asked me to take off my eye shadow and button all my buttons. Why'd you never tell me your real name, Raffaele?

RAFF: I was going to when we got to know each other better.

AGOSTINO: You sleep the same bed, eh?

RAFF: What else you tell him?

AGOSTINO: (*Laughing.*) Everything.

JANICE: Raff, no.

AGOSTINO: The way you ask her to marry. Everything.

JANICE: Raff, you know I didn't.

AGOSTINO: "My sweet baby . . . " (*AGOSTINO laughs.*)

JANICE: He's lying, Raff.

AGOSTINO: C'mon, put the gloves.

JANICE: C'mon, Raffaele.

RAFF: You're drunk.

JANICE: Bullshit.

AGOSTINO: Tell him, pasta ajuta!

JANICE: Put the gloves.

RAFF: Forget it.

AGOSTINO: Look, pasta ajuta, he's afraid.

RAFF: Of what?

AGOSTINO: Put the gloves.

JANICE: Put the gloves, Raffaele.

RAFF: No more wine for her.

AGOSTINO: Let her drink. She don't have a meeting.

JANICE: That's right. I love this wine.

AGOSTINO: Drink, drink.

JANICE: In Italiano?

AGOSTINO: Beva.

JANICE: Beva vino.

AGOSTINO: C'mon, like before. See what you marry, pasta ajuta?

JANICE: C'mon, let me see how you fight.

RAFF: When I put the gloves on, I play for keeps.

AGOSTINO: Me, too.

RAFF: I don't go in for this pansy-ass love-tap bullshit.

AGOSTINO: Me, too.

JANICE: Put the gloves, puppy dog! (*AGOSTINO laughs.*)

RAFF: I can't hit him.

AGOSTINO: Wha's he say?

JANICE: He can't hit you because he loves you so much.

AGOSTINO: He don't fight because he don't want you to see he's a creampuff.

RAFF: What?

AGOSTINO: Creampuff. Maybe she see a creampuff and change her mind, eh?

RAFF: Put the gloves!

AGOSTINO: Andiamo!

RAFF: One round.

AGOSTINO: Can't do two rounds, eh?

RAFF: I don't need two rounds to knock you down.

AGOSTINO: You don't make one round with me, creampuff. (*RAFF takes his shirt off.*)

RAFF: You hear this guy?

AGOSTINO: You don't last one minute with me.

RAFF: I don't talk. I just fight.

AGOSTINO: We see! Tie the gloves, pasta ajuta. (*While she does this, Raff shadow-boxes.*) Showoff.

RAFF: It's been a long time.

AGOSTINO: Just give me one punch.

RAFF: Try and get near me!

AGOSTINO: One punch! One!

RAFF: Hey, I got only one kind of punch—K.O.

AGOSTINO: Me, two kinds— (*Holding up his left hand.*) Hospital. (*Holding up his right.*) And graveyard. Andiamo!

RAFF: Janice, take my watch. Clock us for one minute rounds.

AGOSTINO: C'mon, c'mon, c'mon. (*JANICE gets a pot and wooden spoon for a bell; sounds it.*)

JANICE: Gentlemen! In your corners!

AGOSTINO: Make the bell!

JANICE: Stazit. Gentlemen, center of the ring. All right, no hitting below the belt. And when I say break, you break. Shake and back to your corners. I want a clean fight.

AGOSTINO: How you know all this!

JANICE: I take Raff to opera, he takes me to fights. (*JANICE sounds the pot and spoon. The men enter the ring. AGOSTINO claims the center. RAFF dances around him. AGOSTINO pivots on his heels.*)

AGOSTINO: C'mon, get close to me.

RAFF: I'm gonna dot your eye.

AGOSTINO: Come and do it. (*RAFF attacks with a flurry of wild but meaningless punches. AGOSTINO laughs. RAFF backs off when AGOSTINO presses him.*)

AGOSTINO: You dance nice, but no punch. (*RAFF attacks again and backs off, alternating clockwise and counter-clockwise circles, bobbing and weaving, but throwing weak punches.*)

RAFF: You're getting old.

AGOSTINO: What're you gettin'? (*RAFF corners AGOSTINO—or so he thinks. AGOSTINO allows himself to be backed into a corner where RAFF works the body. AGOSTINO throws his first punch—a solid gut-buster. RAFF backs off, hurt and covering up badly. AGOSTINO laughs and pursues. JANICE hits the bell. RAFF drops his guard. AGOSTINO sucker-punches RAFF and knocks him down after the bell. RAFF goes down hard with a groan.*)

JANICE: Hey! I rang the bell!

AGOSTINO: Wha bell?

JANICE: How many bells are there?

RAFF: You bastard.

AGOSTINO: Wha bell? Do it louder! I'm old!

RAFF: Okay, okay, you wanna street fight? Okay, okay.

AGOSTINO: See, pasta ajuta? Temper, temper. Think about the marriage.

RAFF: Next round, you'll be prayin' for the bell!

AGOSTINO: I'm scare.

RAFF: You're gonna pay for that.

AGOSTINO: Watch out. Maybe I break your nose again, eh?

RAFF: Yeah, and maybe I just might break yours this time.

AGOSTINO: Do it, creampuff.

RAFF: Let's go, let's go! (*RAFF begins round two with a head-long attack. For a brief moment they go toe to toe. AGOSTINO goes down and laughs.*)

JANICE: One, two, three—

RAFF: You hit the canvas, chump. You had enough?

AGOSTINO: Don't make me laugh!

JANICE: Gentlemen! Let's box! (*They fight. RAFF moves in fancy backward circles, keeping his guard at a cocky low. AGOSTINO pivots and waits till RAFF's back is to JANICE.*)

AGOSTINO: Pasta ajuta, no more wine. (*RAFF looks at JANICE, who's just standing there. AGOSTINO clips him in the jaw and sends him to the floor.*) One! Two! Nine! Ten! The winner!

JANICE: What happened to the rest of the numbers?

AGOSTINO: I leave one out?

JANICE: In your corner till the man is up!

AGOSTINO: Where'd ja get this girl? What I teach you when you was this big? Never let you guard down, eh?

JANICE: You okay?

RAFF: Just grazed me.

JANICE: That why you turn green? (*AGOSTINO laughs.*)

RAFF: C'mon, let's go, let's go, let's go.

AGOSTINO: Pasta ajuta, temper, temper, see?

JANICE: Okay, gentlemen, let's box. (*They fight. RAFF comes out with a new stratagem—peek-a-boo style—keeping his gloves up around his face, peeking at his opponent through the small space between the gloves. AGOSTINO keeps his distance. Both are hurting and therefore afraid of each other now.*)

AGOSTINO: Wha's this?

RAFF: It's called peek-a-boo, I got you.

AGOSTINO: Peek-a-boo, ba fungoul.

RAFF: Make a mistake and you're mine.

AGOSTINO: You knew more when you was a kid . . . What happened, eh? (*RAFF attacks, forces AGOSTINO into a defensive position.*)

RAFF: You're goin' down.

AGOSTINO: Knock me down.

RAFF: You think I can't?

AGOSTINO: Do it.

RAFF: Watch out.

AGOSTINO: It takes guts to knock your father down.

RAFF: I guess I got guts.

AGOSTINO: Eh, Mr. Mayor? (*RAFF looks at JANICE. AGOSTINO takes advantage, throws a punch when RAFF's head is turned but misses.*) She tell me everything.

RAFF: Oh, yeah?

AGOSTINO: You run for Mayor, how you ask her to marry—

JANICE: You know I didn't, Raff.

AGOSTINO: Everything.

JANICE: Raff, no.

AGOSTINO: Why you come here—everything. (*RAFF stops boxing.*)

RAFF: What's going on here?

AGOSTINO: Everything. (*He laughs. JANICE rings the bell. Both men go to their corners.*)

JANICE: Raff, he's kidding.

AGOSTINO: Am I?

JANICE: Raff, believe me. (*AGOSTINO laughs.*)

AGOSTINO: What's the matter, Mr. Mayor? You quit now? You look sick.

RAFF: You're out of your mind.

AGOSTINO: Pasta ajuta, pour two glasses!

RAFF: No wine.

AGOSTINO: Drink! (*JANICE hands them both a glass of wine center.*) Cin'd'ano.

RAFF: Cin'd'ano. (*They drink from brim to lees never taking their eyes off each other. JANICE rings the bell. Round three begins when both charge out and streetfight toe to toe, hurting each other, both backing off and feinting.*)

AGOSTINO: C'mon, Mr. Creampuff! Hit your father! Knock me down! You have guts to hit your father!

RAFF: Sometimes it's the easiest thing in the world.

AGOSTINO: Breathe hard, Mr. Mayor? Eh, Mr. Mayor in you fieldstone house? I make trouble and maybe nobody vote for you, eh? That why you come her, Mr. Mayor?

RAFF: Can't hold your wine, eh?

AGOSTINO: Hit your father. (*AGOSTINO hurts RAFF with a punch. RAFF returns it.*) Wait.

RAFF: What?

AGOSTINO: My heart.

RAFF: Too bad.

JANICE: Raff! Stop!

RAFF: It's bullshit. (*AGOSTINO laughs and gives up his little ruse.*)

AGOSTINO: He smart for a dope . . . Now I can smell you, Mr. Mayor . . . You smell scare . . . You scare of me, eh? . . . Or maybe you stay out too late over Uncle Frank and Uncle Lou . . . (*Getting no answer, AGOSTINO pounds RAFF. JANICE sounds the bell. AGOSTINO ignores it. RAFF defends himself. JANICE continues to ring the bell. It's no longer a game. JANICE separates them, gets hurt in the process. The men go back to their corners.*)

JANICE: Sweetheart, it's a little rough out there.

RAFF: Rough? This ain't rough. I could be a lot rougher.

AGOSTINO: She afraid I hurt you? How nice. Just like your mother. (*JANICE rings the bell. The match takes on a new seriousness. The two fighters stand toe to toe, throwing left and right leads, jabs, roundhouse punches, uppercuts, throwing elbows, shoving, and every other dirty trick. Both are tired and hurt. Out of panic, JANICE rings the bell before the time's up.*)

RAFF: It's not two minutes!

JANICE: C'mon, you guys! It's just a game! (*They fight. Both men are breathless and hurt. RAFF takes off his gloves.*)

RAFF: That's all.

AGOSTINO: You quit, Mr. Mayor?

RAFF: Yeah, you win.

AGOSTINO: No. (*AGOSTINO takes off his gloves.*) Bare hands!

RAFF: You're nuts.

AGOSTINO: Like before—bare hands!

RAFF: Get away from me!

AGOSTINO: Hit me! Bare hands! Chicken, eh? C'mon, Mr. Mayor! Bare hands! (*AGOSTINO provokes RAFF.*)

RAFF: If I ever hit you, I'd kill you. (*Beat.*)

AGOSTINO: That's my boy. Mi Piace uomo forte. That's good. That's good. He don't want to hurt me. That's why he don't tell me Lupo send him. For wha? For wha he send you?

RAFF: They're taking the house today.

AGOSTINO: Today?

RAFF: The police are outside. (*RAFF turns his back; AGOSTINO turns him around.*)

AGOSTINO: Why you don't say me this before? Why he don't say this when he come in the door?

RAFF: My guys'll be here with a truck to help you move out.

AGOSTINO: Wha?

RAFF: We can store everything in my warehouse. You can stay with Uncle Lou till you decide what to do. (*AGOSTINO takes the shotgun.*)

AGOSTINO: We see.

RAFF: The shells are no good.

AGOSTINO: We see.

RAFF: They're wet.

AGOSTINO: Wha?

RAFF: I wet 'em.

AGOSTINO: Heh?

RAFF: I poured wine on 'em. (*RAFF shows AGOSTINO the wet shells in a pot. AGOSTINO breaks open the shotgun, sees it empty.*)

AGOSTINO: Brutta bestia . . . Even a rat feel something for where it was born. And you? Wha? Your mother is in this house. She's in the glass pasta ajuta drink. Her hand touch the switch. her feet go up the stairs. She wait by the window for you to come—and when you come home—you a traditore! (*AGOSTINO moves towards RAFF. They stand toe to toe. Neither flinches. Beat. AGOSTINO steps back. RAFF takes the shotgun. AGOSTINO throws the gate key on the floor. RAFF picks it up.*) When people ask you, say you got no family. Change the name. Basta. (*RAFF stands by the door waiting for JANICE.*)

RAFF: Janice.

JANICE: Yes?

RAFF: Let's go.

JANICE: Bye.

RAFF: Hey, I'm talking over here. (*Beat. JANICE pours wine for herself and AGOSTINO. Exit RAFF. Beat. They listen to the bulldozer for a moment.*)

AGOSTINO: Maybe they make a mistake at the hospital and give me the wrong kid. (*Beat. Exit JANICE to backyard.*) Where you go? (*AGOSTINO goes to door, watches her.*) Don't let go the birds! Manage a madone! (*Enter JANICE. A trap goes off somewhere.*) You hear that!

JANICE: Hear what?

AGOSTINO: The rats. They laugh to me. Because they win. (*Beat.*) When the bulldozer come, this house don't go down so easy. I make the walls like this, capice? My sweat is in the cement. I see all the other house go down easy. Like nothing. No this house. This new road, where it goes?

JANICE: It's an off-ramp of the freeway.

AGOSTINO: Wha?

JANICE: When the office buildings downtown get out at five o'clock, the off-ramp will make less traffic. They think.

AGOSTINO: So that's whereas, eh? I hate to lose that tree.

JANICE: Plant it at our house.

AGOSTINO: Eh.

JANICE: Really.

AGOSTINO: Eh.

JANICE: Why not?

AGOSTINO: Eh.

JANICE: Tell me why not?

AGOSTINO: Who take care of it?

JANICE: I will.

AGOSTINO: You forget, morto.

JANICE: I won't forget.

AGOSTINO: Eh.

JANICE: I promise.

AGOSTINO: You break the roots.

JANICE: Hey! I said I'll take care of it. (*Beat.*)

AGOSTINO: Acqua buona?

JANICE: Well water. The best.

AGOSTINO: Sun?

JANICE: Dawn to dusk.

AGOSTINO: But it's all fieldstone, the ground.

JANICE: We'll truck in some topsoil. (*Enter RAFF. Beat. JANICE begins to exit. RAFF takes her by the arm and stops her. Beat. She hands him her empty glass. JANICE to RAFF as she exits.*) He needs help with the tree.

AGOSTINO: Wha help? Pasta ajuta? Where she go? (*RAFF shrugs. AGOSTINO pours himself a glass of wine. He looks at RAFF's empty glass. Beat. He offers to pour. RAFF holds the glass out while AGOSTINO pours. They drink. Long beat.*)

RAFF: Janice? (*Beat. They drink. RAFF looks at the wine against the light. AGOSTINO looks at his.*)

AGOSTINO: Sedimento.

RAFF: Bottom of the barrel?

AGOSTINO: I start the last barrel now.

RAFF: Janice? (*Beat.*) You should take the wine press.

AGOSTINO: You marry that girl.

RAFF: Where's it, in the cellar?

AGOSTINO: You hear me?

RAFF: Yeah.

AGOSTINO: And treat her right. (*Beat.*)

RAFF: You wanna take all the barrels?

AGOSTINO: Wha the hella you think? (*Beat.*) Where she go?

RAFF: Janice? (*Beat.*) I'll go find her.

AGOSTINO: Sit down here and shut up. (*He pours RAFF more wine. They drink. Silence. RAFF works his jaw.*) Can't take a punch, eh?

RAFF: Why, did you throw one? (*They drink. Silence.*) You wanna do the tree?

AGOSTINO: I do it.

RAFF: Where's the shovel?

AGOSTINO: You dirty your suit.

RAFF: Don't worry about it. Where's the shovel?

AGOSTINO: You break the roots, morto.

RAFF: Where's the shovel?

AGOSTINO: Here. (*AGOSTINO throws a square shovel on the floor at RAFF's feet.*)

RAFF: Give me the spade.

AGOSTINO: No spade.

RAFF: Da—.

AGOSTINO: No spade. Use that.

RAFF: This is too wide.

AGOSTINO: The spade's too sharp. You break the roots—

RAFF: I dug it up before.

AGOSTINO: When?

RAFF: When? What about every year.

AGOSTINO: Never once.

RAFF: Give me the spade.

AGOSTINO: I do it myself.

RAFF: Take it easy. (*RAFF muscles AGOSTINO aside, takes the spade, defiantly throws the square shovel on the floor. Enter JANICE.*)

AGOSTINO: Where you go?

JANICE: Lupo would like to speak to you outside. (*Beat.*)

AGOSTINO: I don't talk to nobody. (*Beat.*)

RAFF: I can't believe I still work for this guy. (*Exit RAFF. JANICE looks out the back door. AGOSTINO looks over her shoulder. Beat.*)

JANICE: Why don't we save what we can of the garden?

AGOSTINO: Pick everything. Tomato, pepper, garlic, onion, arugula. It's too much for a girl. I do it. (*JANICE takes the basket from him.*)

JANICE: Aspet. (*Exit JANICE. AGOSTINO looks on for a moment.*)

AGOSTINO: Raffe, too fast! Be careful! (*RAFF obviously ignores him. He goes to the statue, takes a file to the corner of an eye, makes a fine touch, looks over his shoulder—*) Eh? (*Beat.*) Emma? (*Beat.*) Sta qui? Dov'e? (*Silence. She's not there anymore. Beat.*) Brutta bestia. (*He turns to the statue, puts the file down and touches the face, not as a stone carver, but as a man saying goodbye. Lights fade to black.*)

END

THE WOOLGATHERER

Dedicated to Carole Brigantine Shambora, I think.

THE WOOLGATHERER was first produced in July 1979, at Rutgers Theatre Company, New Brunswick, NJ. The play was directed by John Bettenbender with the following cast:

CLIFF .... Ray Baker
ROSE .... Mary Beth Fisher

THE WOOLGATHERER was subsequently produced in May 1980, at the Circle Rep, New York City. The play was directed by John Bettenbender with the following cast:

CLIFF .... Peter Weller
ROSE .... Patricia Wettig

Characters

CLIFF
ROSE

Setting

TIME: Now
PLACE: South Philadelphia
SET: Efficiency apartment.
A single bed, neatly made.
A small table.
A chair.
An orange crate.
A door leading to a hallway.
A closet.
A boarded-up window hidden by cheap curtains.

Property List

ACT I
OFF RIGHT
Six pack Schmidt's beer in brown paper bag
ONSTAGE
Stage Right:
    Waste basket
    Cover for bathtub
    Hot plate
    Steam kettle
    Kitchen towel
    Bar of soap
On Shelves Over Sink:
    Can of sardines
    Magic Mountain herb tea
    Corn niblets
    Artichoke hearts
    Asparagus tips
    Gherkins
    Fruits and nuts
    Seaweed soup

Cinnamon sticks
Bouillon cubes
Drinking glass
2 cooking pots
2 plates
UPSTAGE
Near Refrigerator:
Mop
Broom
Dustpan
In Refrigerator:
Bowl with 4 hardboiled eggs
1 stalk of old celery
Half filled bottle cranberry juice
Box of baking soda
1 stick of butter
Near Closet:
Fruit crate (reinforced)
STAGE LEFT
On Shelves Up Left:
Dying ivy plant
Dying cactus plant
Make-up mirror
Hand lotion
Lipstick
Perfume in spray bottle
Hairbrush
DOWN LEFT
Trunk
Suitcase
Lamp
Good Housekeeping magazine
Flower book
Book with handwritten poem on piece of paper inside book
Dinosaur pamphlet
PERSONAL PROPS
ROSE: Apartment keys
CLIFF: Chewing gum, plastic film can with herbal tobacco, rolling
papers in metal case, cigarette lighter, matches, pack of
Marlboro cigarettes, eyedrops
ACT II
Replace fruit crate with breakaway crate.

THE WOOLGATHERER

ACT I

Darkness. Footfalls in the hallway. Inaudible talking. Lights up slowly.
Keys fumbling in the doorlock. Enter ROSE followed by CLIFF
swinging a six pack in a paper bag.

ROSE: And there was this girl . . . She was a poet . . . And she lived here . . . In this room . . . Before, you know, I moved in . . . And she committed, you know, suicide, right here in this room.
CLIFF: Did she die?
ROSE: Of course she died.
CLIFF: How'd she do it?
ROSE: Rope.
CLIFF: Overdose of rope?
ROSE: No. She, you know, hung herself.
CLIFF: Just kidding.
ROSE: That's not funny.
CLIFF: So why'd she do it?
ROSE: Nobody knows. It's a big mystery.
CLIFF: Big mystery. Didn't she leave a note?
ROSE: No. She left a poem.
CLIFF: Lucky she was a poet.
ROSE: Why's that?
CLIFF: Suppose she was a novelist.
ROSE: This is it. The poem she left. It's called "Death is my lover."
CLIFF: Beautiful.
ROSE: Want to hear it?
CLIFF: Yeah. Just what I need. Something to lift my spirits.
ROSE: "Death is my lover,
    You say it's not right,
    But his love's forever
    Day and night, day and night.
    We've gone to elope,
    Away from the light
    In his cozy house,

Day and night, day and night.

CLIFF: Hey, hey, whoa, whoa. Look, kid, I had a rough day and I don't want to hear about no weirdo's suicide note.

ROSE: O, you don't like poetry?

CLIFF: Hey, I'm nuts about it.

ROSE: Really?

CLIFF: Hey.

ROSE: Do you write poetry?

CLIFF: Hey, everyday.

ROSE: Really?

CLIFF: Hey.

ROSE: I'd like to read some.

CLIFF: I don't write it down. I talk it. Here ya go:
ROSES ARE RED
VIOLETS ARE BLUE
I DIG SHOTS AND BEERS
DO YOU LIKE ICE HOCKEY?

ROSE: That's it?

CLIFF: Like it?

ROSE: It's very . . . very interesting.

CLIFF: It's about my mother who was run over by a garbage truck.

ROSE: O. I'm sorry.

CLIFF: What can I say?

ROSE: Did she suffer?

CLIFF: Hey.

ROSE: I'm really sorry.

CLIFF: Me too, being that I pushed her under the wheels. Rose, that's a joke. You know, ha-ha?

ROSE: I don't joke around about that kind of stuff because it was very tragical the way that poor girl kicked the chair out from under herself and then changed her mind.

CLIFF: How do you know that?

ROSE: The police said. And the papers.

CLIFF: How could they know that unless they was here?

ROSE: They said she kicked the chair out from under but changed her mind and reached up for the rope and tried to save herself and they found rope fibers in her palms but her arms got tired and she, you know . . .

CLIFF: She must've been hung up about something.

ROSE: I don't think that's funny.

CLIFF: Well I don't think it's a good subject to make conversation with.

ROSE: Well it's true.

CLIFF: Alotta things are true, but you shouldn't talk about 'em.

ROSE: Why not?

CLIFF: Because no cops and no paper and no poem can give you the bottom line on what's going on in some weirdo's brain when she puts on the rope and leaps into the great ever-after. Even when you got all the facts in your hands, they don't add up to the leap. There's something missing. Maybe she just didn't fit. She added up the pluses and minuses and figured life ain't worth the hurt. So she turned in her scruples and checked out. And you and the cops and the papers want to know something? She had guts. And I respect that. Alotta people come up with the same figures but they buy insurance. So who knows? Maybe she did the right thing. Maybe she's happy now. Ever think of that?

ROSE: No.

CLIFF: Well you should.

ROSE: I was telling you about the room.

CLIFF: Well I don't want to hear about it.

ROSE: Then drop the subject.

CLIFF: Who brought it up?

ROSE: Me.

CLIFF: Then you drop it. Talk about something nice.

ROSE: Like what?

CLIFF: Like anything.

ROSE: I can't think of something nice.

CLIFF: I can.

ROSE: What?

CLIFF: I can think of something real nice.

ROSE: What?

CLIFF: I can think of something fantastically nice.

ROSE: What?

CLIFF: You.

ROSE: What're you doing?

CLIFF: Taking your poncho.

ROSE: O.

CLIFF: What'd you think?

ROSE: O, I just didn't know why you snuck up on me.

CLIFF: I didn't sneak up.

ROSE: I can take it off.

CLIFF: I know you can.

ROSE: Thank you just the same.

CLIFF: Hang it in the closet?

ROSE: No!

CLIFF: Sorry.

ROSE: Just lay it on the bed.

CLIFF: How come you whisper?

ROSE: The old lady next door, Mrs. Mancuso. She listens on the wall with a glass.

CLIFF: *(Indicating a spot on the wall.)* Here? *(ROSE shakes her head yes. CLIFF slaps the wall.)*

ROSE: No! Don't! She'll hear us!

CLIFF: *(To the wall.)* I don't care if she hears me.

ROSE: I do! She'll tell the landlord and I'll get evicted.

CLIFF: For talking?

ROSE: We're not allowed to have visitors.

CLIFF: How do you know she listens on the walls?

ROSE: I can hear her move the glass.

CLIFF: Beautiful.

CLIFF: How comes the window's all boarded up like that?

ROSE: That girl did it. The one who, you know, the rope? My landlord said he would take it down.

CLIFF: Why didn't he?

ROSE: You'll get mad if I tell you.

CLIFF: No I won't.

ROSE: Yes you will.

CLIFF: Why should I get mad?

ROSE: It's not something nice.

CLIFF: C'mon, tell me.

ROSE: You sure?

CLIFF: Yeah.

ROSE: He died.

CLIFF: Don't tell me. Rope?

ROSE: No.

CLIFF: Aspirins?

ROSE: No. He was old.

CLIFF: He died of old age?

ROSE: Yes.

CLIFF: Well, that's all right to die of old age. How old a man was he?

ROSE: O, I don't know. Old.

CLIFF: How old?

ROSE: He was up there.

CLIFF: Give me a rough idea.

ROSE: Over forty.

CLIFF: He must've took good care of himself.

ROSE: I only met him once. He never came around because he couldn't get up stairs so good.

CLIFF: I know. Once you hit forty, stairs are a big problem. So what's the story? You don't have a landlord now?

ROSE: His daughter took over.

CLIFF: So is she gonna take the boards off? Don't tell me! On the way here she was gored by a rhino!

ROSE: No! She said if she hires somebody to take it down, she has to raise the rent, and since I can't afford more rent, I told her leave it up.

CLIFF: I'll take it down.

ROSE: That's all right. I'm used to it.

CLIFF: But you don't have a window. You're missing out on all that wonderful scenery out there.

ROSE: There's nothing but an air shaft.

CLIFF: But you could at least get some fresh air up here.

ROSE: I go for a lot of walks.

CLIFF: But you know that smell in this building?

ROSE: I don't smell nothing.

CLIFF: That's mildew.

ROSE: I'm used to it.

CLIFF: It's bad for you. If the window was open it would go away.

ROSE: It's too much trouble.

CLIFF: What trouble? A couple eight penny nails. I could rip them boards off with bare hands.

ROSE: No! I'm sorry. It's all right.

CLIFF: I won't hurt your curtains.

ROSE: I'm used to it.

CLIFF: Rose, it's a fire hazard.

ROSE: How can it cause a fire?

CLIFF: It can't cause a fire. But if a fire broke out, how you gonna split?

ROSE: The door.

CLIFF: Suppose the stairs catch fire?

ROSE: They're cement.

CLIFF: It's against the law to board up a window. The landlord has to take it down by law. Not only that, he has to build a fire escape when there's only one means of egress. Not only that, he can't raise the rent because of it. I know the law. Let me take it down in case of fire.

ROSE: What good's that? I'd have to jump five stories.

CLIFF: Hey, would you rather have two broken legs or look like a meatloaf?

ROSE: I don't want to talk about this.

CLIFF: You want to talk about some weirdo who lynched herself but you don't want to talk about saving your life.

ROSE: So you think they're gonna fix your truck today?

CLIFF: Speaking of fire, are they gonna fix your truck. Depends.

ROSE: On what?

CLIFF: Whether the mechanic had a fight with his wife this morning.

ROSE: I don't understand.

CLIFF: Neither do I. And speaking of mechanics, I hate to break the news, but this weed's had it. (*Crumbling a dry, brittle leaf from an obviously dead plant in a flowerpot.*)

ROSE: Nothing grows up here.

CLIFF: No sun.

ROSE: Even the cactus shrivelled up, and they guaranteed it could live anywhere.

CLIFF: Why don't you just throw 'em in the garbage?

ROSE: Well, you never know. They might come alive again.

CLIFF: Come alive again? Never happen.

ROSE: Maybe. I always wanted a lot of plants in my room. You know, long ivy vines curling around things and growing up the wall.

CLIFF: Never happen. No sun.

ROSE: You never know. Did you ever hear of Our Lady of Fatima?

CLIFF: Ever hear of Forget About It? No sun, no plants. Now if I took the boards off . . .

ROSE: No sun ever came in the air shaft anyways.

CLIFF: How would you know if the boards were up when you moved in?

ROSE: So what happened to your truck?

CLIFF: Speaking of plants, I dropped reverse gear.

ROSE: Plants?

CLIFF: Gears?

ROSE: Huh?

CLIFF: Reverse?

ROSE: I don't understand.

CLIFF: No reverse, can't back up to the loading dock to unload. Bananas, very delicate, bananas. Too cold, too hot, or standing too long, they develop a rot inside. Then you can't give 'em away. You even have to pay to dump 'em. And speaking of bananas, want a beer?

ROSE: No.

CLIFF: What's wrong?

ROSE: Nothing.

CLIFF: Mind if I have one?

ROSE: No.

CLIFF: I do something wrong?

ROSE: You drink a lot.

CLIFF: What's a lot?

ROSE: You get drunk?

CLIFF: Nawwwww.

ROSE: O, good.

CLIFF: Have one with me.

ROSE: No, thank you. I'll have tea.

CLIFF: You don't like beer?

ROSE: One beer wipes me out.

CLIFF: No kidding? C'mon, just one.

ROSE: No, thank you.

CLIFF: It makes you smart.

ROSE: Beer does?

CLIFF: Hey, it made Bud wiser.

ROSE: You like to joke around, huh?

CLIFF: Hey, it's nice to get a little buzz on now and again. C'mon.

ROSE: Nah.

CLIFF: C'mon, just half.

ROSE: OK. But just half.

CLIFF: And look, if you change your mind about the window, I got a crowbar in my truck.

ROSE: Crowbar?

CLIFF: Yeah.

ROSE: What's that for?

CLIFF: Kill crows.

ROSE: What?

CLIFF: Sure. Alotta people don't realize that in certain remote parts of this country there's what they call the Killer Crow.

ROSE: Never heard of it.

CLIFF: Course not. Washington gave the word to the papers and TV, play down the Killer Crow. Otherwise you'd have panic in the streets.

ROSE: Really?

CLIFF: Hey, ask any Joe who ever trucked through Arkansas, or worse yet, the Dakota Badlands. Killer Crows as big as doberman pinschers with wingspan as wide as this room.

ROSE: Really honest to God?

CLIFF: Hey.

ROSE: Do they attack people?

CLIFF: Attack? Hey, that's all they do. Anything that moves. You don't have to believe me. Go ask the farmers out there. They sit on a cow's head and peck the eyes out.

ROSE: Eughhhhhhh.

CLIFF: That's why they equip us with what they call in the business—a crowbar. When it lands on the hood of the truck and tries to peck your eyes out through the windshield, you grab the crowbar and whack it on the beak—BAM! And it shrieks . . . (*Imitating the crow shriek.*) And flies off.

ROSE: Don't you get ascared?

CLIFF: Hey, I keep a change of underwear in the glove compartment. But very rarely do you kill one because they got skulls as thick as—pizza crust.

ROSE: Mrs. Mancuso says she sees the landlord's ghost walk through the building the first night of every month.

CLIFF: Here we go.

ROSE: Because he was dead almost two weeks before they found his body and his ghost wandered out his body and that's why they have to bury people right away. Do you think that's true for animals too?

CLIFF: Don't know. It's a little outside my neighborhood.

ROSE: You believe in ESP?

CLIFF: No, I believe in STP.

The Woolgatherer / 65

ROSE: What's that?

CLIFF: Forget it. Turn on the radio.

ROSE: Don't have one.

CLIFF: What's that? tapes? records?

ROSE: No.

CLIFF: You don't dig music?

ROSE: I hate that music. Hate it. Would you like a glass for your beer?

CLIFF: Hey. Thanks. Where's your glass?

ROSE: I only have one glass.

CLIFF: You entertain much?

ROSE: Beg your pardon?

CLIFF: Forget it. Use the glass.

ROSE: No, you.

CLIFF: (*Putting the glass on her side of the table.*) Now Rose, don't make a big deal. (*Sitting in the chair.*) Sit down. (*Noticing she has no seat.*) What do you do for another chair?

ROSE: The crate. I'll use the crate, you the chair.

CLIFF: No, you the chair, me the crate.

ROSE: No, me the crate, you the chair.

CLIFF: No, you Jane, me Tarzan.

ROSE: You make a joke out of everything, huh?

CLIFF: Hey. (*Pause, to the wall.*) Hey, Mrs. Mafusco, can we borrow your glass?

ROSE: STOP IT!

CLIFF: I was just asking her . . .

ROSE: I'm sorry I ever told you that!

CLIFF: She bugs me that woman.

ROSE: Don't talk then.

CLIFF: She don't bug you?

ROSE: She can't help it. She's on Social Security.

CLIFF: (*Pause. He crinkles the cellophane of his cigarette pack, to wall.*) FIRE!

ROSE: You want me to get evicted?

CLIFF: Naw, I wouldn't want you to lose a place like this.

ROSE: Well?

CLIFF: Well, it's getting late.

ROSE: Guess where I got that chair?

CLIFF: In a chair store.

ROSE: No. C'mon.

CLIFF: Where you work at the Five and Dime.

ROSE: We don't sell chairs. Guess.

CLIFF: Box of crackerjacks?

ROSE: No, c'mmmon.

CLIFF: Rubbed up against your leg and followed you home.

ROSE: No, c'mon.

CLIFF: The weirdo with the rope left it in her will.

ROSE: That's not funny.

CLIFF: Sorry. Where'd you get it?

ROSE: I don't want to tell you now.

CLIFF: Why not?

ROSE: I just don't. You ruined it all when you said that.

CLIFF: Look, I'm really sorry.

ROSE: Some things aren't funny.

CLIFF: Yeah, I'm getting the hang of it. So tell me where you got this wonderful chair of yours.

ROSE: No.

CLIFF: Please?

ROSE: Sometimes you joke around too much.

CLIFF: May God strike somebody dead if I should ever do it again. Now c'mon, where'd you get it?

ROSE: I was on my way to the Salvation Army to buy a chair and I saw these people putting garbage on the curb and this old man put this chair on the curb and I asked him if I could have it and he was retired and had diabetes and was cleaning his cellar out and I took the chair home.

CLIFF: Big deal.

ROSE: What?

CLIFF: Big deal.

ROSE: Don't you see? Like it was meant to be.

CLIFF: Meant to be. Hey, tomorrow I'm supposed to see a man about another job. Easier. More bread. More benefits. Closer to home. Bla bla bla bla bla. But my rig broke down and I can't be there, so he'll give the job to somebody else. Now was that meant to be?

ROSE: You can't tell till later.

CLIFF: Hey, c'mon, c'mon, c'mon, meant to be. This morning I'm on the turnpike doin' the limit plus to make up for lost time. I get in back of a chicken truck in the passing lane. Big truck with wooden cages tied on the back filled with chickens. That's why

The Woolgatherer / 67

they call it a chicken truck. You know, big chickens, little chickens, white chickens, brown chickens, gray chickens. Alotta chickens. And feathers streaming out the back hitting my windshield. Well the driver pulls over so I can pass, but something catches my eye. There's this chicken trying to squeeze between the bars. It has its wing spread full and trying to slip between the bars of the cage. Now I could've passed the chicken truck, but I wanted to see the chicken escape. Don't know why. Just a crazy urge. So I hang back. Sometimes you get so cooped up in the cab you do crazy things. So I start rooting for the chicken. Hey! C'mon! Jump! You chicken punk! Jump!

ROSE: Shhh!

CLIFF: Jump!

ROSE: The old lady!

CLIFF: Hell with the old lady! So I said Jump, baby, jump!

ROSE: Shhhh!

CLIFF: (*To wall.*) Hey, Rosie, I can't find my underwear.

ROSE: Stop it!

CLIFF: Give the old lady a thrill.

ROSE: That's disgusting.

CLIFF: I was just kidding around.

ROSE: I hate that.

CLIFF: Take it easy.

ROSE: She thinks I'm nice.

CLIFF: I think you're nice too.

ROSE: Well you can go if you want to talk dirty. (*Pause.*) So what happened to the chicken?

CLIFF: The story ends right there.

ROSE: Did it get out?

CLIFF: Yeah.

ROSE: O, good.

CLIFF: Hit the road in front of my wheels. I swerved but it got caught in the back wheels inbetween the double tires. In the rearview all I saw was this feather ball spinning red and white, red and white, feathers spinning off the wheels red and white.

ROSE: (*Pause.*) Did it die?

CLIFF: Very likely with 36,000 pounds rolling over it.

ROSE: Did it suffer?

CLIFF: Nah. Was quick.

ROSE: Did you, you know, go back?

CLIFF: For what?

ROSE: To, you know, pick it up?

CLIFF: No, I left it flat. Pick it up? What am I? a scavenger?

ROSE: No, you know, to bury it.

CLIFF: It was only a chicken.

ROSE: You should of gone back.

CLIFF: Go back shit. I was doin' 75. What's amatter?

ROSE: Nothin.

CLIFF: Itchy sweater?

ROSE: Hives.

CLIFF: What from?

ROSE: I just get 'em.

CLIFF: So sudden?

ROSE: Yeah.

CLIFF: Let me scratch.

ROSE: No, it's all right.

CLIFF: Hey, I'm an expert.

ROSE: NO! I'm all right. Thank you just the same.

CLIFF: You scratch like you're tearing off flesh.

ROSE: I hate this.

CLIFF: Maybe you're allergic to wool.

ROSE: It's mohair.

CLIFF: You got mohair than me.

ROSE: It was longer. I just got it cut.

CLIFF: Did your man give you his sweater?

ROSE: What man?

CLIFF: That's a man's sweater you're wearing.

ROSE: No it's not. How do you know? So what if it is?

CLIFF: No big deal.

ROSE: No. Why'd you say that?

CLIFF: I was curious.

ROSE: About what?

CLIFF: Why a girl wears a man's sweater.

ROSE: A lot of girls wear men's sweaters.

CLIFF: You don't have to get so touchy.

ROSE: I'm not touchy.

CLIFF: All right, drop it.

ROSE: You brought it up.

CLIFF: Well suppose I had on a girl's sweater. Wouldn't you ask why?

ROSE: No. It would be none of my business.

CLIFF: Excuse me. I must be abnormal.

ROSE: Everybody always asks personal questions.

CLIFF: I'm not everybody. I'm Cliff. How ya doin'? Nice to meet you. So forget the sweater.

ROSE: Good.

CLIFF: You see, where I come from, men wear men's sweaters and girls . . .

ROSE: I got it from Brenda.

CLIFF: Ahhh, Brenda. Now I understand.

ROSE: I used to live with this girl Brenda.

CLIFF: And was this girl Brenda a man?

ROSE: No. Some guy gave it to her to remember him by.

CLIFF: So why'd she give it to you? Or is that too personal?

ROSE: She didn't give it to me. One night she went down the corner for a pack of cigarettes and never came back no more.

CLIFF: What happened?

ROSE: Nobody knows.

CLIFF: Another mystery. Did you call the police?

ROSE: Of course.

CLIFF: And what'd they say?

ROSE: They put her on the missing persons list.

CLIFF: Good idea. So if she reads the list she'll know she's missing.

ROSE: How she going to see the list if she's missing?

CLIFF: That's the problem. If somebody could find her and give her the list, then she'd know.

ROSE: Know what?

CLIFF: She's missing.

ROSE: I don't think you understand.

CLIFF: Hey, Rose, Rose, Rosie, don't make a big deal. Relax.

ROSE: I can't tell when you kid around because your face is so serious. (*Pause.*) Do you want to have kids?

CLIFF: We got time?

ROSE: Me, I wouldn't want to have kids today, the world being what it is.

CLIFF: What is it?

ROSE: Messed up. Really messed up. I feel sorry for mankind.

CLIFF: Mankind?

ROSE: How it suffers.

CLIFF: Jesus. How come you ask me if I want kids?

ROSE: I don't know. (*Pause.*) Where you from?

CLIFF: Ever hear of Elizabeth?

ROSE: Yeah.

CLIFF: I don't live nowhere near it.

ROSE: C'mon, where?

CLIFF: Trenton.

ROSE: I know Trenton! I went through Trenton once on the train. Trenton has that bridge with that big red neon sign: TRENTON MAKES, THE WORLD TAKES.

CLIFF: They changed it.

ROSE: To what?

CLIFF: WHAT THE WORLD SECRETES, TRENTON EATS.

ROSE: They did not! I saw this farm from the train window. Just outside Trenton. Someday I want a farm. I want to raise rabbits. Not in cages. Just, you know, free. Running around wherever they want. And a little house with red and white curtains and a coop where the rabbits go when it's cold.

CLIFF: Rabbits.

ROSE: They don't have claws, and they can't run that fast, but they zig-zag, and that's what saves them when they're chased.

CLIFF: I bag a few every years in gunning season. They make good stew.

ROSE: I wouldn't sell them for that.

CLIFF: How the hell you gonna make a living? They ain't good for much else except good luck charms to keep keys on.

ROSE: Don't talk about that. Do you ever have dreams like that about a farm or something?

CLIFF: I don't waste my time. I dream of getting from one minute to the next. Beer?

ROSE: A little.

CLIFF: So how you gonna latch onto a farm?

ROSE: I don't know.

CLIFF: You think the deed to a farm comes in the morning mail?

ROSE: No.

CLIFF: "Congratulations. You are the happy owner of a sixty acre farm."

ROSE: I don't think that.

CLIFF: You think you could wish it to happen?

ROSE: I was just saying.

CLIFF: It takes scratch, honey. And by the time you earn it you'll forget you ever wanted it. And if you get it, how you gonna make the mortgage payments? the taxes? the upkeep? water, gas, electric? How you gonna feed yourself? And you think it's easy working a farm?

ROSE: No.

CLIFF: It's ass-bustin' labor and you're in no shape to do it. Rabbits. How you gonna feed 'em?

ROSE: I was just saying. I know I'll never get it. But I can dream if I want.

CLIFF: You can but you can't. It catches up with you. You love something that ain't there and then you start hating what is there, and that's hell.

ROSE: What's your Zodiac sign?

CLIFF: You believe in that crap?

ROSE: It's not . . .

CLIFF: Not what?

ROSE: What you said.

CLIFF: Crap?

ROSE: They proved it's true.

CLIFF: Who proved it?

ROSE: Scientists. When were you born?

CLIFF: Soon after my mother had contractions, and tell you the truth I don't want to hear no bartalk zodiacs with a rising Scorpion on the cusp of diddlydo. Just a bunch of crap some lazyass cooked up to sell a book.

ROSE: You want to go the museum and see a dinosaur? It's about, O, I don't know, fifty or forty feet high. Tyranosaurus.

CLIFF: Do they let you feed it?

ROSE: No! It's dead.

CLIFF: Rope!

ROSE: No! It's all bones. Bones this thick all wired together. I made friends with the curator and he took me in the cellar and showed me how they wire the bones.

CLIFF: In the cellar, eh?

ROSE: Of the museum.

CLIFF: And did he show you his bone?

ROSE: No. The bones belong to the museum.

CLIFF: O, I see.

ROSE: He told me the dinosaurs disappeared off the face of the earth very suddenly.

CLIFF: How come?

ROSE: Nobody knows.

CLIFF: Mysterious.

ROSE: They think it was the temperature.

CLIFF: They died of fever?

ROSE: No. The climate changed and the dinosaurs couldn't get used to it. It was called The Great Ice Age.

CLIFF: Why didn't they go to Florida?

ROSE: You want to hear this? This is a serious subject.

CLIFF: I know. Never know when you might come across a dinosaur.

ROSE: And guess what? They just found a wooly mammoth in Siberia, or Algeria, or, I don't know, someplace far. And it was froze in ice in perfect condition! like it was in a refrigerator for ten thousand years! C'mon. We still have a chance before the museum closes.

CLIFF: That's romantic as hell. Go look at bones.

ROSE: People who can't appreciate culture are just ignorant.

CLIFF: I must be people.

ROSE: Mankind does not understand its past.

CLIFF: That what the museum guy says? Tell him if he wants to know about mankind, tell him stop playing with his bone down in the cellar there and go in a city where you don't know anybody and have your truck break down and try and get somebody give you ahand! Don't tell me about bones.

ROSE: It's interesting.

CLIFF: Yeah, so are rock fights. Look, Rose, I'm not too big on culture, see. Now I can get all hepped up over a t-bone or prime rib, but that's about it for bones.

ROSE: I don't think you understand.

CLIFF: Hey, look, sweetheart, I understand. I got a few hours to kill in Philly and I'm not gonna spend it looking at bones. Hey, why don't we hoof it to a joint, lay out some frogskin, do a pizza with the works to go, jump on some vino, bring it here, chow down, talk about the moon, acouple laughs, sing, dance, waterski, la la la, whatever.

ROSE: I have food here.

CLIFF: I don't want to use your food.

ROSE: I have a lot of food.

CLIFF: C'mon, what do you want to do—it's up to me.

ROSE: I'd rather stay here.

CLIFF: Terrific. What do you got?

ROSE: This.

CLIFF: Boneless sardines.

ROSE: Magic mountain herb tea. And this.

CLIFF: Cranberry sauce. Dusseldorff mustard.

ROSE: Bouillon cubes. Cinnamon sticks. And this!

CLIFF: My favorite! Seaweed soup!

ROSE: I got that in a health store.

CLIFF: I though maybe a pet shop.

ROSE: Dried fruits and nuts. Corn niblets. Artichokes hearts. Asparagus. Jerkins.

CLIFF: Jerkins? (*Opening the refrigerator, coming up with a limp celery stalk. ROSE grabs it out of his hand and tosses it in the garbage.*) Hey! Don't!

ROSE: It's wilted.

CLIFF: (*Picking it out of the garbage.*) Never know. It might come alive again. (*ROSE throws it back in the garbage.*) You live on this stuff?

ROSE: I get fruits and vegetables on Ninth Street when they close.

CLIFF: What, steal it?

ROSE: No, you should see the good stuff they throw away.

CLIFF: Garbage?

ROSE: I wash it off. They throw away lettuce leaves just because it has a brown edge. Or if a peach has a bruise, I cut it out. And stick bread this long. A day old. But I don't eat it all. I break it up and feed the pigeons on the roof.

CLIFF: Get your poncho. I'll take you out for steak.

ROSE: I though you wanted to make something here?

CLIFF: Out of this shit? I'd have to be a goddamn magician.

ROSE: You don't have to curse.

CLIFF: What'd I say?

ROSE: You cursed.

CLIFF: No shit.

ROSE: If you want to curse, you can do it somewheres else.

CLIFF: You don't curse.

ROSE: No.

CLIFF: Bullshit.

ROSE: I don't. And don't say I do.

CLIFF: You never cursed?

ROSE: Never. Not once.

CLIFF: No shit? Why not?

ROSE: Because.

CLIFF: Why because?

ROSE: Because I don't. That's all.

CLIFF: What do you say when you stub your toe? O chocolate kisses?

ROSE: I say ouch. And I don't like people who curse.

CLIFF: So you don't like me.

ROSE: Not when you curse like that.

CLIFF: So what are you, a nun?

ROSE: No.

CLIFF: Eh, Sister Rose?

ROSE: If you don't like it . . .

CLIFF: Stick it?

ROSE: No.

CLIFF: Sit on it?

ROSE: No!

CLIFF: Shove it?

ROSE: No!

CLIFF: Fry it with onions? what? if I don't like it what? Eh, Sister Rose?

ROSE: If you don't like it you can go.

CLIFF: For cursing?

ROSE: Yes.

CLIFF: Why?

ROSE: It's ugly.

CLIFF: I didn't invent it.

ROSE: You use it.

CLIFF: It's part of the language.

ROSE: Not my language.

CLIFF: Hey, sorry, I meant to say all shucks and golly gee.

ROSE: Don't make fun of me.

CLIFF: I'm not.

ROSE: I hate when they make fun of me.

CLIFF: You make a big deal out of every fuckin thing.

ROSE: STOP IT! I hate that!

CLIFF: I'm sorry.

ROSE: No you're not! I hate when they curse. Like them kids at the zoo. I hate it.

CLIFF: Here we go.

ROSE: Their radios up against their ears and that wild ugly music and cursing! I hate that!

CLIFF: What kids?

ROSE: I hate that.

CLIFF: They cursed at you?

ROSE: No. At those birds.

CLIFF: O, they cursed at those birds, eh?

ROSE: I forget their names.

CLIFF: O, so you're on a first-name basis with those birds, eh, Rose?

ROSE: Those tall birds with the long thin legs.

CLIFF: Ah, yes. The tall thin-legged bird of North America.

ROSE: Derricks!

CLIFF: Derricks?

ROSE: No. Cranes. Some kind of cranes.

CLIFF: And what did the derricks say, Rose?

ROSE: Stop making fun of me.

CLIFF: Did the derricks ask you if you needed a lift?

ROSE: You may think it's funny but I was the last one to see them alive last summer. There was only seven of them in the world and the zoo had four of them. I used to walk there every night just to watch them stand so still in the water. And they walked so graceful, in slow motion. And they have legs as skinny as my little finger. Long legs. And there was only seven in the world because they killed them off for feathers for ladies hats or something. And one night a gang of boys came by with radios to their ears and cursing real bad, you now, F, and everything. And I was, you know, ascared. And they started saying things to me, you know, dirty things, and laughing at the birds. And one kid threw a stone to see how close he could splash the birds, and then another kid tried to see how close he could splash the birds, and then they all started throwing stones at the birds, and I started screaming STOP IT! and a stone hit the bird's leg and it bended like a straw and the birds keeled over in the water, flapping wings in the water, and the kids kept laughing and throwing stones and I kept screaming STOP IT! STOP IT! but they couldn't hear me through that ugly music on the radios and kept laughing and cursing and throwing stones, and I ran and get the zoo guard and he got his club and we ran to the place of the birds but the kids were gone. And there was white

76 / *William Mastrosimone*

feathers on the water. And the water was real still. And there was big swirls of blood. And the birds were real still. Their beaks a little open. Legs broke. Toes curled. Still. Like the world stopped. And the guard said something to me but I couldn't hear him. I just saw his mouth moving. And I started screaming. And the cops came and took me the hospital and they gave me a needle to make me stop screaming. And they never caught the gang. But even if they did, what good's that? They can't make the birds come alive again.

CLIFF: (*Long pause.*) Yeah, well. I'm really sorry to hear about it. But the fact of the matter is . . . it's a rough-tough world out there, and like everything else, if the birds can't hack the jive, maybe it's better they're not around gettin' in the way because if you want to survive you got to be rough and tough right back.

ROSE: But they don't have a way to be rough and tough.

CLIFF: Then maybe it was meant to be for 'em to bite the dust.

ROSE: That's mean.

CLIFF: That's life.

ROSE: That's not life.

CLIFF: That's the way Niagra Falls.

ROSE: You're just as bad as them.

CLIFF: I'm not them. I'm me.

ROSE: You stick up for them, you mise well be them!

CLIFF: Hey, did I kill the birds? Did I?

ROSE: You mise well if you stick up for them!

CLIFF: But did I kill the fuckin birds?

ROSE: No! (*Pause. Apologetic for screaming.*) No. (*Pause.*) I think you should go.

CLIFF: Yeah, me, too. Afterall, you don't want it to get around you hang out with bird killers. Well, kid, it was nice.

ROSE: You think they fixed your truck?

CLIFF: No. Wasn't meant to be.

ROSE: I hope you get the new job.

CLIFF: As they say when you can't stop your rig—them's the breaks.

ROSE: What kind of job is it?

CLIFF: Testing parachutes.

ROSE: What kind of job is that?

CLIFF: Fifty bucks an hour plus they let you keep the chutes that don't open.

ROSE: What would you do with a parachute?

CLIFF: Make handkerchiefs. Big ones. (*Pause. They face each other. CLIFF offers a handshake. She slowly accepts.*) Cold hands.

ROSE: I'm anemic.

CLIFF: Know what's good for that?

ROSE: What.

CLIFF: Boneless sardines. Hey, Rosie-posey, mind if I smoke?

ROSE: No, but don't call me that.

CLIFF: Why not?

ROSE: You're making fun.

CLIFF: No I'm not. Honest. I just can't believe somebody like you exists.

ROSE: What do you mean somebody like me?

CLIFF: I mean you're beautiful.

ROSE: Don't say that kind of stuff to me. I know I'm not beautiful. You're making fun.

CLIFF: I'm afraid to talk. Everything I say hurts you. Maybe I don't use the right words. Hey, I'm gonna watch myself from now on. Wanna do some stuff?

ROSE: Beg your pardon?

CLIFF: You dig the weed?

ROSE: What weed?

CLIFF: C'mon, you're joshin me now.

ROSE: I don't understand.

CLIFF: Wanna do a joint?

ROSE: I don't understand.

CLIFF: Would you like a cigarette?

ROSE: I don't smoke, thank you. What's that?

CLIFF: Paper.

ROSE: What for?

CLIFF: Make cigarettes.

ROSE: Like the cowboys?

CLIFF: Yeah, the cowboys. Ride 'em cowboy. Hey.

ROSE: What?

CLIFF: Yippi hi ho kai yea!

ROSE: I don't see why you don't just buy 'em out a machine like everybody else.

CLIFF: I may have to. My grocer went on vacation for three to five years.

ROSE: Isn't that a long time for vacation?

CLIFF: That's what he told the judge.

ROSE: Eughhhhhhhh.

CLIFF: Eh?

ROSE: Smells.

CLIFF: Do a drag.

ROSE: No. It's awful. What's that?

CLIFF: Roach clip.

ROSE: What's that for?

CLIFF: Kill roaches. You grab 'em by the antenna and twist. Screws up their radar and they start walkin' crooked and bump into things and die of multiple bruises.

ROSE: Get out!

CLIFF: Take a toke.

ROSE: No thank you.

CLIFF: It makes the world go bye-bye.

ROSE: What do you mean?

CLIFF: I mean I want to hold you, Rosie Rosie.

ROSE: So why do you want to change jobs?

CLIFF: Do you scrub yourself with a wire brush? You are so immaculate.

ROSE: So it's a better job.

CLIFF: How's a man supposed to get near you, Rosie?

ROSE: I think I'd like to be a trucker—I mean, you know, if I was a man.

CLIFF: If I was me, I'd want to be a refrigerator. What problems can a refrigerator have? OK, a little defrosting every six months. Big deal. Ok, a few mouldy cucumber and slimy heads of lettuce to throw away. But outside of that, what? So what am I saying? A wish's just a detour. Skip it.

ROSE: How come you make that noise?

CLIFF: To get all the vitamins out.

ROSE: You don't make sense. (*CLIFF goes to wash off dirt from the beer can.*) Hot is cold and cold is hot.

CLIFF: Yeah. I got one something like that, except on mine, hot is cold and cold is also cold.

ROSE: What's your place like?

CLIFF: A floor that leads to walls that lead to a roof that mostly keeps off the rain. And dust that looks like furniture.

ROSE: You don't dust?

CLIFF: Never home.

The Woolgatherer | 79

ROSE: Why even have an apartment?

CLIFF: I need an address.

ROSE: What for?

CLIFF: So people could send me bills.

ROSE: Bills for what?

CLIFF: For the rent and the phone and the electricity and the heat I never use.

ROSE: That's crazy.

CLIFF: Hey.

ROSE: What?

CLIFF: Touch me.

ROSE: What for?

CLIFF: I'm not sure you're really there.

ROSE: You're silly.

CLIFF: You remind me of somebody I never knew.

ROSE: I hate that noise. Don't you hate people who make noise when they eat soup.

CLIFF: Only if it's my soup.

ROSE: It must be nice to be a trucker.

CLIFF: Beautiful.

ROSE: Different restaurants everyday . . .

CLIFF: Sunnyside ulcers with a side of ptomaine . . .

ROSE: Always moving . . .

CLIFF: Always a stranger . . .

CLIFF: Hitchhikers. Every other one, Charles Manson, the ones in between, some runaway moonie . . .

ROSE: Ocean to ocean . . .

CLIFF: Roads that lead to highways that go on forever . . .

ROSE: I never saw the ocean.

CLIFF: Never?

ROSE: Nope.

CLIFF: Where you been all your life?

ROSE: What's it like?

CLIFF: The ocean?

ROSE: Yeah.

CLIFF: (*Making an expansive gesture. Pause.*) Alotta water.

ROSE: Big?

CLIFF: Pshew.

ROSE: Really?

CLIFF: Hey, like the sky, but down here.

ROSE: Unhuh . . .

CLIFF: Blue water, white water . . .

ROSE: Unhuh . . .

CLIFF: Seagulls flying low over the water . . . (*Imitating the cry of the gull.*)

ROSE: Is that how they sound?

CLIFF: No, that's me when I'm stuck in a hot truck. You come down a mountain and see them heat waves rollin' off the asphalt, and then you see all that cool clean water out there, and you'd like to pull off the road and run across that beach and let them foamy waves take you under. But you can't.

ROSE: Sharks.

CLIFF: No. You got deadlines. You got schedules.

ROSE: But at least you see the ocean.

CLIFF: Just enough to tease.

ROSE: It must be wonderful.

CLIFF: Beautiful.

ROSE: Free as a bird.

CLIFF: Free. What's free? Pushin' an eight-year-old played-out dog on retreads that drops a gearbox when you get a little ahead of schedule? Free. You say free cause you're stuck behind a candy counter all day and a five and dime don't move. Free. When a dispatcher slips you an extra yard to overload your rig, you ain't free to turn it down, because it's your bread and butter. Without the butter. So now you got to sneak past the scale stations where these jerky little guys with clipboards and 27 pens in their shirt pocket wait for you and your freedom to come 18-wheelin' down their pike. Flags you over. Weighs the rig. You get a fine that wipes out the bribe you just took. Click a button and you got a thousand good buddies who map you a snakepath on backroads that never heard of rules and regulations. But then, out of nowhere, a little yellow flasher comes up in the rearview. Motor vehicle inspector out looking for his afternoon quota. Pulls you over. You know he's gonna weigh the rig and slap another summons on you. You know he's gonna crank up his portable scales. Gets out his car like John Wayne with an A-bomb in his holster. Sunglasses so you can't see his eyes. Asks for your logbook, please. Always says please. Looks at it. Scans your eyes that look more like roadmaps than roadmaps. Closes it. Hands it back. Knows it's all faked up. Knows you wrote

The Woolgatherer / 81

"rest" every 450 miles even when you took no rest because that's the law. But he can't prove it. So to show his boss he wasn't stokin' the breeze, he gets you for something else. Dead tail light. Missing mud flap. Dirty license plate. He's a bonafide specialist in smallness. "Take a seat in the back of the car, please." "Hey, look, buddy, could you give me a break?" He pretends he don't hear. And you got to sit there and listen to his pen skip. And trucks are passing you. Trucks with no tail lights. Trucks with no mud flaps. Trucks with bond papers expired. Trucks with last year's license plates. But he's got you. And you sit there. And you think. You think of the money. You think of the doctor who said rattling around in that bucket of clankity junk's giving you the bladder of a 75 year old. You think of your woman. Wonder what she's doing. And who she's doing it with. For a second you don't blame her. Then he hands you the summons. Puts you in the hole half a yard. Gun the engine. Pop a benzedrine. Hit the road. You never turn around. Never. Tires up on the curb on a narrow street in Baltimore. Stacking the load on the curb. A rusty old man who's been cheating death for 10 years comes running out the store waving his arms. "Hey, buddy, could you bring it in the door for me?" "Sorry, pal, bill of lading says sidewalk delivery." "But can't you just wheel it in for me, buddy. Take you two seconds." "I do what the order says, pal." You really want to help the guy, but why should you? Hey, sometimes you're the bird, and sometimes you're the windshield. Today, you get to be the bird. "Sorry, pal, I go by the bill." And he slips you a sawbuck. Stuff it in your shirt. And you say: "Where would you like it, sir?" Score's even. Next stop, the docks. Pull in. Dispatcher stands there pencil and clipboard checking off unicorns. Pretends he don't see you. You snap on your smile: "Hey, how ya doin', champ?" "What can I do for you?" "Look, buddy, I'm running a little late and I got to blow this town in an hour." "You got an appointment?" "Appointment? What're you? a frickin dentist? Why can't I pull in that spot and unload?" "No room." "No room? What's that empty space there?" "That docks reserved. You got to wait." "How long?" "Till there's room." "How long's that about?" "You tell me." Here's another punk you want to bust in the snotbox. But, hey, you asked to get in the game, so play by the rules. You hand him the sawbuck the old man slipped you. And you get a little surprise. He hands it back and walks away. Slow. Now you want to rip his arm off and slap him across the face with it. But that ain't in Murphy's Law. You can't quit, you can't win, you can't break even. So you peel off a double saw. He takes it like he grabbed an ass. Like it never happened. Says like an old beer buddy: "Back it in, Amigo. Have you truckin in a snap." You swear this is your last run. Breeze through the want ads. You're not ACCOUNTANT. DISHWASHER AND GRAVEDIGGER don't appeal. Only thing you're really qualified for is PLASMA DONOR URGENTLY NEEDED. Next thing you know, you're upshifting through an amber light. And not to hear a personal question you're about to ask, you turn up the radio. But they don't play the good songs no more. They just play them new songs. "O baby o baby o baby o baby I want you o baby I need you o baby drop your laundry." They got shoemakers making songs. Fidgit on the CB. Talk ice patches. Radar traps. See a phone booth. Choke it with quarters, dimes, nickels. She's not there. Do a hundred miles. Blinking neon. Diner. Pull over. Coffee, danish, small talk. Do your little routine. Make a waitress laugh. Find out Johnny Blade fell asleep at the wheel out Nevada. Through a guardrail. Now he's truckin in a wheelchair. Do a hundred miles. You think of that waitress in the last diner and sleep. And if you had a choice, you'd take sleep. But you don't. Drink black coffee till you can't taste nothin' but the hotness. You get used to your own stink. No bath, three days. Phone booth. Let it ring thirty times. She's not there. Four in the goddamn morning. Not home. You start talkin' to yourself. You argue with yourself. Whether she this, me that. Whether you should pull over and sleep or do another hundred miles. You argue, you lose, you win, you doze. Rig edges into the other lane. Guy in a Volkswagon beeps like crazy. You see his mouth moving behind the windshield. He's in the right, but you curse him, his family, his car, his dog, kids that ain't born yet. Pull over. Lay on the front seat. Tell yourself you're just resting your eyes because the load's got to be in San Jose in 6 hours or they don't want it, and by rough calculations you can't make it in less than seven and a half. Lay your arm over your face to block out the sun. You see the veins in your wrist, red and blue, like roads on the map. And that question you been giving the slips for the last thousand miles catches up,

The Woolgatherer / 83

and you whisper to nobody in particular, "What am I doing? What am I doing?" And you fade. Wonderful. It scares you. You spring up. You think you slept 10 hours. It's only 2 minutes. The Volkswagon passing you. Other trucks passing you. Leap to the wheel. Pop a benny. Peel off. Insect hits the windshield. Leaves its soft green smear on top a thousand others. Count the white lines shooting past. Lose count. Lose touch. Lose yourself in the road. And you're caught. You move with the pack. Keep it between the lines. That's what it comes down to. Keep it movin' even though the road funnels into some gigantic meatgrinder and every robot's over the limit to be the first one inside where it's all mangled and mixed and you holler, SLOW DOWN! but they only see your mouth movin' behind the windshield. Bulldog tailgating, poundin' foghorn to make you go faster into the grinder. Sign reads NO STOPPING OR STANDING. Radio's goin' "O baby o baby." Three lanes merge into two. The broken white line becomes a solid yellow line, and the solid fades and two lanes merge into one. You floor it. Into the tunnel. Engine echoes off the walls, drowns out your brain. Air goes rancid. Roll up the window. Radio goes dead. Turn on the lights. Lights dim out. Flying down into the tunnel. You look for a miracle. You see a diner ahead. You notice your right blinker clicking.

ROSE: (*Long pause.*) You're right. Get the parachute job. (*Pause.*) The furtherest I ever been was Newark, New Jersey.

CLIFF: Beautiful.

ROSE: I saved up to see the Statue of Liberty, and I asked the ticket man for a ticket to New York, and he thought I said Newark, and I spent the whole day there, in the train station.

CLIFF: Someday I'm gonna take you cross country in my truck.

ROSE: Are you joking now?

CLIFF: Hey.

ROSE: Do they allow that?

CLIFF: It's my truck. I'll let you hold the crowbar.

ROSE: Get out.

CLIFF: Hey, just when you think you had it, you come around a mountain and the Pacific Ocean kicks you right in the eyeballs.

ROSE: People always promise things, but they don't really mean it.

CLIFF: Hey, once more: I'm not people. I'm me. And speaking of nothing in particular, you got a beautiful mouth, but the only thing I don't like about it is I'm not close enough. (*He kisses her*

with a kind of sublimated violence, but breaks gently. Pause.)
ROSE: Thank you.
CLIFF: You don't have to say thank you when a man kisses you.
ROSE: Do you have to make fun of everything I do?
CLIFF: Hey.
ROSE: What?
CLIFF: You like me?
ROSE: Yes.
CLIFF: I don't blame you. I'm a hellava guy. Hey, I need to hold you.
ROSE: What for?
CLIFF: I don't get much exercise.
ROSE: Everybody wants to touch and say nice things.
CLIFF: Hey, it's normal.
ROSE: And then you never see them no more.
CLIFF: It's natural.
ROSE: Says who?
CLIFF: The world.
ROSE: If it's natural, what am I?
CLIFF: You tell me.
ROSE: A freak?
CLIFF: You said it, not me.
ROSE: All right, so I'm a freak.
CLIFF: I need to hold you. Can't you see that?
ROSE: I'd rather be a freak than end up like Brenda.
CLIFF: Here we go.
ROSE: Some guy stopped his car when she was walking down the street. He had a beautiful white car with furry seats. And he said all these things. Took her for a ride, saying all these things, you know, nice things. And they drank this wine (*Showing her Mateus bottle.*) which costs, for your information, $179 a bottle! And he said these things and she, you know, got crazy for him. And the night was beautiful. And he said he'd come by the next day but he didn't, so she went to his apartment and his car was there and she knocked on the door but he wouldn't answer because he had another girl in there. And Brenda kicked the door, and he still wouldn't open it, and she got sick and vomited on his porch and let herself fall in the snow. In the snow. And she felt the snow freezing her fingers and toes, and she didn't care what happened anymore, and the cops came in the

The Woolgatherer / 85

morning and found her almost dead and dragged her in their car and took her the hospital and she almost got killed of pneumonia and frost-bite and they gave her a needle to make her stop screaming and put her on the eighth floor and psychiatrists asked Brenda why she did it, lay in the snow, and she told them and they didn't believe her and they found her father but he didn't want her and used to beat her and curse at her and other stuff and he was an alcoholic and they kept her up there two months and she lost her job and they . . . And that's what happened to Brenda.

CLIFF: So what.

ROSE: What do you mean so what?

CLIFF: That's English for so what.

ROSE: So that's true love.

CLIFF: O don't make me barf. She was a true asshole.

ROSE: When you love somebody, you don't curse or make fun and even when they cheat you make a fool of yourself even if you have to sit in the snow and die.

CLIFF: O, cut the shit, huh? There's no such thing as true love. True love's when you got a fat bankbook.

ROSE: Maybe for some people.

CLIFF: Hey, one thing counts out there, Rosie-schmosie. Scratch! And you gotta leap in the fuckin dogfight and grab all you can grab. And while you're out grabbin' it, true love's screwin' the guy next door. And if you lose it, you get true love's consolation prize—alimony payments! So don't hit me with this bullshit about true love because I been there and I know better. (*Pause.*) Alls I said was I want to hold you and you gotta make a big deal.

ROSE: It's not my fault I'm this way!

CLIFF: Look, I don't want to hear about no bad childhood.

ROSE: I have to be very careful because of my hemophilia.

CLIFF: Your what?

ROSE: I happen to have a very very rare blood disease. If I get cut I could bleed to death.

CLIFF: This ain't happening.

ROSE: Just a little scratch bleeds for days! And if I get a deep cut, that's it!

CLIFF: I said I want to hold you, not bite you!

ROSE: So I have to be very careful!

CLIFF: So how's a flesh and blood man supposed to get near you? I talk, I draw blood. I touch, you go icy. I mean, hey, maybe we should carry this thing on over the telephone. Germless. And when it starts to hurt, you could hang up.

ROSE: I don't have a phone.

CLIFF: I'm not talking about phones! I'm talking about me and you! I'm here, you're there, and there's no wall between us except the one you keep building up in that head of yours!

ROSE: I don't know what wall you're talking about.

CLIFF: Hey, Rosie, I didn't order a pound of nonpareils because I got a sweet tooth. I didn't come up here to discuss Brenda or seaweed soup or homophilioes or dinosaurs or flamingoes. I came up here to be with you. You. And hold you. Make love to you.

ROSE: (*Pause.*) I don't want to cheat.

CLIFF: So you do have a man, eh?

ROSE: Yes.

CLIFF: So why the fuck did you invite me up here.

ROSE: And he doesn't curse or smoke or pretend he wants to talk when he wants to touch and doesn't make fun!

CLIFF: What's he, a priest? Sister Rose and Father Clean!

ROSE: Shut up!

CLIFF: What do you guys do for thrills? Whip each other with the rosaries?

ROSE: Go to hell!

CLIFF: You cursed! O, what a trashmouth!

ROSE: FUCK YOU!

CLIFF: Rose, you don't watch your mouth, I'm leavin'.

ROSE: Now for the rest of my life, I could never say I never cursed!

CLIFF: O big fuckin deal! That your only problem in life? You been cooped up too long, Rosie-dozie!

ROSE: If I never met you, this would've never happened!

CLIFF: If! If! If! If my aunt had balls, she'd be my uncle! (*Pause.*) Well, look, champ, I was lookin' for a little wham-bam-thank-you-m'am, but I guess I turned over the wrong rock. So, catch ya later.

ROSE: Can I have your sweater?

CLIFF: Come again?

ROSE: Nevermind.

CLIFF: No no no no no. What did you ask me?

ROSE: Nothing . . . I was just . . . Nothing.

CLIFF: Could you have my sweater?

ROSE: If you don't want it.

CLIFF: Well, yeah, I was just about to toss it in the garbage on the way out.

ROSE: You must think I'm crazy.

CLIFF: Noooooooooooooooooooooo.

ROSE: Nevermind.

CLIFF: Can I ask what for?

ROSE: I don't know. To remember you by.

CLIFF: Remember me by.

ROSE: But nevermind.

CLIFF: It's my work sweater.

ROSE: I should've never asked.

CLIFF: It's dirty and I slept in it. Blew my nose in it.

ROSE: Nevermind.

CLIFF: You don't want me to stay but you want to remember me by. That's one that goes way over my head, champ. So let's just leave it at that. Take good care of it. It's used to travelling across country at 65 m.p.h.

ROSE: Thank you.

CLIFF: And be careful. It goes through amber lights.

ROSE: Thank you.

CLIFF: It's 100% virgin wool. Meant to be. For you.

ROSE: Thank you.

CLIFF: The label fell out. But see this hole?

ROSE: Yes?

CLIFF: I burned it there so I know which's the front. But I don't want to assume anything, Rosie. Maybe you like the front on the back. Me myself, I like the front on the front.

ROSE: Thank you.

CLIFF: Rose?

ROSE: Yeah?

CLIFF: Can I have your shoe?

ROSE: I thought you was different.

CLIFF: It was all in your head. Catch ya later.

ROSE: Bye.

CLIFF: Yeah.

ROSE: Hope you get the new job.

CLIFF: Yeah.

ROSE: Think your truck's fixed?

CLIFF: What's it matter?

ROSE: Will you ever drive through Philadelphia again?

CLIFF: Who knows?

ROSE: Bye.

CLIFF: Yeah.

ROSE: Thank you.

CLIFF: Yeah.

ROSE: Bye. Cliff?

CLIFF: Yeah?

ROSE: Will you be cold without your sweater?

CLIFF: Me? Cold? Hey, Rosie, you're lookin' at the only survivor of the Great Ice Age. (*Exit CLIFF. His footfalls fade down the stairwell. ROSE rushes to the door.*)

ROSE: Cliff? (*Lights fade quickly.*)

END OF ACT ONE

ACT 2

The same. Almost complete darkness. ROSE hardly visible in bed.

ROSE: Shhh! The old lady! Hear her move the glass? (*Pause.*) You have cold feet. You should cut your toenails. (*Pause.*) If your truck ever crashes through a guardrail off a mountain, and you get all crippled up in a wheelchair, don't worry. Everything will still be the same. (*Pause.*) And I don't cheat. Shh! Hear her move the glass? She's hard-of-hearing until you whisper. And then she hears the flowers growing on the wallpaper. Around Christmas she goes a little berserk. Screams at her son for not visiting her. Throws things. Pots and dishes. But he's not there. Nobody's there. And then it gets real quiet, and if you listen close, like with a glass, you can hear her whimper, like a hurt animal. (*Pause.*) You should rub your hands with cold cream to make 'em soft. You scratch me. (*Pause.*) When you was asleep, I dreamed we were in your truck, riding up this mountain, you know, cross country. (*Pause.*) If you don't mean something, don't tell me, all right? Because it makes me dream, and one dream makes another, and I'm lost in the bigness of the

The Woolgatherer / 89

mountain and the curve of the road, and the engine was chugging hard, and there was this thin guardrail this far away and the breeze carried the scent of grass and wild flowers and I got ascared because we got higher and higher and held tight to the seat and you laughed and said, "what's that funny noise?" and I said, "what noise?" and you said, "o no! the truck's gonna explode!" and I punched you and we laughed and this cool breeze, this different breeze touched us, this salt breeze, and we came around the bend in the mountain road and all of a sudden this tremendous light hit us, and it was so big you couldn't see the beginning or end and it was the Pacific Ocean glimmering like tin foil rolled out forever, and we couldn't speak for a long time, and way down below us we saw the cities along the coast, like beads on a necklace, and we went down the mountain. And at the bottom we got out the truck and you took my arm and pulled me across the sand and into the waves and I screamed at the touch of the water and you laughed and we both went under and tasted the salt of the ocean and it was so good and we came up and kissed me hard on the mouth and I tasted your salt and a wave came over our heads and dunked us under and we laughed and got water in our mouths and spit it at each other and everybody on the beach thought we were crazy but we didn't care because we felt new again. (*A knock at the door.*)

CLIFF: Rose?

ROSE: Yes?

CLIFF: It's me.

ROSE: Yes?

CLIFF: I want to see you. (*Pause.*) Rose? (*Pause.*) Can I see you? (*Pause.*) Huh? Rose?

ROSE: Yes?

CLIFF: You alone? (*Pause.*) Rose?

ROSE: Yes?

CLIFF: You alone?

ROSE: Yes.

CLIFF: You sure?

ROSE: I know if I'm alone or not!

CLIFF: Can I see you?

ROSE: What for?

CLIFF: I don't know I don't know I don't know. (*Pause.*) Can I?

ROSE: I have to get up early for work.

CLIFF: Me too, but I have to see you tonight, Rose.

ROSE: What for? Slam-bam and thank you ma'm?

CLIFF: Hey, Rose.

ROSE: Well I'm not a slam-bam!

CLIFF: That was just all mouth . . .

ROSE: There's a lot of slam-bams in the world!

CLIFF: I know, I know . . .

ROSE: But I am not a slam-bam!

CLIFF: I never thought you was . . .

ROSE: You said you came here for slam-bam.

CLIFF: Rose, can we talk?

ROSE: I don't want to hear about your waitresses or your frickin truck. (*Pause.*) You there? (*Pause.*) Cliff? (*She opens the door. The door stops with a jerk when the chain runs out. Through the long space, a rude slice of hallway light glares on ROSE and CLIFF.*)

CLIFF: Hey, Rosie, you're wearin' my sweater.

ROSE: Truck break down again?

CLIFF: Not the truck.

ROSE: I though you never go back.

CLIFF: Yeah, me too. Can I come in?

ROSE: No.

CLIFF: What?

ROSE: No.

CLIFF: That's what I thought you said. Rose?

ROSE: What?

CLIFF: You don't open up and I pee in the hallway and you get evicted.

ROSE: (*She tries to close the door but for CLIFF's foot.*) Goodbye.

CLIFF: Have a good life.

ROSE: It's over.

CLIFF: Over? Where was I?

ROSE: Get your foot out please?

CLIFF: Did I enjoy it?

ROSE: Your foot, please!

CLIFF: If it ever gets started again, let me know, eh?

ROSE: Goodbye. (*She slams the door, listens to the silence, pause.*) I know you're there.

CLIFF: No sir.

ROSE: Will you please leave?

CLIFF: All right, but before I go, I have one last and final thing to say to your face.

ROSE: (*Opening the door.*) What?

CLIFF: I'm not leaving.

ROSE: I wish I never met you.

CLIFF: That's why you wear my sweater.

ROSE: So.

CLIFF: So.

ROSE: So what?

CLIFF: To remember me by.

ROSE: I thought you had deadlines and schedules.

CLIFF: Remember what about me?

ROSE: It's all ruined now, so nevermind.

CLIFF: Remember what?

ROSE: You won't understand.

CLIFF: Try me. In school, you know, I was the fastest one in the slow group.

ROSE: It's personal.

CLIFF: So's my sweater.

ROSE: You want it back?

CLIFF: Remember what about me?

ROSE: That look you had in the Five and Dime.

CLIFF: What look?

ROSE: That look when you came up to my, you know, candy counter. When I was cleaning the glass, dreaming a man would come in that door out of the cold, with a smile you could hang onto, and he would notice me and we could talk without words. And the door opened and you walked in, came up to my counter and pressed your greasy finger on the glass and said, "Hey, sweetheart, gimme a pound of them things, nonpareils," and I looked at your fingerprint, and you did a beautiful thing: wiped it off with your sweater sleeve.

CLIFF: I did? O yeah sure.

ROSE: And nobody does that. Nobody. And I got ascared, you know, that I could make a thing come true, and you started to walk away and I made a dream you'd stay and you turned around with this look . . . But all it said was, she's a slam-bam!

CLIFF: How do you know?

ROSE: She's a cooped-up whacko!

CLIFF: Rose . . .

ROSE: That's all it said.

CLIFF: Maybe I'm a cooped-up whacko myself. (*Pause.*) It's just you in there, eh?

ROSE: You keep asking me that!

CLIFF: And you keep telling me yes, but look, Rose, I understand and it's late and I'm double-parked out there and if you got company tonight I could always drop in another time and I guess it just wasn't meant to be tonight.

ROSE: You think I invite people up here?

CLIFF: You invited me up here.

ROSE: Everybody always throws stuff back in your face.

CLIFF: Hi. We're everybody.

ROSE: (*Slamming the door.*) Everytime!

CLIFF: Ever slam this door on the museum guy?

ROSE: I never took the curator up here!

CLIFF: Yeah, he brings you down in the cellar to talk about mankind!

ROSE: Why don't you get some quarters, dimes, and nickels and go choke a phonebooth!

CLIFF: You bleed for mankind! But when a real live man's at your door, you give him splinters in the nose! (*Long pause. ROSE opens the door a little.*)

CLIFF: I was halfway home, flat-out on 95, the road empty, radio goin' baby o baby, and I notice my blinker winkin' at me and the rig threaded a jughandle with a mind of its own, and I don't know if I paid the tolls or ran red lights or stopped at STOP signs or ran over a dog, but I'm back like a homing pigeon. (*Pause. ROSE shuts the door. Pause. She undoes the chain, opens the door a little, looks in the hallway. No CLIFF. She opens the door wide. No CLIFF. She goes into the hallway Right. CLIFF, hiding hallways Left rushes into the room and locks ROSE out.*)

ROSE: Hey!

CLIFF: Who's there?

ROSE: Open this door!

CLIFF: I'm not that kind of guy.

ROSE: Cliff! (*He opens the door. ROSE enters scratching.*) See what you did!

CLIFF: Sorry.

ROSE: You always say you're sorry!

CLIFF: I'm always sorry for something around you.

ROSE: Talk low!

The Woolgatherer / **93**

CLIFF: Sorry.

ROSE: The old lady's all over the wall tonight.

CLIFF: What's to listen to?

ROSE: Me.

CLIFF: But you're alone.

ROSE: I really hate this. Always where I can't reach.

CLIFF: Let me.

ROSE: You caused 'em! You kid around too much!

CLIFF: You don't know how to itch. Let me show you.

ROSE: What do you know? You never had hives.

CLIFF: Hey, I know a bee with hives.

ROSE: You never stop.

CLIFF: Let me teach you. We'll start from scratch. Easy. Gentle. See? How's that?

ROSE: More in the middle.

CLIFF: Eh?

ROSE: Up a little.

CLIFF: Better?

ROSE: Harder.

CLIFF: Was I right?

ROSE: Mmmm.

CLIFF: Admit it.

ROSE: Mmmm.

CLIFF: Mmmm. What do you do when you're alone?

ROSE: Doorknob.

CLIFF: What's nicer?

ROSE: I don't know.

CLIFF: Don't know. You smile and the world goes away. (*He kisses her head.*)

ROSE: Don't, ok?

CLIFF: You bring it out in me.

ROSE: I'm not trying to.

CLIFF: Then why'd you get all specialed up?

ROSE: Just washed my hair, that's all.

CLIFF: Ribbon in your hair.

ROSE: Really?

CLIFF: Expecting company?

ROSE: No.

CLIFF: Going someplace?

ROSE: Bed.

CLIFF: Bed?

ROSE: It's late.

CLIFF: All specialed up for the dead cactus to look at?

ROSE: It's not really that dead.

CLIFF: Does this corner of your mouth know what the other's up to?

ROSE: Don't, please?

CLIFF: Hey, I'm sorry but I'm not, see, because I can't get over how this lip is so different from this one, or how your cheek pulls back the skin and all of a sudden there's a smile, and I look, it's there, I blink, it's gone, and everytime I see it, it's always the first time, see, so I'm sorry, but I'm not, because I want it, I want it in my coffee in the morning, I want it in my afternoon beer, and I want it in my nighttimes, I want it, and if the door's locked, and the curtain's drawn, if one mouth found another quiet and sweet and wonderful, maybe it's not as good as money in the bank, but it can't be as bad as smoking two packs aday, so I'm sorry, but I'm not because I could be wherever I want right now, but I'm here and you're there, and all the travellin' I want to do is from here to there . . .

ROSE: (*Pause.*) So how've you been?

CLIFF: Fine, thanks.

ROSE: Good.

CLIFF: And you?

ROSE: Fine, thank you.

CLIFF: Rosie, do you believe in life before death?

ROSE: You mean life after death.

CLIFF: No, I mean life now, here, tonight.

ROSE: Shhh! That was her just then!

CLIFF: (*To the wall.*) But what should we do with the body?

ROSE: Shhh! (*She pushes him on the bed, his face lands on the pillow.*)

CLIFF: That your hair that scent?

ROSE: No. Perfume.

CLIFF: Perfume?

ROSE: Like it?

CLIFF: Mmmmm.

ROSE: It's imported.

CLIFF: Beautiful.

ROSE: From New Orleans.

CLIFF: You always splash on perfume before you hit the sack?

ROSE: Makes me dream.

CLIFF: Of what?

ROSE: Things.

CLIFF: Things.

ROSE: Sniff.

CLIFF: Mmmmm.

ROSE: What's it remind you of?

CLIFF: Lug nuts.

ROSE: No.

CLIFF: Jerkins.

ROSE: No, sniff again. (*She squirts his eyes.*) It's called Tooch Mwa. I get twenty percent off at the Five and Dime.

CLIFF: Beautiful.

ROSE: What's it remind you of?

CLIFF: Bullshit.

ROSE: (*Long pause.*) You always ruin everything.

CLIFF: Brenda, did she wear lipstick to bed too?

ROSE: Brenda?

CLIFF: Yeah, you know, eighth floor Brenda.

ROSE: What's wrong?

CLIFF: You know, die-in-the-snow Brenda.

ROSE: I don't understand you.

CLIFF: How comes the bed's all messed up?

ROSE: I was sleeping.

CLIFF: In a sweater.

ROSE: I was cold.

CLIFF: And lipstick? and perfume?

ROSE: So what?

CLIFF: Hair fixed and ribbon?

ROSE: So what?

CLIFF: SO WHAT? I do a u-turn. So what!

ROSE: Will you lower your voice?

CLIFF: Why'd you take so long to answer the door?

ROSE: It takes me awhile to wake up.

CLIFF: I'm in the hall, ask if you're alone, I get a big stall-out, hear funny things goin' on in here . . .

ROSE: Shh! Mrs. Mancuso!

CLIFF: You got somebody in there, don't you?

ROSE: What?

CLIFF: C'mon, c'mon, you got somebody in the closet, don't you?

ROSE: No.

CLIFF: Move.

ROSE: No.

CLIFF: Look, Rose, I don't give a shit, understand?

ROSE: I don't know what happened to you.

CLIFF: You stash some idiot twerp and then let me pour my guts out?

ROSE: You must be crazy.

CLIFF: Me, not you, me!

ROSE: Will you lower your voice?

CLIFF: Sure. How's this? Move.

ROSE: I don't know you now.

CLIFF: Tell him to come out.

ROSE: Who?

CLIFF: C'mon, c'mon, c'mon!

ROSE: There's nobody!

CLIFF: How come I don't believe you?

ROSE: I don't care if you don't believe me.

CLIFF: Would you care if I rip the door off the hinges?

ROSE: You have to go. I have to go to work.

CLIFF: After midnight? What's at the Five and Ten? The whacko rush?

ROSE: Goodnight.

CLIFF: Tell chickenass to come out so I could say goodnight.

ROSE: There's nobody. Why can't you just believe me?

CLIFF: Because everywhere I go I find I been there before.—MOVE!

ROSE: You just have to believe me.

CLIFF: Do me a favor?

ROSE: What?

CLIFF: Open the door and show me nobody's there?

ROSE: There's nobody!

CLIFF: Show me! Look, Rose, I'm not gonna throw no hands. If you got another man, what's that to me? Who's there? (*He smashes the crate against the wall.*) Who'd you think I was? Johnny Gallant on a white horse ready to pick up the tab for every dipshit that ever got a rod for you? (*CLIFF opens the closet. Inside, men's sweaters on hangers. Long pause.*) Nice selection. (*Pulling a sweater off a hanger.*) Got anything in a turtleneck?

ROSE: They're Brenda's.

CLIFF: And the one you got on, that Brenda's too?

ROSE: No, this one's yours.

The Woolgatherer / **97**

CLIFF: So when's mine get to hang with these, eh, Brenda?

ROSE: What?

CLIFF: When you ask some other asshole for his, eh, Brenda?

ROSE: No.

CLIFF: What was this guy's name, eh, Brenda? (*Drops sweater on floor, kicks it at ROSE.*)

ROSE: Don't!

CLIFF: Was it true love?

ROSE: Please don't. (*She retrieves the kicked sweater.*)

CLIFF: (*Throwing a sweater at her.*) You dippy fuckin gooney-bird!

ROSE: Please?

CLIFF: And what was this guy's name? (*Throwing a sweater at her.*) Was he a truck driver or screwdriver? And this one with the little reindeers and snowflakes! Was it meant to be? (*Throwing a sweater.*)

ROSE: STOP IT!

CLIFF: Did this one die in the snow for you? (*Throwing a sweater.*)

ROSE: Stop it! Stop it!

CLIFF: And what was this guy's name, eh, Sister Rose? (*Throwing a sweater.*) And this one? How long did this one last? (*Throwing a sweater.*)

ROSE: Killing the birds!

CLIFF: I always get the fuckin loonies.

ROSE: Legs snapped like straws!

CLIFF: Fuckin birds.

ROSE: Wings flapping in the water!

CLIFF: What a fuckin Jonah! (*About to throw a sweater, but seeing ROSE frozen in the image of the birds, he drops it, begins to exit.*)

ROSE: Mangled and bloody and broken in the water. Beaks a little open. Still. And one with the eye open. Making a baby sound. Eye open making a baby sound. Its breast beating hard. Hard. Hard. Hard. Hard. Hard. And less hard. And less hard. And not so hard. And not so hard. And a little less hard. And then a little bit. And a little bit. And then very little. And soft. And soft. And very soft. And then nothing. Soft. The feathers. Soft. The breast. Soft. (*She imitates this sound.*)

CLIFF: (*Re-entering.*) Rose, get off the floor.

ROSE: Look what they did! Look!

CLIFF: Rose, get up.

ROSE: Animals! How could you punish them? You can't make the birds come alive again!

CLIFF: Rose, up!

ROSE: I don't want to go there!

CLIFF: (*She backs away from him.*) Rose, I'm sorry.

ROSE: No needle!

CLIFF: What needle? I don't have a . . .

ROSE: I don't want to sleep. I want to run out in the street and scream, They killed the birds! They killed the birds! They stoned the birds! And nobody cares! Nobody!

CLIFF: Rose . . .

ROSE: So I have to care for everybody . . .

CLIFF: Shhh! Ok, ok, shhh!

ROSE: And I asked the zoo guard where they buried the birds, and he said they didn't bury them and I said what did you do with them? and he said they put 'em in the garbage!

CLIFF: Ok, ok . . .

ROSE: Like coffee grinds and old beer cans and milk cartons and orange peels in the garbage!

CLIFF: That's too bad.

ROSE: Beaks a little open . . .

CLIFF: That's all over with, Rose . . .

ROSE: Toes curled up like they was cold . . .

CLIFF: OK, OK . . .

ROSE: In the garbage!

CLIFF: All right, so what the fuck can I do about it?

ROSE: Why couldn't they bury them with a stone and flowers?

CLIFF: You sicko jerkoffed whacko fuckin dippy bitch! I must be flipped out of my gourd to come back to this.

ROSE: Four rare beautiful birds! In the garbage!

CLIFF: Rose! You still got three of 'em left in the world!

ROSE: They killed the birds!

CLIFF: You said there were seven cranes.

ROSE: They stoned the birds!

CLIFF: Didn't you say there was seven fuckin cranes in the world?

ROSE: They dumped 'em in the garbage!

CLIFF: So how much is seven cranes minus four dead cranes, Einstein?

ROSE: And I called the paper and said why don't you put that in the paper! That they dumped four rare beautiful birds in the garbage! Why don't you put that in your headlines!

The Woolgatherer / 99

CLIFF: Hey! Hammerhead! You got crap in your ears! Seven cranes minus four dead cranes! How much!

ROSE: They killed the birds!

CLIFF: Seven minus four! How much goddamnit! (*Shaking her.*) How much! How much! Seven minus four!

ROSE: I don't know!

CLIFF: Seven minus four!

ROSE: I don't know!

CLIFF: SEVEN MINUS FOUR!

ROSE: THREE!

CLIFF: (*Exasperated, going to the floor with her, soft.*) Right. Three.

ROSE: Three!

CLIFF: Three what?

ROSE: Birds!

CLIFF: What kind of birds?

ROSE: Cranes.

CLIFF: Dead cranes or live cranes?

ROSE: They killed the birds!

CLIFF: Alive or dead?

ROSE: And dumped 'em in the garbage!

CLIFF: Alive or dead! There was seven! They killed four! Three left! Alive or dead! ALIVE OR DEAD!

ROSE: ALIVE!

CLIFF: Alive. Three live birds. What's that mean?

ROSE: I don't know.

CLIFF: What happens when you put a male with a female? Or you sayin' you don't know?

ROSE: Suppose there's three males.

CLIFF: Never happen.

ROSE: Or three females.

CLIFF: Eighty-six, champ. Birds hang out in mixed groups.

ROSE: But suppose there's no offspring and they die?

CLIFF: Then they call a taxidermist and stuff 'em and stand 'em next to the dinosaur bones.

ROSE: Dead.

CLIFF: No, just standing still forever.

ROSE: Once I watched the cranes standing so still in the water when the sun was going down. So still. But more alive than anything moving. And so graceful. And beautiful. And I watched the last of the light brush up against their feathers, their pure feathers, and edge 'em with a dandelion glow, like a halo, gold and white. Wings spread, standing like magnificent angels in the dark water, and how they stepped so graceful! Like they thought about each step! And it was like being in church, and I thought I heard music, and I wanted to sing or pray or I-don't-know-what . . . because if you look at them in a certain light, if you look at them and let them inside you, it makes you graceful and alive and beautiful too.

CLIFF: Hey, Rose, you ever hear of the laws of nature? Here ya go: If you're a bird, right, and your folks didn't beget no offspring, chances are, you won't either.

ROSE: But if the parents didn't beget offspring . . .

CLIFF: Right! Now what do you suppose comes down when the zookeepers go home? You think them birds stand around counting each other's fleas? Hey, the place turns into a regular Sodom and Gomorrah. And before you blink, you got a couple eggs on your hands. Long eggs, you know, to accommodate them stilts.

ROSE: How many could they have?

CLIFF: Hey, maybe five, six at a clip.

ROSE: That many?

CLIFF: Well it's a little outside my field of endeavor, but hey, if you're dealing with hustling independents, maybe seven or eight eggs.

ROSE: How long's it take?

CLIFF: You're talkin' acouple of weeks.

ROSE: More than that.

CLIFF: All right, so you get stuck with union birds and they drag it out acouple months. The whole foul-up's them legs. I mean, hey, if you had normal legs, that's one thing, but when you got to grow legs this long for a body this big, hey, you're in a ditch and a half, unless of course you luck out and get hold of a leg-stretcher.

ROSE: A what?

CLIFF: Leg-stretcher.

ROSE: Never heard of it.

CLIFF: It's an adjustable leg-brace on the end of a eye-screw you turn to stretch things out. I used to haul 'em from the factory in Phoenix to a zoo out Sacramento where they got a big population of birds with stubby legs.

The Woolgatherer / 101

ROSE: Where?

CLIFF: Hey, Sacramento.

ROSE: Any killer crows attack, champ?

CLIFF: You got to see it, Rose—something that escapes when you try and nail it down. I want you to be there when we come round that mountain and there's nothing between you and a thousand-foot fall but a guard rail made of popsicle sticks, and you catch whiff of a batch of air sprinkled with salt and turn the mountain and the big, deep, wide Pacific Ocean slams you in the old chops and blinds you with a light-flash that makes you dizzy tipsy, and you look around wonderin' where you're gonna steal your next breath from . . .

ROSE: It's like you get new eyes, and nothing looks the same . . .

CLIFF: And there it is: colors like nothing you saw before, like some delinquent went nuts with blue fingerpaints and smeared 'em as wide and deep and far as the eyeball can roll . . .

ROSE: So pretty, its scares you it might go away . . .

CLIFF: And you're up in that truck rounding the mountain and you're awake like never before, like after a life of catnaps, and you sing and make happy silly noises because there's nobody there . . .

ROSE: Nobody, but you don't want it to go to waste . . .

CLIFF: And you crave the sound of a human voice, even your own . . .

ROSE: But you want a voice different from your own to come back to you . . .

CLIFF: And you see cities along the coast . . .

ROSE: Likes beads on a necklace . . .

CLIFF: And the breeze finds a way inside you . . .

ROSE: So salty . . .

CLIFF: So fresh . . .

ROSE: You can taste it . . .

CLIFF: And the sun . . .

ROSE: So close . . .

CLIFF: So warm . . .

ROSE: You feel it touch you . . .

CLIFF: Like a hand on your shoulder, that warm . . .

ROSE: And it goes through you . . .

CLIFF: And you're never the same again . . .

ROSE: And you think somehow it happened before . . .

CLIFF: So beautiful . . .
ROSE: So so beautiful . . . (*Lights fade.*)

END

EXTREMITIES

EXTREMITIES was first produced in March 1981 at the Fifth Annual Festival of New American Plays at Actors Theatre of Louisville. The play was directed by John Bettenbender with the following cast:

MARJORIE .... Ellen Barber
RAUL .... Danton Stone
TERRY .... Peggity Price
PATRICIA .... Kathy Bates

EXTREMITIES was subsequently produced on December 22, 1982 at the Westside Arts Center, Cheryl Crawford Theatre. The play was directed by Robert Allan Ackerman with the following cast:

MARJORIE .... Susan Sarandon
RAUL .... James Russo
TERRY .... Ellen Barkin
PATRICIA .... Deborah Hedwall

The part of Marjorie was subsequently played by Karen Allen and Farrah Fawcett.

Characters

MARJORIE
RAUL
TERRY
PATRICIA

Setting

TIME: The present. September.
PLACE: Between Trenton and Princeton, New Jersey, where the cornfield meets the highway.
SET: The livingroom of an old farmhouse.
Dining table and three chairs.
Sofa and table.
A fireplace.
A large window before which hang plants of every description. A door leading outside.
A door leading to the kitchen.
Stairs leading to other rooms in the house.
A locked bicycle against the wall.

Properties

Wicker settee
Swivel arm chair
End table
Pedestal oak table
Three side chairs
Bench
Two area rugs (padded)
Metal headboard
Three throw pillows
Bicycle (wheel off)
Phone
Cassette player w/cord
Tea kettle
Hunting knife w/sheath
Scoop shovel
Insecticide

Hammer
Paint brush
Trowel
Metal ashtray
Ammonia bottle w/water
Bleach bottle w/water
Tool box
Ceiling paint roller
Paint box w/dressing
Wooden box matches
Hanging plants
Plant mister
Wine glasses
Wine bottle
Key hook
Pad of paper
Pencils
Iodine
Bite bandage
Bucket
Breakfast (dressing)
Plate w/cold cuts, bread
Bookshelf dressing
Planting dressing
Painting dressing
Bookshelf dressing
Mantle dressing

PERSONAL PROPS
MARJORIE: Cigarettes, matches, lighter
RAUL: Knife harness (padded), vest, belt, noose rigging
TERRY: Bags of groceries, keys, purse (Act II: Drugstore bag
    w/medicine)
PATRICIA: Cheesecake box, purse, keys, briefcase

EXTREMITIES

ACT I
Scene 1

*Bright sunlight through the window. Enter MARJORIE in a bathrobe.
She surveys the breakfast dishes left on the table, sips a cup of tea. It's
cold. She puts on a large kettle of water. She makes a phone call. No
one answers apparently. She hangs up. Don't rush the action. It's a
lazy day. There are no pressing priorities. She rises after noticing a
wilted plant. She touches it affectionately, sprays it with water,
rearranges it among the healthier plants. Still not satisfied, she carrys
it out of the front door, placing it on the outside sill. A wasp attacks
her. She swipes at it. The plant drops. We hear the pottery crack. She is
stung by the wasp.*

MARJORIE: Dammit to hell! (*She enters the house, slams the door
closed. She inspects the inner side of her thigh just above the knee; two
red circles. She bolts for a box of tools near the plants. She find an
aerosol can of insecticide. She shakes the can. She opens the door. An
unseen wasp hovering near the threshold makes her give a little scream
and slam the door closed. She shakes the can. She opens the door
quickly, sprays the wasp, shakes the can, opens the door, sees no wasp,
opens the door wider, sees no wasp, opens the door all the way, looks
down, sees the dead wasp. She kneels down to it. Pause. She sprays it
too much, takes a scoop shovel from the tool box, scoops up the wasp,
closes the door, drops the wasp in the ashtray on the coffee table, sits,
lights a cigarette, takes one puff while studying the wasp, glances at its
wings, and without thought touches the wasp with the cigarette. Enter
RAUL.*)

RAUL: Joe? Hey, Joe? It's me. O. How ya doin? Joe in?

MARJORIE: (*Rising quickly, tying her robe.*) There's no Joe here.

RAUL: He said he'd be in.

MARJORIE: No Joe lives here.

RAUL: O.

MARJORIE: You always just walk in people's houses?

RAUL: O, I'm sorry. Excuse me. I'm really sorry.

MARJORIE: It's ok.

RAUL: Have a good day.

MARJORIE: You too.

RAUL: Thank you very much.

MARJORIE: You're welcome.

RAUL: You live here?

MARJORIE: Good guess.

RAUL: What, Joe move out?

MARJORIE: Joe who?

RAUL: Joe—I forget.

MARJORIE: There never was any Joe here.

RAUL: What's this, all one house, or apartments?

MARJORIE: All one house.

RAUL: He said he had a room here.

MARJORIE: Apparently he lied.

RAUL: Yeah, him or somebody else.

MARJORIE: I'm sorry, you have to go.

RAUL: Can I use the phone, please?

MARJORIE: No, I'm sorry.

RAUL: It's a local call.

MARJORIE: No, you have to go.

RAUL: (*Stroking the bicycle seat so gently.*) You ride a bike?

MARJORIE: No, I use it to collect dust. There's the door.

RAUL: I know where the door is. You don't have to tell me where the door is. This is a real bitch. The guy owes me alotta money. Said come pick it up.

MARJORIE: Well there's no Joe here.

RAUL: You sure, sweetheart?

MARJORIE: Maybe my husband knows. He's upstairs.

RAUL: Why don't you ask him, babe?

MARJORIE: He's busy right now.

RAUL: Busy.

MARJORIE: Sleeping.

RAUL: Sleeping.

MARJORIE: He's a cop.

RAUL: No kidding?

MARJORIE: And I have to wake him up in five minutes for work.

RAUL: Shh! You might wake him up.

MARJORIE: You better go now.

Extremities / **109**

RAUL: Cop, eh? Go ask him if he knows a guy named Joe.

MARJORIE: I told you he's sleeping.

RAUL: I dropped Joe off at this house last week.

MARJORIE: I think you have the wrong house.

RAUL: No. This house. He's about six two. Rides a Harley. Red beard. Wears cowboy boots. Short guy.

MARJORIE: There's no guy here.

RAUL: Except the cop.

MARJORIE: Honey, come down here please?

RAUL: Boy, that cop's a sound sleeper.

MARJORIE: Honey?

RAUL: What's amatter?

MARJORIE: Honey.

RAUL: Just like a cop: never there when ya need 'em.

MARJORIE: Honey!

RAUL: Honey! Honey! What's amatter wit him? Maybe he ain't here. Maybe you're tellin me a little lie eh, pretty momma? Maybe you think I scare easy. Go 'head. Go for the door. Let's see who's faster. So where's the other two chicks that live here?

MARJORIE: Kitchen.

RAUL: House full of people, and when you holler, nobody comes. (She bolts for the door; he cuts her off.)

MARJORIE: Get out!

RAUL: You got a lousy bunch of friends.

MARJORIE: Get out right now!

RAUL: Take it easy, lovely. I saw the other two chicks leave this morning. The one wit the ratty car should get here about five-thirty. The one wit specs, 'bout six. Today's gonna be a triple header.

MARJORIE: Get out! (Long pause. RAUL goes to door, looks at MARJORIE, laughs, goes to phone, rips the wire out.)

RAUL: Your move.

MARJORIE: I'm expecting people anytime now. Anytime.

RAUL: No kidding? Dressed like that? Mind if I stick around for the fun? Your move.

MARJORIE: Don't touch me!

RAUL: Don't fight me. I don't want to hurt you. You're too sweet to hurt. Be nice. You smell pretty. Is that your smell or the perfume? Be nice. Wanna take a shower together first? I'll soap you up real good? Flip me a little smile, babe. I'm gonna fuck you frontways, backways, sideways, and ways you never heard of. (*She runs. He latches onto her hair, brings her down, mounts her, forces a pillow to her face. We hear her muffled screams.*) You gonna be nice?

MARJORIE: (*Muffled.*) Yes!

RAUL: You sure?

MARJORIE: (*Muffled.*) Yes!

RAUL: (*Removing the pillow slightly.*) Please don't wreck it. You made me hurt you, and I don't want to hurt you, but if you kick and scream and scratch, what else can I do, eh, babe? (*She tries to escape once more; he subdues her with pillow.*) That pisses me off!

MARJORIE: (*Muffled.*) Please!

RAUL: See what you made me do!

MARJORIE: (*Muffled.*) Please don't!

RAUL: Want me to put out your light?

MARJORIE: (*Muffled.*) No!

RAUL: You gonna be nice?

MARJORIE: (*Muffled.*) Yes!

RAUL: What's that?

MARJORIE: (*Muffled.*) Yes! Yes!

RAUL: Heh?

MARJORIE: (*Muffled.*) Please don't kill me!

RAUL: Can't hear you.

MARJORIE: (*Muffled.*) Please! Don't kill me!

RAUL: If you're nice! Be nice! (*Removing the pillow.*) You don't want me to do it again, eh? (*Shaking her head no.*) Maybe you like to get hurt, eh? (*Shaking her head no. Pause. He smothers her again out of whim. She goes limp.*) Holy mother of god. A freckle. I didn't know you had freckles. I love freckles. I want to kiss 'em all. Give 'em names and kiss 'em all goodnight. Yeah. The first time I saw you I knew it was gonna be beautiful, but I didn't think this beautiful. I didn't think anything could be this beautiful . . . Not anything . . . Beautiful. (*He kisses her gently.*) Don't make your lips tight. They always make their lips tight. Do it nice. No. They're still tight. Kiss me nice. Yes. Yes. Nice. Smile. Smile! Nicer! How ya doin? Answer me!

MARJORIE: What?

RAUL: How ya doin? Say good.

MARJORIE: Good.

RAUL: Good. Invite me in.

MARJORIE: In where?

RAUL: Your house.

MARJORIE: We're already here.

RAUL: Nice place. Say thank you.

MARJORIE: Thank you.

RAUL: Kiss me and tell me you love me. Tell me!

MARJORIE: Please don't.

RAUL: Don't make it get ugly. Tell me you love me. Tell me!

MARJORIE: I love you.

RAUL: Say it nice.

MARJORIE: I love you.

RAUL: Tell me again and keep telling me.

MARJORIE: I love you I love you I love you . . .

RAUL: Yeah . . .

MARJORIE: I love you I love you I love you . . .

RAUL: More, more . . .

MARJORIE: I love you . . .

RAUL: How much?

MARJORIE: What?

RAUL: How much!

MARJORIE: How much what?

RAUL: You're trying to wreck this for me.

MARJORIE: No . . .

RAUL: Fuckin bitches always got to make it ugly!

MARJORIE: I love you!

RAUL: How much?

MARJORIE: A lot.

RAUL: More than what?

MARJORIE: I don't understand.

RAUL: You're gonna make me do something ugly.

MARJORIE: More than anything in the whole world! I love you!

RAUL: I love how you say that. Sweet.

MARJORIE: I love you.

RAUL: Touch me. All over. Nice. Again. Nicer. Touch my hair. My mouth. My neck. Keep telling me and don't stop.

MARJORIE: I love you I love you I love you . . .

RAUL: And keep touching me . . .

MARJORIE: I love you I love you . . .

RAUL: And touch me down there . . .

MARJORIE: I love you I love you . . .

RAUL: Touch me down there!

MARJORIE: I love you I love you . . .

RAUL: And tell me you wanna make love . . .

MARJORIE: I love you I love you . . .

RAUL: You're makin it ugly again!

MARJORIE: Please don't do this? Take anything you want. I've got jewelry upstairs.

RAUL: (*Slapping her.*) See! See! See what you made me do! Now touch me down there and say you wanna make love!

MARJORIE: I love you . . .

RAUL: And what else?

MARJORIE: I love you.

RAUL: Yeah, and what else?

MARJORIE: Make love.

RAUL: Who?

MARJORIE: You.

RAUL: And who else?

MARJORIE: Me.

RAUL: You wanna make love?

MARJORIE: Yes.

RAUL: Say it.

MARJORIE: I want to make love.

RAUL: You say that beautiful. Again.

MARJORIE: I want to make love.

RAUL: When?

MARJORIE: I don't know.

RAUL: Now!

MARJORIE: I don't know.

RAUL: This is your last chance.

MARJORIE: I love you and I want to make love.

RAUL: Scream.

MARJORIE: What?

RAUL: (*He clamps her leg just above the knee and squeezes.*) Scream! Louder! More! See? Nobody hears. Just me and you, puta. Say you're my puta.

MARJORIE: Puta?

RAUL: Puta, puta, whore, my whore, my puta! Say it!

MARJORIE: I'm your puta.

RAUL: Say it and smile!

MARJORIE: I'm your puta.

Extremities / **113**

RAUL: You like to tease me, eh, puta?

MARJORIE: No. Yes. Yes.

RAUL: You like to tease everybody.

MARJORIE: No.

RAUL: Know what you need, puta? You need acouple slashes here and here and here, stripes t' make you a zebra-face t'scare the shit outta anybody you go teasin', puta, cause you're mine, all mine. Say it!

MARJORIE: Yours!

RAUL: Undo the belt.

MARJORIE: Please! God!

RAUL: Undo it! This is gonna be beautiful, so you keep telling me, puta, and don't stop . . .

MARJORIE: I love you, I love you . . .

RAUL: You smell so pretty . . .

MARJORIE: I love you . . .

RAUL: You put perfume on for me?

MARJORIE: (*Seeing the aerosol almost in reach.*) Yes!

RAUL: Just for me!

MARJORIE: (*Reaching furtively, still too far.*) Yes! Yes! I love you! I love you!

RAUL: You say that more and more beautiful!

MARJORIE: (*In order to reach the aerosol, she must embrace RAUL.*) I love you! I really really love you! I wanna be your puta!

RAUL: This is too beautiful!

MARJORIE: Yes!

RAUL: See! It don't have to be ugly, does it?

MARJORIE: No! No! Beautiful! I love you!

RAUL: I love when you hug me like that!

MARJORIE: I love you!

RAUL: Your perfume makes me drunk!

MARJORIE: I love you!

RAUL: You put it on for me?

MARJORIE: Yes!

RAUL: Just for me?

MARJORIE: (*Grabs the can.*) Just for you! (*Sprays his face. He screams, holds his eyes. MARJORIE pushes RAUL away with her foot and tries to run for the door but RAUL latches onto her leg. Struggling to escape, she yanks an extension cord from the socket, loops it around his neck and pulls. He screams. Blackout. The sound of a wasp, or wasps,*

114 / *William Mastrosimone*

to cover the blackout.)

Scene 2

In the blackout RAUL's cry is more animal than human. Lights up slowly. RAUL is blindfolded and bound in a tangle of extension cords, clothesline, belts, and other household implements. He kicks and bucks and bites at his restraints. MARJORIE staggers to the sink. She turns on the water, splashes some on her face and wasp bite, turns on the kettle.

RAUL: You there? My eyes burn! I need a doctor! You there? I'm hurt bad! Help me! You there? Where are you? (*MARJORIE dials the phone.*) Call the cops, pussy! You can't prove a fuckin thing! (*Realizing the phone is dead, she drops it and watches RAUL buck.*) Why don't you fuckin answer me! You bitch! I'll kill ya! Get the cops! They gotta let me go! (*MARJORIE runs up the stairs.*) Your Honor, I goes out looking for work cause I got laid off the car wash and I sees this farmhouse and goes t'ask if there was any work cause I get three babies t'feed, and this crazy lady goes and sprays me with this stuff, Your Honor. (*MARJORIE rushes down the stairs holding her clothes in hand, opens the door, but stops upon the mention of her name.*) Go on, Marjorie, go down the road and stop a truck on the highway and tell 'em get the cops. You got no bruises, no witnesses, no come up your snatch. You got nothin, pussy. (*MARJORIE inadvertently lets the door slam.*) This is a civilized fuckin country, pussy! You don't go around tyin up innocent people, Marjorie!

MARJORIE: How do you know my name?

RAUL: I demand my rights! I want medical attention! I wanna call my attorney! Palmieri! The fuckin best!

MARJORIE: How do you know my name?

RAUL: And when you're alone in the room wit the pigs and tell 'em what happened, and they say, You sure, sweetheart? They don't believe no pricktease, Marjorie.

MARJORIE: Don't say my name.

RAUL: And little Margie gets a little write-up in the paper and wit Daddy's heart condition that could be real sweet if the old fucker croaks . . .

MARJORIE: My father?

RAUL: And me, I'm sippin o.j. in some nice clean hospital bed jawin with the candy-stripers and every freako-scuz-fuck and happy headhunter who rake the papers for hits come pussy-sniffin out here like a pack o junkyard dogs after a bitch in heat and maybe drop in unannounced for a wet dick . . . (*The tea kettle begins to whistle.*) What's that! Siren? You call the cops? (*MARJORIE gets the kettle. We must see the steam.*) You don't got a fuckin case! They gotta miranda me! and let me go! (*MARJORIE is about to return the kettle.*) And then one day I come back . . . (*She stops.*) Get you in some parking lot and carve up that teasin face . . .

MARJORIE: No!

RAUL: Who the fuck you think you're playin wit, bitch? (*MARJORIE snaps and dumps hot water on him. He screams. She screams. Blackout. The sound of wasps cover the blackout.*)

Scene 3

Lights up slowly. RAUL is in the fireplace. MARJORIE has lashed the bicycle to the fireplace. It is locked with the bicycle chain.

RAUL: Where am I? Marjorie? Where am I?

MARJORIE: How do you know my name?

RAUL: Where am I?

MARJORIE: (*Tugging his noose.*) Answer me.

RAUL: I can't talk! Marjorie!

MARJORIE: Don't you ever say my name again! How'd you know me?

RAUL: I read it on a letter.

MARJORIE: (*Tugging his noose.*) What letter?

RAUL: Heartless bitch!

MARJORIE: What letter?

RAUL: I took some letters from your mailbox by mistake. This guy Joe asked me to come pick up his mail.

MARJORIE: Who were the letters from?

RAUL: One from your father. One from a collection agency. A couple from guys.

MARJORIE: Who?

RAUL: Some guy Tony. He wants you come live with him in New York. He don't want you to tell Terry.

MARJORIE: Who else?

RAUL: Your brother in Marine boot camp. Says they're beatin the shit outta him down there. He thinks he's got it bad.

MARJORIE: Why me? Answer me. Why me?

RAUL: Don't know. Crazy whacko bitch! What the hell!

MARJORIE: Why me?

RAUL: I saw you around.

MARJORIE: Where?

RAUL: Around! I don't know! Please! (*She pokes him with a fireplace implement.*)

MARJORIE: Answer me!

RAUL: I don't know what to say!

MARJORIE: Try the truth!

RAUL: O, the truth! Why didn't you say so! All right! Here it goes. The truth. This guy Joe . . . (*She pokes him.*) That's the truth! I swear on my mother's grace! Whattaya nuts or what! You said the truth, I told the truth, and you go poke me! (*She stops poking.*) You wanna hear this or not?

MARJORIE: Go ahead.

RAUL: You won't poke me?

MARJORIE: I said go ahead!

RAUL: All right. The truth. There was this guy Joe . . . (*He flinches in anticipation of a poke.*) He's a pimp. Said for half a yard he'd fix me up with a knock-out pussy. Said walk right in and ask for him and you'd know what I meant but I guess he was playing a joke on me. (*She pokes him.*)

RAUL: Please! Stop! Marjorie!

MARJORIE: Don't say my name!

RAUL: You are the boss, Jack! You are the man! Whatever you say! Ok? No panic. Listen, can I ask you one little question, Marjorie?—It slipped! I swear on my grandmother's milk!—One little question. Where am I?

MARJORIE: Fireplace.

RAUL: Where?

MARJORIE: The fireplace.

RAUL: What for?

MARJORIE: Why do people put things in the fireplace?

RAUL: People put things in the fire . . . (*Pause.*) Hey, c'mon, don't joke around.

MARJORIE: (*Shaking a plastic bottle of ammonia.*) And I have some gas.

Extremities / **117**

RAUL: Gas? What, for your car?

MARJORIE: No. For you.

RAUL: I don't even own a car.

MARJORIE: (*Shaking a box of wooden matches.*) And matches.

RAUL: Whoa, jack!—Listen, I been doin some deep thinkin here and now I'm ready for the truth. I mean the real truth. I'm a narco. We got a tip there was drugs in this house. Open up. I'll show you my badge. (*She douses him with ammonia.*) Hey! What the hell! Hey! I got a wife and three kids!

MARJORIE: (*Striking a match very near.*) Maybe you'll tell the truth when you're on fire! (*RAUL coughs uncontrollably. He fights for breath in the chemicalized air. MARJORIE strikes a match, holds it close to his face.*)

RAUL: All right! This is it! The honest-to-god truth. I don't know why I didn't tell you this from the beginning because this is it. (*Pause.*) I used to work on the pothole crew. For the County. We went around patchin up potholes. One day we was patchin up potholes on the highway. In front of your driveway. Bitchin day. In the nineties. Working with hot tar. Sweatin. Thirsty. Gettin dizzy. Foreman bustin balls. Somebody says, look at this. And you come ridin down the highway on your bike in your little white shorts and everytime you pedal you could see what was tan and what wasn't and your blouse tied in a knot and the sun shinin off your hair, beautiful. And that's it.

MARJORIE: So why'd you come here?

RAUL: I just told you. You was beautiful.

MARJORIE: So what?

RAUL: You know what that does to a man. It was hot. You had on little white shorts.

MARJORIE: You're gonna burn. (*MARJORIE flicks matches wildly.*)

RAUL: Please! We had a deal! On the milk of Mary! You rode by in your shorts! I said How ya doin? You didn't say nothing. Looked at me like I was a dead dog. You pissed me off so I came back here to fuck you! (*MARJORIE stops flicking matches. RAUL whimpers and slumps down. MARJORIE sits. Long pause.*) You there? (*Pause.*) Whattaya gonna do wit me?

MARJORIE: (*Pause. With perfect aplomb.*) Nothing.

RAUL: Nothing?

MARJORIE: Nothing.

RAUL: You mean—let me go?

118 / *William Mastrosimone*

MARJORIE: No. Nothing.

RAUL: I don't catch what you're talkin.

MARJORIE: (*Silence.*) You will.

RAUL: When.

MARJORIE: You'll see.

RAUL: Starve me?

MARJORIE: Good idea.

RAUL: Why don't you just call the cops?

MARJORIE: Why should I?

RAUL: That's what they're there for! (*Pause.*)

MARJORIE: Two days. No food. No water.

RAUL: You can't do this!

MARJORIE: I am doing it.

RAUL: I really think you should call the cops.

MARJORIE: You said I have no proof, they'll let you go.

RAUL: No. Marjorie, I swear, I was just talkin. Get the cops.

MARJORIE: It's too late.

RAUL: Mother of god! I don't want to die like this! Answer me! Talk to me! Please.—What will you do wit, you know, my body?

MARJORIE: Bury it.

RAUL: Bury it?

MARJORIE: I started a graveyard near the woods for the animals that get killed up on the highway. This time I dig deeper.

RAUL: You're jerkin me off.

MARJORIE: I got a shovel.

RAUL: Don't shit around! I got a weak ticker! (*Pause.*) My wife's eight months pregnant. She won't let me touch her. I'm goin nuts. I got to get it everyday. I need help. Honest to fuckin god. I want to go straight.

MARJORIE: You will. Straight in a fuckin hole.

RAUL: You ain't got the nuts, cunt.

MARJORIE: You say that when you're in the bottom of the hole and the first shovel of dirt hits you in the face!

RAUL: When they come home, the other chicks, they'll stop you!

MARJORIE: You think so? One helps me dig the hole, the other helps me drag you out!

RAUL: You can't do this!

MARJORIE: I want to hear you scream under the dirt, like me under the pillow. (*Exit for a shovel.*)

RAUL: Mother of god!

Extremities / **119**

MARJORIE: And you suck in for air, and dirt fills your mouth and nose!

RAUL: Send me your angel, mother of god!

MARJORIE: Suck for air! Under the dirt! with possum skulls! and dog bones!

RAUL: Get the cops! I want to tell 'em everything! This is it! (*MARJORIE pretends to leave by slamming the door.*) Marjorie! Marjorie! Marjorie!—She's diggin the hole, diggin the hole, she's really diggin the hole! (*Pause.*) O mother of god, do the miracle! Break these chains! (*He tries.*) Break these bars. (*He tries.*) What's amatter? Send me an angel like before! How can you let me die like this? (*Pause. Singing.*)

Found peanut
It was rotten
Ate it anyway just now
Then I died
Went to heaven . . .

(*Pause.*) What I do this time? What I do? I didn't do nothin. (*Pause. Singing.*)

Broke the statue
Knocked it over
Broke the Virgin just now
Got a beatin
Locked the closet
Wit the spiders just now.

(*Pause.*) You there? I know you're there. Marjorie. Please be there. How can you just sit there after alls between us? How can you do this to me? (*He thrashes about, gags, falls down, becomes still.*)

MARJORIE: Is it too tight? You all right? (*No answer. Pause. She probes him with the shovel, nothing. MARJORIE reaches to loosen the noose. RAUL bites her hand. She screams, cries, picks up the stick, but getting a better idea, hurls it at the cage, storms the kitchen.*)

RAUL: Bit the big bitch!
Bit the big bitch!
Bit the big bitch just now!
She was rotten!
Rotten! rotten!
La la la la! la la! (*MARJORIE enters running with the plastic container of ammonia and douses him.*) I'm on fire! I'm good! I'm

good! I'm gonna learn to tell the truth! the whole truth! nothing but the truth! I swear to fuckin god! Car! Car! Please, mother of god, let it be the cops!

MARJORIE: (*Pulling him against bars by noose.*) Talk again and I smash you like a fuckin bug! (*MARJORIE looks out the window, sees TERRY with full arms, opens the door. Enter TERRY with grocery bags.*)

TERRY: What a day! (*Exit TERRY in the kitchen.*) That guy Danny I told you about? He cornered me by the water cooler and said, I'm taking you out to dinner tonight and not taking no for an answer, so I can't help you guys scrape and paint tonight, and look, Margie honey sweet lovely cutie-pie good friend, can I borrow your red dress, the one with the spaghetti straps and slit up the . . . (*Discovering RAUL.*) There's a man in the fireplace.

MARJORIE: Don't get scared. He tried to rape me.

TERRY: O Mother Mary.

MARJORIE: He's been watching us. He knows all about us, when you work, when you come home, when Pat comes home, our cars, everything.

TERRY: Who is he?

RAUL: Please help me! She hurt me bad!

MARJORIE: (*Poking him.*) What'd I say about talking?

RAUL: Not to!

MARJORIE: And what'd you do?

RAUL: I talked.

MARJORIE: And what do you deserve?

RAUL: Help me!

MARJORIE: What do you deserve?

RAUL: The stick. (*She hurts him, he screams.*)

TERRY: Marjorie! It's over now! We'll get the police and lock him up!

MARJORIE: On what charge?

TERRY: Rape.

MARJORIE: There was no rape.

TERRY: Attempted rape.

MARJORIE: Prove it. (*Pause.*) You can't. So they let him go and he said he'd come back to get me. So it's him or me. Him or me. Choose. Him or me.

TERRY: I'd rather call the police.

MARJORIE: Do it.

TERRY: It would make me feel safe.

MARJORIE: Then do it.

TERRY: What should I say?

MARJORIE: Whatever makes you feel safe.

TERRY: Phone's dead.

MARJORIE: Animal ripped it out of the wall. I got lucky. If I didn't you would've come home and found my body . . .

TERRY: Don't talk like that.

MARJORIE: You try and run. He catches you by the hair. Smothers you off and on till you're too weak to move.

TERRY: All right!

MARJORIE: And then he toys with you. Makes you beg for a breath. Makes you undo his belt.

TERRY: Stop it!

MARJORIE: Makes you touch him. All over. His mouth. His neck. Between his legs . . .

TERRY: Why are you doing this to me!

MARJORIE: So it won't happen to you!—Terry, if it happened to you, I'd say, Terry, tell me what to do.

TERRY: Tell me what to do.

MARJORIE: Be with me.

TERRY: I am with you. (*Pause.*) What can I do?

MARJORIE: Help me make him disappear.

TERRY: Let's wait for Pat.

MARJORIE: We don't need her. We only need the shovel.

TERRY: Shovel?

MARJORIE: To dig a hole in the garden.

TERRY: Hole?

MARJORIE: And that's the end of it.

TERRY: O God.

MARJORIE: Him or us. Choose. Say him and I open the cage and let him go. But if he gets you, don't blame me because you chose him. So decide now. Him or us. (*Pause.*) Decide! (*Pause.*) Say it. Him or us.

TERRY: Us.

MARJORIE: Good. Just dig the hole. I'll do the rest.

TERRY: Don't let me see it, all right?

MARJORIE: See what?

TERRY: The blood.

MARJORIE: What blood? There's no blood. We drag him out, throw him in the hole and cover it up.

TERRY: O God.

MARJORIE: Is the world better or worse without him?

TERRY: I don't want to touch him.

MARJORIE: All right, I can drag him myself. You just dig the hole. (*TERRY takes the shovel.*) Dig between the tomatoes and the flowerbed. The ground's soft there.

TERRY: I'd rather you dig.

MARJORIE: Then you watch.

TERRY: I'd rather you watch.

MARJORIE: I can't do both.

TERRY: You dig.

MARJORIE: Then watch him and don't leave the room.

TERRY: Marjorie? Let's think about this some more?

MARJORIE: What's to think about? It's simple. Him or you. Choose. (*Pause. TERRY sits. Exit MARJORIE with shovel.*)

RAUL: Pst! Pst!

TERRY: Be quiet, please.

RAUL: She gone? Is she?

TERRY: Yes.

RAUL: C'mer. C'mer.

TERRY: You will have to not talk.

RAUL: Terry, I need help. She sprayed me with stuff. My eyes're killin me! Please help me. I'm serious.

TERRY: Just shut up.

RAUL: So you're gonna help whacko poof me, eh?

TERRY: You better not let her catch you talking.

RAUL: Terry, Terry, my Good Humor truck broke down the highway. I wanted to call the office before the ice cream melted. I just asked to use the phone . . .

TERRY: I'll tell her you talked.

RAUL: Then share the crime. It's called complicity. That means you sit there like an asshole and watch somebody do a crime.

TERRY: Look, I'm not interested in what you have to say.

RAUL: How about my attorney? Interested in what he has to say? eh? when you're up in that witness chair? in front of the Big Twelve? and he goes, Tell the court what you did, Terry, when whacko was diggin the hole and my client was sufferin terrible and begged you open the cage? And Terry says, Nothin, and His Honor hits ya wit Croak One, and you go the iron Hyatt.

The wall. So you gonna open this up or not? (*Pause.*) Ok, asshole. The wall. Ever hear of my attorney? Palmieri?

TERRY: Yes.

RAUL: The best, right? (*He takes her silence for consent.*) For two g's the man walks on water, so think about it, jailbird. Open it, Terry—you don't want no record. (*Pause.*) Ok. Palmieri. Complicity. The wall. (*TERRY pours herself a glass of wine; at these sounds.*) Can I have a little swig of that? Parched from screaming. (*Pause.*) Hang it up, jailbird! You ride with whacko! The wall. Know about the wall? Noooooooooooo. Jailbird don't know diddly shit bout no wall. That why you sit there doin complicity when you could be givin me a little swig o juice so's I could tell Palmieri, Lay off the chick Terry, she's all right, she did what she could. (*Pause.*) Not even that, eh? (*Pause.*) Now I know how Christ felt. (*Pause.*) Whattaya say at confession this week? eh, Terry? Bless me father for I have sinned. I buried the Good Humor man. Ain't goin over too big, Terry. What do you think father's gonna say? say three hail Mary's and don't do it again? The fucker'll break out handcuffs on the spot! But I understand. You're doin it for Marjorie, good friend Marjorie.

TERRY: Will you shut up?

RAUL: Tight with Marjorie, eh? Friends to the ends, eh? You borrow her dress, she borrows your boyfriend. (*Pause.*) Tony.

TERRY: What?

RAUL: Forget it.

TERRY: No. What did you say?

RAUL: O, you want something from me, but when I ask you for a little drink, you gimme a cup o dust. Get lost, you and your fuckin drink.

TERRY: You're a goddamn liar.

RAUL: Am I?

TERRY: What'd she say?

RAUL: Don't believe me. I'm a liar. Go believe your good friend out there diggin a hole. She's nice. She buries people.

TERRY: What'd she tell you.

RAUL: Look, nobody likes to be the one to bring the bad news. (*Pause.*) She fuckin' him.

TERRY: He doesn't even live round here anymore!

RAUL: New York. (*Pause.*) Photographer. (*Pause.*) She goes see him every Wednesday. You drop her off the train station. (*Pause.*)

Think what you're doin, Terry. She get raped? She got broken bones? I pinched her ass, she took a freak and mangled me. Ever get your ass pinched? Course you did. Did you mangle the guy? Course not. Think, sweetheart, think.

TERRY: Tell me everything she said.

RAUL: Just wet my lips a little? please?

TERRY: All right.

RAUL: Thank you so much. I want to light a candle for you. God bless you . . . (*He latches onto her wrist.*) You scream and I bite your hand the fuck off.

TERRY: Please don't hurt me!

RAUL: I'm not that type person, babe. Undo the lock. (*TERRY blows her rape whistle.*) You fuckin asshole! You fucked yourself real good! They're gonna eat you alive at the wall! (*Enter MARJORIE. RAUL releases TERRY's hand.*)

MARJORIE: What happened?

RAUL: Marjorie! I'm sorry! She gave me a drink of wine.

MARJORIE: Why?

TERRY: I did not!

RAUL: How'd the glass get in here?

MARJORIE: Goddamit. (*MARJORIE bangs the firescreen with the shovel.*)

TERRY: I'm leaving!

MARJORIE: What'd he say?

TERRY: Where are my keys?

MARJORIE: The hole's half dug!

TERRY: I don't care.

MARJORIE: We're halfway there!

TERRY: Move.

MARJORIE: You said you would help me.

TERRY: I don't care what I said.

MARJORIE: Why can't you help me?

TERRY: I don't know what happened here and I don't care. You're alive. So what's it matter? Just get him out of this house. (*Sound of a car. Enter PATRICIA with briefcase and bakery box tied up neatly with a string.*)

PATRICIA: What's up with you broads?—Look, cherry cheesecake!—Did somebody die on the soaps? (*RAUL rattles his cage. Pause. PATRICIA laughs.*) Ok, what's the joke? C'mon, c'mon, you guys! I'm not falling for this one! Who's that?

TERRY: He tried to rape Marjorie.

PATRICIA: O, dear. (*Pause.*) You ok?

MARJORIE: I think so.

PATRICIA: Are you?

MARJORIE: Yes.

PATRICIA: How'd he get like that?

MARJORIE: I did it.

PATRICIA: You?

MARJORIE: Yes.

PATRICIA: Alone?

MARJORIE: Yes.

PATRICIA: And you're ok?

MARJORIE: Yes.

PATRICIA: When?

MARJORIE: Before—an hour—two—I don't know.

PATRICIA: Where's the police? Did you call?

MARJORIE: No.

PATRICIA: Why not?

MARJORIE: I'm going to fix him.

PATRICIA: Fix?

MARJORIE: Fix.

RAUL: Don't let her torture me no more!

MARJORIE: Shut the fuck up!

PATRICIA: What are you doing?

MARJORIE: I want him to hurt like me!

RAUL: Please help me.

PATRICIA: Stop it!

MARJORIE: I want him to hurt like me!

PATRICIA: Looks like you've done that. Now we have to put him away.

MARJORIE: I have no proof! They'll let him go! He'll come back and slash up my face!

PATRICIA: The fact that he's on the premises should put him away.

MARJORIE: Is that true?

PATRICIA: Honest. Honest. (*Pause, disarming her gently.*) It's going to be all right, honest. We'll take care of everything. You relax. Lie down. There. There. Yes. Here is a nice pillow . . .

MARJORIE: No!

PATRICIA: Ok. Everything is fine. Terry, would you call?

TERRY: Phone's dead.

PATRICIA: Ok. Would you get the police?

TERRY: What do I say?

PATRICIA: Tell them to come quickly.

TERRY: What do we say about him?

PATRICIA: Tell them to come and take him away.

TERRY: No, I mean if they see him like that, she's in trouble.

MARJORIE: What kind of trouble?

TERRY: Big trouble.

RAUL: A&B, mayhem, AD&W.

MARJORIE: Is that true?

PATRICIA: We'll get a lawyer.

MARJORIE: Lawyer?

TERRY: You have to, Marjorie.

PATRICIA: For your protection.

TERRY: They'll crucify you.

PATRICIA: Terry, please.

TERRY: We better get a lawyer before we get the police.

PATRICIA: You don't need a lawyer. The state prosecutes. You're only a witness.

MARJORIE: I want a lawyer.

PATRICIA: Ok. Look in the phonebook under P for Palmieri.

TERRY: Holy shit.

PATRICIA: What?

TERRY: That's his lawyer.

PATRICIA: How do you know?

TERRY: He told me.

MARJORIE: You talked with him?

PATRICIA: We'll take care of everything.

TERRY: I think we should make up a story.

PATRICIA: What?

TERRY: I'll say I was with Marjorie when he broke in.

PATRICIA: That's perjury.

TERRY: If it comes to his word against hers, he wins.

PATRICIA: We tell the truth. Now will you please hurry?

TERRY: You know his lawyer's going to file countercharges and haul her downtown.

MARJORIE: Is that true?

PATRICIA: It's just a formality.

TERRY: That's all. But bring a toothbrush.

PATRICIA: Don't worry about jail.

MARJORIE: Jail!

TERRY: Listen! Me and Marjorie are watching t.v., animal breaks in, there's a struggle, we hogtie him, he resists, we're afraid he'll escape, we stuff him in the fireplace, and went for the police.

MARJORIE: Police. Charges. Arraignment. Lawyers. Money. Time. Judge. Jury. Proof. His word against mine. Defendant's attorney—a three-piece button down summa cum laude fresh from Harvard fuck-off: Did my client rape you? No. Assault you? Yes. How? With a pillow. Did you resist? Yes. Evidence? None. Witnesses? None. Did you tie him up? beat him? lock him in a fireplace? Six months for me, that animal goes free. And if I survive being locked up, then what do I do? Come home and lock myself up. Chainlock, boltlock, deadlock. And wait for him. Hear him in every creak of wood, every mouse in the wall, every twig tapping on the window. Start from sleep, 4 A.M., see something in the dark at the foot of my bed. Eyes black holes. Skin speckled gray like a slug. Hit the lights. He's not there. This time. So then what do I do? Wait for him? Or move three thousand miles, change my name, unlist my phone, get a dog. I don't want to taste my vomit everytime the doorbell rings. I don't want to flinch when a man touches me. I won't wear a goddamn whistle. I want to live my life. He's never leaving this house.

PATRICIA: (*Pause.*) Marjorie I think you're in shock and don't know what you're saying. I'm going to a phonebooth and call the police and everything's going to be all right.

MARJORIE: I'm not in shock, and more than ever I know exactly what I'm saying, and you're not going anywhere. (*Snatching up their car keys.*)

PATRICIA: My keys, please.

MARJORIE: No.

PATRICIA: Then I guess we'll have to walk. (*MARJORIE takes a claw hammer from a toolbox near the door.*)

MARJORIE: You leave this house, animal dies.

PATRICIA: O, Marjorie, you don't really mean that.

RAUL: She means it! Please don't leave me! (*MARJORIE locks the door. PATRICIA and TERRY sit.*)

RAUL: Mother of god. (*Lights fade. End of Act I.*)

ACT II
Scene 1

The same as end of Act I. Lights up quickly.

PATRICIA: Ok, everything's fine. (*MARJORIE barricades door.*) Let's relax now and sit down and talk.

MARJORIE: I'm done talking.

PATRICIA: Ok, let's have a drink and some food.

MARJORIE: You eat.

PATRICIA: Ok, I'll open some wine. (*Exit PATRICIA to kitchen.*)

MARJORIE: What are you doing!

PATRICIA: I just opened the window.

MARJORIE: Close it!

PATRICIA: Ok.

MARJORIE: Lock it!

PATRICIA: Ok. (*MARJORIE runs around locking the windows.*)

RAUL: Thank you, Terry.

MARJORIE: What? (*Pause.*) Thank you for what?

TERRY: I don't know.

MARJORIE: What'd you say?

RAUL: Thank you.

MARJORIE: For what?

RAUL: Not you.

MARJORIE: Thank you for what?

RAUL: To Terry.

MARJORIE: For what? (*MARJORIE jerks the noose.*)

RAUL: Please, I can't breathe!

MARJORIE: Thank you for what!

RAUL: For making the noose looser.

MARJORIE: Goddamit!

TERRY: Pat, did I move from this chair?

MARJORIE: You keep away from the animal!

TERRY: Marjorie, I never went near him!

MARJORIE: Do you understand that!

PATRICIA: Terry! please!

TERRY: Sonofabitch!

MARJORIE: No more!

PATRICIA: Let's calm the hell down, please! everyone!

MARJORIE: Where do you think you're going?

TERRY: My room.

MARJORIE: Stay here.

TERRY: Why?

MARJORIE: I said so. Sit down. Now. (*TERRY sits.*)

RAUL: God bless you, Terry.

MARJORIE: Shut up!

PATRICIA: Ok, Ok, Terry, would you please fix something to eat? Please? Cold cuts and cheese. Put it on a plate and bring in some bread.

TERRY: Let's send for a pizza.

PATRICIA: Terry!—Please? (*Exit TERRY to kitchen.*) Wine?

MARJORIE: You know wine makes me sleepy.—Or is that what you want?

PATRICIA: Coffee?

MARJORIE: No.

PATRICIA: Anything?

MARJORIE: Silence. Thank you. (*Pause.*)

PATRICIA: (*Touching MARJORIE who doesn't respond.*) You're welcome. (*Pause.*) Sweater?

MARJORIE: I'm hot.

PATRICIA: You're shivering.

MARJORIE: I have to go to the bathroom.

PATRICIA: Well—go. O. Ok. You want me to go with you?

MARJORIE: That guy you were supposed to see tonight, does he know where you live?

TERRY: No. Yes. I think.

MARJORIE: Does he or not?

TERRY: Yes.

MARJORIE: Would he come here to see why you stood him up?

TERRY: How should I know?

MARJORIE: What do you think?

TERRY: Maybe. He'd call first.

MARJORIE: If he calls with the phone broke, what would he hear?

TERRY: Busy signal.

PATRICIA: He'd just hear dead air. Nothing.

TERRY: Or a recording: The number you have reached is being held hostage.

PATRICIA: Ok, Terry!—I'll call the phone company from work tomorrow.

MARJORIE: Tomorrow. You both have to take the day off tomorrow.

TERRY: Bullshit.

PATRICIA: Marjorie, tomorrow's staff meeting.

MARJORIE: I'm sorry.

TERRY: I used all my sick days. One more and I'm fired.

MARJORIE: Tough shit.

PATRICIA: Let it go.

TERRY: You let it go. I'm talking to you. One more thing and I'm fired. Then I could be like you and polish my nails and read glamour magazines all day.

PATRICIA: Terry.

TERRY: Patricia!

MARJORIE: If he comes here, I want you in the kitchen until I get rid of him. Do you understand?

TERRY: Your wish, Ayatollah. (*Exit TERRY to kitchen. TERRY brings in food, pours wine, hands one to MARJORIE, who doesn't take it.*)

TERRY: Wine? (*Pause.*) So what'd you do in the City yesterday? (*Pause.*)

PATRICIA: Ok, let's just eat now? Sandwich?

TERRY: Roastbeef's dry.

PATRICIA: Somebody didn't seal it properly. (*RAUL moans.*) I can't eat with him in there. (*PATRICIA lights a cigarette. Upon hearing the match struck.*)

RAUL: Please don't burn me again!

PATRICIA: Burn you? I only lit a cigarette.

RAUL: O, it's you, the nice one. I thought it was, you-know-who. She said she was gonna burn me alive. She dumped gas on me!

MARJORIE: It was only ammonia.

RAUL: And she flicked matches at me!

TERRY: I don't believe it! (*RAUL throws a few matches out in front of the fireplace. PATRICIA picks them up.*)

TERRY: How could you do that?

MARJORIE: No more talking with the animal!

PATRICIA: Why not?

MARJORIE: Because he's mine and I say you can't. (*PATRICIA drops the matches on the table and then takes a plate, puts some food on it, brings it towards the fireplace.*)

MARJORIE: What's that?

PATRICIA: He must be hungry.

RAUL: I am! (*MARJORIE bangs the firescreen with hammer.*) I'm not.

PATRICIA: Let me remind you—he's a human being like you or me.

MARJORIE: Is that right? Did you learn that from a book?

PATRICIA: I wouldn't think of going over your head.

MARJORIE: So, what's your analysis? Is it his childhood? His environment? his Greek traumas? Let's hear the dimestore psychiatrist explain this sick creep animal fuck.

PATRICIA: Exactly who is the animal here is not entirely clear to me.

MARJORIE: Is this clear? Don't mess with the animals.

PATRICIA: Nobody dies in my house. (*PATRICIA and TERRY sit. Long pause.*)

RAUL: Excuse me.

MARJORIE: Shut your face, animal.

RAUL: Can I talk to Patti?

MARJORIE: Don't call anyone's name as if you knew us!

PATRICIA: What do you want?

RAUL: Me?

PATRICIA: Yes.—What's your name?

MARJORIE: NO! Say it, animal, and I smash your head.

PATRICIA: Why can't he say his name?

MARJORIE: Because if I hear it I'll put him under!

PATRICIA: Ok. What'd you want to tell me?

RAUL: Can I have a little glass of water please? My throat . . .

MARJORIE: No.

RAUL: I feel sick.

PATRICIA: What kind of sick?

RAUL: Bad sick. Dizzy. Headache. My eyes burn bad. She sprayed that stuff in my mouth.

PATRICIA: What stuff?

RAUL: I'm holdin my vomit because I didn't want to, you know, mess up the place.

PATRICIA: (*Reading the aerosol can.*) "Harmful or fatal if swallowed. Harmful if inhaled or absorbed through skin. Get immediate medical attention. Atrophine is antidotal."

RAUL: What's that mean?

PATRICIA: "Do not spray toward face. Avoid breathing spray mist. Do not apply to humans, pets, dishes, or utensils. Keep out of reach of children." What's wrong?

RAUL: Nothin.

PATRICIA: Why are you gagging?

RAUL: I feel like, I don't know, like I absorbed something through my skin.

PATRICIA: I would like to go to the drugstore and get the atrophine.

MARJORIE: No.

PATRICIA: This stuff could be fatal. (*Putting the can on the table, next to the matches.*)

MARJORIE: No.

PATRICIA: Then what exactly are your intentions?

MARJORIE: What?

PATRICIA: What are you going to do with him?

MARJORIE: I don't know.

PATRICIA: Oh, you don't know. Thank you for being honest.

MARJORIE: Hey, look, I'm not one of your fuckin socialworker cases.

PATRICIA: Ok.

MARJORIE: So don't come off with this superior bullshit.

PATRICIA: Ok.

MARJORIE: And don't run your routine over me.

PATRICIA: Ok, ok, relax.

MARJORIE: I don't want to relax

PATRICIA: Ok, then we've established you don't want to relax and you've admitted you don't know your intentions.

MARJORIE: I didn't "admit" it. I said it.

PATRICIA: Ok, you said it.

MARJORIE: I didn't admit it like it was a crime. I said it.

PATRICIA: Ok, it was a poor choice of words on my part. I'll be more careful. Now, how do you feel about your situation?

MARJORIE: Wonderful. I think it should happen to everyone.

PATRICIA: Sarcasm won't help assess the reality of the problem.

MARJORIE: Fuck reality.

PATRICIA: And the reality is—a man is hurt and you don't have a case.

MARJORIE: That's why I have a hammer.

PATRICIA: Ok, you have a hammer. Let's talk about the hammer.

MARJORIE: My favorite subject. Hammer. One good swing can do more than judge, jury, and prosecutor! (*She whacks a plate on the table.*)

PATRICIA: Ok, let's define our terms. What do you want from him?
MARJORIE: A confession.
PATRICIA: Good.
MARJORIE: In front of you both.
PATRICIA: Excellent.
MARJORIE: To protect me from the law.
PATRICIA: Wonderful.
MARJORIE: What happened today fact for fact.
PATRICIA: Ok, that's something solid.
RAUL: I didn't do nothin.
PATRICIA: This is your chance to save yourself.
RAUL: I didn't do nothin, Patti.
PATRICIA: She's giving you a chance.
RAUL: Chance for what? Go the wall for a bit I didn't pull? Thanks.
MARJORIE: You tell them what you did to me.
RAUL: Look at her and look at me. Who did what to who?
MARJORIE: Tell them. Please?
RAUL: I wanna call my attorney. I want my rights. This country's
   got a fuckin constitution!
MARJORIE: Tell them how you smothered me.
RAUL: This land got laws, jack, and nobody's above the law!
MARJORIE: You made me touch you!
TERRY: Pat! Do something!
MARJORIE: Tell them. Please. Let's end it.
RAUL: No innocent person's got nothin to fear in this country. I
   demand my fuckin rights! (*MARJORIE bangs RAUL's hand with
   the hammer. He screams.*)
MARJORIE: If you knew what it was like under the pillow, sucking
   for breath that wasn't there.
PATRICIA: Tell me—talk about the pillow.
MARJORIE: Talk, hell, let me show you. (*Forcing a pillow to
   PATRICIA's face.*)
PATRICIA: Get the hell away from me with that thing!
MARJORIE: This is not a thing! This is a pillow! Let's define our
   terms!
PATRICIA: It'll all come out in court!
MARJORIE: Before they believe a woman in court, she has to be
   dead on arrival!
PATRICIA: You are not the law! You are not God! You have to
   bring it to court!

TERRY: We can't just keep him like a pet.

PATRICIA: Why don't you shut the hell up!

MARJORIE: Yeah! You're interrupting Patricia's routine!

PATRICIA: I hope we can rise above this personal bullshit.

MARJORIE: It's very personal. It's between me and him. So keep out of it.

PATRICIA: When will you be satisfied? When you become like him?

MARJORIE: Like him? I crave to be like him! Then I'd strike, tear, slash, and reduce him to splinters of bone! Don't stare at me! Forgive me for surviving. Maybe you'd care if you came home and tripped over my body and found animal waiting for you! What's going on here! Don't I count? What about me? Don't I count?

PATRICIA: I'm sorry. If you have to take off tomorrow, we take off. We're going to do the best thing for Marjorie.

RAUL: You're all gonna burn. One, two, three.

PATRICIA: Be quiet, please.

RAUL: Burn. One, two, three.

PATRICIA: Ok. Let's relax. Wine? O, forgot. Ok. Now I'm sure the three of us can come up with something positive.

TERRY: This has nothing to do with me.

PATRICIA: I can understand how you feel.

TERRY: No you can't . . . Only I understand how I feel.

PATRICIA: Ok, I can relate to that.

TERRY: And I'm not taking off tomorrow, because you're not worth it.

PATRICIA: Ok, Terry seems to feel alienated. Ok. Let's look at the facts. We got a man here. He's tied up. He's injured. What does this mean? God, I can't think today. Ok. The problem is this: what laws are violated? Do we all agree on what the problem is? (*Pause.*) Ok, let's stick with the facts. Do you have any bruises?

MARJORIE: He bit me.

PATRICIA: Wonderful!—I mean, you know, for court. It shows.

RAUL: She's right, Patti. I bit her because she was chokin me with a wire!

PATRICIA: Did you put anything on it?

MARJORIE: Peroxide.

PATRICIA: Ok. What's with your leg?

MARJORIE: I got stung. Wasp. It's all right.

PATRICIA: Ok, facts. There was an attempted rape. But you can't prove that. And then there was torture. You can prove that. Torture. You can't do that. But you did it.

TERRY: They'll throw the key away.

PATRICIA: Shut up, idiot!—I'm sorry. I appreciate your opinions, but they do not throw keys away. They have suspended sentence, plea bargaining, parole, probation. They have a lot of things! Ok. We have isolated the problem. I don't know what to do. But I do know your lives are joined now. If he goes under, so do you. If he's kept well, so are you. And that's all I care about. You. Use the hammer, or don't use the hammer. At the moment you have a choice. But if he dies—and he could be dying right now—you have no more choice. And neither do I. So giving him a little bread, to absorb the poison in his mouth, would be one very powerful witness of your humanity, and you need all you can get. One roll. Half a roll. For you.

MARJORIE: Do it.

PATRICIA: Thank you.

RAUL: That goes for me too. Could I have a little sip of wine?

MARJORIE: No!

RAUL: Thank you just the same.

MARJORIE: If I hear that voice again, I'll tear him to pieces.

PATRICIA: Did you hear that?

RAUL: Pieces.

PATRICIA: Will you shut up please?

RAUL: Whatever you think's best, honey.

PATRICIA: I have bread for you.

RAUL: My hand's broke. Could you feed me, please?

TERRY: Don't put your hands in there!

PATRICIA: Why not? What can he do?

TERRY: He said he'd bite my hand off.

MARJORIE: I thought this had nothing to do with you.

TERRY: Kiss off.

PATRICIA: Okay, okay.

TERRY: Okay your ass.

PATRICIA: Marjorie? Do you think we could unlock it?

MARJORIE: No.

PATRICIA: We'll be careful.

MARJORIE: No.

PATRICIA: This bread's for you, not him.

MARJORIE: No.

PATRICIA: If and when I'm asked what I saw here, I truthfully don't know what I could say in your favor.

MARJORIE: That's good to know.

TERRY: Open it, goddamit! I'm not going to prison for you!

MARJORIE: Prison? You? Never. You do exactly what good little girls are supposed to. Nothing.

TERRY: You didn't get raped so don't tell me you can do something because you can't because I know because I got raped once and it was all my fault because I was dressed up like Tinkerbell in pink tights one size too small and half shot in the ass on beer and grass and my best girlfriend's father offered me a ride home and he took a shortcut through a cemetery and stopped behind this mausoleum . . . (*Pause.*) So what could I do? Tell? Ruin everybody? What for? You can't undo it. It's over. I lived. Besides, you know what they'd say. I asked for it. So I went to bed that night and made believe it was just a bad dream. But you, you didn't even get raped, and I'm not committing complicity for you. (*Pause.*)

MARJORIE: Open it.

PATRICIA: Thank you. (*Pause.*) What's the combination?

MARJORIE: Right 31, Left 40 . . .

PATRICIA: And the last number?

MARJORIE: I'll do it. (*MARJORIE undoes the lock. PATRICIA secretly butters a roll. MARJORIE wears the chain about her neck.*)

PATRICIA: I'll feed you.

RAUL: Thank you very much.

PATRICIA: May I loosen the noose? He won't be able to swallow.

MARJORIE: Do it!

RAUL: Thank you very much.

PATRICIA: There.

RAUL: You're a very kind lady.

PATRICIA: Open up. Let me feed you.

RAUL: Thank you. You're very kind. Very kind lady. God bless you. Mmmmm. Good bread. Thank you for putting butter on it.

MARJORIE: You buttered it?

PATRICIA: Just a little.

RAUL: Very kind. Beautiful person. Good bread. Best bread I ever ate. Where do you get bread like this? I'd like to pick up a loaf for my mother. Good crust. But not doughy inside. And so good with butter. You wouldn't happen to have a little slice of meat with this bread, would you? Not good meat. Something that fell on the floor. Or a piece with a lot of fat on it. Something nobody else would eat?

MARJORIE: Would you prefer ham and cheese or roastbeef?

RAUL: Roastbeef, thank you very much, please.

MARJORIE: Lettuce and tomato?

RAUL: Hold the lettuce.

MARJORIE: Mustard?

RAUL: You got mayo?

MARJORIE: (*MARJORIE prods him against the wall and gently touches his head with the hammer. Pause.*) Who the fuck you think you're playin wit, bitch. (*Pause. She spits in his face. Pause. She walks away. PATRICIA feeds RAUL. She lifts the edge of his blindfold.*)

PATRICIA: O my God. His face.

RAUL: What?

PATRICIA: Bubbled up. Blood's running out his nose. The ammonia burned his nose linings.

RAUL: You three are gonna get a snapshot, front and profile, down at the cop shop, jack.

PATRICIA: I'm going to the drugstore. For the atrophine.

MARJORIE: For my good, right?

PATRICIA: Why don't you look under the blindfold? Or is that why you covered it? You can't stand to see the damage you caused? I want that atrophine.

MARJORIE: I'll let Terry go.

TERRY: Where should I go?

MARJORIE: Drugstore at the mall.

TERRY: I'm broke.

PATRICIA: I blew my last few bucks on the cheesecake. Do you have any money?

MARJORIE: You want me to pay for the animal's medicine?

PATRICIA: Can I borrow it?

MARJORIE: I should've crushed his skull in the first two seconds. But I let myself talk, and in talk I squandered it. Talk, talk, talk, talk, talk. No phone calls.

TERRY: All right.

MARJORIE: Say it.

TERRY: No phone calls.

MARJORIE: If you bring the police, I'll do it, Terry, and it'll be just like you did it. When I see 'em pull up, one hit, he's out, two, he's dead. Two seconds. That's all it takes. And I'll be watching every second. (*Handing her the keys and money.*) It should take seven minutes to get there, five in the store, seven to get back, even if you catch the light both ways. I give you one extra minute for the unaccountable. Seven, plus five, plus seven, plus one . . . Twenty minutes.

PATRICIA: Don't speed. You might get stopped. Get atrophine and something for burns.

TERRY: Astrophine . . .

PATRICIA: Atrophine. I'll write it down.

MARJORIE: One second after twenty and he's dead. And it'll be just like you did it. You. (*PATRICIA writes on a pad, hands it to TERRY. MARJORIE snatches it from TERRY's hands.*)

PATRICIA: Don't you trust anybody?

MARJORIE: Myself.

TERRY: Typical Leo.

PATRICIA: Just go.

RAUL: (*As TERRY opens the door.*) Complicity. (*TERRY pauses in the door, exits. MARJORIE locks the door, marks the time, sits by the window. Long pause.*) Excuse me. Can I say something? (*Silence, which he takes as consent.*) I want to thank you very much for the bread. And for putting up that money for my medicine. I think that was very kind of you. Most people wouldn't go that far. But you went all-out and I'm all choked up and want to thank you from the bottom of my heart because it was generous and it was kind and it was nice. So nice of you. You wouldn't have an extra cigarette, would you? Or maybe one that was smoked halfway?

MARJORIE: Menthol filter all right?

RAUL: Thank you very much.

MARJORIE: Reach your hand out and I'll give it to you.

RAUL: No thank you. Bad for the lungs. (*Lights fade.*)

Scene 2

Fifteen minutes later. MARJORIE sits at the window picking at her wasp stings. PATRICIA cleans the supper debris.

PATRICIA: Does it hurt bad? (*MARJORIE shakes her head no. Pause.*) Would you like a cup of tea? (*MARJORIE shakes her head no. Pause.*) Anything?

MARJORIE: Seventeen minutes.

PATRICIA: Did you pull the stinger out? (*MARJORIE shakes her head no. Pause.*) Would you like me to get the tweezers?

MARJORIE: Please. (*Exit PATRICIA.*)

RAUL: Excuse me.

MARJORIE: Shut up.

RAUL: Can I say one thing?

MARJORIE: No.

RAUL: It's about stings.

MARJORIE: Want me to put your lights out?

RAUL: Forget it.

MARJORIE: (*Pause.*) What?

RAUL: Talkin to me?

MARJORIE: What do you think?

RAUL: What do I know?

MARJORIE: What about stings?

RAUL: Ain't no stinger in there.

MARJORIE: Says who?

RAUL: Wasp don't leave no stinger. A bee leaves a stinger and croaks. But a wasp keeps on stingin.

MARJORIE: How do you know that?

RAUL: I know what I know. A wasp don't sing, a bird don't sting. They're gonna call you Hammer. And one night them hefty lesbies are gonna test your mojo, jump you in your roachy piss-smellin six by ten, bust your nose, make it flat, spit your teeth in a toilet bowl, and when bull says get down in the bush, Hammer jumps in the weeds smokin dry beever, cause you're like me, you do what you gotta do to keep alive. And don't holler cause them hacks get a sudden case of deaf cause they don't get involved in petty in-house business. So keep your ass close to the wall or some cannibal puts a dull screwdriver in your back and nobody hears nothin when them showers are splashin and them radioes are blastin them funky tunes and your blood washin down the drain reminds you of once upon a time in a cozy little house, me and you, to have and to hold, forever.

PATRICIA: (*Entering.*) Here.

MARJORIE: There's no stinger.

PATRICIA: You pulled it out?

MARJORIE: Wasp doesn't leave a stinger.

RAUL: Best thing's to rub it with alcohol.

PATRICIA: We don't have rubbing alcohol.

RAUL: Got any hundred proof whisky or vodka?

PATRICIA: Hundred and fifty-one proof rum.

RAUL: Beautiful. Let me taste it first to make sure.

PATRICIA: Does it work?

MARJORIE: Very well, thank you.

RAUL: You're welcome. Anytime. I mean if we can't help each other out, what the hell are we on this earth for? (*MARJORIE looks at the time.*)

PATRICIA: That's a busy drugstore. Sometimes there's a long line. You've been there before. When did you ever get service right away?

MARJORIE: Twenty minutes.

RAUL: Maybe she stopped for gas.

MARJORIE: She's a traitor.

RAUL: Maybe she ran into traffic. Her car needs a valve job. Ten to one she broken down.

MARJORIE: I'll make sure they put you away!

RAUL: Come in here motherfucker, I bite your throat! (*MARJORIE grabs RAUL's noose, raises the hammer.*) Hail Mary, full o' grace, smoke this loony bitch! (*PATRICIA grabs the hammer. They struggle. PATRICIA is hurt.*)

MARJORIE: I'm sorry.

PATRICIA: Don't touch me! (*TERRY's car pulls up.*)

RAUL: I'm fuckin saved! Blessed art thou among women! (*MARJORIE opens the door. Enter TERRY with a white drugstore bag.*)

MARJORIE: You're fuckin late, goddamn you!

TERRY: You killed him? For two minutes? (*Discovering RAUL.*) O.

PATRICIA: Where's the atrophine?

TERRY: You can't buy it over the counter.

Extremities / **141**

PATRICIA: Why not?

TERRY: You need a doctor's perscription.

MARJORIE: Did they ask questions?

TERRY: Why I needed it.

MARJORIE: And what'd you answer?

TERRY: Emergencies.

MARJORIE: Did they believe you?

TERRY: How should I know?

MARJORIE: What did you think?

TERRY: I don't know!

PATRICIA: Did you suggest a substitute antidote?

TERRY: You didn't say to do that.

PATRICIA: You should've figured that!

TERRY: I told 'em we live in a farmhouse and have a lot of wasp trouble . . .

MARJORIE: Why'd you tell them where we live?

PATRICIA: Now what do we do without the antidote?

TERRY: They said see a doctor or go to the emergency room.

MARJORIE: Why were you so long?

TERRY: I ran into Sally in the parking lot. She's getting divorced.

MARJORIE: You talked with her?

TERRY: She wouldn't let go of my arm!

RAUL: Talkin in a parkin lot! You dippy bitch! She's gonna hammer me and you're talking in the parkin fuckin lot!

PATRICIA: This isn't for burns! It's for cuts!

TERRY: That's all they had!

PATRICIA: I know they have it!

TERRY: Then go got it! I'm sick of being the goddamn gofer around here!

PATRICIA: A damn moron would've got a substitute antidote!

TERRY: Then send a damn moron! And if you can't find one, you'll do just fine!

PATRICIA: I'll apply this for whatever it's worth.

MARJORIE: Four dollars and fifty cents to be exact.

RAUL: Let me chip in. I pay my way.

PATRICIA: Shut up! May I take off the noose to apply the medicine?

MARJORIE: Why don't you just fuck him. Maybe that'll make him feel better.

TERRY: You both make me sick. (*Patricia seats RAUL with great*

142 / *William Mastrosimone*

difficulty.)

RAUL: Thank you.

PATRICIA: Shut the fuck up! (*With great delicacy, PATRICIA removes the blindfold. TERRY gasps at the bloody sight.*)

RAUL: What was that? Terry? Why'd she do that? Am I ugly?

PATRICIA: No.

RAUL: Liar. I'm a fuckin monster.

PATRICIA: Open your eyes.

RAUL: I'm afraid.

PATRICIA: Open them.

RAUL: They open?

PATRICIA: Yes.

RAUL: I can't see. I can't fuckin see. Mother of God.

PATRICIA: I'm sorry.

RAUL: Go tell my babies sorry.

PATRICIA: Is there anything I can do?

RAUL: Give me a crown of thorns and finish me off!

PATRICIA: Why don't you have the honors! (*Picking up hammer, handing it to MARJORIE.*) Finish what you start!

RAUL: What the fuck's goin on here? Patti! You snake-face traitor! I pray for an angel, but what's god send me? A fuckin traitor! Fuck you and your bread! And fuck god! Fuck 'em! You're all gonna burn, baby! one, two, three, burn!

PATRICIA: How can I stop the pain?

RAUL: Give me back my eyes!

PATRICIA: What's your name?

RAUL: Mike.

PATRICIA: Mike what?

RAUL: Mentiras.

MARJORIE: How many women have you raped and murdered?

PATRICIA: You don't have to answer anymore.

MARJORIE: Tell them about the pothole crew.

RAUL: The what?

MARJORIE: When I rode by on my bike! Tell them why you came here!

RAUL: Use the phone. (*MARJORIE slaps his raw wounded face. He almost screams from his raw wounds but holds it in.*)

MARJORIE: I'm sorry.

RAUL: She said, sure, come in and use the phone, and she was walkin around with her robe open, the red robe, with nothing much on underneath.

MARJORIE: Why are you looking at me like that?

PATRICIA: I'm not looking in any special way.

RAUL: And I'm usin the phone and she comes struttin pretty and ok, she turned me one, I admit it. I'm just a man. God made me that way. Something happens inside. Boom. And when I tried to go, she goes nuts, sprays me with this stuff, pulls the phone, starts yellin rape.

MARJORIE: Mother of God! You believe him!

RAUL: If that's a lie, let God off me on the fucking spot! Now tell 'em about the hole, Marjorie! Tell 'em about the grave! My grave!

PATRICIA: What grave?

RAUL: O! I don't hear Marjorie talkin now!—Terry comes home and they decide to dig a grave in the garden and bury me!

PATRICIA: Is that true?

RAUL: Between the tomatoes and the flowers! With the possums and the dogs! A fuckin grave!

PATRICIA: That can't be true!

RAUL: Don't believe me. Let the grave talk!

PATRICIA: Is there a grave out there?

TERRY: Ask her.

PATRICIA: I'm asking you! The one who wanted to make up a story!

TERRY: I didn't dig it!

RAUL: See! See! Bury me alive, Patti! Alive! Whacko and Terry!

TERRY: Alls I did was watch him! Marjorie said she would drag him out, throw him in and cover it herself!

PATRICIA: Did you get enough justice today? Two eyes enough? Burn a man alive? Is that savage enough?

MARJORIE: Not as savage as a human roach forcing your legs apart!

RAUL: Awwwww, c'mon, c'mon, c'mon! What would I go do that for? Get some ass? I got poontang home.

MARJORIE: I thought your pregnant wife won't let you touch her?

RAUL: Don't talk about my sick wife, especially you, wit a sick father in the hospital.

MARJORIE: He stole our mail!

RAUL: I can't win wit this woman! First I'm a killer! Then I'm a raper. Now I'm a thief! What next?

MARJORIE: Don't you see what he's doing?

PATRICIA: Leave the man alone! Can't you see he's in pain?

RAUL: Don't say one bad thing about Marjorie. We're all human. We do things we don't mean, and I forgive her everything. All I wanted was a kind word, a little closeness, to forget my troubles; all she wanted was to forget about some guy in New York. Tony.

MARJORIE: Tony wrote to me and animal took one of the letters.

TERRY: He wrote you?

MARJORIE: I never answered.

TERRY: Why didn't you tell me?

MARJORIE: I didn't want to hurt you.

TERRY: Is that why he came here when he knew I was at work?

MARJORIE: Terry, please believe me.

TERRY: Is that why you changed from jeans to bathrobe when I brought him here.

MARJORIE: I must've been ready for bed.

TERRY: You're always ready for bed!

PATRICIA: You do dress loose, you know.

TERRY: Everytime I'd have a guy over, I'd have to shout in to see if you're decent.

PATRICIA: You parade around this house like it was a centerfold. A man enters the room and you go all statuesque. How you cross your leg at just the right moment—how you butterfly through a room—You're not happy until you're got every man in the room begging for it. And this one did. And now you want to fix him. One man pays for every letch and wolf whistle. You go through men like most women go through kleenex, and then you complain about the come-ons you provoke! The man is blind. Look at what you've done to yourself, to us, to him. Can't you look in blind eyes. Let's see what else you've done! (*She opens RAUL's jacket. Hanging from a leather thong is a curved hunting knife in a sheath. MARJORIE rushes to it, draws it out slowly. She lays the flat of it on RAUL's shoulder.*)

RAUL: I use it for work. (*Pause.*) I cut open boxes in a warehouse.

MARJORIE: Cut boxes, eh?

RAUL: Yeah.

MARJORIE: I thought you didn't have a job.

RAUL: O, I meant, you know, before I got employed.

MARJORIE: Cuts 'em good, eh?

RAUL: Yeah, pretty good.

MARJORIE: Sure, it's so sharp.

RAUL: Patti.

MARJORIE: And strong.

RAUL: Patti? You there?

MARJORIE: The kind of knife they use to gut a deer. Your move.

RAUL: Please.

MARJORIE: Smile. Nicer. Don't make your lips tight.

RAUL: Please!

MARJORIE: What's the matter?

RAUL: Patti! Terry! Make her stop!

MARJORIE: Know what you need? Acouple slashes here and there. Tell me you want it. Say it.

RAUL: O Mother of god, please!

MARJORIE: You're wrecking this for me. Say it.

RAUL: I want it.

MARJORIE: What?

RAUL: I want it.

MARJORIE: Want what?

RAUL: Please!

MARJORIE: Want what? Say it.

RAUL: The knife.

MARJORIE: Where do you like me to touch you? I forget.

RAUL: Nowhere.

MARJORIE: Remind me.

RAUL: Nowhere.

MARJORIE: Here?

RAUL: Nowhere.

MARJORIE: Or here?

RAUL: Nowhere.

MARJORIE: Ah, now I remember.

RAUL: Please! I beg you on my mother's milk!

MARJORIE: Down there! (*Putting the blade in RAUL's crotch and lifting him off the chair an eighth of an inch. Pause.*) Tell me you love it. Say it!

RAUL: I love it.

MARJORIE: Say it nice.

RAUL: I love it.

MARJORIE: Say it sweet.

RAUL: I love it . . .

MARJORIE: Sweeter!

RAUL: I love it.

MARJORIE: You say that beautiful. Again.

RAUL: I love it.

MARJORIE: Now tell me cut 'em off.

RAUL: I can't say that!

MARJORIE: This is your last chance.

RAUL: You can't make me say that!

MARJORIE: You say it and you say it nice and sweet and beautiful and you smile, you fucking bug!

RAUL: Mother of god! I stole letters! Watched the house! Came here to fuck yous all!

MARJORIE: Who!

RAUL: You and Terry and Patti, like Paula Wyshneski and Linda Martinez, Debbie Parks and some I forget. They screamed. I begged 'em not to scream. I hate when they scream. (*MARJORIE runs a stiff hand across RAUL's throat. Thinking himself slashed, he writhes on the floor.*) Mother of god! (*Realizing he's not slashed.*) Thank you. (*Pause.*) Everytime I do it, it's in the papers, and I gets up in the morning and my wife and her mother they're talkin about it and I says, what happened? and they says, the raper got another girl last night, and they show me the paper and a picture of the dude somebody saw runnin away, but it don't look nothin like me. And my wife says, fix the back door, Raul, cause I don't want no raper comin in here, and I says, don't worry, he don't want you, and she bitches and I fix the door real good so the raper can't get in. (*Pause.*) Tell 'em lock me in a room. Not with locks. I know about locks. I can pick 'em. A room with nobody else. And maybe if I could have a little radio so's I could listen the ball game so it won't be so quiet because I hate the quiet because the dark, I don't care, but the quiet, please don't let it be quiet.

MARJORIE: (*Long pause.*) I think you should go get . . . help.

PATRICIA: Ok.

MARJORIE: Keep Patricia company?

TERRY: Won't you be afraid?

MARJORIE: No.

PATRICIA: What do we say?

MARJORIE: Say a man is hurt.

PATRICIA: Ok.

MARJORIE: Say a man needs help.

PATRICIA: Ok.

RAUL: Marjorie?

MARJORIE: Yes?

RAUL: Can I say your name?

MARJORIE: Yes.

RAUL: One big favor?

MARJORIE: Yes.

RAUL: Don't make 'em put the siren on?

MARJORIE: Tell them no siren.

RAUL: And no red light?

MARJORIE: And no red light.

PATRICIA: Ok.

RAUL: Thank you very much. (*Exit PATRICIA and TERRY. Upon hearing the door close.*) You there?

MARJORIE: Yes.

RAUL: Thank you. Don't leave me alone?

MARJORIE: I'm right here.

RAUL: Thank you. They comin?

MARJORIE: Yes.

RAUL: Don't let 'em beat me?

MARJORIE: No.

RAUL: Thank you very much. You there?

MARJORIE: Yes.

RAUL: Marjorie?

MARJORIE: Yes?

RAUL: Can I wait in the fireplace?

MARJORIE: If you want.

RAUL: Thank you. (*Getting to his knees.*) Show me. (*MARJORIE puts the knife down, directs him to the mouth of the fireplace. He crotches inside, closes the screen. Lights fade slowly.*) Thank you. Thank you very much. (*He rocks slightly. Almost imperceptibly he sings slowly, MARJORIE weeps.*)

Found a peanut
Found a peanut
Found a peanut just now
Just now I found a peanut
Found a peanut just now
Cracked it open
Cracked it open

148 / *William Mastrosimone*

Cracked it open just now . . .
(*Lights fade to darkness.*)

END

The Making of Extremities

In May of 1978 I met a fifty-five-year-old woman. For convenience, let's call her Mary. Her face was cut, swollen and bruised. She told me she was raped the night before. Perhaps because I was a complete stranger, she told me about her bizarre ordeal. A nineteen-year-old man broke into her apartment with intent to rob. Thinking no one home, she startled him when she awoke. He raped her, beat her with a lamp and fled. Hours later, when she was able to pick herself up, she called the police and gave a description. She was given a humiliating pelvic exam at the hospital and taken to police headquarters to look at several suspects. Out of a line up of six, Mary made a positive identification of the rapist. He was arraigned and a court date set.

Months later the trial began. Mary was made to retell the rape before her peers, the public, the press. The rapist sat quietly in a three-piece suit, white shirt and tie. He looked like the son of a minister. When he was cross-examined he made amusing remarks. The jury laughed. There was evidence of rape but no evidence that he was the rapist. The case was dismissed. Mary left the courtroom. On the courthouse steps the rapist walked up behind Mary and said, "If you think that was bad, wait until next time."

Mary informed the police. They told her that they would keep regular patrols near her home, that she should call them on the slightest suspicion. But there are many hours in a minute. The house plays such cruel little pranks. A board creaks in the middle of the night. The dripping faucet sounds like a man coming up the stairs on tip-toes. The wind. A cat. Mary slept with the light on. Next to the phone. With a butcher knife. It was too much. She quit her job, lost her pension, and bought a one-way ticket to the opposite coast.

On her way to the airport, Mary stopped by to say goodbye to me. If she hadn't, *Extremities* would not exist. She thanked me for listening. We shook hands and parted. As she walked through the door, something possessed her to stop and turn and say: "There was a moment during the rape when the animal stopped and reached for one of my cigarettes on the night table . . . He couldn't reach it . . . He put one foot on the floor . . . At that moment I knew I could kick him and hurt him . . . The moment waited for me . . . But I just lay there . . . Paralyzed . . . Maybe it was that I was just brought up not to hurt anybody . . . Maybe it was that I was too afraid that if I didn't hurt him enough, he'd kill me . . . I don't know . . . I did nothing . . . He lit a cigarette, raped me again and then beat me with a lamp . . . I will think about that moment for the rest of my life . . . I will fantasize about what would have happened . . . Now I can see myself hurting him . . . And hurting him some more . . . It's hard for me to admit that I love to hear his scream . . . I should have acted . . . I would've got real justice . . . Not to act is to have to live with a coward for the rest of your life . . . If I had five minutes in a locked room with him now . . ."

Mary did not finish her sentence. *Extremities* was written to fill in the blank she left. I had never seen such anger in a woman except on stage in *Medea*. Something screamed in me. I was sick and angry. Sick because the woman's life was ruined. Angry because her peers let a guilty man go. *Extremities* came out of me like an overdue baby. I began writing that night at midnight. I worked all night. I thought it was a two-character play, but then Terry and Patricia walked in. I slept two hours at the end of Act One. By three that afternoon I had finished.

In the ensuing months, I began my research. When I heard of a rape trial, I would sit in the court all day. I talked to spectators, lawyers, sometimes defendants and plaintiffs. I learned that one out of three women in the U.S. are sexually assaulted by age eighteen. That of all rape cases that are able to pass strict rules of evidence, only 2 percent result in conviction, which means that it's easier for a camel to pass through the eye of a needle than for a rapist to go to prison. That the average rapist rapes 29 times. That means 29 women. Most rapes go unreported due to embarrassment or fear. That juries are so fearful of sending an innocent man to prison many guilty men are set free. Now I began to fathom Mary's urge to rip the rapist to pieces.

I spoke with a lawyer who was defending a rapist. The conversation went something like this:

Q—How do you defend a rapist?

A—A man is only a rapist after he's convicted. At that time, defense is impossible.

Q—How do you defend a man who's been charged with rape?

A—Of course it's always different, but there's a certain recipe that helps—put as many women on the jury as possible.

Q—Women? Don't you mean men?

A—Women. Women attack other women. I don't know why. A man

on the jury sees in the plaintiff his mother, sister, wife, lover, and that brings out the white knight in him. You can actually watch him strap on the armor and go to the rescue of a lady in distress. A woman, on the other hand, lives in constant fear of rape. I don't know if a man can really understand it. She tends to distance herself from the victim . . . She thinks, There, but for the grace of God, go I . . . Why didn't she lock her door? . . . What was she doing there? . . . Why was she dressed like that? . . . Women tend to blame other women for being raped because most women have accepted the male myth that some women like it, want it, crave it, in fact.

No producer dared to put *Extremities* on stage for two years. *Extremities* went where it was welcome. The first production was in a community college by amateurs. The town council made a motion to ban the play—for which I now take time to thank them for the priceless advertisement. As a result, there was a playwright's dream every night—standing room only. The next production was in a hole in the wall in Philadelphia. The reviews ran the gamut. Audiences were less fickle. They loved it. Sometimes they threw things at Raul. One night several women ran on stage and tried to stop the attempted rape. Then there were two university productions, and then it went to one of the best regional theatres in America, Actors Theatre of Louisville, where it received worldwide attention. From there, the movie rights were sold and a New York production was planned. The New York critics ran the gamut again, but the public voted at the box office in overwhelming favor. From there *Extremities* travelled around the world—Norway, Denmark, Sweden, Canada, Mexico, Australia, South Africa, France, Italy, Spain, Germany and Greece.

All because Mary had stopped to tell me her dark fantasy—to be alone in a locked room with the rapist. In giving her the five requested minutes—giving her, in fact, two hours—I had given thousands of women a fantasy that affects real behavior. Fantasy gives permission to reality. That is, what we allow ourselves to fantasize encroaches upon our everyday behavior. I know this because after every show, women, hundreds and hundreds of women, sought out the playwright, director, actors, to tell us of their rape experiences. There was a time in China's history, Confucius remembers, when historians left blanks in their books for what they didn't know or weren't sure of. That's the epitome of integrity. I

152 / *William Mastrosimone*

wish playwrights could do the same. As I learned about this epidemic phenomenon, I changed the play. In one instance in Philadelphia, a woman in the audience screamed during the show. The actors stopped until she seemed to be all right and then continued. Later, the woman came to me and said, "I'm sorry I ruined your play. I was raped 20 years ago and forgot until tonight." That was the basis for Terry's monologue which I wrote that night and appended into the script.

As a man I have been reeducated about rape. The most dangerous teaching is the unconscious acceptance, the insidious little assumptions one makes while growing up. I have, through the play, freed myself of the two lethal myths. One, that women cause rape, and two, that rape is for sex. A woman can never cause rape. That is a male excuse for the desire to rape projected into the victim. Rape is done to degrade, humiliate and intimidate. It is a confusing issue because the tenderest act of man and woman is used to disguise the most brutal and sadistic. The extremities of the spectrum are brought together. Based on interviews of victims, the worst part of rape is not the physical. It is the fear, the threats, real or imagined, the degradation, the helplessness. *Extremities* has focused on the latter. Audiences often have to be reminded that no rape occurs in *Extremities*. But audiences often think that a rape has occurred because of the mental cruelty of the first scene. We see Raul tossing Marjorie about like a rag doll. We cannot know what is happening in her head. We can only surmise. We can only do that by giving something to the play, by investing emotion, by empathy. A play can only work when the audience is willing to project themselves into the protagonist in order to understand the character's thoughts and emotions. The audience must pay twice: once to get past the box office, and again to get beyond the footlights. When empathy comes easy, that is what we call a commercial play. *Extremities* is not a commercial play. There is no initial sales pitch to get empathy. But the audience gives it voluntarily. The fact that *Extremities* has gone so far is a tribute to audiences who think and feel for themselves. *Extremities* contains the seeds of all the things that interest me as a writer—politics, ethics and morals, and psychology. A woman alone, a man enters, the play begins. From the very first, we see a contagion of violence pass from Raul, to Marjorie, to Terry, to Patricia. It grows in the language and in the action like a germ culture. The monster in all of us is just under the skin. Scratch the skin deep enough and it comes leaping out full-blown. In order to survive Raul, Marjorie has to become like Raul. To do that is to lose herself. The victim and victimizer, the cager and the caged, form each other. Thus, the psychological play leads to the moral play—How does one deal with evil without becoming evil oneself? Marjorie has a choice—to act or not to act. To turn Raul over to the police is a choice which would result in his release which would result in her death. Marjorie's self-preservation forces her to make another choice—to not release him, to bury him and assure herself he will never return. Standing so long on the verge of that choice, Marjorie equally fears what she will become after Raul is six foot under. There is no safe choice. On the one hand, her life is jeopardy. On the other, her sanity. She must act and act strongly, decisively. There is no help. Neither the authorities nor friends can lend a hand. Marjorie's helplessness leads to the politics of *Extremities*, the idea of the violated social contract. Every individual and society make a deal: let's all surrender our state of nature, our animal impulses, in return for protection, in order to form an orderly society of rules by which we can all have freedom from each other. In *Extremities*, Marjorie's actions are based upon the perception that society violates the social contract by not keeping up its end of offering protection. Sure, the police say, call us when there's a problem and we'll come running, but what's that mean to a phi beta kappa prison graduate like Raul? Marjorie feels abandoned and therefore must defend herself against the most privileged citizen in our society—the recidivist criminal And those who criticize me for Terry and Patricia's unfriendly reaction to Marjorie's dilemma had better turn their daggers to the 2 percent conviction rate first. Sadly enough, Marjorie's roommates' reaction is all-too-true. If *Extremities* could change anything, I would have it alter the perceptions of the people who sit in the jury box; I would have them hear testimony through the ear of the social contract. A play does not have to say anything. But it must do something. *Extremities* has changed people's perception of rape. The rest follows.

What some people have applauded or booed as "comic relief" in *Extremities* is no such thing. I set out to recreate Mary's experience. I wanted to write a courtroom drama, not in court, but in a living room (where a woman is most likely to be raped, in her house). I wanted to create a psychic trial where all characters shift roles and become plaintiff, defendant, prosecutor, judge, jury, witness, etc. I wanted to show how the rapist can turn the jury around. In our society, we are all guilty of a prejudice. If someone makes us laugh, we think well of him. The rapists I have seen, and talked to, were cleverly rehearsed in their lawyer's offices, given a Sunday suit and a spitshine, and after an amusing remark, had spectators and jury saying, "My, he's such a nice fellow—I don't think he could have done such a terrible thing"—That's the goal of every defense attorney, to let one positive trait through and let it begin that chain reaction that ends in a reasonable doubt. The result is a 98 percent chance of freedom for the rapist. To the horror of misunderstanding critics of *Extremities*, audiences laugh. A lot. Where there is tension, there is need for release. Laughter is the most accessible form of release in the theatre. Raul has a certain devil-may-care variety of humor, but it's not for the sake of making mirth, but to turn people around, give doubt, divide, manipulate and finally destroy. He represents no social class or ethnic group. He only represents the men who know the law and how to beat the system. I have observed it countless times in courts and who doesn't like it, don't kill me. I'm only the messenger. All theatre, in my opinion, is about change. We pay to see a character change. In change there is hope, and that is what I think an artist must do—not create false hope but dig as hard and deep as he or she can to find the best part of human beings. In the last scene of *Extremities* Marjorie's cycloptic drive to tear Raul apart results in a communication between victim and victimizer that goes beyond revenge. Marjorie does for Raul what all the social scientists, psychiatrists, police and prisons have failed to do—she gives him a conscience, and a soul. She makes him see himself from the other end of the knife. She makes him face himself. That is the beginning of change. Marjorie is exorcised of psychic torment, at the same time she gives Raul a soul. All theatre in my opinion, should be wish fulfillment tempered in reality. Women don't apprehend their rapists. Marjorie is the exception. But we can learn about the rule by examining the exception. So many rape victims have told me that *Extremities* has provided the catharsis that rape, police, lawyers, courts have not provided. That alone has made the entire experience worthwhile.

Down through the ages *Extremities* has been performed millions of times in the psyches of raped women who have mutely suffered the same brutalization and humiliation, and have, I am sure, in the

Extremities / 155

privacy of their nightmares wielded hammers and broomsticks and brought about a justice that society denied them. I am only the one who wrote it down.

William Mastrosimone
Trenton, NJ
1984

NANAWATAI!

This play is dedicated to ...
the greatest of human beings, the freedom fighters,
who draw the line with their blood to say, no further.
To the memory of David Earling
And to Kjetil Bang-Hansen and Tom Remlov.

NANAWATAI! was first produced in the Norwegian language, January 1984, at DEN NATIONALE SCENE in Bergen, Norway. The play was directed by Kjetil Bang-Hansen with the following cast:

TAJ AMAN	Sverre Rossummoen/Helge Jordal
KHASAMAR AMAN	Lars Steinar Sorbo
AKBAR AMAN	Kaare Kroppan
MUSTAFA IDA GIL	Thor Hjorth-Jenssen
AFZAL	Ulf Borge
SHORANA	Ragnhild Hiorthoy
ROXANNE	Eva Sevaldson
GUL	Inger-Johanne Rutter
MARGHALAI	Wenche Kvamme
ABIDA	Eva Danielsen
GEORGI DASKAL	Rold Soder
KONSTANTIN KOVERCHENKO	Bentein Baardson
NIKOLAI KAMINSKI	Gjert Haga
ANTON GOLIKOV	Kim Haugen
MALIK SAWAD	Kim Kalsas
MUSICIANS	Magne Lunde and Harald Maeland

NANAWATAI! was subsequently produced in English, September 1985, in Los Angeles, at the Los Angeles Theatre Center. It was directed by Lamont Johnson with the following cast:

SHERINA .... Gina Gershon
GEORGI DASKAL .... Philip Baker Hall
ANTON GOLIKOV .... Tommy Swerdlow
NIKOLAI KAMINSKI .... Adam Arkin
SAMAD .... Gerald Papasian
KOVERCHENKO .... Bill Pullman
SHAHZAMAN .... Edwin Gerard
TAJ MOHAMUD .... Steven Bauer
AKBAR .... Stefan Gierasch
ISKANDAR .... Mark Petrakis
MOUSTAFA .... René Assa
VILLAGE WOMEN: Ariana Delaware, Setara Begum, Fahila Delawari, Soraya Delawari, Yasmine Delawari, Roya Fahmy, Khorshied Machalle Nusratty, Zarmina Popal.
STANDBYS:
KOVERCHENKO & DASKAL .... Kevin Bash
TAJ MOHAMUD & ISKANDAR .... Edwin Gerard
SHAHZAMAN & GOLIKOV .... Carmine Iannaconne
SHERINA .... Khorshied Machalle Nusratty
MOUSTAFA & AKBAR .... Gerald Papasian
SAMAD & KAMINSKI .... Mark Petrakis

Characters

THE AFGHANS:
SHERINA, AND VILLAGE WOMEN OF VARIOUS AGES
TAJ MOHAMUD
SHAHZAMAN: his younger brother
AKBAR: his uncle
MOUSTAFA: mortal enemy of Taj's tribe
ISKANDAR: Moustafa's tribesman, a mystic
SAMAD: Afghan Tank trainee

THE SOVIETS:
GEORGI DASKAL
KONSTANTIN KOVERCHENKO
NIKOLAI KAMINSKI
ANTON GOLIKOV

Setting

TIME: Spring.
PLACE: Between Kabul and Jalalabad, Afghanistan.
SET: An empty space and some kind of representation of a Soviet T-72 tank.
SOUND: At least a drum. Ideally, use Afghan instruments to begin, move, and conclude the drama. The director should use the native sounds of Afghanistan, and the Middle East in general. Use the chorus of women to chant like Meuzzins in a minaret. When the audience arrives, they will hear the sounds of Afghanistan: A goat with a bell around its neck, sheep, birds, dogs, running water. These natural sounds will be interrupted now and then by the sounds of war in increasing intensity and danger. A rifle report, a machine gun, artillery shells, faraway at first, but increasingly near. Jets streak by. Helicopters. Rockets.
LIGHTS: The play takes place from dawn to dawn.
COSTUME: The Soviets wear simple jumpsuits and boots. The Afghans wear traditional garb—all variations upon a theme. War has favored an eclectic utilitarian mixture—part Soviet uniform, part traditional. Samad wears an Afghan army uniform, old fashioned probably bought wholesale from some minor Western power.

ACT I

"This was one of the most beautiful battles I ever saw. Not one of the enemy escaped."

—Napoleon, letter to General Dugua

"Where I have passed, not a blade of grass will grow again."

—Attila the Hun

"Defend yourself against your enemies but attack them not first. Allah hateth the aggressor."

—KORAN (II, 190)

NANAWATAI!

ACT I
Scene 1

The tank stands silently at dawn. Enter the Afghan women. They attack the tank with sticks, screaming insults and roving about the tank, looking for something to tear or break off. From under the tank, a yellowish-greenish gas pipes out and engulfs the stage. The women scatter. One of them is overtaken. She collapses, coughing, gagging, vomiting, crawling by inches, writhing in agony. The searchlight on the tank focuses on the body. The body twitches (throughout this scene). The gas stops emanating and gradually dissipates. The turret hatch opens. The head of a man wearing a gas mask. (Insectlike goggles, an elephantine hose apparatus.) It's KOVERCHENKO. He looks about in a 360 degree pattern, like the searchlight, and then emerges with an AK-47, walking about on the tank top. He jumps off the tank, touches the twitching body with his boot tip. He takes out gas meter. It flickers red in the presence of lethal gas. It flickers on and off and then off. Another man in a gas mask peers out of the hatch. He emerges from the tank. It's DASKAL.

DASKAL: Is the gas gone?

KOVERCHENKO: Yes, sir. (*They remove gas masks, leaving them hang from their necks.*)

DASKAL: How many dead?

KOVERCHENKO: One.

DASKAL: How old?

KOVERCHENKO: Just a girl.

DASKAL: What kind of weapon?

KOVERCHENKO: A stick.

DASKAL: Outside! (*KAMINSKI, GOLIKOV, and SAMAD climb out of tank.*) Samad, cyanide the well.

SAMAD: Yessir. (*SAMAD gets cyanide canisters from the rear of the tank, exit. DASKAL inspects a blackened spot near antenna.*)

KAMINSKI: My piss is green.

DASKAL: Fill out the gas report, Koverchenko, then we can move on.

KOVERCHENKO: Yessir.

DASKAL: Kaminski?

KAMINSKI: Yessir.

DASKAL: Golikov.

GOLIKOV: Yessir.

DASKAL: Get to the next tank in the cordon. Tell them we took a hit early in the battle and our radio's out. Then I want you to send up a blue flare when we get orders to rejoin the convoy.

GOLIKOV and KAMINSKI: Yessir. (*Exit KAMINSKI and GOLIKOV with AK-47's. Enter SAMAD.*)

SAMAD: The well is cyanided, sir.

DASKAL: Do you know how to do the gas report?

SAMAD: No, sir.

DASKAL: Teach him, Koverchenko.

KOVERCHENKO: Yessir. (*With pen and clipboard.*) This is the form. Use a ballpoint, clearly. TYPE OF OPERATION: Pacification of mountain village. CODE NAME OF OPERATION: leave that blank. What's wrong?

SAMAD: She's alive.

KOVERCHENKO: No.

SAMAD: She made a sound.

KOVERCHENKO: Trapped air escaping through the esophagus.

SAMAD: Are you sure?

KOVERCHENKO: Next blank. TANK NUMBER: 5447. COMMANDER: Georgi Daskal. TYPE OF GAS: Check the canister in the rear end loader. You have to specify irritant, incapacitant, nerve agent, myco-toxins, mustard gas, lewisite, or toxic smoke. In this particular case, phosgene oxime.

SAMAD: How do you know that?

KOVERCHENKO: I loaded it myself. I'll teach you that later on. ONSET: This means . . . (*One of the woman's arms begins to flail about spasmodically.*)

SAMAD: She's breathing! She's alive.

KOVERCHENKO: Nerve gas breaking down the spinal cord. ONSET: Are you paying attention? You've got to learn this.

SAMAD: I'm sorry.

KOVERCHENKO: ONSET: This means the time at which you turn on the gas, which was 0600 hours. NON-FUNCTIONALITY:

Means the time it takes for the body or bodies to be rendered incapable of activity, which was about three minutes, which you add to the time of onset. So write 0600 plus three.

SAMAD: 0600 plus three. How does one know when the enemy is nonfunctional?

KOVERCHENKO: After you see four or five, it's second nature.

SAMAD: Sir?

KOVERCHENKO: They look like puppets. They start flopping around. Then the legs go. When they vomit, that's usually it. Next item, BLEEDING: Turn her over. Don't touch her! Not with your hands! Use your foot! There's residue of poison on her clothes and skin. Now just checkmark the appropriate blanks under BLEEDING FROM: MOUTH: NOSE: EARS: VAGINA: or ANUS: Doesn't apply to the first three. Lift up her dress. (*SAMAD hesitates, then does so. He holds his mouth and rushes behind the tank and vomits his guts out.*)

DASKAL: What's wrong with him?

KOVERCHENKO: Queasy stomach.

DASKAL: Get up, and do your job!

SAMAD: Yessir.

DASKAL: Our Afghan comrades want technology, but can't even fill out a simple report. Move!

SAMAD: Yessir. Does one make report for every enemy killed?

KOVERCHENKO: Only for experimental weapons. Negative—Vagina. Negative—Anus.

SAMAD: Sometimes I think I am not capable.

KOVERCHENKO: Of what?

SAMAD: I feel captive when I am inside the tank.

KOVERCHENKO: When you're down in the bowels of the machine, you are in the presence of the best minds the twentieth century has produced. A machine whose power is more than the sum of its parts. Xenon searching—from Japan. Asimuth indicator—made in Britain. Infrared periscope—Italy. Laser rangefinder—France. Metascope—West Germany. Dynamic gyroscope—Canada. And the entire computer instrumentology made in the U.S.A. A United Nations inside a shell made in the Union of Soviet Socialist Republics.

SAMAD: But without a man, the machine is only fifty tons of iron. It needs me. I have a brain. I can think.

KOVERCHENKO: Until you overcome your self-importance, you will never succeed as a tank driver. As driver, I can have no self. When I resist the machine, I am its slave. When I submit to it, I become its master. When I embrace this paradox, my skin is nickel-chrome steel. I can hide submerged underwater. I can spit flame seventy-five feet. I can hurl incendiaries, shrapnel, concussion and armor-piercing projectiles, and eleven kinds of lethal gases 2.3 miles. The moment I think of myself as cog, not flesh, think of myself as servomechanism, I'm liberated from useless reactions, and at that moment, I am the machine.

DASKAL: You finished?

KOVERCHENKO: Almost, sir. NUMBER OF ENEMY DEAD. One.

DASKAL: Include those others who ran off.

KOVERCHENKO: Why, sir?

DASKAL: They breathed the gas. Therefore they died.

KOVERCHENKO: I'm not certain about that, sir.

DASKAL: If you looked, you'd find 'em up there dead among those rocks. I won't risk the lives of my men on body counts.

KOVERCHENKO: Yessir. How many were there?

DASKAL: Nine or ten.

KOVERCHENKO: I'll write nine.

DASKAL: Write ten. (*Enter KAMINSKI and GOLIKOV dragging SHAHZAMAN. KAMINSKI carries the latter's old ornamented rifle.*) Who's this?

KAMINSKI: We captured him.

DASKAL: When are we getting out of here?

GOLIKOV: Sir, the convoy's gone.

DASKAL: Gone?

GOLIKOV: Yessir, we saw the last few tanks moving far down the Kabul Road.

KAMINSKI: Towards the base.

DASKAL: They left us here?

KOVERCHENKO: Sir, perhaps they took our dead radio to mean we've been destroyed.

DASKAL: How could they go? We haven't accomplished the rest of our mission! Samad, translate for me—where are the rebels hiding?

SAMAD: Where is the Mujahadeen camp? My commander demands to know?

SHAHZAMAN: There are no Mujahadeen here.

SAMAD: We have aerial photographs of Mujahadeen taking food in this village.

SHAHZAMAN: The Mujahadeen are all around you and one Shuravi will die for every hair upon every head that was butchered here today.

KOVERCHENKO: What's he say? Translate.

SAMAD: He says he does not know, sir.

DASKAL: Where's the cache of rebel arms?

SAMAD: Where do the Mujahadeen hide their weapons? (*SHAHZAMAN laughs.*)

DASKAL: Help him remember. Put him under the tank track. I don't want that recorded.

KOVERCHENKO: Sir?

DASKAL: Run him over, Koverchenko.

KOVERCHENKO: Sir, shouldn't we rejoin the convoy immediately?

DASKAL: Drive.

KOVERCHENKO: Yessir.

SAMAD: Say your prayers. You are about to die.

SHAHZAMAN: Allah Akbar. Nanawatai!

DASKAL: Translate.

SAMAD: The man is asking for nanawatai, sir. Sanctuary.

DASKAL: You ever see what they do to Russian prisoners? Ready, Koverchenko?

KOVERCHENKO: Yessir.

SHAHZAMAN: Do you not hold sacred our nanawatai?

SAMAD: I do but my commander does not.

SHAHZAMAN: An Afghan has but one commander in Paradise.

DASKAL: Is he telling us where the rebel arms cache is? (*Enter the Afghan women.*)

SHERINA: Give us our clansman!

DASKAL: Cut them down on my command.

KAMINSKI and GOLIKOV: Yessir!

GOLIKOV: Jesus.

KOVERCHENKO: Don't look in their eyes. Look at their feet and shoot up.

DASKAL: Samad, tell them to go or die.

SAMAD: Afghan women—leave this place or you will know the wrath of my commander.

SHERINA: You are also Afghan?

SAMAD: I am.

Nanawatai! / **165**

SHERINA: And you fight with the Shuravi?

DASKAL: What are they saying, Samad?

SHERINA: Give us our clansman, and then we shall leave.

SAMAD: Do not offend this commander. He prefers bullets to words.

SHERINA: Tell your shit-eater of a commander to give us our clansman.

DASKAL: Translate!

SAMAD: Sir, she humbly begs you for the prisoner.

SHAHZAMAN: Do not add blood to blood! Go! (*KAMINSKI gives SHAHZAMAN a rifle butt in the face.*)

DASKAL: Tell them to watch what happens to rebels.

SAMAD: My commander begs your forgiveness for this most unfortunate death.

SHERINA: Why must he die?

SAMAD: He is a rebel.

SHERINA: Rebel? The man defends his hearth. The man is a patriot. And what are you, snake?

DASKAL: Do it, Koverchenko.

KOVERCHENKO: Yessir. (*SHAHZAMAN gets on his knees, holds out his arms, facing the tank.*)

SHERINA: You are Satan. Rejoice Shahzaman. Allah's closer than the vein in your neck.

SHAHZAMAN: Allah Akbar! La Ilaha Illa Allah!

DASKAL: Koverchenko! Forward! (*The tank engine starts. SHAHZAMAN laughs.*)

SHAHZAMAN: Mohamed Rasullah. (*The tank moves forward. Blackout. The women scream in the dark.*)

Scene 2

Morning. Where the village was. Enter TAJ MOHAMUD and AKBAR.

TAJ MOHAMUD: This is where my village stood. There my house. There, yours. There my milk-goat ate a circle in the grass. Dogs barked, babies cried, boys with sticks played men at war. All my people—vanished!

AKBAR: How to begin again? How?

TAJ MOHAMUD: Do we flee to Pakistan? Or Persia? (*Pause.*) Must

I be the cursed son to surrender the tribal home of my father's father's father?—Follow misery's spoor to Pakistan? Where millions—millions!—waste away. Here I was born. On that day my father put a nail in the wall over my crib. On the nail he hung this rifle. My mother rocked my crib and sang the names of enemies that I should slay when I should come of age. Sing now, dear mother, the names of these Shuravi who come in diabolical engines out of the sky and drop one bomb that rips the earth's bowels, and makes the mountains groan, then flee like jackals. Oh father! I have taken the rifle off the nail. But here is nothing to strike at! Allah, give me a man to tear apart! Give me Badal—blood for blood!

AKBAR: No grieving till the barbarian makes a death cry. No sleep, no food, no talk, till equal blood is spilled.

TAJ MOHAMUD: How does one take Badal?

AKBAR: Let us petition Allah. (*AKBAR and TAJ MOHAMUD spread their prayer rugs. They stand facing Mecca. Their hands on either side of their faces, thumbs touching ear lobes. They go gently to their knees, place hands and face to the ground.*)

TAJ MOHAMUD and AKBAR: Allah akbar.

MOUSTAFA: (*Offstage.*) Taj Mohamud. (*TAJ MOHAMUD and AKBAR rush for their weapons.*)

TAJ MOHAMUD: Moustafa and a tribesman.

AKBAR: Ambush.

TAJ MOHAMUD: They come openly.

MOUSTAFA: (*Offstage.*) I come in peace. Salaam alekum, Taj Mohamud.

TAJ MOHAMUD: He gives us salaam. (*Enter MOUSTAFA and ISKANDAR. MOUSTAFA lays his rifle, a pistol, and two hidden knives on the ground.*)

ISKANDAR: Salaam.

MOUSTAFA: Look, I lay my weapons on the ground.

TAJ MOHAMUD: What assassins in the trees?

MOUSTAFA: No plots, cousin. Salaam, Uncle.

AKBAR: Salaam, Moustafa.

ISKANDAR: Salaam.

AKBAR: Salaam.

TAJ MOHAMUD: Do you have a weapon?

ISKANDAR: I am a dervish. We do not touch weapons. The Holy Koran is my weapon. (*TAJ MOHAMUD points his rifle at*

MOUSTAFA's head—puts his hand in MOUSTAFA's shirt, pulls out a hidden pistol.)

MOUSTAFA: I always said, have faith in Allah, and keep a hidden pistol . . . Salaam.

TAJ MOHAMUD: I tell you the truth, Moustafa, as you stand before me, every part of me screams for your blood.

MOUSTAFA: You steal my thoughts, cousin.

TAJ MOHAMUD: One cannot steal from a thief for nothing is his. I have seen you and your scavengers picking gold from the teeth of the dead Shuravi. Did you come to pick my teeth?

MOUSTAFA: Truce.

TAJ MOHAMUD: I have such a spleen, if I slayed you, I would cry you back to life to kill you again, knife you, disembowel you, dismember you, feed you to diseased pigs and punish their shit.

AKBAR: Taj Mohamud, your father would never dishonor the truce.

MOUSTAFA: In happier times we ate and drank at your father's table. Then disputing a brook, which Allah made for all, we drew each others' blood. Enough. Who is not weary of endless vendetta? We are warriors who kill by the ancient codes. Lay down your weapon, cousin. Let us talk. (*Pause. TAJ MOHAMUD looks to AKBAR who nods. They lay their weapons down.*)

ISKANDAR: Allah akbar. (*MOUSTAFA produces a gold cigarette case.*)

MOUSTAFA: Cigarette? (*TAJ MOHAMUD and AKBAR decline.*) Lucky Strike. From the pocket of a Russian major I found dead in a helicopter. (*They take one each.*) The barbarian has made us one in grief this day. That snake of smoke twisting up in the sky . . . they took my village too! We are all Shuravi game. (*Pause.*)

TAJ MOHAMUD: Why does Allah forsake us?

AKBAR: To see who will forsake him.

ISKANDAR: Not a leaf falls without Allah's design.

AKBAR: Allah akbar. He sends Shuravis like a wind to separate the faithful from the unbeliever.

MOUSTAFA: That same wind separated one tank from fifty others.

AKBAR: What are you saying?

MOUSTAFA: My tribesman and I, while at prayer, saw the many tanks returning to Kabul. A lone tank, lost from the many, came to the place where the Kabul road forks . . .

ISKANDAR: And Allah could not bear the cries of the Afghan

dead, (*He starts to whirl.*) and his wrath was loosed and the winds collided and made whirlwinds and the whirlwinds collected dust and blinded the Shuravis in the tank . . .

MOUSTAFA: And the tank went right, not left, into the Valley of the Hyena.

AKBAR: You know that valley, Taj, it has only one way in and one way out. You killed your first antelope there, when you were eleven.

ISKANDAR: Allah filled us with oxen strength. We moved rocks that moved bigger rocks that moved rocks as big as tanks. We could have moved the mountain.

MOUSTAFA: We tumbled rocks, caused a landslide . . . and sealed the Shuravi tank in the valley. Cousin, Uncle, let us put aside old hatreds and kill the tank. We will follow the new Khan.

TAJ MOHAMUD: A man is a man. A tank is a tank. (*MOUSTAFA unwraps an RPG from a blanket.*)

MOUSTAFA: I took this from a dead Shuravi.

AKBAR: Look. Three rockets.

MOUSTAFA: A very proper weapon, Taj.

AKBAR: What do you say, Taj?

MOUSTAFA: Allah has tossed a peach in our laps! Take it! (*TAJ MOHAMUD sits, inspects the RPG.*)

ISKANDAR: Allah akbar.

TAJ MOHAMUD: How close to the tank must the user be with this weapon?

MOUSTAFA: From here to the camel-thorn.

TAJ MOHAMUD: That is too close.

AKBAR: I will do it.

TAJ MOHAMUD: Must the user of the weapon sacrifice himself to kill the tank?

MOUSTAFA: No sacrifices!—I want the tank's treasures, Taj.

AKBAR: If this is my time, so be it. I am ready.

ISKANDAR: Who is born to hang shall not drown.

TAJ MOHAMUD: I have seen such rockets bounce off tanks like rotten cabbages.

MOUSTAFA: I have seen such rockets explode tanks—hit in the right place.

TAJ MOHAMUD: Do you know that place?

MOUSTAFA: A tank contains many treasures, Taj. Machine guns. Ammunition. Bombs. Food. Who knows what treasures we

Nanawatai! / **169**

could sell in Peshawar for things we need to live.

AKBAR: The smallest tank gun could take down a helicopter, Taj.

TAJ MOHAMUD: Shuravis will send more helicopters.

AKBAR: We are the sons of Afghan warriors who with blood and faith alone expelled Alexander, Darius, Ghengis Khan, Tamerlane, and British Grenadiers. Taj Mohamud! We are no shaking feather to the godless Soviet tank! What do you say?

MOUSTAFA: Let us be the brothers Allah made us, and hunt the tank.

TAJ MOHAMUD: Our fathers fought men, eye to eye, and in that, an Afghan has no equal. There is no fighting a tank.

AKBAR: In agony, you called to Allah to give you a man . . . give you some flesh to tear apart! You have been heard. It is given. A tank full of Shuravi.

MOUSTAFA: Jihad!

ISKANDAR: When David chose five smooth stones from a brook, did he not tremble when he beheld mountainous Goliath? And remember that Allah's loving hand guided the stone from David's trembling sling and cracked the giant's skull and brought Goliath down.

MOUSTAFA: David, a great Afghan.

TAJ MOHAMUD: Without this, we cannot take the tank.

MOUSTAFA: Taj, Iskandar is a holy man. I saw him fix a car once with a prayer.

TAJ MOHAMUD: The RPG is broken!

MOUSTAFA: Iskandar, what can you do?

ISKANDAR: I prayed to Allah once and raised a dead camel. But a weapon—never.

MOUSTAFA: Faith, Taj, faith.

TAJ MOHAMUD: Faith! We might as well bomb the tank with camel shit!

ISKANDAR: Go first and Allah will follow.

TAJ MOHAMUD: You are boys with a new slingshot hunting wounded tiger. As for me, I am for Pakistan.

AKBAR: Do you ask for manna before you go into the wilderness? This is how we begin again.

MOUSTAFA: Let my son murder me with my own gun before I leave my land for Pakistan. Pakistan is a dry woman giving suck to a screaming baby.

AKBAR: It was I who whispered "Allah Akbar" four times in your ear when you still had your mother's birthing slime upon you, and I knew you would be a Khan measured by mountains.—When will the new Khan avenge his people?

TAJ MOHAMUD: Remember the Afghan who took revenge after a hundred years and said—'I took it quickly.' (*Enter the Afghan women.*) Allah has chosen some to live and some to perish. My father is in paradise. I am Khan. It is Allah's will.—Go and hide yourselves in our caves. Give thanks and wait for our return. (*The women begin to exit. SHERINA steps out of the throng. The others stop when she addresses TAJ MOHAMUD.*)

SHERINA: Why do you walk with Moustafa our enemy?

TAJ MOHAMUD: You will call our former enemy our friend.—In war all things change.

AKBAR: These are the last days when women question the Khan. (*The women take this as a threat and try to pull SHERINA among themselves, but she resists.*)

SHERINA: We go, too, Khan, and fight with you. (*The other Afghan men laugh.*)

AKBAR: Do you stand for this? How she looks directly in your eye!—No shame!—Has no one ever taught you to avert your eyes when you speak to a man?

SHERINA: In war all things change.

AKBAR: Backtalk today, rebellion tomorrow, Taj.

SHERINA: There is no disrespect, Khan. Let us fight, too.

TAJ MOHAMUD: You have no weapons.

SHERINA: We have no fear.

TAJ MOHAMUD: Is that enough?

SHERINA: We attacked the tank with sticks.

TAJ MOHAMUD: Sticks.

SHERINA: Sticks.

TAJ MOHAMUD: Did you destroy the tank? (*The men laugh.*)

SHERINA: The tank, no. The valor and honor of the Shuravi inside the tank—utterly.

TAJ MOHAMUD: And how was their honor and valor destroyed?

SHERINA: Shuravi hid inside like boys. They sprayed the yellow vapor at us, and we could not fight that with sticks. We ran but restored honor to our village.

TAJ MOHAMUD: (*Privately.*) What are you called?

SHERINA: Sherina.

TAJ MOHAMUD: Your father?

SHERINA: Zaman the gunsmith.

TAJ MOHAMUD: He was blind.

SHERINA: Yes.

TAJ MOHAMUD: Have you inherited your father's blindness? Do you not know a tank has a thousand kinds of death?

SHERINA: Who fears Allah fears nothing.

TAJ MOHAMUD: Nothing?

SHERINA: Nothing.

TAJ MOHAMUD: No man?

SHERINA: Nothing.

TAJ MOHAMUD: (*Privately.*) Not even your Khan? (*She shakes her head no.*) Why do you not fear me?

SHERINA: I cannot fear the eyes of a fawn.

TAJ MOHAMUD: Most men would strike you for that.

SHERINA: Allah wills it, or Allah does not.

TAJ MOHAMUD: If you insult me, I promise I will strike you.

SHERINA: I promise I will not feel it.

TAJ MOHAMUD: Anger me and I promise you will feel it.

SHERINA: I will think of it as a kiss.

TAJ MOHAMUD: It will be the hardest kiss of your life.

SHERINA: And my only one.

TAJ MOHAMUD: (*Breaking privacy.*) Go back to the caves with the women, and prepare for the trek to Pakistan.

SHERINA: We will carry your weapons, my Khan.

AKBAR: Outrageous woman! Obey your Khan!

TAJ MOHAMUD: Did you hear me?

SHERINA: My Khan, your brother's spirit sits in the shade of palm and pomegranate, on brocade couches, with all the Afghan martyrs in paradise, served honey wine by black-eyed and bashful virgins in green silk, and he gazes upon our lord of the two easts and two wests . . .

ISKANDAR: Allah akbar.

SHERINA: Allah chose us to witness his martyrdom when he faced the tank and showed Shuravis how a P'tan dies . . . As the evil engine crushed his flesh, his unbroken spirit laughed, and truly the Shuravis blanched and quaked . . . We buried with prayers and wailing his mortal part . . . Azrael claimed the rest . . . His rifle . . .

AKBAR: The rifle I gave him when he came of age.

SHERINA: The crow is fat in cold Afghanistan. (*He hands TAJ*

MOHAMUD *a bent rifle.*)

TAJ MOHAMUD: Allah, Allah, Allah. If you do not have a heart of flesh you cannot comprehend a man.

AKBAR: The tank, Taj.

TAJ MOHAMUD: From this time forth, I am a stone in Allah's sling.

ISKANDAR: Allah Akbar!

MOUSTAFA: Allah Akbar! (*He picks up the RPG.*)

TAJ MOHAMUD: Fling me, Allah! Fling me! (*The women make the zagharit. Blackout.*)

Scene 3

Afternoon. Lights up. DASKAL climbs out of the tank.

DASKAL: All out! Where've you led us? I don't see the convoy's tracks.

SAMAD: Sir, I think we made the wrong turn at the fork in the road.

DASKAL: You think? You don't know? You're dismissed from your post. Why do I need an Afghan navigator? To get me lost in enemy territory? Record it.

KOVERCHENKO: Yessir.

DASKAL: Hand me the map and a rifle. How's the petrol?

KOVERCHENKO: Three quarters tank, Sir.

DASKAL: Run a check. (*KAMINSKI, GOLIKOV, and SAMAD exit the tank. DASKAL walks a distance from the tank. KOVERCHENKO sees that Daskal would speak with him privately.*)

KOVERCHENKO: Golikov, check the track for impacted stone. Kaminski, secure the arsenal and see what's been rattling around back there. Samad, clean the portals and lenses.

ALL: Yessir.

DASKAL: Watch Samad.

KOVERCHENKO: Why, Sir?

DASKAL: Sabotage.

KOVERCHENKO: I think that was an honest mistake, Sir.

DASKAL: There are no honest mistakes. I can't believe they just left us here!—If I were convoy commander and thought one of my tanks were hit, I'd send to see if there were survivors. That's why I'm not convoy commander.—I'm going to see if I can see

Kabul Road from that rock and get a bearing.

KAMINSKI: Sir, this shell's got a damaged casing.

DASKAL: Discard it.

KAMINSKI: Yessir. There goes my mother's refrigerator.

DASKAL: What?

KAMINSKI: Nothing, Sir.

DASKAL: No. What did you say about a refrigerator?

KAMINSKI: My mother can't get a refrigerator, and we throw shells away.

DASKAL: At Stalingrad we ran out of shells. Too bad we didn't have refrigerators to throw at the Nazis.

KAMINSKI: Sorry, Sir.

DASKAL: Keep them busy.

KOVERCHENKO: Yessir. (*Exit DASKAL.*)

KAMINSKI: Prick.

KOVERCHENKO: Check the crankcase.

KAMINSKI: After I have a smoke.

KOVERCHENKO: Now.

KAMINSKI: What's the hurry?—We're all dead anyway.

KOVERCHENKO: You want a write-up?

KAMINSKI: I don't give a shit.

KOVERCHENKO: Move. (*KAMINSKI does so.*)

GOLIKOV: We got a leak here somewhere.

KOVERCHENKO: What is it?

GOLIKOV: I can't tell.

KOVERCHENKO: Check the transmission fluid line gauge. Samad, check the computer under Engine Check.

SAMAD: Yessir. (*Exit SAMAD into tank. KAMINSKI lights up a wad of hashish and plays a tape cassette—rock and roll.*)

KAMINSKI: Hash? (*GOLIKOV sneaks a toke.*)

GOLIKOV: This is the best hash we ever got.

KAMINSKI: Next time, the dealer wants two Kalashnikous and five clips. (*KOVERCHENKO sees smoke behind the tank.*)

KOVERCHENKO: Is that hashish?

KAMINSKI: Hundred percent Cuban tobacco.

KOVERCHENKO: Get rid of it.

GOLIKOV: Konstantin, it's our first one today.

KOVERCHENKO: Don't let Daskal see you.

GOLIKOV: Thanks. (*GOLIKOV takes a toke of KAMINSKI's cigar. KAMINSKI drinks from his canteen, offers it to GOLIKOV who* *drinks and spits it out. KAMINSKI laughs.*)

SAMAD: (*Appearing through a hatch.*) Sir, computer registers no malfunction.

KOVERCHENKO: Clean off the oil line.

SAMAD: Yessir.

KOVERCHENKO: And the transmission fluid line.

GOLIKOV: Right.

KOVERCHENKO: And we'll see if it's traveling along the lines.

KAMINSKI: Where are we, Samad?

SAMAD: I do not know.

KAMINSKI: Don't you know your own territory?

SAMAD: Do you know every inch of your territory?

KAMINSKI: I know my foot from my ass. Next time you navigate, don't think Allah, think left and right, and look at the fucking map.

KOVERCHENKO: Get off him, Kaminski. (*KAMINSKI turns on a tape player and dances to the rock music.*) Turn that music off! (*KAMINSKI turns it off.*)

KAMINSKI: That's what I hate about war. No fun. (*GOLIKOV takes a rag and cleans the line. He stands the way SHAHZAMAN was killed. He lies down to see what SHAHZAMAN must have seen.*)

KOVERCHENKO: What the hell are you doing?

GOLIKOV: Did you see the way that rebel stretched out his arms?

KAMINSKI: Bastards go around looking for somebody to make them a martyr.

GOLIKOV: We didn't even have to hold him down. I saw his fucking eyes pop. Could you let a tank run over you?

KOVERCHENKO: We took an oath never to surrender.

GOLIKOV: But if by surprise . . . ?

KOVERCHENKO: Check the line.

GOLIKOV: What did that rebel say?

SAMAD: Nanawatai. It's a custom of the P'tan tribe—Afghan code of honor. If you ask your enemy for Nanawatai—Sanctuary—he must spare you.

GOLIKOV: But he laughed. I saw his face. He wasn't scared. He looked happy.

SAMAD: He knew he would go straight to paradise and sit at banquet with all the martyrs of history.

KAMINSKI: Horseshit.—It's a banquet of maggots.

GOLIKOV: How could he do that?

SAMAD: That's Islam. The word itself means "surrender."

GOLIKOV: Surrender to what?

SAMAD: Allah's will.

KAMINSKI: How do you know what's Allah's will?

GOLIKOV: What was that other thing he said?

SAMAD: What thing?

GOLIKOV: La La La La La La.

KOVERCHENKO: La ilaha illa Allah.

SAMAD: Do you speak Arabic?

KOVERCHENKO: No.

SAMAD: You said that so well.

KOVERCHENKO: I heard it before.

SAMAD: Where?

KOVERCHENKO: Kabul.

GOLIKOV: What's it mean?

SAMAD: Allah is the only God.

KAMINSKI: These people got no regard for life. I hate those spooks in the minarets. They sound like ghosts with a finger up their ass. (*He imitates the Azan.*) "Kill a Russian and you will go to paradise."—We should level every fucking minaret in this fucking country.

KOVERCHENKO: What'd you find?

GOLIKOV: It's still dropping from the same spot.

KOVERCHENKO: Check the hydraulic fluid. (*KAMINSKI stands on the tank with the cannon between his legs.*)

KAMINSKI: I need a woman.

GOLIKOV: There must be sheep around here, Kaminski.

KOVERCHENKO: Check the track.

KAMINSKI: Golikov did. I think.

KOVERCHENKO: Don't think. Do it.

SAMAD: Where in Kabul did you hear la ilaha illa Allah? The Mosque?

KOVERCHENKO: I used to organize the firing squads there. They used to stand, eyes open, looking in the muzzles, smiling, la ilaha illa Allah. All day. All night. I found myself repeating it, though I didn't know what it meant. Until now.

GOLIKOV: Sir, I think I found the leak.

KOVERCHENKO: Where?

GOLIKOV: Just left of the master link. (*KOVERCHENKO checks for the leak between the links of the tank track.*) Oil? (*KOVERCHENKO*

176 / *William Mastrosimone*

dabs his finger in the liquid, rubs it, smells it.)

KOVERCHENKO: Blood. (*He kneels, reaches up in the tracks with his fingers and pulls out the bloody severed hand of Shahzaman.*)

GOLIKOV: Jesus.

SAMAD: What is that?

KOVERCHENKO: The rebel's hand. (*KOVERCHENKO drops the hand.*)

KAMINSKI: We can use an extra hand around here. (*KOVERCHENKO flings it away.*)

GOLIKOV: Jesus Christ—They never said we'd have to kill women or run people over with the tank.

KOVERCHENKO: You only had to watch—I had to press the accelerator and feel the bones crack through the steel. (*Long pause. GOLIKOV and KAMINSKI smoke hashish. GOLIKOV reads an old letter. KOVERCHENKO writes in his log. SAMAD lays out his prayer rug and prays in a low whisper.*)

SAMAD: Allah akbar. (etc.)(*KAMINSKI snatches the letter.*)

KAMINSKI: "My dear little rabbit—" (*KOVERCHENKO grabs the letter from KAMINSKI and hands it to GOLIKOV.*) My dear little rabbit!

GOLIKOV: I can't understand why Anna wants to have the baby baptized. My babushka must have been talking to her.

KAMINSKI: Why doesn't she get the abortion?

GOLIKOV: There's benefits for having a Slavic baby.—We're outnumbered in our own country.

KAMINSKI: How do you know it's yours?

GOLIKOV: Of course it's mine.

KOVERCHENKO: How many months?

GOLIKOV: Four.

KAMINSKI: You've been here three. All those weeks of travel. Somebody's been keeping your little rabbit warm at night. (*KAMINSKI laughs. GOLIKOV attacks KAMINSKI. KOVERCHENKO stands in between.*)

KOVERCHENKO: Sit down. (*Pause. KAMINSKI and KOVERCHENKO square off.*) Sit down. (*Pause. KAMINSKI sits.*) I'm sick of you and your mouth. When we get back to barracks, I want you out back.

KAMINSKI: Wouldn't miss it. Just watch out for snipers. Sometimes ambitious officers are found with a bullet in their back. (*Enter DASKAL.*)

DASKAL: What's going on?

KOVERCHENKO: Just talk, sir.

KAMINSKI: A lot of talk.

DASKAL: Can't you keep order here?

KOVERCHENKO: Yessir.

DASKAL: Samad.

SAMAD: Sir?

DASKAL: Stop.

SAMAD: I am in my prayers, Sir.

DASKAL: Get up. (SAMAD quits praying.)

SAMAD: May I ask why, Sir?

DASKAL: I said so.

SAMAD: Yessir.

DASKAL: Read the last entry.

KOVERCHENKO: "1200 hours. Fuel, three quarters tank. Separated from convoy due to navigator error."

DASKAL: Record this: the pass we entered into this valley has been blocked by a landslide. Four rebels follow in our tracks. They have an RPG. (*KAMINSKI, GOLIKOV, and SAMAD listen.*) Considering the terrain, and being without flank support, I have decided to—(*Pause.*)

KOVERCHENKO: To what, Sir?

DASKAL: —to wait for rescue gunships! Samad! You idiot! I will see to it you never command a tank! (*DASKAL climbs on the tank.*) On watch, Kaminski!—Keep flares on the ready.

KOVERCHENKO: Yessir.

DASKAL: When you hear the gunships, send up a flare every ten seconds.

KOVERCHENKO: Yessir. Do you want to finish the entry, Sir? (*DASKAL enters the tank. The periscope turns.*)

SAMAD: I don't understand this commander. If I am able to justify Allah and dialectical materialism in the same brain, what should it matter to him?

KOVERCHENKO: Let it go.

SAMAD: Does he not trust me?

KOVERCHENKO: I don't know.

SAMAD: He knows I am a member of the Party. My oldest son is in the cultural exchange in Moscow. Does he think I would compromise my son?

KAMINSKI: You turned on your own people.

SAMAD: Sir! I think you do not know me very well!—I did not "turn" on my people! I am trying to educate my people!—That Afghanistan is a flea on the tail of a bear and will never overthrow the bear. And Afghans must accept that. And when they do, I will be there knowing technology and Russian, to lead them—

KAMINSKI: Hope you lead them better than you led us.

GOLIKOV: What are we waiting for? The Afghans to find us? Why's he not doing anything?

KOVERCHENKO: For instance?

GOLIKOV: Turn around and attack the rebels.

KOVERCHENKO: In this terrain, they have the advantage.

GOLIKOV: We have a tank! What do they have?

KOVERCHENKO: Inside the tank, we've got a 70 percent visual and weapons deadspace. That's why tanks always operate in tandem—to cover each other's blind spots. In this terrain the rebels could crawl up to us and fire the RPG point-blank.

GOLIKOV: If we abandoned the tank, we could get back the same way we came.

KAMINSKI: They'd get us out there.

GOLIKOV: Five of us? With AK's? With that kind of firepower, we could hold off an Afghan army. We could dismantle the machine gun and carry it.

SAMAD: Why do we not suggest this to Commander Daskal?

GOLIKOV: It's the only sane thing to do. Let's save our lives.

KOVERCHENKO: Abandoning armament to the enemy could get him a court martial.

KAMINSKI: Explode the tank.

KOVERCHENKO: They'd never entrust him with another tank.

KAMINSKI: He's retiring in six months.

KOVERCHENKO: He envisions himself driving this tank back to command post compound, if we have to push, pull, or carry it on our backs.

KAMINSKI: Fuck this. Fuck this tank. Fuck this country. It stinks. It fucking stinks. (*DASKAL climbs out of the tank. He walks to KAMINSKI, takes the canteen from which he drinks, drinks from it, spits it out.*)

DASKAL: What is this?

KAMINSKI: Something I made, Sir.

DASKAL: Made? From what?

KAMINSKI: Brake fluid, Sir. It's got alcohol in it.

DASKAL: Where'd you get it?

KAMINSKI: I bled the brake line, Sir. Mix it with raisins, leave it out in the sun. Those Moslems in the minarets, cramped up in this tank, this fucking war.—I get the shakes. Calms me down.

DASKAL: Do you still have a liver?

KAMINSKI: I don't know, sir.

DASKAL: This will kill you.

KAMINSKI: Doesn't matter, Sir.—I breathed nerve gas once. I cough up blood and pieces of my lungs. I'm a walking deadman, Sir.

DASKAL: Koverchenko.

KOVERCHENKO: Yessir.

DASKAL: Record this. Kaminski says he's dying. He volunteers for all the dangerous missions. (*DASKAL flings the canteen away.*) Take over the watch.

GOLIKOV: Yessir.

DASKAL: What were they talking about?

KOVERCHENKO: Gunships.

DASKAL: Is Samad talking against me?

KOVERCHENKO: Nosir.

DASKAL: If under attack, I want you to get him.

KOVERCHENKO: Get him?

DASKAL: We'll write it up as a sniper's bullet.

KOVERCHENKO: I think you misread him, Sir.

DASKAL: Don't write that down. This is not algebra. This is war. Let me see the log.

KOVERCHENKO: Yessir.

DASKAL: You're always writing.

KOVERCHENKO: I was taught in academy that the logbook is the junior officer's bible.

DASKAL: You record in the log unnecessarily.

KOVERCHENKO: I only want to be a good soldier, Sir.

DASKAL: Good soldier? And what do you suppose that is?

KOVERCHENKO: Like you, Sir.

DASKAL: Me? Academies don't make soldiers like me. I was made in the rubble of Stalingrad. I was eight. My mother sent me to look for wood to burn. I returned home and the house was leveled. Everybody dead. I lived in the streets. Some defenders gave me some broth of a boiled belt. I helped carry the machine gun ammo. They tied a rope about my waist, lowered me from windows on top of Nazi tanks. I stuffed molotov cocktails between the cannon and turret, and they'd pull me up quick before it exploded. They called me the Tank Boy. I took a lot of tanks. That was the last good war. (*Pause.*) And then Kabul. A boy, no more than ten, jumped in front of my tank, shouting that thing they shout, Allah this, Allah that, playing chicken with me!—With me! After Stalingrad—After Berlin and Budapest— After Prague and a People's Medal for action on the Mongolian border! You tell me what's a good soldier. I don't know anymore. But I do know you can't be a good soldier in a rotten war. (*SAMAD looks at GOLIKOV and KAMINSKI, who give him encouraging glances and gestures.*)

SAMAD: Sir, excuse us, Sir.

DASKAL: What is it?

SAMAD: May I have a word with you alone?

DASKAL: A word, yes, alone, no. Speak.

SAMAD: Some of us wonder if the most expedient course would be to abandon tank and make our way over to the Kabul Road, Sir, by foot.

DASKAL: So, our scout loses us in the wasteland, and now wants us to walk away from the tank. Give it to the enemy.

SAMAD: Explode the tank, Sir.

DASKAL: Explode the tank, in violation of Soviet Military Law. (*Pause.*) Who's some of us?

SAMAD: I, for one, Sir.

DASKAL: Who else?

SAMAD: I would rather each man speak for himself, Sir.

DASKAL: Kaminski?

KAMINSKI: Sir?

DASKAL: Are you part of this?

KAMINSKI: Well, Sir, it's an interesting idea but I don't know how feasible it is.

DASKAL: Golikov?

GOLIKOV: Well, I really haven't thought it through, Sir.

DASKAL: So this some of us whittles down to you, Samad.

SAMAD: Yessir.

DASKAL: Well, the idea does have some merit.

SAMAD: Thank you, Sir.

DASKAL: I'm going to see that you get a commendation for this,

Samad. It shows you're officer material.

SAMAD: Thank you, Sir.

DASKAL: Take the maps up that ridge and map out a tentative travel route.

SAMAD: (*Going to get an AK.*) Yessir.

DASKAL: You don't need an AK. Take my binoculars.

SAMAD: Yessir. (*Exit SAMAD.*)

DASKAL: What's this, mutiny?

KAMINSKI: Nosir.

DASKAL: Record this in the log, Koverchenko.

KOVERCHENKO: Yessir.

DASKAL: That Kaminski and Golikov took part in a mutiny to abandon tank.

KAMINSKI: Sir, that wasn't mutiny. We just talked. That's all.

DASKAL: Ten years hard labor if the judge is lenient.

GOLIKOV: Sir, Samad suggested it and we told him to bring it to you.

DASKAL: And if the judge wants to make an example, you get a blindfold, a cigarette, and a three gun salute.

KAMINSKI: Sir, please it was just talk.

DASKAL: Koverchenko. Stop writing. I can see they're sincere.

KAMINSKI: We are, Sir.

DASKAL: Why ruin their lives with this?

KAMINSKI and GOLIKOV: Thank you, Sir.

DASKAL: Why make it bad for their families?

GOLIKOV and KAMINSKI: Thank you, Sir.

DASKAL: Now I know where you two stand.

KAMINSKI: With you, Sir.

DASKAL: Do you have anything to do with this?

KOVERCHENKO: Nosir.

DASKAL: Where do you stand on this?

KOVERCHENKO: Whatever you say, Sir.

DASKAL: Abandon tank or no?

KOVERCHENKO: Whatever you say, Sir.

DASKAL: I want your opinion.

KOVERCHENKO: It's obvious they trapped us in a cul-de-sac. Petrol's low. Kaminski drank our brakes. We have half a day's rations. If not rescued within 24 hours, we have no choice, Sir.

DASKAL: In other words—abandon tank.

KOVERCHENKO: Yessir. And it's been my experience that rescue crews don't like to stick their necks out for anybody.

DASKAL: No!—Our comrades-in-arms would never throw us to the wolves!—Never!

KOVERCHENKO: Yessir.

DASKAL: Yessir, yessir, yessir!—Don't give me yessir!— (*DASKAL takes out his pistol, offers it to KOVERCHENKO.*) You want to be a good soldier? Take Samad. He's a traitor. He's bringing this tank over to the enemy. They'll make him a Major. Do it, if you got the juice.

KOVERCHENKO: Sir, this is a mistake. He wants to be a good soldier. Let me have a talk with him, Sir.

KAMINSKI: Don't think, Koverchenko. Do it.

KOVERCHENKO: He's loyal, Sir. Under fire, I'd take Samad over Kaminski any day.

DASKAL: You have an order. (*KOVERCHENKO takes the gun.*)

KOVERCHENKO: Sir, please, understand. (*Enter SAMAD.*)

SAMAD: (*Out of breath.*) Sir, rebels, two kilometers.

DASKAL: Koverchenko? (*Pause. KOVERCHENKO hands the gun back.*)

DASKAL: Take your posts. (*The men scramble about. DASKAL shoots SAMAD in the back. He screams.*)

KOVERCHENKO: No! (*KOVERCHENKO lunges at DASKAL but is restrained by KAMINSKI.*)

SAMAD: Sir! Sir! I'm hit! (*SAMAD falls. DASKAL finishes SAMAD.*)

DASKAL: Kaminski, drive.

KAMINSKI: Yessir.

DASKAL: Load and navigate, Golikov.

GOLIKOV: Yessir.

DASKAL: Get some wire and tie him.

KAMINSKI: Yessir.

KOVERCHENKO: You have no right!

DASKAL: Don't tell me about rights! We're fighting for our lives! Get the logbook. Tie him and leave him in our tracks.

KAMINSKI: Kill him, Sir.

DASKAL: The Afghans can do that better, and buy some time for us.

KOVERCHENKO: Anton! (*KAMINSKI moves to tank, stops, turns back to KOVERCHENKO and takes his cigarettes.*)

DASKAL: Let's go!

KOVERCHENKO: Golikov! (*DASKAL stands upon the tank looking down. KAMINSKI climbs up. GOLIKOV hesitates as KOVER-CHENKO bucks.)*

KOVERCHENKO: Golikov!

DASKAL: Let's go! (*GOLIKOV climbs up and in. The hatch shuts. The tank withdraws.*)

Scene 4

Evening. Enter the Afghan women. They first see the body of SAMAD, rush for it, turn it over, remove his boots. They see KOVERCHENKO, rush for him. Pause)

KOVERCHENKO: Nanawatai. (*The women look at each other in consternation. Lights fade. End of Act I.*)

Act II

"When you're wounded an' left on Afghanistan's plains,
An the women come out to cut up your remains,
Just roll to your rifle an' blow out your brains,
An' go to your Gawd like a soldier."

—Kipling.
("The Young British Soldier")

" . . . an overweening self-confidence, bred by this mistaken belief in their own invincibility, then leads them on to court disaster by rashly attacking still unbroken peoples whose spirit and capacity for resistance takes them by surprise."

—Arnold Toynbee

ACT II
Scene 1

No time has passed. Evening.

KOVERCHENKO: Nanawatai. (*SHERINA circles KOVERCHENKO. She covers his face with her veil.*)

SHERINA: Your bombs made dust of all our kin, our homes, our sheep,—and now, Shuravi, you sing our sacred word?

KOVERCHENKO: Nanawatai.

SHERINA: Stop my ears, Allah. I am so at war with the softness of my sex. I am no more a woman, no more one of Adam's race.—We ourselves must be all of our brothers, fathers, husbands to ourselves. One of us is nothing. Together we are the pack of hunting dogs that chase the buck with frothing mouths and drag it down and tear it all to pieces! (*She gathers two stones.*) Turn your grief to stone, Afghan woman, and make a song of this Shuravi's death-cry, and let it echo cliff to cliff and call hyenas to a putrid supper. (*The women make the zagharit and take up stones. SHERINA removes the veil from KOVERCHENKO's eyes. He sees the women all about him clicking the stones together.*)

KOVERCHENKO: No. No!

SHERINA: Allah, who made the stones, sanctify the stones, sanctify us to cleanse the earth of the Shuravi unbeliever.

KOVERCHENKO: Nanawatai!

SHERINA: I teach you another word: BADAL! (*The women chant "Badal,' working up into a frenzy, making feints with the stones, laughing when KOVERCHENKO ducks the unthrown stones. Enter the Afghan men. Long pause. TAJ looks at SHERINA, KOVERCHENKO, SAMAD's corpse.*)

TAJ MOHAMUD: Afghan women! How did you take the Shuravi captive?

SHERINA: We found him in the tank spoor, Khan.

TAJ MOHAMUD: Tied up?

SHERINA: Yes, my Khan.

TAJ MOHAMUD: How did you find him before we?

SHERINA: We went around you, Khan.

TAJ MOHAMUD: I told you—back to the caves!

SHERINA: It was Allah's will.

TAJ MOHAMUD: You will heed my will!

SHERINA: Yes, my Khan.

TAJ MOHAMUD: The other one?

SHERINA: He was dead when we found him.

AKBAR: By all feature, one of us, Khan.

SHERINA: An Afghan traitor!

ISKANDAR: Shot in the back.

SHERINA: A fit farewell for one who walks with his enemy.

ISKANDAR: A sign from Allah. No mercy for the unfaithful.

AKBAR: You asked Allah for a man to tear apart. Allah has delivered the man. Do it, Taj.

MOUSTAFA: You take the honor, Taj. Do it for all of us. (*MOUS-TAFA hands TAJ his knife.*)

KOVERCHENKO: Nanawatai.

TAJ MOHAMUD: Do you speak Afghan?

KOVERCHENKO: Don't cut me. Please.

TAJ MOHAMUD: Is that all you know, nanawatai?

KOVERCHENKO: I prefer to be shot.

TAJ MOHAMUD: How do you know this Afghan word nanawatai?

KOVERCHENKO: As a P.O.W. I invoke the Geneva Convention.

TAJ MOHAMUD: Why are you abandoned?

KOVERCHENKO: I don't understand.

TAJ MOHAMUD: What is your name?

KOVERCHENKO: Nanawatai.

AKBAR: Taj! You asked for Badal. Take it!

TAJ MOHAMUD: He asked for Nanawatai.

SHERINA: A crow can speak a word, but I call no crow a Khan. Your father would have slain him.

TAJ MOHAMUD: I am not my father.

SHERINA: I am very sure of it. Your father's memory groans.

TAJ MOHAMUD: My father's son groans, too. Where is your veil?

SHERINA: I lost it.

TAJ MOHAMUD: Find it, and get back with the women.

SHERINA: Outside of their machines Shuravis beg like puppies. But in their tanks, in their helicopters, they are archangels that kill us with gas that smells like flowers, kill our children with bombs that look like little green butterflies, and then they flee away in the sky or hide in all their iron, and leave us to scream Badal. For once we hold one in our hands! I say if you have sucked of an Afghan mother, if you be men, rip his bowels with happy knives and rejoice when his miserable life passes out of him. (*The women make the Zagharit.*)

TAJ MOHAMUD: Without codes, we are hyenas fighting for a carcass.

MOUSTAFA: Nanawatai is for Afghans, not Shuravis. (*The women make the Zagharit.*)

TAJ MOHAMUD: Why do we war? . . . To keep our code . . . How do we keep it if we be the violators of it?

AKBAR: The Shuravi gives us death! Should we give back life? (*The women make the Zagharit.*)

TAJ MOHAMUD: Who are we to slay a man Allah spared three times?

SHERINA: How, three times?

TAJ MOHAMUD: From the Shuravis who shoot in the back, from your sudden rage, and from mine.—I call you Thrice Blessed!

MOUSTAFA: As children of a slain people, we are obliged to take Badal!

TAJ MOHAMUD: Why was he abandoned?

MOUSTAFA: How can we know this?

TAJ MOHAMUD: Because he was a friend to Shuravis? Or Foe? (*Pause.*) If you are foe to the Shuravis, then perhaps you are friend to us.

AKBAR: He does not speak our tongue, Taj. Why do you persist?

TAJ MOHAMUD: Why would the Shuravis leave him for us to find?

MOUSTAFA: Our vendettas make the foreigners think us blood-lovers. Perhaps he was left for us to disport ourselves in gore and let the tank spoor grow cold.

AKBAR: There is something in this, Taj.

KOVERCHENKO: A drink?

ISKANDAR: I think he wants water.

SHERINA: Give me your knife and I will give him a cup of his own blood.

TAJ MOHAMUD: Would you drink his blood, too?

SHERINA: I cannot live under the same sky with him.

TAJ MOHAMUD: Eat his heart?

SHERINA: His corpse would smell sweet to me.

TAJ MOHAMUD: Here is my knife.

AKBAR: Taj.

TAJ MOHAMUD: If you would be the slayer of our code, declare yourself pure before your clan and Allah.

SHERINA: I am pure!

TAJ MOHAMUD: Are you a virgin?

SHERINA: As I am female.

TAJ MOHAMUD: Do you keep the faith?

SHERINA: I know the Holy KORAN by heart.

TAJ MOHAMUD: Then do it.

ISKANDAR: Our most Glorious KORAN demands decent conduct in war! Fulfill promises. Never slay women or children. Spare orchards and crops and sacred objects. Never mutilate wounded or disfigure the dead! These things Mohamud has set down. (*SHERINA raises the knife.*)

KOVERCHENKO: La ilaha illa Allah!

ISKANDAR: Allah akbar!

KOVERCHENKO: Mohamud Rasul'llah!

ISKANDAR: The man was spared for he embraced Allah! (*TAJ MOHAMUD cuts KOVERCHENKO loose.*) Jonah, too, was lost, deep in the bowels of the leviathan, and when he cried out, Allah heard him and Allah delivered him. A sign! Devils shall be converted! Allah akbar!

KOVERCHENKO: (*Removing his uniform.*) Kill this, not me. I am no longer this.

AKBAR: Shuravi forsakes Shuravi.

SHERINA: Even a viper slips from its skin when the season changes.

KOVERCHENKO: Nanawatai.

MOUSTAFA: Maybe your boots would fit me.

TAJ MOHAMUD: Give him water. (*AKBAR takes the goatskin.*) No. You. (*AKBAR hands the goatskin to SHERINA. She does not take it. She glares at TAJ. TAJ glowers at SHERINA. She takes it and gives the goatskin to KOVERCHENKO and screams.*)

KOVERCHENKO: Thank you. Thank you. La ilaha illa Allah.

ISKANDAR: I never heard the mullah sign it more beautifully.

TAJ MOHAMUD: Let us look to our guest.

SHERINA: Guest. (*TAJ MOHAMUD removes his vest and extends it to KOVERCHENKO.*)

TAJ MOHAMUD: Cover yourself. (*KOVERCHENKO looks up, takes it, puts it on. AKBAR calls to women to bring SAMAD's pants.*)

AKBAR: Cover yourself. (*KOVERCHENKO takes it. MOUSTAFA hands his scarf.*)

MOUSTAFA: Cover your neck. (*KOVERCHENKO takes it. TAJ MOHAMUD spreads a cloth before KOVERCHENKO. From every pocket and pouch, an assortment of bread, pieces of mutton, almonds, raisins, and the goatskin are put before him. Being more astonished than hungry, he touches nothing.*)

TAJ MOHAMUD: Eat.

SHERINA: Choke.

TAJ MOHAMUD: Learn your place or I will have you tied to a tree.—Do you have no appetite? Eat. (*KOVERCHENKO cannot eat.*)

KOVERCHENKO: You let me live? (*TAJ shows KOVERCHENKO the RPG's broken trigger.*)

TAJ MOHAMUD: Can you fix this?

KOVERCHENKO: RPG.

TAJ MOHAMUD: RPG!

AKBAR: RPG!

MOUSTAFA: RPG!

TAJ MOHAMUD: Can you fix the trigger of the RPG?

KOVERCHENKO: I don't understand.

TAJ MOHAMUD: Trigger! Trigger! This!

KOVERCHENKO: Kaput?

TAJ MOHAMUD: Kaput!—RPG kaput!

AKBAR: Kaput!

KOVERCHENKO: No problem.

TAJ MOHAMUD: No problem!

AKBAR: No problem!

MOUSTAFA: No problem!

KOVERCHENKO: I need a screwdriver.

TAJ MOHAMUD: What?

KOVERCHENKO: Give me your knife.

TAJ MOHAMUD: What?

KOVERCHENKO: That!

MOUSTAFA: Careful!

TAJ MOHAMUD: No problem.

KOVERCHENKO: No problem. (*TAJ gives KOVERCHENKO his knife. KOVERCHENKO begins to take the RPG apart.*) It's the spring.

TAJ MOHAMUD: What?

KOVERCHENKO: Spring—kaput.

TAJ MOHAMUD: Kaput. (*KOVERCHENKO makes a raspberry. All* *the Afghans do it.*)

KOVERCHENKO: I can take the spring from your rifle.

TAJ MOHAMUD: What do you say?

KOVERCHENKO: Give me your Enfield.

TAJ MOHAMUD: Enfield!

AKBAR: Enfield!

KOVERCHENKO: Lee Enfield.

MOUSTAFA: Lee Enfield!

KOVERCHENKO: Give it. To me. Give. (*KOVERCHENKO takes the rifle apart.*)

SHERINA: What's he doing?

TAJ MOHAMUD: I do not know.

SHERINA: You let a Shuravi take your gun apart?

TAJ MOHAMUD: He is Allah's favorite Shuravi.

AKBAR: Enfield.

KOVERCHENKO: Lee Enfield.

AKBAR: RPG kaput. No problem.

KOVERCHENKO: Yes. Enfield's spring. Won't fit.

TAJ MOHAMUD: Put it back together.

KOVERCHENKO: If it doesn't fit, it doesn't fit.

MOUSTAFA: The trigger coil is different in the old guns.

KOVERCHENKO: Look. I can rig up a wire or something and you can still fire it.

TAJ MOHAMUD: What do you say?

KOVERCHENKO: Give me some wire or string or—that. Your rosary.

ISKANDAR: He wants my prayer beads.

KOVERCHENKO: You want it to work? I need your rosary.

TAJ MOHAMUD: Give him your beads. (*ISKANDAR reluctantly gives KOVERCHENKO his prayer beads. KOVERCHENKO ties the beads to a mechanism in the RPG.*)

ISKANDAR: Sacrilege.

MOUSTAFA: Allah is forgiving.

TAJ MOHAMUD: Will it work? (*KOVERCHENKO goes down on one knee, aims the RPG, tugs on the prayer beads and the weapon makes a click.*)

KOVERCHENKO: Boom boom.

TAJ MOHAMUD: Boom boom?

ISKANDAR: Ah!—Boom Boom!

KOVERCHENKO: Yes! Boom boom!

AKBAR: Boom boom!

KOVERCHENKO: Boom boom—vooom!

MOUSTAFA: Boom boom—vooom! (*The Afghan men laugh.*)

TAJ MOHAMUD: How many Shuravis in the tank?

KOVERCHENKO: Tank!

AKBAR: Tank! (*KOVERCHENKO picks up a stone and draws a tank in the dust and makes an engine noise.*)

KOVERCHENKO: Tank?

TAJ MOHAMUD: Yes! Tank! Tank! How many Shuravis in the tank?

KOVERCHENKO: Shuravis? Soldiers? (*KOVERCHENKO draws stick figures next to the tank.*) Shuravis?

TAJ MOHAMUD: Yes! Shuravis?

ISKANDAR: I have seen the carcasses of the tanks. There are five chairs. Five minus Thrice Blessed and the traitor—three.

AKBAR: Thrice-Blessed has drawn three Shuravis in the dust.

KOVERCHENKO: (*Draws in the dirt.*) Golikov, Kaminski, and . . . (*He draws and salutes.*) Daskal. (*All the Afghans salute and repeat "Daskal."*)

TAJ MOHAMUD: Shuravis.

AKBAR: Shuravis. RPG boom boom tank. Tank kaput.

TAJ MOHAMUD: Teach us to boom boom tank?

KOVERCHENKO: What?

TAJ MOHAMUD: RPG—tank—where?—Show us.

KOVERCHENKO: Oh!—Design weaknesses!—RPG—in arsenal— here. Never hit the front. Ah—no boom boom tank in front— here. Strong. (*Demonstrating.*)

TAJ MOHAMUD: Strong.

KOVERCHENKO: Put RPG rocket here—under cannon—weak. (*Demonstrating.*)

TAJ MOHAMUD: Weak.

KOVERCHENKO: Ah men in tank are almost blind. (*Hands over eyes.*)

TAJ MOHAMUD: Why does the tank go deeper in the wilderness?

KOVERCHENKO: I don't understand.

TAJ MOHAMUD: Tank.

KOVERCHENKO: Yes.

TAJ MOHAMUD: Wilderness.

KOVERCHENKO: Yes.

TAJ MOHAMUD: Speak in the dust.

KOVERCHENKO: Look. (*He draws in the dust.*)

AKBAR: More pictures.

MOUSTAFA: The moon.

SHERINA: Sun.

AKBAR: What is this?

TAJ MOHAMUD: Horizon.

SHERINA: Dawn.

MOUSTAFA: A bird.

AKBAR: Eagle.

SHERINA: Helicopter.

AKBAR: So it is, but very like an eagle.

TAJ MOHAMUD: What does this mean?

SHERINA: At dawn the helicopters will come to save the Shuravis in the tank.

ISKANDAR: All shall face judgment. Some will know the honey wine of paradise, and some will know the unquenchable fire.

TAJ MOHAMUD: We take the tank now. Afghan women, gather stones and build a shrine here in honor of our dead, and return to the caves.

SHERINA: Just a shrine? Not a mosque?

TAJ MOHAMUD: You are more rock than all the Hindu Kush! Obey me!

SHERINA: I will.

TAJ MOHAMUD: Sherina, prepare yourself. I take you for my wife. The blood of my ancestors passes to you. I want sons.

SHERINA: Consult Allah.

TAJ MOHAMUD: Husband is another name for God.—We go. Carry that one in the field for the crows.—Badal, come.

MOUSTAFA: Badal.

KOVERCHENKO: What? What?

TAJ MOHAMUD: Badal.

KOVERCHENKO: What are you doing?

TAJ MOHAMUD: Badal.

KOVERCHENKO: But you let me live, Taj. Nanawatai. La ilaha illa Allah. (*Pause.*) Shoot me in the head. Savages.

AKBAR: He thinks we mean to slay him.

TAJ MOHAMUD: Tank. Badal.

KOVERCHENKO: Oh! Tank Badal!

TAJ MOHAMUD: Shuravi Badal!

KOVERCHENKO: Daskal. (*Exit KOVERCHENKO and the Afghan*

men. The women stand in silence.)

SHERINA: Allah! The Compassionate, the Merciful, Protector of Orphans—I have recited your ninety-nine beautiful names.— What is your one hundredth name?—Abandoner of women? (*The other women move away from SHERINA.*) Crusher of the Defenseless?—If I have sinned, take me now with terrible fire! (*The other women scream, but when SHERINA is not taken, they subside.*) But if I have not sinned,—bless me! (*She stands looking up at the moon, arms out, accepting Allah's blessing. Lights fade.*)

Scene 2

Night. A river bank. Lights up slowly. The hatches open. KAMINSKI and GOLIKOV scramble out. DASKAL follows.

DASKAL: Prepare for fording.

GOLIKOV and KAMINSKI: Yessir. (*GOLIKOV opens a compartment, gets the cannon cover, stops to regard a pair of gloves.*)

DASKAL: What's the matter?

GOLIKOV: Koverchenko's gloves, Sir. (*Pause.*)

DASKAL: Your concern for Koverchenko is touching. Too bad he thought so little of you. Of course you don't know what he wrote about you two in the log.

GOLIKOV: Koverchenko?

DASKAL: It's all there in his neat style. If I let this be seen by Command Post, and it gets passed on up the line, do you know what doors it will close for you both the rest of your lives? (*He tosses the log away.*)

KAMINSKI: Thank you, Sir.

DASKAL: I've seen his dossier. Demoted from Intelligence to Military Policy. Demoted from that to Rescue Operations. Demoted from that to Tank Driver. Each case for insubordination. I don't apologize for anything. I am only thankful that I had the courage to do what's necessary to preserve the group.

KAMINSKI: You did the right thing, Sir.

DASKAL: I appreciate that, Kaminski.

KAMINSKI: And I think I speak for all of us.

GOLIKOV: He does, Sir.

DASKAL: What happened to Samad, Kaminski?

KAMINSKI: Sniper, Sir.

DASKAL: To Koverchenko, Golikov?

GOLIKOV: Land mine, Sir.

DASKAL: Seal the cannon. Close all vents. Button it all up.

KAMINSKI and GOLIKOV: Yessir.

DASKAL: Go upstream and see how deep the river is.

GOLIKOV: How, Sir?

DASKAL: Walk in it.

GOLIKOV: Yessir.

DASKAL: Where are you going?

GOLIKOV: To get an AK, Sir.

DASKAL: You don't need one. (*Pause.*) Well, move.

GOLIKOV: Sir, I just want to go home.

DASKAL: So do we all. Move.

GOLIKOV: Yessir. (*Exit GOLIKOV.*)

DASKAL: Know what I like about you, Nikolai?

KAMINSKI: Nosir.

DASKAL: You're not weak like Golikov.

KAMINSKI: Nosir.

DASKAL: Listen. I'll go in and fidget on the periscope. I'll leave the underhatch open so that I can hear you two outside. Close the vents so that it appears I can't hear.

KAMINSKI: I understand, Sir.

DASKAL: Talk about Samad and Koverchenko. See how Golikov feels about me. Then offer him your AK—to get me. Offer to keep your mouth shut. Egg him on.

KAMINSKI: Yessir.

DASKAL: Good.

KAMINSKI: Here he comes.

DASKAL: You idiot, Kaminski!

KAMINSKI: Sorry, Sir. (*Enter GOLIKOV. His pants are wet up to mid thigh.*)

DASKAL: You know the heater exhaust pipe has to be plugged. Do you want to flood the engine?

KAMINSKI: Nosir.

DASKAL: Cows! Cows! You should have rings in your noses! Do it!

KAMINSKI: Yessir!

GOLIKOV: About three feet, Sir. Like ice.

DASKAL: I didn't ask the temperature. What's the bottom?

GOLIKOV: Sir?

DASKAL: Stone? Pebbles? Mud?

GOLIKOV: Pebbles, Sir.

DASKAL: Good. Help Kaminski.

GOLIKOV: Yessir. (*DASKAL climbs down in the tank, closes the hatch.*)

KAMINSKI: That lousy bastard.

GOLIKOV: Shh!

KAMINSKI: Vent's closed. So's the hatch.

GOLIKOV: Sure?

KAMINSKI: Old man's deaf to begin with. Koverchenko said Daskal was in a tank that took a direct hit once.

GOLIKOV: I pissed myself.

KAMINSKI: Why?

GOLIKOV: Why!—Couldn't you hear my heart pound? I'm standing out in the water waiting for him to machine gun me. Words came out of my mouth, "The Lord is my shepherd I shall not want"—and I couldn't remember the rest.

KAMINSKI: He wouldn't do that.

GOLIKOV: That's what Samad thought. And what about Koverchenko?

KAMINSKI: A troublemaker.

GOLIKOV: Because he wouldn't shoot Samad?—I'm next.

KAMINSKI: Next for what?

GOLIKOV: What do you think? The next bullet in Daskal's gun has my name on it.

KAMINSKI: You think so?

GOLIKOV: Just tell me one thing: If Daskal gave the order, would you tie me and leave me for the Afghans? (*Pause.*)

KAMINSKI: If I'd thought he'd back-bullet me, I'd do something about it.

GOLIKOV: What do you mean?

KAMINSKI: What do you think?

GOLIKOV: Jesus Christ.

KAMINSKI: Why not?

GOLIKOV: Jesus Christ, Kaminski.

KAMINSKI: Who'd find out?

GOLIKOV: Oh, Jesus Christ.

KAMINSKI: Afghan snipers.

GOLIKOV: Jesus Christ.

KAMINSKI: We blow up the tank, backtrack to Kabul Road.

GOLIKOV: You're crazy.

KAMINSKI: Why?

GOLIKOV: He's our commander.

KAMINSKI: He was Koverchenko's commander, too.

GOLIKOV: We need him.

KAMINSKI: For what?—He got us in this! If he didn't stop to run over a rebel, we'd be with the convoy!

GOLIKOV: I don't want to hear this, Kaminski.

KAMINSKI: That Bolshevik can't do anything else. He's not looking forward to sitting on a park bench feeding the pigeons and watching May Day parades. He's going out a People's Hero!

GOLIKOV: No. No. No.

KAMINSKI: Here's my rifle if you change your mind.

GOLIKOV: I won't. Give me some hash.

KAMINSKI: What?

GOLIKOV: Hashhish.

KAMINSKI: Forget it.

GOLIKOV: You smoked it all?

KAMINSKI: I don't smoke it anymore.

GOLIKOV: What?—What'd you do with it?

KAMINSKI: Threw it away.

GOLIKOV: Threw it away?—You risk your neck to steal a Kalashnikov for hash and then throw it away? What for?

KAMINSKI: It's bad for you.

GOLIKOV: It was half mine.

KAMINSKI: Just keep your mouth shut and obey Daskal.

GOLIKOV: I don't understand you. First day I'm assigned to this tank, I ask you how's the commander and you said he'd trade his mother for a rat's asshole.

KAMINSKI: I never said that! When did I say that?

GOLIKOV: Do me a favor. Put a bullet in my head so the Afghans don't torture me.

KAMINSKI: I was talking about the other commander. (*DASKAL climbs out of the tank.*)

DASKAL: Ready for fording?

KAMINSKI: Yessir.

DASKAL: Let's go. (*KAMINSKI and GOLIKOV climb on the tank.*) Enter the water slowly. At mid-stream, cut hard upstream and keep a middle course.

KAMINSKI: Yessir.

GOLIKOV: Sir? What if the gunships don't come?

DASKAL: Then you can lead us in prayer. The rest goes "He maketh me to lie down in green pastures." (*GOLIKOV looks at KAMINSKI and slips down in the tank. DASKAL smiles at KAMINSKI, who smiles back, and puts a hand on KAMINSKI's shoulder, which is taken for an affectionate pat. But DASKAL grabs KAMINSKI's AK.*) You don't need this to drive. (*KAMINSKI sinks down in the tank.*)

Scene 3

Night. The river bank. Enter the Afghans and KOVERCHENKO.

MOUSTAFA: We have lost the tank spoor in the river. Which way Taj? (*Exit KOVERCHENKO.*)

AKBAR: Where does he go, Taj?

TAJ MOHAMUD: He looks for the tank spoor underwater.

MOUSTAFA: Watch him. He looks to escape from us.—Thrice Blessed! On horseback I can hit the eye of a gnat!

TAJ MOHAMUD: Uncle? With or against the water?

AKBAR: Whatever you choose, you will be either right or wrong.

MOUSTAFA: I have a strategy. Two of us go with the water. And two of us go against the water.

TAJ MOHAMUD: Divide ourselves? We have one RPG. What will two of us do if we find the tank and have no RPG? We remain as one. (*Pause.*) Uncle, what would my father do?

AKBAR: Your father never stood on this river bank looking for a tank. Therefore do what you would do.

MOUSTAFA: Now I know why the Shuravi who owned these boots was dead—the boots killed him. (*Enter KOVERCHENKO with a stone.*)

KOVERCHENKO: The bottom's stone . . . Can't find the tracks.

AKBAR: What does he say, Taj?

TAJ MOHAMUD: The tank spoor does not show on rock.

MOUSTAFA: It is finished.

TAJ MOHAMUD: Thrice-Blessed, Allah speaks with your voice. Which way? With the water or against the water?

MOUSTAFA: Speak oh voice of Allah.

KOVERCHENKO: And if I choose wrong, he'll send me off to paradise. You choose. I don't know.

MOUSTAFA: What, is Allah speechless today?

ISKANDAR: All the world is Allah's open book. Allah speaks, not in words, but signs, that only true believers may read.

MOUSTAFA: I see nothing.

TAJ MOHAMUD: Iskandar, ask Allah for a sign.

ISKANDAR: A hawk carries a rat in its talons!

TAJ MOHAMUD: What does it mean?

ISKANDAR: We will capture the tank!—Allah akbar!

MOUSTAFA: How many rifles are in the tank? (*ISKANDAR gestures for silence as he looks and listens for signs.*)

ISKANDAR: A fish!

AKBAR: What sign is that?

ISKANDAR: The wind moved the cloud. The cloud made a shadow. The shadow moved upon the water. The fish thought it a bug. (*Pause.*) But it was nothing.

TAJ MOHAMUD: Which way did the tank go? (*ISKANDAR gestures for silence.*) With the water—? Or against the water—? (*ISKANDAR becomes a whirling dervish.*)

ISKANDAR: Speak, Allah, speak. Reveal yourself. Speak, Allah, speak. Reveal the answer. Speak, Allah, speak. Reveal the wonder. (*He stops. Pause.*)

MOUSTAFA: Sit down and catch your breath.

TAJ MOHAMUD: (*Privately.*) Uncle, why does Allah toss mountains and rivers in my way?

AKBAR: He loves you.

TAJ MOHAMUD: Am I worthy of this rifle?—Uncle, am I fit to be Khan?

AKBAR: To ask this question makes you khan. A khan lives and sleeps on a hill of red ants.

TAJ MOHAMUD: Then I am khan indeed! (*Shaking KOVER-CHENKO violently.*) With or against the water, Thrice Blessed!

MOUSTAFA: We are thrice cursed.

TAJ MOHAMUD: Answer!

MOUSTAFA: I see a sign . . . The tank escaped!—Because we have spared, fed, clothed, and companioned the unbeliever! We have corrupted the jihad! Therefore Allah has allowed the tank to escape. Therefore, let us heed the sign and return. (*Pause.*) Without the Shuravi.

TAJ MOHAMUD: Has Allah blessed you or am I a fool? Help me.

KOVERCHENKO: All right, there is an open plain. If I were Daskal,

I'd go upstream to the open plain. The helicopters could see the tank better. Upstream.

AKBAR: He points against the water, Taj.

TAJ MOHAMUD: Allah has spoken.

ISKANDAR: Allah akbar.

TAJ MOHAMUD: We go.

MOUSTAFA: He points against the water to allow his fellow Shuravis to escape with the water! (*Pause.*) We return. Allah will crack this tank like a mildewed nut, and the Shuravis will pass through the bowels of the wilderness.

TAJ MOHAMUD: Let the doubters go back and learn to sing Shuravi songs!

MOUSTAFA: The RPG goes with me.

TAJ MOHAMUD: The RPG has no doubts. It goes with us.

KOVERCHENKO: Taj, look, look, tank oil floating downstream!

AKBAR: Oil, Taj.

KOVERCHENKO: The tank went upstream!

ISKANDAR: Allah akbar! All the world is a snare to catch unbelievers who doubt the unseen! Allah gave us Thrice Blessed to show the way!

TAJ MOHAMUD: Come, cousin, let us heed the sign! (*As they begin to exit, KOVERCHENKO puts his hand on the RPG.*)

KOVERCHENKO: Taj. Tank strong. Daskal strong. Tank boom boom Afghans. Afghans kaput. I know tank, there is a spot this big under the cannon. Tank heart. RPG boom boom tank. Shuravis vavoom! Tank kaput. Daskal kaput. Afghans (*Pause.*) —Allah akbar. (*TAJ MOHAMUD hands the RPG to KOVER- - CHENKO. Blackout.*)

Scene 4

Night. In the dark, the sound of an engine running out of fuel. The Afghanistan plain. KAMINSKI, GOLIKOV and DASKAL scramble out of the tank.

DASKAL: What's the problem?

KAMINSKI: Computer says we're out of fuel.

DASKAL: The computer's wrong. Check the fuel tank with the dipstick. See if the exhaust pipe's clogged with debris from the water.

GOLIKOV: Yessir.

KAMINSKI: It's empty.

GOLIKOV: Oh God.

DASKAL: Both of you, get the reserve tanks and fuel up.

KAMINSKI: What reserve? We used them hours ago.

DASKAL: As driver, it's your duty to keep me informed!

KAMINSKI: I'm not trained to drive. I'm a gunner and I don't know how to work the computer.

DASKAL: You will call me Sir!

KAMINSKI: What's the difference, Sir? We're out.

DASKAL: If you told me, I would have positioned us on higher ground, idiot! (*DASKAL scans the horizon with binoculars.*)

GOLIKOV: Gunships, Sir? (*Pause.*) What do we do, Sir?

DASKAL: Inside.

GOLIKOV: But you said we're in a bad position here, Sir.

DASKAL: Inside.

GOLIKOV: But we're an open target here, Sir!

DASKAL: This tank is the most sophisticated front-line armament in the world. (*Unseen Afghan women make the zagharit.*)

GOLIKOV: They don't even have to fire at us, Sir. They could just wait out of range. We have to come out.

DASKAL: As tankmen, we have standing orders: Tank out of petrol, become a pillbox. Out of ammo, lock the hatch, become a bunker. After that—heroes.

GOLIKOV: Sir—I'm not dying in that thing, Sir. (*Zagharit.*) I'm going crazy. I can't get in that thing. Shoot me, Sir, but I'm not getting in that tank.

DASKAL: My son and some paratroopers tried to surrender to the Afghans in the Panjsier Valley—And they were hamstrung, blinded with a knife, and with their eyeball fluid running down their cheeks, stoned and fed to starving dogs. Alive. (*DASKAL and KAMINSKI go down into the tank. Zagharit, closer, louder. GOLIKOV runs back to the tank, kneels before it, pounds on the hatch, crying.*)

GOLIKOV: Sir! Please! (*Long pause. The hatch opens. Lights fade.*)

Scene 5

Dawn. Enter KOVERCHENKO with the RPG. A moment later, enter the Afghan men.

TAJ MOHAMUD: The plain holds the tank in its hand like an offering.

ISKANDAR: Allah works his will through this man, truly.

TAJ MOHAMUD: May Allah bless his aim.

MOUSTAFA: One beautiful rocket—that kills all the Shuravis, but not the tank, Taj.

TAJ MOHAMUD: Do you ask for a miracle?

MOUSTAFA: A burning tank would please us for the hour, but those Shuravi guns would give the war another year.

AKBAR: Many young Afghans would be your Mujahadeen if we had guns for them.

TAJ MOHAMUD: How sweet to kill Shuravis with Shuravi guns. (*To KOVERCHENKO; pause.*) Thrice Blessed. Boom boom Shuravis . . . No boom boom tank. (*Pause.*)

KOVERCHENKO: Boom boom Shuravis? No boom boom tank?

TAJ MOHAMUD: Speak to the tank.

KOVERCHENKO: You want me to talk to them?

TAJ MOHAMUD: Three times Allah gave you nanawatai. You are Thrice Blessed with power over them. Speak. (*TAJ takes the RPG.*)

KOVERCHENKO: Speak?

TAJ MOHAMUD: Speak. (*Long pause. KOVERCHENKO moves about the tank in the dark.*)

KOVERCHENKO: Tank Boy! (*The tank's searchlight turns on and looks for KOVERCHENKO in the dark. He eludes the light.*) Over here! Tank boy! (*He continues to elude the light.*) The rocket's aimed at your arsenal! I taught the Afghans what to hit! (*The light finds KOVERCHENKO. He thrusts his arms out wide, defiantly, to make himself a bigger target.*) Do you have me in the crosshairs, Sir? Not a very good tank position, Sir. Can you hold off the Afghans till the gunships come? You know no gunships are coming! You have no food, no water. How long can you last! Two, three days! Then do you pull grenades in unison? You know you can't do that, Kaminski. And after the pins are pulled, Golikov, when you're waiting out those seven awful seconds, you know you'll wish you had sat at your kitchen table watching Anna breastfeed your baby. And if they can't pull the pins, will you do it for them, Daskal? Is that how Tank Boy makes good soldiers in a rotten war? Oh, what heroes we'll be when urns of our ashes—taken from a common crematorium—

are decorated and sent home with the official telegram that reads—"The heroic crew of tank 5447 has fulfilled its internationalist duties, exploded by an American made rocket employed by Chinese troops in the victorious battle of Jalalabad." (*Pause.*) Sorry, Sir. Not much of a war, Sir. Running over little boys with tanks isn't Stalingrad. That was war. Flying on the end of that rope, your feet touch the Nazi tank, you stuff the molotov cocktail between turret and cannon, your comrades pull you up again!—Tank boy had faith back then! Swinging on the end of that magical rope! Faith that his comrades would be there to pull him up again! Pull him up and away from death!— But this time they left you dangling, Sir. Now I throw you another kind of rope. If you want to live, I know the way. The proof is standing before you now. Answer me. (*DASKAL opens the hatch and half emerges from the Tank. Long pause.*) Do you have your finger on the trigger?

DASKAL: You know I do.

KOVERCHENKO: They only want the guns.

DASKAL: How do I know that?

KOVERCHENKO: They could've exploded you by now.

DASKAL: What do they offer us?

KOVERCHENKO: Your lives for the tank.

DASKAL: Why should I believe you?

KOVERCHENKO: It's all you have left, Sir.

DASKAL: Konstantin, you know my standing orders.

KOVERCHENKO: When I was ten, they chose me to lay the wreath of red and white carnations at the foot of Lenin's tomb. Me. Above all Pioneers in Komsomol to honor our twenty million dead. And I looked up in Lenin's empty sockets and yearned to be a People's Hero and die defending the Motherland.—But gassing women armed with sticks is not the hero I wanted to be, Sir! What about the Tank Boy of Stalingrad? (*Pause.*) For the first time in our lives, let's take an order from ourselves and live! (*Pause. DASKAL stands atop the tank.*)

DASKAL: (*To KAMINSKI and GOLIKOV.*) Keep them in your sights.

KAMINSKI and GOLIKOV: Yessir. (*DASKAL removes his gun belt, holds it up.*)

KOVERCHENKO: (*To TAJ.*) Nanawatai Shuravis? (*Pause. TAJ and AKBAR lower their weapons.*)

MOUSTAFA: Spill their entrails on the ground to make the weeds grow better. (*ISKANDAR stands in front of MOUSTAFA's gun.*)

ISKANDAR: Before our eyes, Allah has turned evil to good! (*KOVERCHENKO stands between TAJ's RPG and the tank. DASKAL stands in front of the tank.*)

KOVERCHENKO: Nanawatai.

TAJ MOHAMUD: That Allah has blessed you, I deny nothing . . . Nanawatai. (*TAJ removes the rocket from the RPG and lays them before the tank.*)

AKBAR: (*Laying his weapon on the ground.*) Allah akbar. (*TAJ and AKBAR look to MOUSTAFA who then lays his weapon on the ground.*)

DASKAL: Golikov, Kaminski, outside. (*Long pause.*) Outside! (*Pause. GOLIKOV and KAMINSKI show their heads.*) Disarm and come out. (*GOLIKOV and KAMINSKI drop their weapons on the tank and climb down. DASKAL hands his gun belt to TAJ and salutes. TAJ returns the salute.*)

TAJ MOHAMUD: (*To KOVERCHENKO.*) Daskal?

AKBAR: He has many battles on his face.

TAJ MOHAMUD: (*Inspecting GOLIKOV and KAMINSKI.*) Boys.— Where are the devils?

DASKAL: What now?

KOVERCHENKO: Walk northwest.

GOLIKOV: You're not coming with us?

KOVERCHENKO: No.

DASKAL: You fight with them?

KOVERCHENKO: Tell the tankmen we know where the machine's soft.

DASKAL: Konstantin—why?

KOVERCHENKO: Go.

DASKAL: Why?

KOVERCHENKO: I found a good war, Sir. (*Pause.*)

DASKAL: We march out in formation.

KAMINSKI: They won't shoot us in the back?

DASKAL: Stand up straight! Attention!—Left! Left! Left! (*Exit DASKAL, KAMINSKI and GOLIKOV.*)

AKBAR: Thrice Blessed fights with us?

ISKANDAR: Allah akbar!

TAJ MOHAMUD: Behold the terrible engine! Where is its lightning and thunder now?

ISKANDAR: (*Becoming a whirling dervish.*) Allah akbar!

204 / *William Mastrosimone*

MOUSTAFA: New AK-47's!

TAJ MOHAMUD: Let them send a hundred thousand engines against us! We who are Allah's engines will meet them on the Afghan plain!

ISKANDAR: Allah akbar!

MOUSTAFA: A radio!

TAJ MOHAMUD: And the little hands of our sons and daughters will know the feel of a trigger as they learn the nipple and the bitter milk of war!

ISKANDAR: Allah akbar!

TAJ MOHAMUD: And they will rise with freedom cries and reach like our mountains and touch the dusty feet of Allah!

ISKANDAR: Allah akbar! (*Enter the Afghan women led by SHERINA. Their hands are smeared with blood. They throw the boots of DASKAL, KAMINSKI, and GOLIKOV, at the feet of TAJ MOHAMUD. Lights fade slowly.*)

SHERINA: Forgive us, my Khan. One escaped.

END

SHIVAREE

This play is dedicated to . . .
Cabby #407
and the man in the window with the disease of kings
Mirko Tuma and Niema.
Special thanks to Don Sullivan

SHIVAREE was first presented on November 9, 1983, by the Seattle Repertory Theatre. The play was directed by Daniel Sullivan with the following cast:

CHANDLER	Steven Flynn
MARY ANN	Diane Kagan
SCAGG	John Procaccino
LAURA	Lori Larsen
SHIVAREE	Maggie Baird

Characters

CHANDLER KIMBROUGH
MARY ANN KIMBROUGH
SCAGG
LAURA
SHIVAREE

Setting

TIME: Now
PLACE: The South
SET: An apartment with:
A small window equipped with an air conditioner French doors that open to a balcony about five feet from another balcony of the next house
A skylight
A telescope mounted on a tripod
An interior door that leads downstairs
A bed
Aquaria with exotic fish, turtles, all with pumps, special lights
A formicary (optional)
Aquarium with hamster with a treadmill (optional)
Tons of books (perhaps the walls are made of books)
Plants and flowers everywhere
A pully connected to a beam which hangs a cluster of bananas
A C.B. radio
A conspicuous I.V. rack with clear plastic tubes hanging
An expensive computer and large screen
Everything is padded or rounded off; nothing sharp; all is white, like a clinic, to detect blood.
MUSIC: Something from the Italian Renaissance

SHIVAREE

Let the stars appear one by one. Give the sky a gradual moon whose light reflects prettily on the white lace curtains of the French doors and open window. Rose-colored heat lightning is the only illumination. No thunder. Wind chimes, of bamboo, lack breeze. Outside the window an occasional bat flits by in pursuit of the greenish glow of fireflies. Faraway, the caterwaul of cats in heat make eerie music. CHANDLER turns the music off, opens a bag, takes out an ascot, peels off sales tag, puts it on, puts on Johnny Mathis, "Misty," stands before his mirror.

CHANDLER: How do you do? Won't you sit down? (*New pose.*) How do you do? Won't you sit down? (*Turns off the music, opens artbook of Botticelli's paintings; to himself—simply because the sound pleases him.*) Simonetta. (*He gets a Playboy out of hiding, compares and recites as if cramming for an exam.*) Mons veneris. Labia majora. Labia minora. Mucus membrane secretes a viscous fluid when stimulated which acts as a lubricant and thus facilitates copulation. (*He takes a skin-magazine out of hiding, opens it up to the centerfold. He opens an artbook of Botticelli's paintings and compares. Caterwaul.*) One hundred and forty million. One hundred and forty million. A million is a thousand thousands. And that times 140 is one hundred and forty million sperms per ejaculation. I am one out of one hundred and forty million. It's like the Boston Marathon! And I won! (*The buzzer rings. He rushes to it.*) Who's there?

SCAGG: (*Over intercom.*) Fudgie wudgie, creamsicle, Eskimo pie, fur pie!

CHANDLER: Are you alone?

SCAGG: Open up, amigo. (*CHANDLER releases the door lock, puts on his suit jacket, preens up. Enter SCAGG in white pants, white shirt, white shoes and panama hat with a feather lugging a white metal box on shoulder straps with cartoon characters painted on the side.*) M'man! m'man! M'main man!

CHANDLER: Where is she?

SCAGG: The whore's in the truck and I'm double parked. —Lay alittle cash on me, bro.

CHANDLER: Let me open the wine so it can breathe. (*SCAGG opens the metal box, takes out a brown liquor store bag.*)

SCAGG: Let there be juice!

CHANDLER: What is this?

SCAGG: The wine.

CHANDLER: This isn't Medoc.

SCAGG: Medoc? I thought you said Mad Dog.

CHANDLER: I never heard of this! Where's the corkscrew!

SCAGG: This is 20th century technology—you don't need one for this wine, Amigo.

CHANDLER: O God, Scagg! This is awful!

SCAGG: What's the button here? Quick k.o.? For a five-spot more you got genuine mountain corn brew. Goes down hot, lays 'em out cold. (*Taking a mason jar of clear moonshine from the metal box.*) —On special.

CHANDLER: I don't want that!

SCAGG: Fudgie-wudgie?

CHANDLER: No! Did you forget the candles?

SCAGG: Only the best for m'man! (*Taking votive candles from the box.*)

CHANDLER: These are used! Where'd you get these?

SCAGG: The church on the corner.

CHANDLER: You robbed these from the church!

SCAGG: Hell, m'man, they had a whole shitload.

CHANDLER: O, God, Scagg.

SCAGG: M'man, these are consecrated.

CHANDLER: Did you tell her about, you know, me?

SCAGG: Yup.

CHANDLER: How'd you tell her?

SCAGG: Just like you told me.

CHANDLER: How?

SCAGG: I said I got a friend, he's a hypodermiac . . .

CHANDLER: Hemophiliac.

SCAGG: Right. Right.

CHANDLER: And what was her reaction?

SCAGG: Gooseegg.

CHANDLER: Really?

CHANDLER: What color's her hair?

SCAGG: Just like you wanted.

CHANDLER: She pretty?

SCAGG: Pretty?

CHANDLER: Really?

SCAGG: Any man with red blood in his veins would crawl five hundred miles on hands and knees over broken beer bottles and armadilla turds just to'hear this enchalada burp.

CHANDLER: O God, Scagg, she's not cheap, is she?

SCAGG: Fifty bucks.

CHANDLER: No! Is she slutty-looking?

SCAGG: In her spare time she poses for madonna pictures.

CHANDLER: How long's her hair?

SCAGG: About here.

CHANDLER: That's—short!

SCAGG: Whattaya gonna do with a hank o'hair?

CHANDLER: I asked you to regard that!

SCAGG: You want hair, I'll get ya a sheepdog cheaper.

CHANDLER: I specifically stipulated length and color.

SCAGG: M'man, it ain't like shopping at the A&P.

CHANDLER: Does she look like this. (*Showing the Botticelli book.*)

SCAGG: That what you want? A born-again Billy Gramm girl?

CHANDLER: She's not like this? What's so funny?

SCAGG: One leg's longer than the other.

CHANDLER: She's not like this?

SCAGG: Alittle. Only thing, she's got a very mild case of herpes.

CHANDLER: O God!

SCAGG: C'mon, bro! I'm only goosin ya!

CHANDLER: Everything's gone awry! (*SCAGG rolls back his long sleeve, revealing a dozen watches.*)

SCAGG: I got a good deal on a watch.

CHANDLER: I don't want a watch! What will the cost be for, you know, just the woman?

SCAGG: Fifty.

CHANDLER: I don't mean to impugn your integrity, but is that normal?

SCAGG: Plus ten for the vino.

CHANDLER: For that?

SCAGG: Candles on me. And five for this. (*Taking out a packet from the box.*) This'll drive her t'loonsville, jack. French tickler.

CHANDLER: I don't want that!

SCAGG: Take the watch, I throw in the tickler.

CHANDLER: No.

SCAGG: Want another magazine?

CHANDLER: No.

SCAGG: Then we're up to fifty plus ten—that's sixty-five dollars.

CHANDLER: Sixty.

SCAGG: Right, plus ten for my time. Seventy. Grass?

CHANDLER: No.

SCAGG: Coke?

CHANDLER: No.

SCAGG: Just askin. (*CHANDLER goes to a hiding place, takes out a pillow case filled with coins of every demonination neatly wrapped. SCAGG takes out a tiny tin.*) Tiger Balm?

CHANDLER: What's that?

SCAGG: Tiger balm. Extract from the horn of the white rhino. Gives ya a stone bone.

CHANDLER: I don't need an aphrodisiac.

SCAGG: 'Course ya don't. Not now. Don't need an umbrella when the sun's shinin, do ya?

CHANDLER: How much?

SCAGG: Now, m'man, there's three, four, maybe five rhinoes rottin on the plains o'Serengeti t'fill this little tin—but it's enough for half a lifetime.

CHANDLER: How much?

SCAGG: Top shelf, m'man. Seventy-five.

CHANDLER: Can I owe it to you?

SCAGG: Nothin' walks 'less the president talks.

CHANDLER: I can't afford it.

SCAGG: My cost—twenty-five.

CHANDLER: Can't afford it.

MARY: (*On c.b.*) Mobile to Home Base, c'mon.

CHANDLER: Stand still! Don't breathe! She's got ears! Home Base to Mobile, over.

MARY: Whattcha doin, babe? Over.

CHANDLER: Reading. Over.

MARY: Want some ice cream? Over.

CHANDLER: Negatory, Mom, but thanks. What's your 10-20?

MARY: Just dropped off a fare downtown, honey babe. Conventioneers are comin' on like locusts. Catch ya on the flip-flop, honey babe.

CHANDLER: Forty roger.

SCAGG: Gimmie the money—I'll bring her up.

CHANDLER: Could we postpone this?

SCAGG: I went out of my way to get you a woman—not just a woman, but one with hair, and this, and that. Damn, boy, you know how much business I lost?

CHANDLER: I'm sorry.

SCAGG: Sorry ain't gonna help me pay your mama the rent tomorrow.

CHANDLER: She suspects something.

SCAGG: Use my room.

CHANDLER: But if I'm not here when she calls, she'll come looking.

SCAGG: She won't look for you there. You leave by the roomer's entrance, come back in your private entrance. Say you went for a walk.

CHANDLER: Oh . . . I don't know . . .

SCAGG: Now you decide now if you wanna ride or slide.

CHANDLER: I planned this for a year!

SCAGG: Ride or slide.

CHANDLER: Ride.

SCAGG: Lay some cash on me bro.—What's that?

CHANDLER: The money.

SCAGG: Don't you have paper.

CHANDLER: I've hoarded loose change for over a year. It's the only way I get money. For the ice cream.

SCAGG: How am I gonna pay her with 97 pounds o'coin?

CHANDLER: Ten, twenty, thirty, forty.

SCAGG: This is a real ass-pain.

CHANDLER: Fifty, sixty, sixty-five, seventy.

SCAGG: This is a real snafu, m'man.

CHANDLER: Should we postpone it?

SCAGG: I don't know if she's gonna take it.

CHANDLER: Wait!

SCAGG: What?

CHANDLER: I have to ask you something.

SCAGG: You want the tickler.

CHANDLER: No! When you bring her up . . .

SCAGG: Yeah.

CHANDLER: And you leave us, right?

SCAGG: Not 'less you want me t'cheerlead . . . Chandler, Chandler, he's m'man, if he can't do it . . .

CHANDLER: Scagg! C'mon! This is important!

SCAGG: Sorry, Amigo.

CHANDLER: When it's just me and her, what do I do?—I mean, I know what to do, but—how would you, say, get things started?

SCAGG: Hang, loose, drink a little juice, and the one-eyed worm'll find its way home.

CHANDLER: Scagg, concerning the actual womanly part?

SCAGG: Yeah.

CHANDLER: Could we possibly discuss that a little?

SCAGG: I can talk all night about the vertical smile. I seen dogs rip open jugglers for it; bulls break down barn doors for it; roosters chew chicken wire t'get in the coop. I seen cowboys get throwed off a brama—o'purpose!—just t'snag the fancy o'some freckled little pony tail up in the bleachers! You can't name the things a male won't do for that little patch o'real estate no bigger than a fried egg.

CHANDLER: What was that?

SCAGG: What?

CHANDLER: My mother's cab. She just pulled up.

SCAGG: Holy shit!

CHANDLER: Go down the back way. We'll do it another night.

SCAGG: No, I'll bring the woman when your mama goes. (CHANDLER hides the wine, shuts out the light, jumps into bed, pulls the covers to his chin, but his shoes are visible. Enter MARY KIMBROUGH dressed as a cabby.)

MARY: Lovy? You asleep?

CHANDLER: Mom?

MARY: Y'up?

CHANDLER: Hmmm?

MARY: Whatcha doin?

CHANDLER: Sleeping.

MARY: How's m'baby? All dressed for bed? Your best suit, eh? Where ya going in your dreams?

CHANDLER: I wanted to see if the suit still fits and must've dozed off. I thought you were downtown.

MARY: I had a nearby fare. You must be roasted out of your mind. Lookie, honey babe, you got the air conditioner off! And the window open!

CHANDLER: I hate the noise, that hum.

MARY: That damn screw's loose again. (Takes out a screwdriver.)

214 / William Mastrosimone

CHANDLER: I'd rather have fresh air.

MARY: Air's not fresh. It's all chemicals.

CHANDLER: There's a river breeze.

MARY: Putrid air. Factory air. Poison air. Nosir. (*She closes the window and turns on the air conditioner; pause.*) You seen that ice cream man?

CHANDLER: No.

MARY: You take plasma?

CHANDLER: Yes.

MARY: What for?

CHANDLER: I scraped my gums with the toothbrush.

MARY: Where?

CHANDLER: It's all right.

MARY: Let's see.

CHANDLER: It's all right.

MARY: Don't brush so hard.

CHANDLER: All right.

MARY: Don't frown on me. Remember your last tooth-pull.

CHANDLER: Every quart.

MARY: So whattcha been doin'?

CHANDLER: After supper I watched a somniferous documentary on TV on Grey Whales. I weeded the garden. We have a big slug problem, you know. One third of the tomatoes are destroyed. I called the library. Mrs. Yarborough gave me a list of books on slug defence.

MARY: Beer.

CHANDLER: Pardon?

MARY: Stale beer attracts 'em. Put it around in little bowls. They smell it, think it's the mating scent, crawl up the bowl, fall in and drown in their own sin.

CHANDLER: O, mom, you made that up.

MARY: Old time remedy, goes way back. Look it up in your books. I know a thing or two, sonny boy. We come from farm people, ya know.

CHANDLER: Drown in sin.

MARY: You shush. I heard ya talking on the c.b. with a trucker.

CHANDLER: Coalminer. "Eh, good buddy, t'day m' dog had pups and et one."

MARY: Well, you can't expect everybody t'be on your level, honeybabe. So you ain't seen that ice cream man anytime today?

CHANDLER: I got an eskimo pie from him when I was in the garden.

MARY: I told you I don't want you buyin ice cream from him. If you want something, just call me.

CHANDLER: I didn't want to bother you.

MARY: It's no bother. Did he come up here?

CHANDLER: No, O, I forgot—Teddy called.

MARY: What's he want? Zif I didn't know.

CHANDLER: He's free to put in the other skylight, which means he wouldn't mind spending a few days here, which means he still wants to marry you.

MARY: Son of a bee! You never mind.

CHANDLER: You promised me a skylight, Mom.

MARY: Skylight—not a daddy. Now you pick out a nice shirt in the Sears and Roebuck Catalogue so you look nice and handsome for the races tomorrow.

CHANDLER: Can you afford to take off?

MARY: Half a day. We'll fix a little chicken and lemonade, park by the gate, see the whole thing.

CHANDLER: O, we can't go inside?

MARY: Now, now sugar. All those uppity ladies swingin brand new handbags, and roughhousers carousin and carryin' on, nosir. We'll park by the gate. You bring your binoculars.

CHANDLER: And then the planetarium.

MARY: OK.

CHANDLER: And then the museum.

MARY: Now, now honeybabe. Little school kids yellin and runnin up and down the stairs? Nosir. How I ever let you talk me into this thing (*Pulling his ascot out of his shirt.*) you look like one o'them Hollywood outlaws. You thumb through and pick out a nice shirt and I'll pick it up in the morning.

CHANDLER: I don't need a new shirt, Mom.

MARY: Sure you do.

CHANDLER: The closet's full.

MARY: This one's frayed on the sleeve, this one's crooked. I swear the way they make clothes today, no pride, no pride in workmanship. These are goin in the rag bag. Now c'mon, lovy, pick one out. Lookie here. Do you like this shirt? (*She tears shirts into rags.*)

CHANDLER: Do they have it in a round collar?

MARY: That's too old fashioned. You like this one?

CHANDLER: Either.

MARY: Blue or white?

CHANDLER: (*Pause.*) Yellow or pink.

MARY: No, no, honey, that's not for you. You want to look distinguished.

CHANDLER: Blue.

MARY: Well, you got a lot of blues.

CHANDLER: White?

MARY: That's a good choice. (*Pause.*) And I'll see if they have a round collar.

CHANDLER: Would you pick up these books at the library?

MARY: Mrs. Yarborough says you got an overdue book. Dollar ninety-five.

CHANDLER: Could we afford to buy a copy of this book?

MARY: You got so many books, lovy. I think next year I'll have that wall knocked out, put up a greenhouse for ya, and that observatory ya want, and your own bathroom so ya don't have to go trudging up and down the stairs.

CHANDLER: Teddy could do a masterful job with that.

MARY: Now you never you mind about Teddy! And hang that suit up!

CHANDLER: And would you stop by Mrs. Vollens? She has some knickknacks for me.

MARY: Like what?

CHANDLER: Jerry's parachute.

MARY: You ain't jumpin outta no airplanes!

CHANDLER: I only want to make a canopy over the bed.

MARY: Son of a bee—she call you?

CHANDLER: No.

MARY: You call her?

CHANDLER: Yes.

MARY: I don't want you talkin' with sucha women.

CHANDLER: All right.

MARY: She oughta be on death row. No mom in the hemophilia chapter even talks to her. Lettin her boy go jumpin outta airplanes!

CHANDLER: Jerry made twenty-seven jumps. He had special shoes and padding, and jumped on sand.

MARY: Did it help him when he landed on that barbed wire fence?

Shivaree / 217

CHANDLER: It was a freak accident.

MARY: She was a freak mother, and why you want a deadman's thing, I'll never know.

CHANDLER: I loved how he talked about his life being cleaved in two, prejump and postjump.

MARY: That's just how her heart's cleaved. I held her hand there in the 'mergency room when they was pumping 23 quarts o' blood in her boy. Nosir. Can't allow it. Nosir. So you get your mind off daring-do. You are what you are. (*Pause.*) Where's the overdue book?

CHANDLER: I'd like to have it renewed.

MARY: This is the third time, lovy.

CHANDLER: Then never mind.

MARY: I will, I will, it's just not like you t'keep a book more than two days. What is this?

CHANDLER: Botticelli. Paintings.

MARY: Nudies, eh?

CHANDLER: Art. That's "Primavera." That's "The Birth of Venus."

MARY: Looks like a naked woman on the half-shell t'me. (*The skin magazine falls out.*)

CHANDLER: That damn Scagg.

MARY: That his?

CHANDLER: He had it.

MARY: Had it?

CHANDLER: It's his.

MARY: Did he give it to you?

CHANDLER: No. He had it with him and he must've left it here by mistake.

MARY: Well you make sure he gets it back.

CHANDLER: Yes ma'm.

MARY: I'll give it him.

CHANDLER: Yes, ma'm.

MARY: That goddamn Scagg! He's a pedigree bum, a drinker, therefore a liar, therefore thief, therefore trouble. What's he get from you?

CHANDLER: Nothing.

MARY: Nosir, I don't buy it. Life's always tit for tat. (*Pause.*) I don't want him up here no more. Or anybody else I rent to.

CHANDLER: Yes, ma'am.

MARY: You're special. (*She hugs him, checks his ears for wax.*) He's out o'here tomorrow, I swear I could rip him apart with my hands!— just the looks of 'im sticks in my craw.

CHANDLER: Then why'd you rent him a room?

MARY: Damn if I wouldn't rent to Beezlebub if he could fork up thirty advance rent and thirty security for damages. I'm just glad your daddy ain't here d'see how I carved up his dream home t'rent rooms by the week. If he saw me now heavin suitcases bigger than me in the taxi?—Your daddy was such a man. Wouldn't let me so much as lift a sugar-spoon. When he carried me over the threshhold, down in the vestibule, I said, what we gonna do with all these rooms? He said fill 'em with kids. And that's just what I did. All the world's socks without a mate, all the shoes without a double, end up here. All the bastard kids of the world—Kiss good night, lovy. Brush you teeth, k?

CHANDLER: I did.

MARY: Brush 'em again for me.

CHANDLER: Going to bed now?

MARY: No. There's some good business at the airport now.

CHANDLER: Don't take any creeps, ok?

MARY: Don't you worry 'bout your momma. I can handle myself. Night night, lovy.

CHANDLER: Night, mom—Bring home some stale beer—we're going to drown 'em in sin!

MARY: Hang up your suit and don't wait up for me. (*Exit MARY with the books. CHANDLER waits for her foot-falls to die away, and begins to undress. He unbuttons his vest, undoes his ascot, etc.*)

CHANDLER: Did you hear about Chandler? (*Pause.*) They found him dead. (*Pause.*) They found him on the walk. They're calling it suicide. (*Pause.*) They're calling it accidental. Someone saw him hanging out the window waving down the ice cream man. They think he slipped. (*Pause.*) What a karma: to die for an Eskimo Pie. (*Pause.*) They're calling it natural causes. (*Pause.*) They found a brain tumor the size of an orange. Not mandarine. Florida. Lodged in the medulla oblongata. Very rare—only kills one out of every one hundred and forty million. (*Buzzer sounds.*) Who's there?

SCAGG: A man and a lady. Open up, amigo. (*CHANDLER pushes the lock-release button. CHANDLER tidies up. We hear footfalls up the stairs. Enter SCAGG.*) Everything's ace high m'man unless your zipper snags.

CHANDLER: I said we'd do it another night! (*Enter LAURA.*)

SCAGG: This is Laura.

CHANDLER: How do you do?

LAURA: You must be Chandelier.

CHANDLER: Chandler.

LAURA: Chandler.

SCAGG: See here, m'man—just like in the book—left leg's longer than the other.

CHANDLER: Shut up!

SCAGG: Adios.

CHANDLER: No, have a drink, Scagg.

SCAGG: Ain't you never heard three's a crowd.

LAURA: In my neighborhood they say three's almost as much fun as four.

SCAGG: Chandler, Chandler, he's m'man—

CHANDLER: Go on! (*Exit SCAGG, laughing.*) How do you do?

LAURA: Hi.

CHANDLER: Won't you sit down?

LAURA: I am.

CHANDLER: At the table?

LAURA: Oh, you like it on the table?

CHANDLER: No. No. I mean . . .

LAURA: Look, I understand. I do a guy who's into closets.

CHANDLER: No, I mean for a drink of wine or tea or . . . that's all I have. Scagg brought this wine. Not having drunk it, I can't testify as to its merits.

LAURA: What's the matter?

CHANDLER: I don't remember where I hid it. I didn't want my . . . well, actually I wanted to put it where it wouldn't get broken.

LAURA: Scagg said it's goodnight if you get cut.

CHANDLER: That's not true.

LAURA: I had a client do a massive coronary on me once. Thing was, I didn't know and kept going.

CHANDLER: I wish I could remember . . . I was here and . . .

LAURA: That's ok. I don't need any wine.

CHANDLER: Do you like music?

LAURA: I'd gut my dog if I thought it'd make a good sound.

CHANDLER: What would you like to hear?

LAURA: Whatever brings ya to a head, sweetheart. (*CHANDLER* *puts on a tape.*) You read all these books?

CHANDLER: Yes.

LAURA: I like brains.

CHANDLER: Pardon?

LAURA: Brains. I like em.

CHANDLER: I'm a bibliophile.

LAURA: O, I'm sorry. (*The music comes on. It's Johnny Mathis singing "Misty." LAURA bursts out laughing.*)

CHANDLER: Would you prefer something else?

LAURA: No, love, it's fabulous. Relax.

CHANDLER: I am.

LAURA: No, you're not. Really. Let yourself go.

CHANDLER: Thank you.

LAURA: Let's sit on the bed and talk about it.

CHANDLER: Momentarily.

LAURA: It's all right, love, 'least you don't want t'pour teryaki sauce all over me.

CHANDLER: Pardon?

LAURA: Nothin'. You still looking for that wine?

CHANDLER: Yes.

LAURA: Wouldn't you rather undress me?

CHANDLER: I would really like to have some wine first.

LAURA: You wanna do this some other time?

CHANDLER: Would that be inconvenient?

LAURA: I'm booked all week what with the A.M.A. and Shriners conventions.

CHANDLER: No. Now. Tonight.

LAURA: So we gotta rise to the occasion 'cause I got other people to see.

CHANDLER: O.

LAURA: You thought I'd stay all night?

CHANDLER: Well, yes.

LAURA: It's a hundred big ones for all night, babe.

CHANDLER: I didn't know.

LAURA: Otherwise, it's thirty-five a throw.

CHANDLER: Thirty-five?

LAURA: For a straight jump.

CHANDLER: What else's, you know, available?

LAURA: Well, there's straight, half and half, doggie-doggie, 'round the world.

CHANDLER: Fine.

LAURA: You want the works?

CHANDLER: Sure.

LAURA: Whoa, wild man,—that's two hundred and fifty plus mucho stamina.

CHANDLER: O. O, I see. Let's . . . just regular.

LAURA: Well, let's get the fish in the pan here, babe.

CHANDLER: I'm not quite ready.

LAURA: Want me to talk filthy?

CHANDLER: No. Thank you.

LAURA: Wis un accent, eh, amor?

CHANDLER: Thank you just the same.

LAURA: Wanna just shoot the breeze awhile?

CHANDLER: Would that be possible?

LAURA: Walter used to have to talk first.

CHANDLER: Walter?

LAURA: Philosophy Proff, Tuesday nights.

CHANDLER: Really? What'd he talk about?

LAURA: Talked about them Greek boys and diabolical materialism. Hooked up a garden hose to the exhaust pipe, sat in the back seat, and there went my education.—So what should we talk about?

CHANDLER: Why did he kill himself?

LAURA: The man had a thing about, you know, reality . . . all that about—I can think therefore I'm here.

CHANDLER: "I think therefore I am."

LAURA: They changed it?

CHANDLER: No. It's still the same.

LAURA: So, let's talk about the planets.—What's that?

CHANDLER: That's an artist's conception of the origin of our universe. It's called the BIG BANG THEORY.

LAURA: I know that theory. Feel better? Good. Let's go.

CHANDLER: Please!—Please don't squeeze my wrist so hard.

LAURA: What'd I do.

CHANDLER: I bruise quite easily.

LAURA: Jesus. What is this thing you've got?

CHANDLER: Blood disorder. Not contagious. Inherited. Actually it's the lack of a protein in the blood plasma which regulates the time it takes for blood to clot.

LAURA: That's a real bitch. Can I undress you?

222 / *William Mastrosimone*

CHANDLER: (*Pause.*) Yes. (*She begins to undress him.*)

LAURA: What a fine ascot. Silk? Relax. Your neck's so tight. Let your arms just hang down. Sure. Yes. Yes. Relax. Touch me. Not there. Somewheres else. Close your eyes. Close 'em. Shh! Don't talk. Touch my belly. Yes. That's where it all is. You are such a lovely man. (*MARY's voice interrupts over c.b.*)

MARY: (*on c.b.*) Mobile to Home Base, copy?

LAURA: Police!

CHANDLER: Don't move! Please! Don't make a sound!

LAURA: I'm on probation. You got a back door here? (*Grabbing her belongings in a rush.*)

CHANDLER: Please! It's my mom!

MARY: Mobile to Home Base, c'mon!

CHANDLER: Home Base to Mobile, copy?

MARY: Wall to wall, treetop tall. Sorry to wake you sugar, but I'm taking some oil people over to the Palm Room and I won't be home till very late, so don't you worry none, k?

CHANDLER: OK.

MARY: Sugar? You brush your teeth?

CHANDLER: Yes, ma'm.

MARY: Dental floss?

CHANDLER: Yes, ma'm.

MARY: Brush 'em again, honeybabe.

CHANDLER: Yes, ma'm.

MARY: Night, night, lovy. Over.

CHANDLER: Good night. Over.

LAURA: Your mama loves ya.

CHANDLER: I really need some wine.

LAURA: You don't need wine. You need to come over here.

CHANDLER: I know it's right here! Somewhere!

LAURA: And after wine you'll wanna brush your teeth and floss! Bonzo's gonna think I'm moonlighting.

CHANDLER: What are you doing?

LAURA: Seducing you.

CHANDLER: O.

LAURA: C'mon now, lay your sweet head down on your nice white pillow.

CHANDLER: Pillow! (*He springs up for the pillow, finds the wine under it.*) Eureka! Would you like some?

LAURA: Just a swig.

CHANDLER: Caps so tight.

LAURA: You have to break the metal band first.

CHANDLER: I can't seem to . . .

LAURA: Here.

CHANDLER: Oh, God.

LAURA: You cut?

CHANDLER: On the cap.

LAURA: Oh, shit, you gonna die now?

CHANDLER: My life is not that exciting.

LAURA: Please don't die on me, cupcake.

CHANDLER: I'm fine.

LAURA: Let me call an ambulance.

CHANDLER: No. I'm fine.

LAURA: You faintin'?

CHANDLER: no.

LAURA: Sure?

CHANDLER: Yes.

LAURA: You look pale.

CHANDLER: I'm Caucasian. Thank you.

LAURA: You're so cold.

CHANDLER: I have to rest now.

LAURA: You ain't checkin out, are ya.

CHANDLER: No. Please go!

LAURA: I'll come back some other time.

CHANDLER: Yes. (*CHANDLER gets into bed. LAURA covers him.*)

LAURA: And we can talk about the stars and all.

CHANDLER: Yes.

LAURA: And maybe you'd like to take Walter's Tuesday night slot.

CHANDLER: Please go.

LAURA: Sweetie babe? I need the money.

CHANDLER: But nothing happened.

LAURA: You pay for the time, not the ride, babe.

CHANDLER: I gave it to Scagg.

LAURA: Scagg? He don't take the squirt, boy. I need some paper t'account my time t'Bonzo.

CHANDLER: Scagg's got it.

LAURA: (*Grabbing his face.*) If you lie, me and Bonzo's coming back. (*Exit LAURA. He turns out his light. The sound of a train. CHANDLER sits up in bed. Sound of a train.*)

CHANDLER: Did you hear about Chander? He's missing. Not a clue. Left no note. Took nothing. He went forth in the world unemcumbered. Someone saw him among the vagabonds. Someone saw him hitch a freight train. (*A faint Guazi belly dancer tune as old as the Nile, wafts through to him. In it, we must feel the heat of the desert and the mystery of the East. CHANDLER uncovers his head, listens, sits up, listens. The moon appears slowly, so slowly. Subtly indicate a passage of time. CHANDLER goes to his balcony, opens doors, sees the music comes from the light apartment across the alley from his own. He sees the moon.*) Cadaverous moon—you pocked-marked thief.—That's not even your own light, but reflected sun. —The only men you ever had left their footprints on you, and never came back.—One side's too cold, one side's too hot. You gloat down with that vicious silence, you swollen lump of a whore's earwax . . . (*Enter SHIVAREE. She wears the traditional garb of the belly dancer—opaque harem pants, coin bra and girdle, long chiffon veil, tiny bells, bangles, beads, chains, rings, bracelets, earrings and zills on her fingers.*)

SHIVAREE: Sorry if my music woke you. (*She begins to exit.*)

CHANDLER: Excuse me!

SHIVAREE: Yeah?

CHANDLER: It didn't wake me.

SHIVAREE: Goodnight.

CHANDLER: Excuse me.

SHIVAREE: Yeah?

CHANDLER: Sorry if my talking woke you.

SHIVAREE: I wasn't asleep.

CHANDLER: That's—wonderful.

SHIVAREE: Goodnight.

CHANDLER: EXCUSE ME!

SHIVAREE: Yeah?

CHANDLER: Exactly what kind of music is that music precisely? Greek? Arabic? Israeli?

SHIVAREE: All o'that, and more.

CHANDLER: O?

SHIVAREE: Oriental dance.—(*She begins to exit.*)

CHANDLER: And what's that on your fingers?

SHIVAREE: Zills. (*She demonstrates, but not too much.*)

CHANDLER: I love that sound!

SHIVAREE: (*She sounds them again, very little.*) Goodnight now. (*After CHANDLER turns to reenter his room, she reappears.*) My name's Shivaree.

CHANDLER: Shivaree.

SHIVAREE: Ain't m'real name.

CHANDLER: Professional name? I'm Chandler.

SHIVAREE: Wish m'arms was longer.

CHANDLER: Just moved in?

SHIVAREE: Sublet. Passin through.

CHANDLER: The occupants don't usually stay long in those apartments.

SHIVAREE: Well, nice t'meet you.

CHANDLER: Hot.

SHIVAREE: Terrible.

CHANDLER: This night affords a crystalline view of the constellation Hercules.

SHIVAREE: Man alive! Throw an eye at that buttery moon!

CHANDLER: Actually, it's the gibbous phase.

SHIVAREE: Say again?

CHANDLER: More than half but less than full. When it's parameters are convex.

SHIVAREE: You some kind of astronomer?

CHANDLER: That's my bailiwick.

SHIVAREE: You boys still anglin to string that unstrung pearl?

CHANDLER: I beg your pardon.

SHIVAREE: Me, I just let it roll around the night unclaimed.

CHANDLER: You'll love this vantage during thunderstroms, St. Elmo's fire dances on that church steeple.

SHIVAREE: When'd you come south, Yank?

CHANDLER: I was born here.

SHIVAREE: Not talkin' like that.

CHANDLER: I taught myself a provincial dialect now in widespread disuse: Standard American English. Perhaps could have tea sometime?

SHIVAREE: Sometime's for dreamers. I'm up for it right now.

CHANDLER: Splendid.

SHIVAREE: But not for tea. You got beer?

CHANDLER: No, but I've got some questionable wine.

SHIVAREE: I know the brand well.

CHANDLER: Out front there are two doors. (*She enters her apartment. CHANDLER shouts at her.*) One for the apartments, and my private entrance on the left—just ring the buzzer and . . .

(*She reenters with a tubular ironing board and makes a bridge between balconies.*)

CHANDLER: What are you doing?

SHIVAREE: Makin' a bridge, sport. Let down your locks, Rapunzel, I'm a' comin over.

CHANDLER: Not on that!

SHIVAREE: Ain't the Golden Gate, but it gets ya there.

CHANDLER: O my God. (*She jumps onto his balcony.*)

SHIVAREE: Hi. Well, ain't this a kick in the ol' wazoo.

CHANDLER: What is this?

SHIVAREE: Coins.

CHANDLER: I've never seen anyone dress like this!

SHIVAREE: Well, there was a time way way back in Egypt when a man was so scarce that a women had to wear her coins and do alittle dance in the marketplace t'attract one.—Woolworths.

CHANDLER: And what's your purpose?

SHIVAREE: I'm warmin up for a show tonight.

CHANDLER: O.

SHIVAREE: Private party.

CHANDLER: Won't you sit down? (*A banana falls from the rafters.*) I hang a bunch up in the rafters, and when they're ripe, they fall.

SHIVAREE: Jus' like ol' what's-his-bucket? An apple fell and he invented the law of gravity?

CHANDLER: Newton. Well, actually, he didn't invent it. He merely described and formulated a law based upon observation.

SHIVAREE: So what are you formulatin' with fallin' bananas?

CHANDLER: It's not an experiment. They're more nutritious when they're ripe.

SHIVAREE: Why don't you just keep 'em down here and eat 'em when they're ripe?

CHANDLER: You never know for sure. You can't tell just by the outer coloring. When it's truly ripe, a chemical reaction occurs, the stem weakens, and it falls when it's ready.

SHIVAREE: Ahhhh.

CHANDLER: Tell me about your profession.

SHIVAREE: You could pluck out m'fingernails and I wouldn't reveal the sacred mysteries of the dance. Disclosure's punishable by artha-ritic hips.

CHANDLER: Why is it sacred?

SHIVAREE: Why, it only celebrates the most important thing in the whole world, that's all, sport.

CHANDLER: Which is?

SHIVAREE: Man and woman.

CHANDLER: O.

SHIVAREE: I saw belly-dancers in the murals on the tombs in Egypt, with zills on their fingers.

CHANDLER: You've been to Egypt?

SHIVAREE: Hell, sport, I danced there, in moonlight before the Temple of Isis.

CHANDLER: Where do you dance now?

SHIVAREE: Wherever the power of woman to bring new life is appreciated. Sometimes I just drop in a nursing home, dance for the infirm and the old. They're really the best appreciators.

CHANDLER: Can you make a living doing that?

SHIVAREE: Well, sport, you can dance for dance and get a flat rate, or you can dance for tips and get what you get. Like after dancin' at the Hyatt last night, seven sheiks from Dubai approach me and said they was throwin' some highbrow shindig up in their suite, would I grace their company with the dance, salam alekum, the whole bit, and I says, Hell yeah, and I walks in and it looks like a sheet sale, all kinds of Mideastern folk jabberin' and the musicians go big for some Guazi tune and I let loose my stuff. I do veil work where I put myself in this envelope like a little chrysalis in a gossamer cocoon listenin' to the beat of my heart, and then I break out with hip shimmies and shoulder rolls and belly flutters, mad swirls, Byzantine smiles and half-closed eyes, and my hands are cobras slitherin' on air, hoods open and I'm Little Egypt, Theodora, Nefertiti, and Salome, all in one skin, and these before me was Solomon and Herod and Caeser and Tutankhamen shoutin' Ayawah, Shivaree, Ayawah, which roughly means, Go for it, Little darlin'—and this young sheik he's clappin hands to my zills, and he rolls up this hundred dollar bill and tries to slip it in my clothes, which makes me stop dancin', which makes the musicians stop, and there's this hush when I fling that hundred dollar bill on the rug, and it gets so quiet you could hear a rat tiptoe on cotton, and I says, Look here, sucker, I'm a dancer, and I'm moved by Ishtar, Aphrodite, Venus, Isis, Astarte, and Rickee Lee Jones, all them sultry ladies of the East. I am the goddess of the feathery foot, and I only take orders from the moon. Direct. I have turned dives into temples, cadavers into footstompers, drunks into believers, and Tuesday night into Sunday mornin' gospel-time, and I don't take tips. It ain't proper to tip a goddess. And I starts to leave in a huff, and the young sheik comes to 'pologize, asks me to Arabia, he would take care o' everything, and then I know he's talkin about the even more ancient horizontal dance of the harem girl, and I says, Tell me, sheik, you got biscuits 'n gravy over there? And he says, What's biscuits and gravy? And I walks out sayin', See there, sheik, you're living a deprived life.—And that's m'story bub, now where's this wine?

CHANDLER: Wine?—O, yes—of course. But what time's your dancing engagement?

SHIVAREE: Fifteen minutes ago.

CHANDLER: So you have to leave soon?

SHIVAREE: After alittle vino? Let 'em wait. Just a pack o' apes lookin for a thrill.—What's this for, Tommy Peeps? (*He pours wine into soft plastic cups.*)

CHANDLER: I observe the stars.

SHIVAREE: And maybe an occasional lighted window?

CHANDLER: I find the movements in the heavens more interesting.

SHIVAREE: I admire your principles. So, you're a starman, eh? What's these pictures here?

CHANDLER: Various heavenly phenomena: nebulae and comets, double stars, Jupiter's moons, star clusters, our moon itself. (*She spins planets in a model of the solar system.*)

SHIVAREE: And what's this big swirly pizza-thing?

CHANDLER: That's our galaxy. Our solar system is a little dot about—here.

SHIVAREE: You mean all those planets is just an itsy-bitsy dot?

CHANDLER: Our solar system is one of billions in this universe.

SHIVAREE: You think there's life out there?

CHANDLER: It's estimated there are 50,000 planets in our galaxy with earthlike conditions.

SHIVAREE: But how'd ya get these pictures?

CHANDLER: I mount a camera on the telescope. It has a self-adjusting device to compensate for the earth's motion. (*Handing her wine.*) Please don't touch the setting. It's fixed on a star.

SHIVAREE: Can I look-see?

CHANDLER: Do you see a cluster of three stars?

SHIVAREE: Yeah.

CHANDLER: That's Eta Carinae, the largest star in our Milky Way.

SHIVAREE: It looks about the same as the others sizewize.

CHANDLER: It's further away.—Nine thousand light years, which is the distance light travels in a vacuum in one sidereal year. About six million million miles times nine thousand.

SHIVAREE: Eta Carinae.

CHANDLER: It's a blue supergiant, one hundred times bigger than our sun, and will explode, soon.

SHIVAREE: Tonight?

CHANDLER: By cosmological standards, soon is anytime in the next one hundred thousand years.

SHIVAREE: How come she's explodin'?

CHANDLER: The star is a supernova: it has consumed itself.— Burned itself up from within.—And is about to collapse at which time it will unleash the heat and light of a billion suns.

SHIVAREE: A billion suns! Explodin' stars! Nine thousand light years! You ever come down here with the rest of us?

CHANDLER: I ceased bein an earthling after my first parachute jump.

SHIVAREE: You do that?

CHANDLER: My life was cleaved in two: prejump and postjump. You hold on the wingbrace waiting for the jumpmaster to nod. You must believe that nylon, folded in a certain way, can subterfuge gravity. He nods. This is it. Let go. One-one thousand, two-one thousand, three-one thousand, you fall away. You leave the heaviness of flesh, become pure spirit, sublime as sunlight shafting through cumulonimbus. Four, five, six one-thousand. The earth nears and reminds you're no more than a gnat whirling. Seven, eight, nine, ten one-thousand. Find the ripcord. Pull. The miracle happens. A fabulous nylon cherry blossom puffs up so pretty overhead and prolongs the ecstasy.

SHIVAREE: Praise the lord.

CHANDLER: You yell like a baby out of womb, and as you drumble towards the earth, you know, this is it, this is really it.

SHIVAREE: Man alive. How do you support all these bad habits?

CHANDLER: I'm a astrobiophycist. (*Pause.*) I'm in the manufacture of life saving drugs that are made in their purest form in a zero gravity environment.

SHIVAREE: But—can you name the Seven Dwarfs?

CHANDLER: Can you name the constellations?

SHIVAREE: I never saw one.

CHANDLER: I'll show you. It's interstellar geometry. It's just connecting the stars with imaginary chalk.

SHIVAREE: You think the maker put each star up there like he was decoratin a wedding cake? or just sorta slung 'em across the sky like popcorn t'pigeons?

CHANDLER: I think he started to fix each one in order but found chaos more interesting. But we imposed order on the chaos, made pictures with the stars, called them Cassiopeia's Chair, Hercules . . .

SHIVAREE: Now just how do you see a Hercules in all that jumble?

CHANDLER: It's between Corona Borealis and the Lyre.

SHIVAREE: Now make believe you're talkin to a centipede.

CHANDLER: Follow my finger. That's the sky.

SHIVAREE: I'm with ya so far.

CHANDLER: Three stars?

SHIVAREE: I'm goin strong.

CHANDLER: That's Hercules' club.

SHIVAREE: Lost me.

CHANDLER: It's like the meaty part of a turkey leg.

SHIVAREE: Got it.

CHANDLER: Follow the finger to one star.

SHIVAREE: I'm there.

CHANDLER: That's his fist, holding the drumstick.

SHIVAREE: If you say so. Where's the rest of 'em?

CHANDLER: (*On bed.*) All right, this is the sky—imagine Hercules on right knee, club raised, left hand before him, left leg thus, all upside down.

SHIVAREE: Still don't see it, bub.

CHANDLER: It's difficult to picture the picture instantaneously. Perhaps if you were to lie down on the bed upside down.

SHIVAREE: Hell, you star-gazers are slicker than hogs in slime.

CHANDLER: Your assumption as to my motive is entirely erroneous.

SHIVAREE: I ain't never seen a pair o'pants who didn't talk true blue who wasn't really thinkin screw you.

CHANDLER: I regard myself as something more than a pair of pants.—

SHIVAREE: Good night, starman.

CHANDLER: No. Think what you want. But I am not that.

SHIVAREE: I'm so used t'apes maulin me when I dance, I can't tell a bonafide man anymore. (*Pause.*) I'll take that wine now. (*Pause, he fills both cups.*) I got a sudden case o' the dancers jimjams.

CHANDLER: What do you mean?

SHIVAREE: That's when you think yourself a temple dancer whirlin through the incense, and look in a the spectators' eye and see a cheap strip-tease.—To starting over. (*She offers a toast. They touch cups, drink, cough.*)

CHANDLER: Sorry.

SHIVAREE: You said it was questionable. Question is: will we live?

CHANDLER: Why do you keep dancing for apes?

SHIVAREE: This is what I was born for. If there's one appreciator among the pack, I'll wear m'feet down to the ankle. Once I was dancin in this Sicilian bistro and this dude Lodovico was pealin an orange in one hand, leavin the rind in one piece, unbroke, and I thought, Damn, any man who could be that gentle with an orange, must be something else with a lady, and he starts talkin cotton-candy and out t'sea on his yacht Il Caprice he slips a Spanish fly in m'wine.

CHANDLER: Then what?

SHIVAREE: Strap on your seat-belt, sport.—I let him have the Roman special.—Stuck a finger down m'throat, upchucked all over that orange-pealin wizzbag, leaped in the Mediterranean, swam t'shore.

CHANDLER: What do you do for excitement?

SHIVAREE: O—I work m'regular job.

CHANDLER: Which is?

SHIVAREE: I read feet.

CHANDLER: Pardon?

SHIVAREE: You heard o' palmistry? Well, this is pedistry. It's more accurate. I see you're from Missouri. Off your shoe and sock, peach fuzz. C'mon, c'mon, I'll read the future.

CHANDLER: That's frivolous.

SHIVAREE: Sure it is, sure it is—till it comes true.

CHANDLER: You don't really set store by it, do you?

SHIVAREE: Off your shoe and sock, infidel, 'less you're afraid.

CHANDLER: Afraid of what?

SHIVAREE: Why, t'have all your shaky beliefs come crashin' down in a stinkin' junkheap—that's what. (*He laughs and takes off his*

232 / *William Mastrosimone*

shoe and sock.)

CHANDLER: Predict one thing, anything.

SHIVAREE: Silence. You've got a real long lifeline, but . . .

CHANDLER: But what?

SHIVAREE: It's crossed.

CHANDLER: By what?

SHIVAREE: A very strong pain line.

CHANDLER: What's that mean?

SHIVAREE: It means you're a damn fool. (*She digs her fingernail into his instep.*)

CHANDLER: No! Stop! Please! I'll bruise!

SHIVAREE: Fool, fool, go back t'school. (*A banana falls, scares them both. They laugh. She grabs his hand and pulls him into a kiss.*) Now don't go fallin' in love with me or your name's just gone straight to the bottom of a long list o'broken hearts. Where'd you ever learn to touch a lady with such angora fingers.

CHANDLER: I read a lot.

SHIVAREE: How many wet-eye damsels do ya got in your pretty little palm?

CHANDLER: I never had a girlfriend.

SHIVAREE: You're gonna so far in this world, peach fuzz, 'cause you lie with such a God-love-ya smile.

CHANDLER: It's the truth.

SHIVAREE: Kiss me, peach fuzz, afore I yawn t'death. Soon, and I ain't talkin' cosmological soon. (*Kiss.*) M'grand-daddy can do better than that. I gotta go.

CHANDLER: Don't go.

SHIVAREE: Give me a reason to stay.

CHANDLER: I got reasons.—I got a hundred and forty million reasons!

SHIVAREE: That's enough for me! Let it take all night. Let's go get some proper vino, and I challenge you to barefoot one handed frisbee on the levee—best out o' three—and I'll dance for you, special. C'mon, peach fuzz! Say yes! Move, statue afore your feet take root!

CHANDLER: I can't.

SHIVAREE: C'mon! Let's break rowdy on a midnight binge!

CHANDLER: I can't go outside.

SHIVAREE: Ol Etna's gonna explode and release enough heat and light t'vaporize us! If I get time, I'll compare ya to the moon.

C'mon.

CHANDLER: I'm a hemophiliac. A bleeder.

SHIVAREE: C'mon, peach-fuzz, you gotta rise before the rooster t'razzle me!

CHANDLER: I wanted to tell you before, but you made me forget. (*Pause.*) I rarely go out. Even then, it's in the backseat of a padded cab that my mother drives to support me. And that's to the Emergency room for transfusion, dentist, museum, library, sometimes restaurants. (*Pause.*) Classic hemophilia. The inability to form a plasma protein, Factor VII. Which makes thrombin. Which converts fibrinogen to fibrin. Which clots blood. Which means you don't run barefoot on the levee. Or jump from airplanes. Or anything else. (*Pause.*) It's a myth you can die from a scratch. You don't die. You ooze for days. You lay still. You read. You think. A lot. Too much. Of a lifetime of premeditated babysteps across a room. All owing to the minutest biochemical snafu on a strand of mom's DNA. You retreat from the world because you bruise easily. You befriend paranoia. The room's full of assassins. A lightbulb. That table's corner. The door jamb. Anything. That's every moment's dread: Bumping. Bruising. Hemorrhage in joints, degradation of bone and cartilage, or within muscle. Rig the I.V., insert the needle. Lie still. Plastic bag of somebody else's plasma. A lot of cab fares. Thus the padding. (*Pause.*) This is my domain. You might call me Master of Insignificance. I know every wall crack, every knot in the wood, the bird nests in the treetops, the coming and goings of every neighbor in my field of vision, and the stars.

SHIVAREE: Take off your shoe and sock.

CHANDLER: Why?

SHIVAREE: To see what I did t' your foot.

CHANDLER: It's fine.

SHIVAREE: Take off your shoe and sock.

CHANDLER: No, it's all right.

SHIVAREE: You will or I will. (*She looks at his sole.*) Why didn't you stop me? Why didn't you tell me? Why didn't you make me stop?

CHANDLER: I wanted you to touch me. (*Enter MARY, with an ice cream bag. An unendurable pause.*)

CHANDLER: It's just a scratch. Of all things, on the air conditioner.

MARY: (*Long pause.*) Who are you?

CHANDLER: I'd like you to meet -

MARY: Chandler!

SHIVAREE: (*Pause.*) My name is Shivaree, ma'am.

MARY: Who are you?

SHIVAREE: I'm your new neighbor.—Chandler just took me on a little tour of the cosmos.

MARY: What are you doing here?

SHIVAREE: I live right across the way, ma'am.

MARY: But what are you doing in this house!

SHIVAREE: Me and Chandler, we're friends.

MARY: How long has this been?

SHIVAREE: O, it's hard to say.

CHANDLER: An hour.

MARY: You know Chandler's condition?

CHANDLER: She didn't know, Mom.

MARY: This is a sick boy here—and I work too long and too hard to keep him in blood or to let him keep company with a whore . . .

CHANDLER: Mom -

MARY: You shush!

SHIVAREE: Ma'am, I happen to take huge exception to your fly-off the handle remarks, but it's no sooner said then overlooked. I am a very high-class terpischorean.

MARY: You will never come in this house again.

SHIVAREE: Ma'am?

MARY: Never. Get out.

SHIVAREE: Chandler? (*CHANDLER turns away. Pause. SHIVAREE walks through the French doors onto the balcony.*)

MARY: Where are you going? (*SHIVAREE walks over to the bridge. SHIVAREE pulls the bridge away and exits. MARY closes the doors, closes the window, turns on the air conditioner. Pause. She looks at CHANDLER's wound, gets the first aid kit, puts on a new dressing, not because it's necessary, but because she has always been the one to do this. Long pause.*) Did you sleep with her?

CHANDLER: No.

MARY: I want the truth?

CHANDLER: NO! (*MARY slaps him.*)

MARY: Baby! (*Blackout. End of Act I.*)

ACT II

SHIVAREE's music plays. The next evening. Lights up slowly. CHANDLER in a robe and pajama bottoms sits with his back to the audience. He is connected to his I.V. and languidly twirls an orange in one hand, trying to peel it with one hand. The rind breaks. The peal drops. He stands as though to look at SHIVAREE's apartment. Listening to her music.

CHANDLER: Did you hear about Chandler? They found him dead. O.D. Vitamin C. (*The buzzer sounds. He ignores it. He answers it, wheeling the I.V. stand with him without disconnecting it. When he turns we see that the side of his face is black and blue.*) Who's there?

LAURA: (*Over intercom.*) I want m'money, cupcake.

CHANDLER: Get it from Scagg! (*He walks away. The buzzer becomes an elongated blare.*) Go away.

LAURA: Open up or I'll ask you mama for it. (*He releases the doorlock, wheels the stand to his desk, sits, picking up orange peels. Enter LAURA.*) I've been took by slick-ass sharpies, I been took by credit card conventioneers, but I never been took by a mother-lovin' zit-face virgin boy. (*LAURA sees his bruise.*) Did I do that? I only just touched your face.

CHANDLER: It wasn't you.

LAURA: What's all this?

CHANDLER: Plasma.

LAURA: My man Bonzo's said you bread or your head.

CHANDLER: I gave the money to Scagg.

LAURA: I ran into Scagg last night. He says he never saw a dime.

CHANDLER: That son-of-a-bitch.

LAURA: Bonzo's pissed.

CHANDLER: Would he take a stereo or radio or something?

LAURA: Bonzo only takes foldin' stuff, kid.

CHANDLER: Can I pay him—in a few months?

LAURA: He's gonna scramble my face.

CHANDLER: I gave all my money to Scagg. Fifteen months of my mother's pocketchange. My ice cream money. Twenty-five cents a day. A dollar-seventy-five a week. About seven dollars a month in quarters, dimes, nickels, that I hoarded, sorted, wrapped, counted, hid, re-counted, and planned down to the

236 / *William Mastrosimone*

penny for nothing.

LAURA: You shoulda ate the ice cream, boy.

CHANDLER: I know.

LAURA: But ya can't put the python t'sleep with a fudgie-wudgie, though. (*The buzzer sounds. CHANDLER goes to it, stops.*)

LAURA: It might be Bonzo. (*Buzzer.*) He chews doors like this for breakfast.

CHANDLER: How did this happen!

LAURA: Answer it. (*CHANDLER wheels standard to door-release button.*)

CHANDLER: Who's there?

SCAGG: M'man!

CHANDLER: Scagg!

LAURA: Let him up! I want my money!

CHANDLER: (*Releasing the door lock.*) Why am I such an invertebrate? Ring bell, salivate. I can't say no. I can't say yes. I'm just a knee-jerk. (*Enter SCAGG in filthy clothes, his right hand wrapped in a bloody rag. CHANDLER stands behind standard.*)

SCAGG: Your ma booted me—garbage-bagged m'threads, put 'em out on the curb, flushed three thou worth o' blow down the john, all cause you went and told her I gave you a magazine. Now the supplier's hatchets shived me in the penny arcade said some up with the paper or the stuff or they're gonna put me t'bed with a shovel tonight. Now I got to skip this dogass town—and don't have no clothes. Gimme some clothes.

CHANDLER: Where's Laura's money? You took fifty. She only charges thirty-five.

SCAGG: M'man! I'm bleedin' 'cause o' you!

LAURA: Simmer down, you. (*CHANDLER grabs the clothes from SCAGG.*)

CHANDLER: Get out.

SCAGG: I need them threads, bro.

LAURA: Give him the damn clothes, dumbass.

CHANDLER: Get out of here. (*SCAGG retakes the clothes.*)

SCAGG: I could put you away so easy. (*CHANDLER pushes SCAGG.*)

CHANDLER: Pussy.

SCAGG: Do it again and see what happens. (*CHANDLER pushes SCAGG.*)

CHANDLER: Pussy.

SCAGG: You gonna die. (*CHANDLER pushes SCAGG.*)

CHANDLER: C'mon, pussy! Put me away! (*SCAGG grabs CHANDLER by the robe, picks him up. Pause.*)

LAURA: C'mon, the boy ain't right in his brain. (*Pause. SCAGG puts CHANDLER down. CHANDLER spits in SCAGG's face. LAURA stands between. SCAGG pushes her away.*) You got no sense, boy.

CHANDLER: You pussy.

SCAGG: You wanna die.

LAURA: Boy, can't you tell your life from a mess o' rags?

CHANDLER: Why don't you put me away, pussy?

SCAGG: (*Pause.*) 'Cause I'm a nice guy. (*SCAGG counts out some money, throws it on the floor. Exit SCAGG. CHANDLER picks it up, hands it to LAURA. Long pause.*)

LAURA: Don't care too much for life, do ya?

CHANDLER: What's a life worth these days?

LAURA: More than this. (*LAURA begins to exit.*)

CHANDLER: So much?—Have a profitable night.

LAURA: I can't give back the money, but I do owe you one.

CHANDLER: Let's call it a transaction without the action.

LAURA: I didn't charge you for the house call.

CHANDLER: Your business ethics are only surpassed by your personal morals.

LAURA: Business is business.

CHANDLER: Tautology is tautology and nonsense is nonsense.

LAURA: I seen so many college boys like you before. They pay me with money daddy set aside for their education, take off clothes and stand naked before life afraid to say, Teach me. In ten minutes I make 'em feel like lusty bulls and off they go. Many a happy female out there owes me thanks.

CHANDLER: Mother Teresa was wrongly rewarded.

LAURA: But for you, I have never failed t'raise the rammer.

CHANDLER: I'm above that.

LAURA: I had 'em all and you ain't no different. You need a good hard toss in the sack. You need alittle woman love in your life.

CHANDLER: Love.—Just another appendix.—Only time you know it's there's when it's ready to burst and kill you.—Love. What you mean's the pedestrian excuse for the exercise of our reptilian physiology—feel-goodism for Cro-Magnon man and woman modernized in permapress polyester—good for a grunt and a squabble, and ulcer, a couple unwanted offspring, and a

238 / *William Mastrosimone*

divorce lawyer's fee . . . Not for me. - I, look down on the chaotic, futile, stinking antheap—and see the human-bugs building Taj Mahals out of orange peels, and I veer off, circumnavigating the scope of human knowledge . . . A universal mind . . . One . . . Hermaphroditic . . . Inscrutable . . . Happy.

LAURA: Underneath all that bookstuff, you're a hot-assed Indian. See that thing there, boy? Looks like a bed, eh? It's more. It's the final exam. If that's good, life's good. If that's dogmeat, nothing else's right. Some things you can't learn between book covers. You can bluff yourself inside out but you never took the final exam. You never had a woman.

CHANDLER: Once.

LAURA: Once upon a time.

CHANDLER: That's right.

LAURA: Who was she?

CHANDLER: A dancer.

LAURA: I was a dancer once.

CHANDLER: She was a real dancer.

LAURA: I worked the Ginger Palace right out o' high school. What style go-go she do?

CHANDLER: Danse orientale.—Egyptian style.

LAURA: Belly dancer?

CHANDLER: Pharaonic.

LAURA: 'Scuse me.—Was it good with her?

CHANDLER: Ineffable.

LAURA: So after the first time, you put the python t'sleep and the whole world can take a flush, eh? (*Pause.*) She dance for ya?

CHANDLER: Of course.

LAURA: Stir ya?

CHANDLER: To the marrow.

LAURA: How'd you meet?

CHANDLER: I met her one night . . . before the Temple of Isis.

LAURA: Is that that pink bar down on Mohamud Ali Boulevard?

CHANDLER: It's a ruins.

LAURA: O.

CHANDLER: In Egypt.

LAURA: O.

CHANDLER: On the Nile.

LAURA: Why was you there?

CHANDLER: I was digging for artifacts. I had just unearthed a bronze statue, utterly lifelike, of goddess Isis, when I heard zills.

LAURA: What's zills?

CHANDLER: Finger cymbals. She was dancing under the moon playing her zills, barefoot on the weathered stone, hair whirling about . . . zills.

LAURA: What's she like?

CHANDLER: She smiles and you'd think the world were a charm on her bracelet. She laughs, throws her head way back, shuts her eyes like she's kissing herself, and you could almost believe she had a summer cottage on the moonshore of Mare Tranquillitatis. (LAURA does a poor Pharaonic dance.)

LAURA: She's dancin Egyptian for ya . . . Pretend it's her.

CHANDLER: That's sick.

LAURA: Everybody does it.

CHANDLER: Stop—stop—stop.

LAURA: What's the matter with you?

CHANDLER: The matter is me that I am matter, and matter, having extension in time and space, exerting gravitational attraction to other such bodies, and having inertia, resistance to acceleration, quantitatively measured by mass which in this case seems to predominate over the impulse to say . . . I want her.

LAURA: Someday, girl, you're gonna need a degree for this work.

CHANDLER: Shivaree!

LAURA: You are fargone.

CHANDLER: If there were world enough and time, I would sweeten the air with eloquence, but for now accept this—Scram.

LAURA: You win, kid.

CHANDLER: Shivaree!

LAURA: Don't chew no razor blades. (Exit LAURA.)

CHANDLER: I am astronomical! (Silence. He rushes to his desk, gets a metal cup, dumps the pencil, seizes the metal garbage can, empties it on the floor, rushes to the balcony and makes a shivaree banging them together.) Hey, hootchy kootch! Get out here, you juicy little enchalada! (Enter SHIVAREE in a plain dress.)

SHIVAREE: What'd you call me?

CHANDLER: I wish I had a bouquet of dirty socks to throw across.

SHIVAREE: What kind o' vino's talkin to me tonight?

CHANDLER: But let this suffice, my apogee, my perigee, my jalapena, my decaffeinated canary! (He grabs a half dozen multi-

colored socks from his dresser and throws them at her.)

SHIVAREE: (*Catching the bouquet.*) And they said romance is dead.

CHANDLER: Shivaree, come back and play your zills? There's nothing in this world more beautiful than you playing your zills.

SHIVAREE: I can't never resist a real live appreciator. I'll get 'em. (*She exists. He unplugs the c.b. She reenters with zills and a shoebox tied up with a hair ribbon. She makes her bridge and crosses.*) Where's you ma?

CHANDLER: Gone.

SHIVAREE: So how's your chromosomes, sport? (*She sees his discolored face. She touches it.*)

CHANDLER: I bumped a door in the dark.

SHIVAREE: You keep practicin that, bub, and maybe you'll fool a fool. I got you a little goin away present.

CHANDLER: Where are you going?

SHIVAREE: (*Picking up an orange peel, eating an orange slice.*) Not bad for a first-timer.

CHANDLER: You can't be unpacked yet.

SHIVAREE: Open it.—I was gonna get you a madras jacket, but hell, if you get caught in the rain, it could bleed t'death. (*He opens the box, takes out a rose.*) I took the thorns off. (*He takes out other things.*) Bull's ears. Dedicated to me by El Matador Juanito at Guadalajara in which he was severely gored in the left cheek o' his butt. That's a tape of them Guazi tunes you like. Camel-bone ring from Kabul which wards off desert jinnis, and brings good luck on caravans and dangerous crossings. It's more of a treasure than a present, ain't it?—And there's a big fat bag o blood waiting for ya down at the clinic.

CHANDLER: You gave blood?

SHIVAREE: What's the proper thing t'say to a hemophiliac on such a grand occasion?—Coagulations. What's it called when they take blood, spin off the plasma, and put the red cells back in ya?

CHANDLER: Plasmaphresis.

SHIVAREE: I was the first one in line. Told 'em put it in your account. They all knew who ya were. Everybody say hi.

CHANDLER: Did it hurt?

SHIVAREE: Them suckers rammed me with a needle big as a telephone pole. But it hurts kind of beautiful when you see your blood coursin' through the clear plastic tubes, how red and rich, how quick it fattens the bag with life, and gives ya a Sunday-mornin after-church kind of feelin when the nurse takes her thick black pen and prints like a first-grader on the bag—CHANDLER KIMBROUGH. Knocks the bejesus outta me to think our plasmas are gonna mix in your veins.—So when you get a transfusion and start shakin those hips and talking twang, don't wonder why.

CHANDLER: Where will you go?

SHIVAREE: Memphis.

CHANDLER: What's there?

SHIVAREE: Home.

CHANDLER: For how long?

SHIVAREE: Till m'vocal cords're stripped from screamin-match with my folks. They don't approve o' no female over twenty who don't have three wailin brats hangin on her leg.

CHANDLER: After that?

SHIVAREE: I'm liable t'chase the first dandylion fuzzball t'come along.

CHANDLER: And then come back.

SHIVAREE: What for?

CHANDLER: What for?

SHIVAREE: That's American for porque.

CHANDLER: It was my distinct impression . . . I thought we had something between us.

SHIVAREE: We do. Your mama.

CHANDLER: I never had this problem before.

SHIVAREE: I'm sorry I'm gummin' up the works here.

CHANDLER: I don't mean problem. It's always been just mom and me. Who I am and who she is—sometimes blurs.

SHIVAREE: When you sit on a tack, who says ouch, you or her?

CHANDLER: I do.

SHIVAREE: Take thought, bub.

CHANDLER: I can't exist in the world on my own. I was born incomplete. I'm attached to a needle, to a tube, to a plasma bag, to her . . .

SHIVAREE: Save it for your diary. You're as free as you want to be.

CHANDLER: So you're leaving?

SHIVAREE: I already broke the lease.

CHANDLER: Perhaps you can reinstate it.

SHIVAREE: New tenant's moving in tomorrow noon.

CHANDLER: You won't come back?

SHIVAREE: I'll fall back here like a Newton banana if I feel some kind of gravity.

CHANDLER: You never danced for me.

SHIVAREE: I was about to—when you come down with a sudden case o' hemophilia.

CHANDLER: Well—you said you would—so—dance.

SHIVAREE: There's a proper way t'ask, and that ain't it.

CHANDLER: I remind you, I have the disease of kings and kings don't ask.

SHIVAREE: I remind you, I ain't no dancin concubine on her toes when the king makes a snappy finger, bub.

CHANDLER: I humbly solicit your pardon.

SHIVAREE: I'll think upon it.

CHANDLER: That would please us immeasurably.

SHIVAREE: I'll dance for an unbroken orange peel.

CHANDLER: It's impossible.

SHIVAREE: Lodovico did it.

CHANDLER: No, no. I can't do it. Therefore he can't. I'm ambidextrous and went through three sacks already. Can't be done.

SHIVAREE: Takes a lifetime.

CHANDLER: The slightest twitch and the rind breaks.

SHIVAREE: If devotion was easy, it'd be a rusty beer can in the gutter.

CHANDLER: Where do you find devotion in a monkey trick?

SHIVAREE: It shows a man willin t'take his sweet time t'denude the fruit.

CHANDLER: It shows a decadent overweening egocentric world-class flim-flam.

SHIVAREE: For all his failings, Lodovico had hands that could teach tenderness to swansdown.

CHANDLER: So tender you jumped ship and swam for your life!

SHIVAREE: Don't get all shook just cause you can't cut the finesse.

CHANDLER: Spare me your fond reminiscences of failed romances. And keep you bulls' ears and your matador lovers. I don't have hundred dollar bills to slip in your clothes and I can't unpeal an orange one-handedly, but for a dance, my eyes will pay tribute.

SHIVAREE: Tribute I will take. Put on that tape, sport. (*She lights votive candles.*) Lie down. There's an ancient healing dance called the Zar. It drives out demons called afreetees, like the one you got in your chromosome. (*The music begins.*)

CHANDLER: Why?

SHIVAREE: No talk. Lie down.

CHANDLER: Where's you learn this?

SHIVAREE: In Istanbul. From an old leper woman with a milky white eye. She sent me t'study the Naja-Naja cobra up there in Punjabi. When some intrudin animal goes near her nest, she stands, puffs her hood, and bobs and weaves and shimmies and sways so pretty, the intruder gets hypnotized and she bites!— And it's beddie-bye for eternity. When I stop, life comes up roses or rhubarb. If this don't grab your butt, you ain't got one. (*She dances to music that mimics the cobra, using a makeshift veil. The belly dance becomes the Zar, the healing dance. She goes to her knees and invites him into the dance, which he joins shyly. They join hands and the healing dance becomes the mating dance.*) All my life I never found that hand that could turn me into eiderdown, till now.

CHANDLER: I was all secret desire.

SHIVAREE: I was all tinder and never found fire.

CHANDLER: You are codeine, morphine, percodan and demerol.

SHIVAREE: Hell, I ain't never been compared to a drugstore before.

CHANDLER: Will you come back?

SHIVAREE: Don't the swallows always fly back to Capistrano?

CHANDLER: Don't go.

SHIVAREE: Beg and bribe me. I'm corrupt like that.

CHANDLER: I'm free-falling and afraid to pull the rip-cord. (*She gently lifts him to his feet and leads him to the bed.*)

SHIVAREE: One one thousand.

CHANDLER: Two one thousand. (*She begins to undress him, only played in silhouette.*)

SHIVAREE: Three one thousand.

CHANDLER: Four one thousand. (*He begins to undress her.*)

SHIVAREE: Five one thousand.

CHANDLER: Six one thousand.

SHIVAREE: Seven one thousand.

CHANDLER: Eight one thousand.

SHIVAREE: Nine one thousand. (*They're in bed under the covers.*) Say it.

CHANDLER: Ten one thousand. (*Pause.*) Look at us!

SHIVAREE: Ain't we something? What's all this?

CHANDLER: Scars from needles.

SHIVAREE: See here? When I was seven, a big ugly purple grackle flew into me. That's where the beak stuck. And this one's from when I was eleven and Bobby Ray tried to kiss me and I said no and he tried to stick a bumble bee in m'ear and I kicked him and he sicked his dog on me and I bit his dog's ear off. (*They look up through the open skylight.*)

CHANDLER: Do you think there's life out there?

SHIVAREE: I think two red-eye Jupiterians are looking down here right now and one's sayin, You think there's life on that greenish-bluish foggy little ball down there?

CHANDLER: And what's the other one say?

SHIVAREE: She says, Aww, fuzzbrain, what's freckles matter on a shaggy dog? Quit your yip-yap and come lay a juicy liplock on your lovin' lady.

CHANDLER: And then what?

SHIVAREE: And he does so.

CHANDLER: If my heart were put on a scale now, it would balance with a feather. (*SHIVAREE takes one of the votive candles, blows it out, takes the other, holds it before CHANDLER, who blows it out, they recline. They hear footfalls up the stairs. They freeze. Enter MARY.*)

MARY: Lovy?

CHANDLER: Mom!

MARY: Don't get up. Here's Jerry's parachute. But don't get no ideas, sonny boy. You ain't never jumpin'. It's only for that canopy you wanted over the bed. But if it collects dust, out it goes. All day, all damn day, drivin' around with my "Occupied" sign lit up, people lookin' in the empty cab, dispatcher callin', where are ya 409?

CHANDLER: Mom?

MARY: I wasn't strikin' you, lovy. I was strikin' my own face.

CHANDLER: Mom, excuse me . . .

MARY: You got your manly urges I suppose. But God knows this world don't need another bleeder.

CHANDLER: Mom? I'm not alone.

MARY: What?

CHANDLER: Shivaree's here. (*Long pause. MARY turns on the swivel light, aims it at the bed. Long pause.*)

MARY: Get your clothes on.

SHIVAREE: M'am, I strongly object on this.

MARY: You object! Object! You! Get dressed and get out!

SHIVAREE: Would you please turn that light off, m'am?

MARY: O! You got sudden modesty!

CHANDLER: Mom, please. It's difficult enough.

MARY: You! You get out of that filthy bed right now, young man.

CHANDLER: I can't stand up right now.

MARY: No baby steps for you! When you go to hell, you leap headlong in the pit, don't ya? (*MARY turns off the light. CHANDLER and SHIVAREE get out of bed and dress.*)

SHIVAREE: M'am, I'm sorry you caught us in all our dishabille.

MARY: Shameless. Like dogs pairin' up on the lawn at noon. With all your learnin, all your knowledge, you fall for the first one-night flirt that comes along.

CHANDLER: Mom, Shivaree gave blood today, and put it in my name.

MARY: Anybody can give blood. I know vagabonds who give blood 'cause they want that eleven dollars and fifty.

SHIVAREE: I really do care for Chandler, m'am.

MARY: For how many hours? You care for him in leg braces? Wheelchair? You'd curdle at the first sight of blood.

SHIVAREE: I do, m'am.

MARY: How much?

SHIVAREE: M'am?

MARY: How much do ya care?

SHIVAREE: I don't rightly know how t'answer that, m'am. As far as I know, ain't no measure for affections.

MARY: Yessir! Yessir, there's a measure! How still can ya sit when incompetent interns are learnin' their trade on your little baby, when he cuts his tongue on a lollipop and bleeds for a week and they're diggin in his veins t'run a transfusion, diggin and searchin' and probin' in your baby's arm—diggin'—? O god. Can ya watch a good man take to bottle and put himself in the ground? Can ya be your baby's skin in a world that's a booby trap for him? How much will ya care when the blood don't stop no matter how much gauze and bandages you throw at it, cause the blood wants out!—His blood and my blood, too! I give blood till they won't let me give no more! Can ya force your unwillin lips back over your teeth t'make a smile t'get a tip? How much do you care, little dancin girl?

SHIVAREE: Enough never t'slap his face, m'am.

MARY: You get gone.

SHIVAREE: Bye, star-gazer. You should be sportin Corona Borealis for a diadem, sittin up there in Cassiopeia's Chair, 'cause your gentle ways makes you the natural-born aristocracy o' men. Hail, peach-fuzz. (*Exit SHIVAREE, withdrawing her bridge. MARY rips the sheets off the bed.*)

MARY: In a night you tumble back nineteen years and animalize. Where was your mind? Answer me. Answer. I will be answered.

CHANDLER: You can't talk to me like that anymore.

MARY: I assumed before tonight that you tucked all this away and came to realize . . . you can't be with a woman.

CHANDLER: Like you realized when they said your sons would be bleeders?

MARY: I thought the world would make an exception in my case. There's not a second of my life I don't regret it.

CHANDLER: Regret me? Too late. I'm here. And this cubic space can't hold me anymore.

MARY: I only want you to have a good long life.

CHANDLER: Good? What's that mean? Sterile? Then it was superlative. Long? I have been sustained for centuries and never lived until tonight.

MARY: You don't have the injuries of other hemophiliacs.

CHANDLER: I'd rather be Jerry Vollens thrashing in barbed wire dying by spurts and gushes! At least once he lived!

MARY: He could've lived longer!

CHANDLER: For what? Live longer for what?—To stuff a coffin?

MARY: Alls I know is this thing, this godawful thing's got to end with us—

CHANDLER: You mean me, end with me!

MARY: You want to watch your grandsons piercin' veins with the hypo? like you did? eh? and when you didn't cry, I did! while that big strong weakling of a father drank it away with sour mash! Chandler, you have an obligation to the unborn.

CHANDLER: The same obligation you couldn't keep?

MARY: I didn't have your high mind.

CHANDLER: I don't have my high mind either . . . Sometimes I want to kill myself . . . but I don't want to be dead . . . For whatever screwup in a chromosome, I am a man . . . and I want her, mom.

MARY: You're my only family. I live for you. You don't know what I do out there. You don't see me fightin' cabbies for a place in the airport line—you don't see me over-chargin out-o'-towners for you! (*SHIVAREE's music wafts across the balconies. Pause.*)

CHANDLER: You don't have to punish yourself with work for me. You don't have to do penance for bringing me in the world—because I love you for giving me life—Look at those stars! burning themselves out!—Me too.—Hell, me too.—I want to hear those zills—listen, one hundred and forty million sweet Egyptian zills.

MARY: I never knew you had so much vinegar in you, Mr. Kimbrough.

CHANDLER: I never knew pigheadness is genetically transmitted.

MARY: I am not pigheaded. I am simply addicted to my beliefs.

CHANDLER: We're taking off tomorrow.

MARY: Off?

CHANDLER: The whole day.

MARY: How can I take off?

CHANDLER: You don't show up, and if the world folds up, to hell with 'em. We're going to the races.

MARY: I have a living to make, honeybabe.

CHANDLER: We have to live, too.

MARY: Let's do.

CHANDLER: In the grandstand.

MARY: All right.

CHANDLER: And then a picnic.

MARY: Chicken and lemonade.

CHANDLER: Enough for three.

MARY: Son of a bee.—Well, Mr. Kimbrough, I'm missin some good business at the airport.

CHANDLER: Why don't you get some sleep?

MARY: No, I wanna drive. I never know what I'm thinkin till I'm driving. (*Pause.*) Looks like we're not gettin no sleep round here what with her playing that hootchy kootchy music all night long.

CHANDLER: It's oriental.

MARY: O yeah? What's her name?

CHANDLER: Shivaree. (*MARY nods and exits. CHANDLER listens to her footfalls die away, listens to the door close. He goes out on the balcony, and softly calls.*) Shivaree? (*He reenters, rushes to a bookshelf, topples books onto the floor, makes a bridge between the balconies, stands on the ledge, puts on foot on the bridge, then another foot, looks down, steps back to the ledge, hears the zills tease. The bats flit. The cats caterwaul. The stars burn as they always have. He rushes back into the room, takes the bedspread, makes an Arabian garb for himself, tying SHIVAREE's ribbon about his head. He begins to rush out again, puts on the parachute, stops again, picks up an orange, tosses it in the air, catches it. He rushes to the balcony, takes in the music, surrenders to it, and begins to make his dangerous crossing, slowly, surely, never looking down, balancing carefully his babysteps in the dark. The lights fade quickly as he surmounts the balcony and enters into SHIVAREE's door.)*

END

TAMER OF HORSES

For George and Midge Thomas

TAMER OF HORSES was first produced November 6 – December 1, 1985 at Crossroads Theatre, New Brunswick, NJ. The play was directed by L. Kenneth Richardson with the following cast:

TY .... Joe Morton
GEORGIANE .... Michele Shay
HECTOR .... Tony Moundroukas

Characters

TY FLETCHER
GEORGIANE FLETCHER
HECTOR ST. VINCENT

Setting

The play is set in rural New Jersey. The 100-year-old barn is fieldstone ten feet up and the rest is heavy wood. The feeling is rugged and masculine. The horse stalls are visible to the actors, not to the audience, and have their own exit to the barnyard. Tools, ropes, rusty farm equipment, saddles, etc. hang on the walls. Somewhere pieces of furniture in various states of disrepair are stacked. One of the pieces is sanded down to the raw wood.

The house is made of the same material, but the kitchen's heavy floor planking and walls have been softened by a definite feminine touch—curtains, throw rugs, hanging plants, flowered pottery, etc. The occupants have kept the best of the old and the best of the new in harmony. A microwave is nestled in the hollow space where a brick oven used to be. The table and chairs are antiques. The chandelier is brightly colored stained glass, also antique.

TAMER OF HORSES

ACT I
Scene 1

Lights up on interior barn. Moonlight is filtered through a horse stall open to the barnyard. The placid night sounds give way to nervous horses snorting and erratic hoof stomping. After a moment, the barn door opens slowly on rusty hinges. Enter Hector with a boom-box in silhouette, backlit by the moonlight. He closes the barn door behind him and stands in the darkness looking at the horses behind a gate, which we cannot see. The horses continue to make nervous noises.

HECTOR: Shut up, man. (*The horse noises become more intense.*) I said shut up, man. (*The horses begin to whinny. Hector impulsively pulls a rake off the wall and throws it at the horses. We hear the horses whinny and stampede into the barnyard. Hector lights a cigarette. His lighter throws a long flame illuminating his face briefly. He looks around, pulls two horse blankets off the gate, lays one over two bales of hay, wraps himself in the other, and lies down to sleep. The barn door opens on creaky hinges. Hector lays low as Ty comes in with a flashlight.*)

TY: Zeus? Hera? (*Not finding the horses in the stall, he whistles, but the horses don't come. He explores the barn with the flashlight. He spots Hector's stubbed-out cigarette, still smoking.*) Who's there? (*Beat.*) Who's there? (*He trains the flashlight on the horse blanket over the bales of hay. Hector leaps to his feet running for the door. Ty cuts him off.*)

HECTOR: Move, man! (*Ty shines the light in Hector's face. Hector pulls a slap-back knife.*) All right, man, time to bleed! (*Ty grabs a pitchfork off the wall.*)

TY: Your move, asshole.

HECTOR: Move, man!

TY: Drop it! (*Ty corners Hector.*)

HECTOR: Don't you be stickin' me wit that, man!

TY: Drop it! (*Ty backs Hector to the wall.*)

HECTOR: You crazy, man!

TY: That's right! Last warning! (*Hector folds up the knife, puts it in his pocket.*)

HECTOR: I'm cool, man.

TY: Drop it!

HECTOR: It's in my pocket, man!

TY: Last warning! (*Ty makes a feint with the pitchfork. Hector drops the knife. Ty picks it up.*)

HECTOR: Shit, man, you crazy.

TY: What're you up to in here?

HECTOR: Nothin'.

TY: Nothin'? You hurt my horses?

HECTOR: No, man.

TY: Why's the rake in the stall?

HECTOR: I don't know, man.

TY: Don't know? Suppose I whip your ass. Think that'll help you remember?

HECTOR: Man, I jus' now walk in here.

TY: I find my horses hurt and you're gonna be sorry, asshole.

HECTOR: I didn't hurt no horses, man.

TY: You alone?

HECTOR: Shit yeah.

TY: You sure?

HECTOR: Shit yeah, man.

TY: My horses better not be hurt.

HECTOR: Go see, man. Why should I go do that for, man?

TY: Then why'd you come in here?

HECTOR: I was cold.

TY: Cold?

HECTOR: No coat, man.

TY: How'd you get all cut up?

HECTOR: Bob wire.

TY: My fence?

HECTOR: Yeah.

TY: How old are you?

HECTOR: Twenty-five.

TY: Oh yeah. What about fifteen?

HECTOR: I look young. Everybody tell me that.

TY: You in trouble?

HECTOR: If you gonna stick me wit that thing I am. (*Ty puts down*

254 / *William Mastrosimone*

the pitchfork.)

TY: What, you run away from home?

HECTOR: Yeah.

TY: Where you headed?

HECTOR: New York.

TY: What's there?

HECTOR: My homies.

TY: What happened to your coat?

HECTOR: Ain't got one.

TY: What's the rake doing in the stall?

HECTOR: I don't know nothin' 'bout no rake, man. Damn. (*Ty removes his down vest and hands it to Hector.*)

TY: Here.

HECTOR: What?

TY: Take it.

HECTOR: What for, man?

TY: It's cold out there.

HECTOR: So what?

TY: Take it.

HECTOR: Forget it, man.

TY: C'mon, take it.

HECTOR: I rather have my shiv.

TY: The knife won't keep you warm.

HECTOR: Shiiiiiiit. (*Hector takes the vest, puts it on.*)

GEORGIANE: (*Offstage.*) Ty?

TY: Yeah?

GEORGIANE: (*Offstage.*) What is it?

TY: It's all right. Go back to bed.

GEORGIANE: (*Offstage.*) Wild dogs?

TY: No. It's all right. I'll be right in. (*To Hector.*) There's a goosedown sleeping bag over there. It's much warmer than the horse blankets. (*Enter Georgiane in nightgown and robe.*) This man needs a place to sleep for the night.

GEORGIANE: What happened to you?

TY: Got caught up in the fence.

GEORGIANE: Oh, dear me, you really tore yourself up. What's your name? (*Silence.*)

TY: He needed a little break from home.

GEORGIANE: I see. Well, I think we should clean up those cuts. All kinds of animals rub up against the barb wire. You could get a serious infection. Why don't you come in the house and we'll disinfect—

HECTOR: I can take care for myself, man.

TY: You hungry? (*Hector shrugs.*) When's the last time you ate? (*Hector shrugs.*)

GEORGIANE: There's some cold roast chicken in the frig. Sweet potatoes. Interested? (*Hector shrugs.*) There's some apple pie, too.

HECTOR: You tryin' to keep me here till the chauffeur come?

GEORGIANE: Chauffeur?

TY: Cops. Nobody called the cops.

GEORGIANE: Would you like to come in? (*Hector shakes his head no.*) I really wish you'd change your mind. (*Hector shakes his head no.*)

TY: Don't smoke in here. (*Ty and Georgiane start to leave.*)

HECTOR: Pie.

GEORGIANE: Pardon?

HECTOR: Pie.

TY: You wanna come in for pie?

HECTOR: No. Bring it here.

TY: No. You have to come inside. (*Exit Ty and Georgiane. Hector throws a few punches in his new vest to see if he can fight in it. Enter Ty. He tosses the knife to Hector and exits. After a moment, Hector follows as lights crossfade to kitchen.*)

Scene 2

The house. Sometime later that night. Hector finishes a piece of pie.

TY: You eat like you're going to the electric chair.

HECTOR: Maybe someday I am, man.

TY: Here. (*Ty puts the pie pan in front of Hector.*) Might as well eat from the pan. (*Hector eats ravenously.*)

GEORGIANE: You sure you don't want some chicken and sweet potatoes? (*Hector shakes his no.*) Glass of milk?

HECTOR: Beer.

GEORGIANE: I'm sorry, you're a minor. Cranberry juice?

HECTOR: Beer.

GEORGIANE: No, I'm sorry.

HECTOR: Any more pie?

GEORGIANE: No, that's it. Why don't you let me disinfect your cuts? They're really bad on your arms. (*Beat.*) It won't take long. (*Beat.*) You could get very sick. (*Beat.*) If you would just take off your shirt, I could dab you with peroxide. (*She shows him the cotton and peroxide bottle. Beat.*) I'm sure you'll feel better when it's done. (*Hector removes his vest, unbuttons his shirt. Georgiane cleans his cuts with cotton and peroxide.*)

HECTOR: It hurt, man!

GEORGIANE: That means it's killing the germs.

HECTOR: Damn!

GEORGIANE: It'll stop.

HECTOR: When?

GEORGIANE: Soon. Some of these are deep.

HECTOR: It ain't stoppin', man.

GEORGIANE: It will. This is much worse than I thought. Ty, I really think we should drive him to the emergency room. (*Hector stands to put his shirt on.*)

HECTOR: Forget it, man! (*Ty eases Hector back into the chair, takes the shirt.*)

TY: I don't think the man wants to see anybody right now. Take it easy. (*Hector calms down. Georgiane continues to clean his wounds.*)

GEORGIANE: Would you like to phone your folks? (*Silence.*) Let them know where you are? (*Silence.*) Don't you want to let them know you're all right at least? (*Silence.*) Your mom must be worried sick. (*Hector laughs.*)

TY: You have folks?

HECTOR: She a nurse.

GEORGIANE: Your mother?

HECTOR: He a doctor.

GEORGIANE: Your father's a doctor?

HECTOR: That's right, man.

TY: Where do they live?

HECTOR: Don't know.

TY: You don't know where your folks live?

HECTOR: New York somewhere.

TY: We can call information. What're their names?

HECTOR: Don't know.

GEORGIANE: You don't know your folks' names?

HECTOR: See, man, some thirteen year old go in for a 'bortion, right? But her stomach too big for a 'bortion, right? But they do it anyway, right? And the baby come out kickin' and screamin', right? And the nurse say, I can't go dump this baby in no garbage, man, 'cause this baby alive, and she bring it to the doctor and he keep it alive and put it up for 'doption. So my mother a nurse and my father a doctor 'cause they had somethin' for me, man. I'm a 'bortion. Can you dig that shit, man? (*Beat. Hector goes to put his shirt on. Georgiane holds onto it.*)

GEORGIANE: Ty, would you give him one of your shirts?

TY: Sure. (*He exits.*)

GEORGIANE: Let me put on a bandage.

HECTOR: Man, you say one thing and then you do a hundred things.

GEORGIANE: Just to stop the bleeding, dear. It's a real deep cut on your back.

HECTOR: Shit, man.

GEORGIANE: Please? (*Hector stands still while Georgiane applies a bandage to his back. Enter Ty with several shirts, hands him one.*)

HECTOR: I don't wear no farmer shirt, man. (*Ty hands him another. He puts it on.*) You gonna call the chauffeur now, man?

TY: No.

GEORGIANE: You do something wrong?

HECTOR: You the FBI, mama?

GEORGIANE: Excuse me. You may call me Georgiane, or you may call me Mrs. Fletcher, but you may not call me mama.

HECTOR: When you get pregnant, you gonna tell you baby not to call you mama?

GEORGIANE: That's a very different thing, isn't it?

HECTOR: Shit, man, everybody look at my face and say, You do somptin' wrong? Everybody look at my face and wanna call the cops.

GEORGIANE: I'm sorry.

HECTOR: Nobody give you a chance in the worl', man. (*He starts to exit.*) I rather sleep in the woods, man.

GEORGIANE: Don't do that, please? There's a pack of wild dogs out there. Stay in the barn.

HECTOR: I don't care, man. 'Least they ain't gonna be raggin' my ass out wit all kinds o' questions! (*Exit Hector with his boom-box blasting a rap song. Ty and Georgiane look at one another. Ty picks up Hector's bloody shirt.*)

TY: Did you have to give him the third degree?

GEORGIANE: Ty, I only asked—

TY: I was here. I heard it. and I saw him run out the damn door.

GEORGIANE: Well, I think he's in big trouble.

TY: I think he needs a refuge, not an inquisition. (He throws Hector's bloody shirt on the floor, exits.)

GEORGIANE: Ty? (She picks up the shirt. Lights fade on Georgiane.)

Scene 3

Darkness. Wild dogs barking. Moonlight comes up gently on a hunter's tree stand. Hector climbs up lugging a tied up blanket full of clanging things. He lies on his back, reaches in the blanket, pulls out a whiskey bottle, drinks deeply, listens to the dogs bark, laughs. Dogs bark. Hector imitates. Dogs answer. He imitates. Dogs howl. He howls. Dogs howl. He howls and pounds out a rhythm to the howling on the boards. He stands, stops howling, listens to the dogs howl. They await his howl. Instead, he makes a monstrous growl. Silence. Hector laughs, drinks deeply, as lights fade.

Scene 4

The house the next night. Georgiane sits at the kitchen table correcting test papers and sipping tea. Loud knocking at the door.

GEORGIANE: Who's there?

HECTOR: Awwww, man! (*Georgiane opens the door. Enter Hector.*) Awwww, man! Awwwww, man! I shoulda listen to you, Mrs. Fletcher! I learn my lesson now, man!

GEORGIANE: What? What?

HECTOR: Awwwww, man! Awwww, man!

GEORGIANE: What happened?

HECTOR: Awwwww, man, them wile dogs try and kill me, man.

GEORGIANE: Oh, dear, are you hurt?

HECTOR: I'm gonna get a heart attack any second now.

GEORGIANE: They killed our dog.

HECTOR: I believe it, man. I'm sleepin' in the woods, right, and them wile dogs come and I say, whoa, jack, and I'm runnin', right, and they right behind me, right—

GEORGIANE: How many?

HECTOR: Man, you 'spect me look over my shoulder and go one, two, three, four? Shit, man, so I climbs a tree, right, and this ugly black dog wit spots grabs my pants wif his teef, right, and that sucker hangin' on my pants while I'm climbin' up the tree, right, and it growlin' and shit I lay some nasty knuckles upside its head, man, I say, bam! and that ugly dog say— (*He howls like a wounded animal.*)

GEORGIANE: Did it bite you?

HECTOR: Bite me? Man, that dog almost eat me!

GEORGIANE: Maybe it was rabid.

HECTOR: It wasn't no rabbit, man! It was a dog!

GEORGIANE: Did its teeth penetrate your skin?

HECTOR: Shit, no, man, I too fast. So, so, so, so, I'm hangin' up the tree and them dogs lookin' up at me like my name's suppertime, all them fangs showin' and drippin' and shit—

GEORGIANE: You were up a tree all night and day?

HECTOR: Shit, yeah. They got tired and went. I hear 'em barkin' faraway so I know it safe and I jump down and run here.

GEORGIANE: You must be all nerves.

HECTOR: Shit, yeah. I could use some wine to calm me down.

GEORGIANE: I'm sorry. What about some apple juice?

HECTOR: I need some wine, man.

GEORGIANE: I'm sorry.

HECTOR: Don't be sorry. Jus' halfa glass.

GEORGIANE: No.

HECTOR: Whatever you say, Mrs. Fletcher. Damn. Who own them dogs?

GEORGIANE: People around here don't spay their dogs, so every few months somebody's dumping a puppy litter in the woods. Most of them die. But a few survive. (*Hector picks up her eyeglasses from the table.*) Those are mine. (*He puts them on.*)

HECTOR: Whoa . . . You a pretty lady . . . (*She holds out her hand. They stare at each other for a moment. He hands them to her.*)

GEORGIANE: Thank you.

HECTOR: What's all this?

GEORGIANE: History tests.

HECTOR: You too old for school.

GEORGIANE: I teach at the prep school in town.

HECTOR: Teach what?

GEORGIANE: History. Ty's a teacher, too.

HECTOR: Of what?

GEORGIANE: Well, he used to teach the classics.

HECTOR: Say what?

GEORGIANE: Literature. Books.

HECTOR: He get fired?

GEORGIANE: No. The school phased out—they cancelled—his classics course. They offered him some other courses, but I guess you might say his heart was broken, so he quit teaching.

HECTOR: Where Ty?

GEORGIANE: Went to get some milk and bread. What's your name?

HECTOR: Hector. Hector St. Vincent 'cause that's the name of the hospital where the girl had the 'bortion.

GEORGIANE: Where'd you run from?

HECTOR: Mrs. Phillips.

GEORGIANE: Foster home?

HECTOR: Yeah. Man, that woman lock the 'frigerator, man. I said, I am hungry, woman, and she say, you wait till supper, and I say, I am hungry now, and she say, too bad, so every day I goes to the store and I got no money, right, and I bust open the baloney, right, and I stuff my jaws, right, and I be chewin' hard, man, 'fore the manager come catch me, 'cause, you know, man, that woman take in kids jus' to get all them checks from the state.

GEORGIANE: Ever report her?

HECTOR: What caseworker gonna believe a street-dog, man?

GEORGIANE: Ty came from a foster home, too.

HECTOR: No mother, no father?

GEORGIANE: They died when he was three.

HECTOR: Who kill 'em?

GEORGIANE: House fire.

HECTOR: Whoa, man.

GEORGIANE: Christmas tree lights shorted out in the middle of the night . . . tree caught fire.

HECTOR: While they all sleepin'?

GEORGIANE: Yeah.

HECTOR: Whoa, man.

GEORGIANE: Ty and his brother, Sam, survived.

HECTOR: They jump from the window?

GEORGIANE: No. His mother carried Ty and Sam outside. His father went for his sister, Emily, and the dog, but when his father didn't come out, his mother went back in.

HECTOR: Shit, man, why she go do that?

GEORGIANE: Any mother would. They never made it back out.

HECTOR: And them little kids just standin' there? Damn, damn, damn. Man, all that fire make me thirsty for some beer. So who took them kids?

GEORGIANE: The state. They put Ty in a foster home with retired teachers. Sam went in a home . . . well, like Mrs. Phillips' house . . . He ended up in state prison. Maximum security. Killed over a pack of cigarettes at the ripe old age of twenty.

HECTOR: Me, when I'm twenty, man, I'm gonna be a millionaire.

GEORGIANE: How's that?

HECTOR: Music. I can think of songs.

GEORGIANE: What kind of songs?

HECTOR: Rap songs.

GEORGIANE: Really?

HECTOR: I rap to girls and they break down and cry.

GEORGIANE: Rap me one.

HECTOR: I gotta be in the mood. I rap to a girl once and she almost tried to kill herself.

GEORGIANE: You must be something.

HECTOR: It's just a gift I have. What can I say, right? I don't know where it come from. I wake up in the middle of the night and I'm doin' a rap, right? Words and everything. The best rap I ever made was about Paloma, my lady.

GEORGIANE: Where's she?

HECTOR: Don't know. She in the last house I stayed, right? Then Esmeralda, this gypsy girl come, right? And she got nuts for me, too.

GEORGIANE: Must be a problem.

HECTOR: Shit, yeah. Womens ohways cryin' and shit for me. I don't know why, man. One night that Esmeralda say to Paloma, you ain't lovin' Hector right. He need a woman like me, so from now on he mine, or you come outside wif me, and Paloma say, Let's go, and they go outside, and Esmeralda say, "We fight gypsy style." And Paloma said, "What's that?" And Esmeralda say, "You find out," and somebody tie their left hands together and put blindfolds, right? And put a knife in their right hand, and they went at it, slashin' and cuttin' and screamin' and bleedin' for half hour. And that Esmeralda got messed up real bad, so did Paloma, but she won me back again. And when I walks down the street with her and somebody say somptin' about scars on her face, I kick some ass 'cause she did it for me, and I kiss them scars, and I love them scars like they was my kids, right, and I touch them scars and I cry because she did it for me, man, for me. (*Enter Ty.*)

GEORGIANE: Hector had a run-in with the wild dogs.

TY: You all right?

HECTOR: That's what all the girls tell me, man.

TY: Hungry?

HECTOR: I'm cool. I ate yesterday.

GEORGIANE: Stay for supper.

TY: You got enough?

GEORGIANE: Oh, sure.

HECTOR: What smell so good?

GEORGIANE: Apple pie in the oven.

HECTOR: Definitely I'm stayin', man.

GEORGIANE: Why don't you stay with us until you know what you're doing?

HECTOR: Whoa, man!

TY: But you have to do chores.

HECTOR: I 'preciate it, man. I do.

GEORGIANE: Your room's down at the end of the hall. There's towels in the bathroom.

HECTOR: Man, you all right, man. (*Exit Hector to look at his room. Long pause. Ty looks at Georgiane.*)

TY: Yeah, man, you all right. (*She smiles. They embrace. Enter Hector.*)

HECTOR: Awwww, man, 'scuse me.

GEORGIANE: It's all right, Hector. Come back in.

HECTOR: Whoa, man, that room beautiful, man. Sheets clean, the blanket warm. Man, I ain't never gonna leave that room. (*Exit Hector. Lights fade.*)

Scene 5

The barn. The next morning. Lights up on Ty as he sandpapers an old rocker. Enter Hector.

TY: There he is, officer. (*Hector looks behind him.*)

HECTOR: Shiiiiiiit.

TY: How'd you sleep?

HECTOR: Bad. Too quiet here, man. (*Ty tries to move a dresser by himself.*)

TY: Give me a hand? (*Hector applauds, smokes a cigarette.*) Don't want to work for your room and board?

HECTOR: Hey, dude, ain't you heard? The slaves was freed. (*Ty drags the dresser himself. Hector sees a pelt hanging.*)

TY: Raccoon. It was killing our chickens. I trapped it with this. (*Shows him a trap.*) There's an old guy at the flea market who could make you a hat out of this.

HECTOR: The kid don't wear no rat on his head, man.

TY: You know anything about two missing beers from the frig?

HECTOR: Raccoons, man.

TY: Don't do it again.

HECTOR: Somebody gonna make me breakfess?

TY: Hey, dude, the slaves was freed. There's cereal in the cupboard.

HECTOR: Cream donuts and chocolate milk.

TY: Donuts are bad for you.

HECTOR: They bad for *you*. They good for me.

TY: You help me load some furniture on the truck, I'll stop at the diner on the way and get you donuts.

HECTOR: We go now?

TY: After I put the finishing touch on this dresser. See, I picked this up at a yard sale for 25 bucks. It was covered with cheap pink paint. Scratches. Missing knobs. It wobbled. I sanded to bare wood, oiled it to bring up the natural grain. Before I can get it off the truck, somebody's waving two hundred bucks in my face. You'll like it there. You can meet a lot of interesting people.

HECTOR: I don't want to meet nobody, man.

TY: Not to mention, some nice-looking tail.

HECTOR: Where is this place, man?

TY: A few miles.

HECTOR: Can you sell stuff over there?

TY: People buy anything over there. What do you have in mind?

HECTOR: Got some old jewelry and shit I don't wear anymore.

TY: I thought maybe you'd sell some of your songs there.

HECTOR: Shiiiiiiit, man, what she tell you?

TY: That you write love songs.

HECTOR: What else?

TY: That you make up the music and lyrics in your head.

HECTOR: The what?

TY: Lyrics. Words. How many songs do you have?

HECTOR: Alot. Someday, man, you be hearin' them tunes on the radio. I gonna be famous . . . (*Ty puts a log in an x-bed, gets a two handle saw, invites Hector to help. They saw. Ty goes slow but Hector wants to punish the log, goes all out, gets winded, has to stop.*)

TY: Who named you Hector?

HECTOR: Maybe that nurse Spanish. Every time I see a Spanish nurse, I think it's her.

TY: The name Hector's not Spanish, you know. It's Greek.

HECTOR: Greek?

TY: You have the name of a famous Trojan.

HECTOR: I don't use no rubbers, man. I ride 'em bareback, jack.

TY: No, before the Trojans were drugstore heroes, they were a fierce tribe in Asia. Hector was the greatest fighter the Trojans had.

HECTOR: Heavyweight?

TY: Not a boxer. Warrior.

HECTOR: He a bad dude?

TY: His soldiers called him Hector of the flashing helmet. He wore a polished bronze helmet that flashed in the sun, with a wave of horsehair, front to back.

HECTOR: Who he fight?

TY: The Greeks. See, Hector had a brother named Paris who kidnapped the most beautiful woman in the world.

HECTOR: Check it out.

TY: Helen.

HECTOR: She fresh?

TY: Huh?

HECTOR: What she look like?

TY: In the entire book, the writer never once describes her. But what's it to say that thousands of men were willing to die to win her back?

HECTOR: Whoa, man.

TY: That's right.

HECTOR: So Paris bone that babe?

TY: Of course.

HECTOR: He all right, man! No wonder they call 'em Trojans! Then what happen?

TY: Well, the Greeks came to get Helen back. The best Greek fighter, Achilles, fought the best Trojan, Hector.

HECTOR: Who won?

Tamer of Horses / 265

TY: I'll lend you the book.

HECTOR: Ain't got time for no books, man. Who won?

TY: Can you read?

HECTOR: Don't be dissin' me, man!

TY: You want to learn?

HECTOR: Shit, no.

TY: It's no big deal.

HECTOR: Then shut up, man.

TY: I had a brother who couldn't read, and let me tell you where he ended up.

HECTOR: If he too dumb to do the big house, man, he deserve to take a shiv for a pack o' smokes, jack.

TY: Georgiane told you that?

HECTOR: The Christmas tree, everything, man.

TY: If you sit with me for a few hours a day, I could teach you to read in a week.

HECTOR: Don't need it.

TY: What kind of job do you think you can get without—

HECTOR: Don't need no job, man. Gonna sell m'songs.

TY: To sell 'em, ya gotta write them down.

HECTOR: Man, I pay somebody else to write 'em down! Then I'm gonna roll in bread and buy me a Harley.

TY: To get a driver's license, you have to take a written test.

HECTOR: Hey, dude, change the station, man, 'cause that tune's raggin' my ass out!

TY: Well, I don't think your head's on right about this. (*Hector pushes Ty violently.*)

HECTOR: You talk that shit you put snakes in my head, man! My teacher say, Read that book to the class, right, and he know I can't read and the other dudes be laughin' at me and shit, right, and he say, Even little kids in kinnygarten can read that book, son, and I say, Whoa, man, if I you son, that mean you be dippin' in my mama? and he say, Time out for you, and I say, Time up for you, and I say bop bop bop bop bop!

TY: You hit him?

HECTOR: Ain't that what I'm talkin' about, man?

TY: You a good fighter?

HECTOR: I'm gonna be world champ, take the crown. Bop bop bop.

TY: How good are you?

HECTOR: Shiiiiiiit, I throw punches you can't even see,

I hit like Tyson and dance like Ali.

Big dudes, bad dudes, never lost a fight,

I stop you wif my leff, smoke ya wif my right.

The bigger and badder, I cut you down to size,

You tangle wif me, jack, and you gonna die.

TY: Maybe you can show me a few moves.

HECTOR: Yeah, well, maybe I ain't got no time.

TY: You got time to help me cut some wood? Cream donuts and chocolate milk.

HECTOR: Just like the Youf House, man. (*Ty hands him a one-man saw.*)

TY: Who's badder, you or the log?

HECTOR: Shiiiiiiit. (*Hector saws at the log. Exit Ty. Hector drops the saw, picks up an axe, hacks at the log. Enter Georgiane.*)

GEORGIANE: Where's Ty?

HECTOR: Out.

GEORGIANE: Out with the horses? (*She begins to exit.*)

HECTOR: You know that book the Classics?

GEORGIANE: The Classics?

HECTOR: You know, Hector and Killies and Paris and Helen.

GEORGIANE: Oh, the "Iliad."

HECTOR: Yeah. Ty tell me the story.

GEORGIANE: Did he?

HECTOR: Know my favorite part?

GEORGIANE: What's that?

HECTOR: When Hector and Killies fight.

GEORGIANE: Bloody scene.

HECTOR: Bet you don't know who won.

GEORGIANE: Achilles.

HECTOR: Damn!—That's right. (*Enter Ty with a wheelbarrow.*)

GEORGIANE: Hector, would you mind if I had a word with Ty?

HECTOR: Go on, man.

GEORGIANE: Alone.

HECTOR: Whatever makes you happy, tickles me to deff.

TY: Hector, there's a dead tree near the creek. See if you can drag it up here. We'll cut it up. Thanks. (*Exit Hector.*)

GEORGIANE: Mrs. Gibbs called me. Her house was broken into last night. The thieves, or thief, made off with some loose cash, about sixty dollars, family heirlooms, rings, lockets, a radio cassette player, some liquor, and a carton of Camel cigarettes . . .

Tamer of Horses / **267**

TY: When?

GEORGIANE: About the time Hector was up a tree.

TY: Fingerprints?

GEORGIANE: None.

TY: Who knows he's here?

GEORGIANE: Nobody.

TY: You didn't tell Mrs. Gibbs he's here?

GEORGIANE: No. How do you want to handle it?

TY: I'll ask him.

GEORGIANE: You ask him. Then I'm searching his room.

TY: Suppose you're wrong? Did you consider how he'll feel if you're wrong?

GEORGIANE: Did you consider how these folks around here'll feel about us when they find out we're harboring a petty larcenist?

TY: This kid's screaming for somebody to treat him like a human being.

GEORGIANE: Listen, Ty—for eleven years we lived in that campus shoebox, clipped coupons, did without so we could afford a down payment for this place and I'm not jeopardizing it. It took too much damn work to get these folks around here to say good morning to us. It's just like Sam snitching money from my purse. Who needs that again?

TY: Why'd you ask him to stay?

GEORGIANE: I thought you wanted it. I thought you needed some company. I worry about you here alone all day long. I just don't know what to do anymore, Ty. We're losing each other. (*Enter Hector dragging a dead tree.*)

HECTOR: Cream donuts and chocolate milk.

TY: Last night, our neighbor's house was robbed . . . You know anything about it? (*Pause.*)

HECTOR: That what the FBI believe?

GEORGIANE: My name's Georgiane.

TY: Answer the question.

HECTOR: Everywhere I go, man, everywhere I go, they jus' blame me for the rain that come down from the sky, man.

TY: Georgiane, may I have a word with Hector?

GEORGIANE: I have to look for something in the house anyway. (*Exit Georgiane.*)

HECTOR: Man, I'm goin' where nobody know me!

TY: You be straight, and I'll defend you no matter what. Did you do it?

HECTOR: If there's a God, let the dude fry me with lightnin' bolts right now if I did. (*Pause.*)

TY: Yes or no.

HECTOR: I can't say more than that, man!

TY: I'm your friend.

HECTOR: If you my friend, say I was wif you all night.

TY: If you didn't do it, why do you have to lie?

HECTOR: I ain't lyin', man! You know if they can't find the fool, they gonna blame somebody!

TY: Not without proof. Jest tell the police what happened. Take them out and show them the tree you were in. Tell them about the dogs.

HECTOR: Man, I can't talk to no chauffeur, Ty.

TY: Why not?

HECTOR: 'Cause.

HECTOR: You are in trouble, aren't you? What'd you do?

HECTOR: What make you think I do somptin'? Sometimes they do shit to me too, man.

TY: Who's they?

HECTOR: The Youf House in Trenton. I 'scaped over the bob wire.

TY: So Mrs. Phillips was a lie?

HECTOR: No, man, I was wif Mrs. Phillips before the Youf House. They catch me now, Ty, and they ain't gonna send me back the Youf House no more. The Judge say, I ain't gonna try you for no juvenile no more, Mr. St. Vincent. Next time you come before my bench, I'm gonna put you in the big house, and I say, Shiiiiiiiit, man, prison can't be no worser than the Youf House, man. They say, Get up. Eat. Go for class. Eat again. Mop that floor. Mop it again 'cause it ain't right. Eat again. Now watch TV. Now do your homework. Now sleep. And I say, S'pose I ain't tired. S'pose I fell like leavin' this bullshit? So I did. I climb that fence and that bob wire say, Whoa, m'man, you ain't gone nowhere, and I say, Shit I ain't, jack, and I fight that bob wire, man, and it cut me to the bone, man, cut me to the bone, and I say, Ain't nothin' gonna keep me here no more. And I 'scaped.

TY: I can't hide you. If the police come, you have to deal with it.

HECTOR: I'll throw myself in front of the train, man, but the kid ain't gonna mop no floor in no Youf House no more.

TY: If you didn't do it, you got nothing to fear . . . Did you?

Tamer of Horses / 269

HECTOR: Awwww, man, Ty, no! What would I go and do that for? I ain't no little time fool no more. The kid don't jump for no chump change, jack. All my life, Ty, I never had no chance. Now I got one here and I ain't gonna blow it over no fifty-seven dollars, man.

TY: Fifty-seven?

HECTOR: Like I'm jus sayin', right? Shit, this a good life here. Good sheets on the bed. Good pie.

TY: Give me a cigarette.

HECTOR: You don't smoke.

TY: I'm just started.

HECTOR: I'm out.

TY: What's that in your pocket?

HECTOR: I got one left, man.

TY: What kind?

HECTOR: Marlboro.

TY: Show me.

HECTOR: What for, Ty?

TY: Show me it's not Camels.

HECTOR: Get off me, man! (*Ty grabs Hector. There's a struggle. Ty sees the pack of Camels.*)

TY: Camels. Where's the stuff you wanted to sell at the flea market?

HECTOR: Get away from me! (*Ty grabs Hector and throws him against the stall.*)

TY: Tell me!

HECTOR: I sold it!

TY: To whom?

HECTOR: Some white guy.

TY: Where?

HECTOR: The diner.

TY: Liar!

HECTOR: I said a hundred. The trucker gave me fifty. (Ty picks us an axe handle.) Look, man! (Hector shows money. Ty counts it.) Fifty from the trucker, fifty-seven from the house . . . I'm really sorry, Ty.

TY: Shut up.

HECTOR: All right, Ty.

TY: Another wasted life. That nurse should've left you a 'bortion in the garbage bag. That's right! And saved the world from another misfit!

270 / *William Mastrosimone*

HECTOR: Ty, man—

TY: Shut up.

HECTOR: All right, Ty.

TY: Maybe I should just call the chauffeur.

HECTOR: Ty, man, it's the big house for me this time.

TY: Then why'd you do it?

HECTOR: I lost my brain, man.

TY: Oh, they're gonna love you in the big house.

HECTOR: Anybody touch me, man, I kill myself.

TY: Sam was so bad catin' around in his Cadillac—till they spread him on the hood of a squad car and cuffed him behind his back. and when they drove him away, he turned with tears in his eyes. Who's going to visit you there?

HECTOR: Nobody, man.

TY: We invite you in our home, treat you like family . . . I don't need this. I don't owe you anything. —I gave him money I didn't have, cigarettes, food, whatever he asked for because I thought I owed him because some state clerk put him in a bad house and me in a good house. And know something, idiot? When they called and told me he was dead, I was relieved! Relieved! that I didn't have to waste my Saturdays visiting that human junkyard. —I don't know you. I don't owe you. I have a nice life here. What do I need you for? Why not just call the chauffeur to pick up your sorry butt?

HECTOR: You do that, man, I'm gonna run.

TY: Where? Where can you go?

HECTOR: Back to Tito's gang.

TY: Why don't you?

HECTOR: 'Cause I do that, man, I ain't never gonna see twenty years old. I like it here, Ty.

TY: Like it here?

HECTOR: I ain't never gonna find this life no more.

TY: Then why'd yo blow it? You had it all for free. Why'd you have to steal.

HECTOR: I go for a walk, right? I get lost. I see a white house. I knock on the back door. That door open, right? Why they go and leave that door open, man? I went in to get a drink. There was chicken, so I took some. And then I took stuff. Man, I don't know why. I don't need that shit. I just did it, man. I wish I didn't do it, man, 'cause I like it here. Shit, I wish I could put it

Tamer of Horses / **271**

back.

TY: You will.

HECTOR: Shit, Ty, I can't survive the big house, man. You know that. You my friend.

TY: We'll give this money back to the woman.

HECTOR: Awww, man.

TY: We'll mail it from another town. She won't know who sent it. But she'll know it was the thief. Then maybe it'll pass. If not, the judge'll take that into consideration.

HECTOR: All right, Ty.

TY: I must be out of my mind. You think I'm a fool, don't you?

HECTOR: No, Ty.

TY: You laugh in my face, don't you?

HECTOR: No, Ty.

TY: Well, laugh at this, tough man: I got you by the balls. This is how it's going to be: You are up at six o'clock every morning.

HECTOR: All right, Ty.

TY: You do your chores.

HECTOR: All right, Ty.

TY: You take classes with me.

HECTOR: Classes?

TY: You learn how to read.

HECTOR: Shit!

TY: Or explain it to the police.

HECTOR: I'm gonna learn, man.

TY: You mess up one time . . .

HECTOR: I won't, Ty.

TY: Just one time . . .

HECTOR: I won't, man.

TY: Just one time and you know what I'm going to do. (*Enter Georgiane.*) He said he didn't do it . . . I believe him. (*Pause. Georgiane nods. Beat. Exit Georgiane. Ty looks at Hector. Hector looks away. Lights fade. End of Act I.*)

ACT II
Scene 1

In the darkness, Hector's voice.

HECTOR: Duh. (*Pause.*) Duh. (*Lights up slowly on the barn. Ty and Hector sit on tree stumps. Hector is wearing a frontier-style raccoon hat and Ty's shirt from Act I. A green blackboard hangs from a post. The word DOG is written on it in white chalk. Nearby, another piece of furniture is half-stripped down to the wood.*) Duh.

TY: Good.

HECTOR: Duh.

TY: Second letter.

HECTOR: Don't know.

TY: What'd you say?

HECTOR: I don't know!

TY: You do.

HECTOR: Man, why do we had to get up a six o'clock in the morning!

TY: If the horses don't eat, they kick the barn down. Sound it out.

HECTOR: Right now, man, it's two o'clock in the morning for me.

TY: What do you mean 'for you'?

HECTOR: I was born in another time zone.

TY: C'mon.

HECTOR: Tell me about Hector and Helen.

TY: You're wasting my time. (*Pause.*)

HECTOR: Oh.

TY: No.

HECTOR: It's oh.

TY: No.

HECTOR: Man, don't tell me no! It's oh!

TY: That's the letter. Not the sound.

HECTOR: Uh.

TY: Right.

HECTOR: Uh.

TY: Right.

HECTOR: Uh.

TY: Good.

HECTOR: Uh.

TY: Yes.

HECTOR: Uh.

TY: You said that.

HECTOR: I just can't get over that I know it.

TY: Now put them together.

HECTOR: Duh, uh.

TY: Yes! And what's this?

HECTOR: Gee.

TY: That's the letter. What's the sound?

HECTOR: This shit hard! You gotta learn when you a baby!

TY: What's the sound?

HECTOR: I'm tired, man.

TY: Make the sound!

HECTOR: My head hurts!

TY: That means it's working.

HECTOR: Man! I can't learn this shit! (*Hector starts to leave.*)

TY: Then no TV tonight.

HECTOR: You said Wile Kingdom's educational!

TY: No TV. Have a good day. (*Hector leaves. Ty throws the chalk at the blackboard. Pause. Enter Hector. Long pause.*)

HECTOR: (*Not so sure.*) Guh? (*Pause.*)

TY: You sure?

HECTOR: (*Positive.*) Guh!

TY: That's right.

HECTOR: Guh, as in guh-night. (*Hector starts to leave.*)

TY: Get back here.

HECTOR: But I can watch Wile Kingdom after supper?

TY: We'll see.

HECTOR: That mean no, right?

TY: It means after you do your lessons, we'll see if you have time.

HECTOR: Man, I am doin' some hard ass time!

TY: C'mon, put all the letters together.

HECTOR: Now my brain can't work, man, 'cause Georgiane know I wait all day for them animals, Ty, and she told you not to let me watch TV.

TY: That's not true and you know it.

HECTOR: Man, she give me looks when I watch it.

TY: You upset her when you sit there and laugh when the lions kill the zebras.

HECTOR: That funny shit, man.

TY: What's so funny about that?

HECTOR: A million zebras go for a drink, right? And one lion make 'em all run, and the slowest zebra say, awwww, man, awwww, man, shit, man, and that lion say, ahhhhhhhh! and dig them claws in that zebra ass and bite that zebra neck and that zebra go— (*He falls down imitating a zebra being killed. He laughs.*)

TY: You find that funny?

HECTOR: Shit, man, you gonna make a new rule? I can't laugh?

TY: No, no, no, you can laugh. It's just that, when I watched it, I thought about the zebra . . . the horror.

HECTOR: But, man, that lion hungry. That lion need zebra meat, jack. You dig, man?

TY: Yeah.

HECTOR: Zebra got legs, man. It can run. (*Singing.*) "If it too slow, that's life, bro."

TY: Where do you get that from?

HECTOR: Streets.

TY: What streets?

HECTOR: My street.

TY: Not my street.

HECTOR: Nothin' happenin' on your street, jack.

TY: Do the word.

HECTOR: You pissed, Ty?

TY: Do the word.

HECTOR: But I can watch it after supper?

TY: Yeah, if you put all the letters together now.

HECTOR: (*Quickly.*) Duh, uh, guh.

TY: Good.

HECTOR: I need sleep, man.

TY: You need school.

HECTOR: I'm too cool for school.

TY: Said the fool.

HECTOR: Man, you cruel.

TY: Bunch o' bull.

HECTOR: Let's go shoot pool.

TY: That's against the rule.

HECTOR: Man, I can't think o' nothin'!

TY: C'mon. Do the word.

HECTOR: Man, when I eighteen, I'm gone where nobody can tell me what to do.

Tamer of Horses / 275

TY: Where's that?

HECTOR: I'm gonna join the Marines.

TY: Good luck. C'mon, c'mon, sound out the word.

HECTOR: Shit, Ty, what I need this shit for?

TY: To survive in the world.

HECTOR: I survive good, man.

TY: Survive by using your smarts.

HECTOR: You ain't usin' your smarts. You hustlin' wood at the flea market and you a *teacher*.

TY: Do you want to run your life? Or do you want somebody to run it for you? If you can't read, you can't get a job. No job, you starve.

HECTOR: You can read, man, and it ain't doin' you no good. You get fired and your wife out there hijackin' groceries and you stay home and cook like a woman. What's that, man? (*Pause.*)

TY: All right. (*Ty goes back to sanding the furniture.*)

HECTOR: What do you mean, all right?

TY: We're done.

HECTOR: You mean, like for a half hour?

TY: Like forever.

HECTOR: What about class?

TY: You said you don't need class.

HECTOR: I need class.

TY: Do you?

HECTOR: Not every day, man. Not six in the morning.

TY: Then come when you feel like it.

HECTOR: Well, shit, I'm here now.

TY: I don't feel like it. (*Hector grabs the sandpaper from Ty's hand.*)

HECTOR: Man, when I said I don't feel like it, you said, you got to learn discipline! (*Ty takes back the sandpaper.*)

TY: What's discipline?

HECTOR: That when some dude make you suffer some terrible shit, man.

TY: No.

HECTOR: I forget.

TY: Discipline is when you have control of yourself.

HECTOR: Oh, yeah, right.

TY: Why do you need discipline?

HECTOR: So you won't be pissed.

TY: No. There's a better reason.

276 / *William Mastrosimone*

HECTOR: So Georgiane won't be pissed?

TY: No.

HECTOR: I don't know, Ty.

TY: Guess.

HECTOR: To talk like you?

TY: No, no, no.

HECTOR: I don't know, man! Just tell me!

TY: You need discipline to be free. (*Pause.*)

HECTOR: Free? Shit, all right. You the boss, man.

TY: Don't hide behind that bullshit. Speak your mind.

HECTOR: You think this free? This ain't free, man. Tito free. Babes, threads, bread, wheels. Shiiiiiiiit. Sleep all day if he want. Stay up all night if he want. Eatin' pizza in Times Square, jawin' wif homes . . . (*Singing.*)

I wanna be like Sam in a Cadillac

My chauffeur in the front

And me in the back.

Wif two fine babes all in fur

When people see ya

They call ya sir.

TY: You want to be like Sam in a Cadillac? They found him in his bunk. A screwdriver in his back. That make sense to you? A life for a pack of smokes? You think life's worth more than a dollar?

HECTOR: Hey, man, Sam break the law, right? You break the law, too, when you let me slide. What's that, man? Same thing.

TY: Is it?

HECTOR: The law's the law, bro.

TY: So I should turn you in?

HECTOR: I ain't sayin' that, man.

TY: What are you sayin', man?

HECTOR: I'm jus' cuttin' alittle breff wif ya, Ty.

TY: Why shouldn't I turn you in?

HECTOR: 'Cause it might wreck my life, man.

TY: So what? What do I get out of this?

HECTOR: I don't know, man.

TY: If you don't know, I should call the cops.

HECTOR: Wait a minute, man! I'm gonna figure it out!

TY: Why should I break the law for you?

HECTOR: Aww, I know! Like you like a dude, right, so it's cool to go and break the law.

Tamer of Horses / **277**

TY: Is it?

HECTOR: Yeah. No. I don't know, man.

TY: Yes, I broke the law. And that's wrong. But if I didn't, you'd be in jail. My conscience spoke to me and said that's more wrong. What's a conscience?

HECTOR: Don't know, man.

TY: You ever do something and feel bad about it?

HECTOR: Yeah. One time this dude Maurice say some shit to me and I popped that sucker in the face and then I walks away, right? and I felt bad inside and I say to myself, Shit, man, I should've choked him, too.

TY: No, no, no, no, no. That's not what I'm talking about. A conscience is a little voice in your head that tells you something is wrong. It tells you to stop and control yourself. You ever hear a voice like that in your head?

HECTOR: Nope.

TY: That's why you need to read. You need to know words. Words. Why? If you don't give your ideas and emotions names, they run wild . . . A horse is a hundred times stronger than you. But with a bit in his mouth and the rein in your hand, you control it. Words are the reins of emotions. You dig that, bro?

HECTOR: Like I ain't sure, man.

TY: Honest answer. Okay, suppose we didn't have language. Suppose we're cavemen. How do you tell me you want . . . this orange?

HECTOR: I say, Yo, bro, flip me that fruit, my man.

TY: You can't say that. There's no language.

HECTOR: They always had a language.

TY: No. It was invented as we went along, to meet our needs. Our language is our history. So how do you get this orange?

HECTOR: I don't need no words, jack. I get up and get it myself.

TY: Suppose you can't.

HECTOR: Why not?

TY: Suppose you fell off a rock and broke your legs and you're lying there dying of hunger. How do you get that orange?

HECTOR: I point to it.

TY: Show me. (*Hector points but Ty looks the other way. Hector points emphatically. Ty doesn't look.*)

HECTOR: Hey, man, I'm dyin' over here!

TY: There's no language. (*Hector grunts. Ty looks. Hector points. Ty imitates him. Note: Let the actors improvise Hector's attempt to make Ty see the orange. It ends in Hector's frustration.)*

HECTOR: The orange! Look what I'm pointin' at!

TY: Huh?

HECTOR: Huh, your ass! Give! Me! Now! Hey! I'm gonna cave in your head, caveman, you don't lay that orange on me, boy! *(Hector jumps up and pushes Ty toward the orange.)*

TY: See? You need words for things. Especially you, a maker of songs. You turn the noise of the world into poetry. You have the sacred fire. That's the poet in you. But the poet wears a mask. The mask is a streetdog because the poet doesn't want homes to see his sensitive soul. Question is, when's the poet gonna chuck the mask? Or is that gonna be his face for the rest of his life? *(Long pause.)*

HECTOR: Duh, uh, guh.

TY: Don't pause between the sounds.

HECTOR: Duh, uh, guh.

TY: Blend 'em.

HECTOR: Duh, uh, guh.

TY: Blend.

HECTOR: Duh, uh, guh.

TY: Blend 'em.

HECTOR: Let's go the flea market and check out the babes.

TY: Keep your mind on the green
And off the in-between.

HECTOR: *(Laughing.)* I know what you mean!

TY: Work and don't dream! Do the word!

HECTOR: I hate this shit, man!

TY: Too bad.

HECTOR: And I hate you!

TY: Let's go.

HECTOR: This shit's for faggots!

TY: Can you read the men's room sign? Or do you have to have a little picture of a man on the door?

HECTOR: Gimmie a hint, man.

TY: You must think I'm dumb as a dog.

HECTOR: C'mon. Ty, one hint.

TY: Let's go.

HECTOR: I can't do this!

TY: Yes you can! What's that sound!

Tamer of Horses / **279**

HECTOR: Duh! Uh! Guh!

TY: Make it one sound!

HECTOR: Duh, uh, guh!

TY: You know what one is?

HECTOR: Duhuhguh!

TY: Heh?

HECTOR: Duhuhguh?

TY: Can't hear you!

HECTOR: Dooooooooooooog! (*Pause. He looks at Ty.*) You dirty dog! (*Ty and Hector leap up and dance around the barn yelping and barking and howling and laughing. Playfully, Ty assumes a boxing stance.*)

TY: Teach me.

HECTOR: Now I'm gonna teach you some discipline! (*Hector responds with a serious street stance. They stalk each other with their guards up, circling, bobbing, weaving. Ty obviously is out of his element but imitates Hector. The action is continuous. He throws some punches.*) C'mon, teacher, time to go to school!

TY: What's that move called?

HECTOR: It called—watch out, sucker! (*He throws some clever combination.*) What you do if some dude jump you?

TY: Give him a final exam. Teach me something.

HECTOR: See, man, you don't let no dude scare you wif words. You look in his eye. His eye tell you what he gonna do, right? Don't look at his hands. Check out his eye. Here I come, teacher!

TY: You ever fight in the ring?

HECTOR: I fight in the subways, jack.

TY: Hoods jump you?

HECTOR: Shit.

TY: You jump people?

HECTOR: Wolfpackin'.

TY: Who do you jump?

HECTOR: Suits, man.

TY: Suits?

HECTOR: Dudes in suits.

TY: How's it done? Show me what you do.

HECTOR: Jump away, man.

TY: Wolfpack me. Teach me.

HECTOR: Things bad at the flea market, eh, bro?

TY: C'mon. I'm a suit. On the subway. Now what?

HECTOR: I don't ride your train, dude.

TY: I knew you were a bullshitter.

HECTOR: You think so? (*Pause.*) First I look you in the eye.

TY: I don't look back.

HECTOR: Then I know I got your cash.

TY: How do you know that?

HECTOR: 'Cause you scared.

TY: Maybe I got a gun.

HECTOR: You ain't got shit.

TY: How do you know?

HECTOR: 'Cause you had a gun, you look back, 'cause when two dudes look each other in the eye, one of them's gonna blink first, and it ain't the dude with the gun.

TY: All right. I got no gun and I don't look back and you know I'm scared. Now what?

HECTOR: So now you ain't looking at me, but I'm lookin' bad at you, so now you think I'm gonna jump you, so now you show me where your cash is.

TY: Why would I do that?

HECTOR: They all do it.

TY: I ain't showing you no cash.

HECTOR: You can't help it.

TY: What do you mean I can't help it?

HECTOR: You just showed me.

TY: I did like hell.

HECTOR: You cash's in your top left pocket.

TY: You can see it?

HECTOR: You showed me. You touched it. See man, when a dude's scared he think he gonna get jumped, he think, Where's my money? And then he touch it. That's why I'm watchin' real close 'cause he gonna teach me where's the goods.

TY: All right, I showed you the goods.

HECTOR: I'm halfway home.

TY: Yeah, well, maybe it won't be so easy.

HECTOR: I'm gonna test you out to see how hard it's gonna be.

TY: How?

HECTOR: I say, what time's it, m'man?

TY: Seven o'clock.

HECTOR: Thanks.

TY: You're welcome.

Tamer of Horses / **281**

HECTOR: Have a good day.

TY: You, too.

HECTOR: Thanks.

TY: You're welcome.

HECTOR: Shit, man, I got your bread.

TY: How do you know that?

HECTOR: By your voice I can tell you a pussy.

TY: How?

HECTOR: I can tell.

TY: How?

HECTOR: I just know. Now if I think a dude's a *big* pussy, I say, "Sir, I like your shoes, I like to get me a pair like that but I got no cash. You think you could help me out?" Sometimes he piss his pants and give me everything he got.

TY: And what can you tell by my voice?

HECTOR: You really want to know?

TY: Yes.

HECTOR: Pussy.

TY: You'd jump me?

HECTOR: Shit, yeah.

TY: So, I'm just a pussy, not a big pussy?

HECTOR: That's right.

TY: How do know I'm not a black belt in karate?

HECTOR: I can tell.

TY: How?

HECTOR: If I ask a black belt what time's it, he look me in the eye first and then he look at his watch, slow and bad, and he just say, "Seven." But a pussy do what you did. Quick, to get it over wif. "Seven o'clock." "Thanks." "You're welcome." And karate don't mean shit when we wolfpack 'em, anyway.

TY: So you're not alone.

HECTOR: Shit, no, man.

TY: How many?

HECTOR: I like three. Can't make nothin' wif four. Two's not enough if you get some crazy dude.

TY: All right, it's my stop.

HECTOR: We follow.

TY: I see you following me.

HECTOR: I want you to see us follow, fool.

TY: There's a cop.

HECTOR: Ain't no cops down there. They're all eatin' donuts in the coffee shop laughin' wif the waitress.

TY: I follow the crowd.

HECTOR: Crowd don't mean shit, dude. Everybody scared, and they ain't gonna do shit because we vic you quick.

TY: You *what* me?

HECTOR: *Vic* you.

TY: Vic me?

HECTOR: You the victim.

TY: And that makes you feel good?

HECTOR: When I get cash, jack, I feel good.

TY: You see nothing wrong with that?

HECTOR: When I hungry, jack, that wrong.

TY: So how you vic me? (*Hector knocks Ty down and mimics a wolfpack.*)

HECTOR: One man yokes you . . . One man caves in your chest . . . One man goes in your left pocket for the cash.

TY: How do you know I don't have more?

HECTOR: 'Cause you don't think you gonna get vic'd so you keep all you money in one pocket.

TY: So I'm down.

HECTOR: We hurt you again.

TY: What for?

HECTOR: Keep you scared.

TY: What do they do when you're down?

HECTOR: Some scream. Some cry. Some beg. And they talk nice. I like that shit. That good as cash, man. (*He keeps Ty in the headlock for a beat.*) Bet you can't get loose. (*Ty tries, but can't. He's out of breath.*)

TY: Let go. (*Hector still holds Ty, tightens the grip.*) Let go. (*Hector laughs. Ty struggles. Beat. Enter Georgiane running. She attacks Hector.*)

GEORGIANE: Stop!

HECTOR: You bitch! (*Georgiane continues to pound him.*)

GEORGIANE: Let him go!

TY: Georgiane!

HECTOR: Get offa me, woman!

GEORGIANE: You animal!

TY: Whoa! Whoa! Sweetheart! (*She continues to attack Hector.*) It was just a game! Georgiane! It's okay.

HECTOR: Look what you did to my head!

TY: Hector, this is my wife. You respect her.

HECTOR: She lay a hurt on me, man!

TY: He was . . . showing me . . . a headlock.

GEORGIANE: Oh.

TY: It's all a misunderstanding.

HECTOR: It's all a hurt on my head!

GEORGIANE: Oh Hector . . . Oh God . . . Let me see. I'm so sorry, Hector. Please forgive me.

HECTOR: Shit no.

TY: Hector.

HECTOR: Shit no, man! I don't have to forgive nobody!

TY: Of course not, but it was a mistake.

HECTOR: Anybody who sneak me, man, that a big mistake.

GEORGIANE: Hector—

HECTOR: Get away from me.

GEORGIANE: Please listen?

HECTOR: No.

GEORGIANE: All I saw was you hurting Ty. He's everything in the world to me. Wouldn't you do the same thing if you saw somebody hurting your best friend?

HECTOR: No.

GEORGIANE: Oh, c'mon.

TY: Why don't we just let it go for now?

HECTOR: I ain't lettin' nothin' go.

GEORGIANE: Well, sometime in your life you might do something wrong and need people to forgive you.

HECTOR: I don't need shit from nobody. (*Beat.*)

GEORGIANE: I'll make you an apple pie. (*Beat.*)

HECTOR: Two pies. (*Beat.*)

GEORGIANE: Three pies.

HECTOR: Shit.

GEORGIANE: Deal?

HECTOR: Shit, man.

GEORGIANE: Three pies and you forgive me.

TY: What a deal.

GEORGIANE: All right? Deal? Four pies. That's my best offer. Yes or no?

HECTOR: Like the pie you made before?

GEORGIANE: The same. Four deep dish apple pies for eternal

forgiveness. Deal? C'mon, Hector. I see you smiling. Shake on it. (*She extends her hand. He holds out his tentatively. She embraces him. He's embarrassed, breaks out of the embrace.*)

HECTOR: Man, your woman crazy, man.

TY: I know all about it.

HECTOR: Four pies and they better be good.

GEORGIANE: The headmaster pulled me out of class today and asked me in his office.

TY: Ah, his lordship speaks with the help now.

GEORGIANE: He asked about you.

TY: I'm touched.

GEORGIANE: Asked if you're still doing furniture. And he went on and on about "the man's a born teacher," and "tragic he's not here now," and—

TY: Enough foreplay.

GEORGIANE: They want you back. This fall. They're going to reinstate the classics program. They ain't got one Ivy League acceptance this year. Those seniors who got early acceptance didn't make the prestige schools, so parents are miffed and aren't sending in donations. (*Pause.*)

HECTOR: Yo, Ty, what's for supper?

TY: Spaghetti.

GEORGIANE: Would you consider it?

HECTOR: Meatballs?

TY: Yeah. Why didn't he call me first?

GEORGIANE: You know him. He's a coward.

HECTOR: Garlic bread?

TY: Yeah.

GEORGIANE: What do you think?

HECTOR: Ty, pudding?

TY: Yeah.

HECTOR: Butterscotch?

TY: Yeah.

HECTOR: Thanks, bro.

GEORGIANE: Hello?

TY: I can't understand why he can't phone *me*.

HECTOR: Yo, Ty.

TY: Hector! Can't you see we're talking here?

HECTOR: I jus' wanna know if you and your woman wanna be private, man.

TY: Thanks.

HECTOR: Hey, man, I'm cool.

TY: We're not done with the lesson. Don't get lost.

HECTOR: Man, you must think I'm dumb as a duh, uh, guh. (*Exit Hector.*)

GEORGIANE: Don't you miss teaching? I used to sit in the hall outside your classroom on my break just to hear the passion in your voice. I miss getting up together, driving to and from school together. It used to be so perfect. Not to mention we could use the money.

TY: Last week I made more money doing furniture than my school salary.

GEORGIANE: But not the week before.

TY: It rained that week. Nobody showed at the flea market.

GEORGIANE: So if we can't make the mortgage one month, I'll give the bank the weather report. Ty, it would kill me to lose this place.

TY: We'll make it.

GEORGIANE: Of course we'll make it. But you're not happy. This isn't you.

TY: What's me?

GEORGIANE: White button-down, wool tie, in front of your students telling them the passage is lovelier in the original Greek. (*Long pause.*) Ty, you miss teaching. Don't say you don't.

TY: So much that sometimes I lecture the horses on the Greeks. And get the same response. I tried to make those horse-dumb eyes see that Hercules wrestling with Apollo for the sacred tripod of the Delphic priestess was more thrilling than the homecoming football games. I recounted all the wondrous things that sprang full-blown from the head of Zeus—and I'd hear their sports car keys jangling in their pockets. How do you talk to kids who know they're inheriting the world? I wanted to educate them against the world, to be worthy of a cup of hemlock. I wanted to produce one thinker, one dreamer, who could make the desert green, make the sea drinkable, or make a line of poetry that would outlast the centuries. One great soul capable of a good deed. But the school's modern education is geared up to mass produce great bellies with great appetites, to make more cogs for the machine . . . At the end of the year, I used to wait in my classroom for one student, the one I got to, to come in my class after exams to say thank you. Thank you for giving me another world a bit better than the one I live in. But no student ever came to visit. Because I never got to one. Not one. I didn't want to just teach students. I wanted to create them. And now, I don't know. I don't know. I just don't know. Whatever it took to stand before that class, it's gone now. I've lost my touch. (*Pause.*)

GEORGIANE: Not so. I saw you come alive teaching your little Calaban. (*Enter Hector.*)

HECTOR: Where's my pies, man?

GEORGIANE: You'll have the first one tonight after supper.

HECTOR: Don't be late, man.

GEORGIANE: I've got a class.

HECTOR: Have a good day.

GEORGIANE: You, too. (*Pause.*) Can I tell the headmaster you're thinking about it?

TY: (*Beat.*) I don't think so.

GEORGIANE: You've got to come down from Mount Olympus sometime. It's getting awful lonely down here. (*Exit Georgiane.*)

HECTOR: You know, bro, you too good for her. That woman gotta be put in her place. She come in the door, take her money first thing, then say, where you been woman, you five minutes late. Now clean the house and make my food and then go wait in the bed for me.

TY: Don't you ever talk about my wife like that again. Ever. Ever. You got it? (*Hector erases the blackboard.*)

HECTOR: So what's my next word, bro? (*Pause.*) Bro? (*Ty turns and sees Hector offering him the chalk. He takes it and writes on the blackboard: "BROTHER". Hector kneels before the blackboard.*) Beh.

TY: Good.

HECTOR: "R."

TY: That's the letter. What's the sound? (*Lights fade.*)

Scene 2

In the darkness we hear a wild rap song. Lights up slowly. Hector mimes a performance of a rap song blaring from his boom-box. Georgiane comes in the front door. The music is so loud Hector doesn't hear her. She watches. After a moment, he sees her. He stops abruptly and turns off the tape.

GEORGIANE: I'm sorry. (*Hector unplugs the radio and starts to go into his room. Georgiane turns on the light.*) They say we're going to have a big snow for Christmas.

HECTOR: You should knock 'fore you come in, man.

GEORGIANE: Why? It's my house. Is that the kind of stuff you write?

HECTOR: I write better stuff, man.

GEORGIANE: When do we get to hear one?

HECTOR: When I'm headliner at Madison Square Garden, man, and it's gonna be sold out, s.r.o., jack!

GEORGIANE: If you'd like, I'll help you write them down on paper.

HECTOR: I can do it myself, man. Almost.

GEORGIANE: That's fantastic.

HECTOR: Ty say he can't believe my progress, man.

GEORGIANE: By the way, don't put wet towels in the hamper. They mildew.

HECTOR: 'Nother rule, man.

GEORGIANE: You know who dipped a finger in the peanut butter jar? (*She shows him the jar.*)

HECTOR: No, who?

GEORGIANE: You.

HECTOR: Why you say me?

GEORGIANE: Because I know you.

HECTOR: No, man, you think you know me. Careful what words you choose, FBI, 'cause words be the reins of emotion. Did you know that shit?

GEORGIANE: Look in this jar. See that? Somebody's finger mark.

HECTOR: Ty did it.

GEORGIANE: Ty wouldn't do that.

HECTOR: You never know, man.

GEORGIANE: I know Ty since high school. He wouldn't do that.

HECTOR: Yeah, well, maybe you don't know him like you think you do. See, man, you never know what a dude's about. Sometimes you think a dude's cool, right, and he turn around and do somptin' whacked. You dig that, man?

GEORGIANE: I dig, man. And you're so right. Now take that dude who ripped off the Gibbs' farm. He went and did something really whacked. He went and mailed the money back to them.

HECTOR: Why would he go do that?

288 / *William Mastrosimone*

GEORGIANE: I don't know. What do you think?

HECTOR: Maybe the dude felt bad or somptin', right? So he sent the money back for the stuff.

GEORGIANE: So he sold the stuff?

HECTOR: He must of.

GEORGIANE: What made him feel bad?

HECTOR: Maybe he wanna change.

GEORGIANE: You think he can?

HECTOR: I don't know.

GEORGIANE: You sure?

HECTOR: You got somptin' on your mine?

GEORGIANE: Where's Ty?

HECTOR: Lookin' for furniture. I sold everything he had. We made almost two thousand dollars, man.

GEORGIANE: Really?

HECTOR: Ty said I a good salesman. Them people be lookin' at a dresser and I say, See this dresser, man? This come from Paris. Look at that oak. Look at that work. See how them drawers slide easy? You don't see such fine work these days. And them people be fightin' to buy stuff. Man, people 'round here be fools.

GEORGIANE: Not everybody.

HECTOR: Reading lessons, man. My brain's tired. I gotta take a nap.

GEORGIANE: You didn't sleep much last night.

HECTOR: How you know?

GEORGIANE: I couldn't sleep myself. I got up to make a cup of tea. I thought you might like some, too, so I knocked on your door, but you didn't answer.

HECTOR: I don't hear nothin' when I sleep.

GEORGIANE: I kept knocking and calling your name, but you didn't answer.

HECTOR: I heard somptin' but I thought it was like a dream, right?

GEORGIANE: Uh-huh. But then I got worried and I thought you might be sick of God knows what and I tried to open your door, but it was locked.

HECTOR: Shit, yeah, don't you lock your door?

GEORGIANE: No.

HECTOR: I ohways lock my door, man. Ohways.

GEORGIANE: Why?

HECTOR: Man, in the Youf House, you know, my foster home, if you don't lock your door, some dude come in and rob your eyes, man. It's jus' like a habit, right? Ohways lock your door, man, ohways.

GEORGIANE: Well, by that time I was in a panic and started pounding on your door.

HECTOR: Oh, man, that what that was? I thought I was dreamin' of horses runnin'.

GEORGIANE: By them I was convinced you were too ill to open the door, so I got our spare key . . . and I opened your door . . . And guess what? (*Pause. Hector gathers up his things.*)

HECTOR: I don't need this shit, FBI. (*He starts for his room. She stands in his way.*)

GEORGIANE: I opened your door—and you weren't there.

HECTOR: Move, FBI.

GEORGIANE: Window wide open—three-thirty in the morning.

HECTOR: I heard a noise in the chicken coop.

GEORGIANE: Uh-huh.

HECTOR: A raccoon was tryin' to kill our chickens.

GEORGIANE: Why didn't you tell us?

HECTOR: Like I didn't want to wake yous up, man.

GEORGIANE: You sell your jive to somebody else in this house, man, 'cause I ain't buyin' it, man, 'cause you were gone till five forty-five a.m., man, and the Henderson farm was robbed last night.

HECTOR: Move! (*Pause. She moves aside.*)

GEORGIANE: Don't make a mistake, Hector . . . 'cause I'm right behind you. (*Exit Hector. Lights fade.*)

Scene 3

Lights up on the barn. Ty reads from a book with gilded edges. Hector listens.

TY: " . . . Dawn came once more, lighting the East with rose hands, and saw the people flock together at illustrious Hector's pyre ..." That's a huge pile of wood on which they burn the body . . . "When all had arrived . . . they began quenching the fire with sparkling wine in all parts of the pyre that the flames had reached. Then Hector's brothers and comrades-in-arms collected his white bones . . . They took the bones, wrapped them in soft purple cloths and put them in a golden chest. This chest they quickly lowered into a hollow grave . . . Then hastily, they made the barrow . . . " That's piling stones to mark the grave . . . "in case the bronze-clad Greeks should attack before the time agreed . . . They went back into Troy . . . and enjoyed a splendid banquet in the palace of King Priam . . . Such were the funeral rites of Hector, tamer of horses." (*Long pause.*)

HECTOR: That it? (*Ty nods yes. Pause.*)

TY: Like it?

HECTOR: Shit no!

TY: Why?

HECTOR: I don't!

TY: But do you know why?

HECTOR: I just said it, man—I don't. (*Pause.*)

TY: Tell me the story.

HECTOR: I can't remember all that!

TY: Tell me what basically happens.

HECTOR: Man, I never even heard of some of them words!

TY: But you understood it.

HECTOR: How you know?

TY: I watched you. You knew what was happening even though you didn't know all the words. You had a sense of it. So now, I want you to tell me in your own way, the plot of the story.

HECTOR: Man, I can't do that!

TY: Try.

HECTOR: Shit. Why you make me do this shit for?

TY: Take your time.

HECTOR: Man, every day you think up some new shit.

TY: Speak in your own words. Don't try to imitate the poet—who is?

HECTOR: Home run.

TY: Homer.

HECTOR: Yeah.

TY: I want you to pretend you just saw a movie called "The Iliad." You come out of the movie house. You walk down the street. On the corner you find your homies. They say, Hey, Hector, where you been, man. Tell 'em about the movie. In your own words. (*This appeals to Hector.*)

HECTOR: Don't see it, man.

TY: Tell 'em the story.

HECTOR: There was this Trojan dude, Paris. Not the city, man. I'm talkin' 'bout the *man*, Paris.

TY: Good.

HECTOR: One day he stay at the house o' some Greek dude wif red hair.

TY: Menaleaus.

HECTOR: Yeah. And the dude had a foxy ass wife, Helen. And Paris take one look at her and say, You the finest shit I ever seen. And she say, Don't be talkin' that shit to me, man. And he say, You know you like it. And she say, My man find out, he gonna mess you up bad. And he say, Shit, man, it be worff it. And she say, Jump away, fool. And he say, Yo, mama, how you like a man of my complexion to walk in your direction and give you a little affection? And she smile, right?, and he know she dig him bad, right?, so he cop that babe, right? Take her back home to Troy.

TY: What's Troy?

HECTOR: Some city on a hill wif a big ass wall around it, man. And ten times a day he be dippin' in that Greek meat.

TY: You've taken a few liberties.

HECTOR: It's 'tween the lines, m'man, it's 'tween the lines.

TY: Just stick to the lines.

HECTOR: So now the Greek gang-bangers say, "Whoa, jack, what's comin' down here, man? Them Trojan fools slicked us, man! Jump in the ships and let's go wax some Trojan ass!"

TY: Good.

HECTOR: So the Greeks bring the baddest dude they could find. Killies of the fast feet. They call this dude the panic maker 'cause when this dude throw his spear, his spear hit what he throw it at. Nobody to be messin' wit, jack.

TY: And what about the Trojans?

HECTOR: Don't be interruptin' me, bro. Get some discipline, man. Now the Trojans had a major dude, too. And we are talkin' about noble lion-hearted Hector o' the flashy helmet, tamer o' horses, a bad ass bro and a righteous dude! (*Hector shadowboxes like a boxer just announced. Ty whistles and applauds.*) Hector brave and Hector strong and Hector handsome and Hector—

TY: All right, all right, get on with the story.

HECTOR: And when Helen see him she say, Whoa, what's happenin', dude? and she drop her cookies right there, man.

TY: That's not in the "Iliad."

HECTOR: I was jus' testin' you, bro. So Hector go to his brother, Paris, and he say, "Paris, why you go and poke that babe, Helen? A lotta dudes gonna die ugly 'cause o' you. But, shit, you my bro and I gotta defend you now."

TY: Excellent!

HECTOR: So the Greeks and Trojans rumble ten years, right? And the Greeks are kickin' ass. But dig this shit: Killies is pissed.

TY: Why?

HECTOR: There was this chick he wanted.

TY: Briseis.

HECTOR: Yeah. But the boss man got her.

TY: Who?

HECTOR: Agamoron.

TY: Agamemnon.

HECTOR: Yeah . . . So Killies say, "Hang it up, you fools! You cop my babe, I ain't fightin' no war, jack!" So Killies cut out, man, and stay in this tent and smoke a little weed, and the Greeks start losin' bad, right?

TY: Very good.

HECTOR: So Killies' main man—

TY: Patroclus.

HECTOR: Yeah. He put on Killies' armor and go out gunnin' for Hector, right? And Hector say, "Shiiiiit, man," and jump off his chariot like a lion and spear that fool, and that dude say, "Ahhhhh."

TY: And the outcome?

HECTOR: So now Killies come gunnin' for Hector, right? The cat beserk, man. He kill the first thousand dudes he see just for chuckles, man, and one o' them dudes be Hector's little brother.

TY: Polydorus.

HECTOR: Yeah. So now—Hector pissed! So check it out, man. Killies and Hector meet, right? And Killies say, "Yo, son, you offed m'main man. Now you get iced." And Hector say, "Shiiiiiiit, you be illin', man. You offed m'bro. Now you gonna go!" And Killies laugh and say, what you gonna do when I'm stompin' all over you? And Hector say, "Maaaaan, you so full o' shit, you should have a toilet flush on your jaw—C'mon, Greek boy, show me what you got!" And they fight, right? . . . And Hector smokes Killies.

TY: Excuse me.

HECTOR: The end, jack! The end!

TY: That's not what happened, and you know it.

HECTOR: Shit.

TY: Tell it the way it really happened.

HECTOR: Killies cheated.

TY: How?

HECTOR: Don't be readin' me no more books, teacher! You puttin' snakes in my head again, man!

TY: Cheated? *Cheated*? What do you mean he cheated?

HECTOR: Jump away from me, jack.

TY: Achilles and Hector met and the best man won.

HECTOR: No, man. He cheated.

TY: Where do you get this word 'cheated'? How'd he cheat?

HECTOR: He just did.

TY: How?

HECTOR: Man, if you don't know, you one dumb fool. (*Exit Hector.*)

TY: Big man beats up people in the subways but he's afraid of an idea! Afraid of words, bro? (*Enter Hector.*)

HECTOR: Killies throw his spear and it miss, right? And that bitch goddess—Athena! She go get it and give it back to Killies! What's that, man? You ever see that shit in the Olympics? But when Hector spear miss, who go get his spear, man? Zip, jack, zip!

TY: Maybe you got a point there.

HECTOR: Not maybe, dude. Definitely.

TY: So it was two against one.

HECTOR: That's right.

TY: Like you and two dudes when you jump a suit.

HECTOR: That's different, man!

TY: How's it different?

HECTOR: It jus' is!

TY: No. It was two against one.

HECTOR: No, man.

TY: Killies wolfpacked Hector.

HECTOR: No, man.

TY: And Hector ran away.

HECTOR: No, man, I don't play that shit.

TY: He didn't run away?

HECTOR: What he gonna do, man? If Killies gonna wolfpack 'em, then, shit, dude, you get some legs, too!

TY: But Killies caught him and killed him.

HECTOR: That goddess help him!

TY: No, bro. Killies had faster feet. Lions and zebras.

HECTOR: For a teacher, man, you some dumb shit.

TY: That lion need meat, jack.

HECTOR: No, man.

TY: Hector have legs, man. If he too slow, that's life, bro.

HECTOR: No, man. Killies a savage. Hector noble!

TY: What's noble?

HECTOR: Hector loves his wife, love his kid, defend his bro. That noble, man.

TY: Noble is bullshit. Lions and zebras.

HECTOR: No, man. Then why Killies drag Hector 'round Troy by his ankles in front of his wife and mother and father and all his soldiers, man?

TY: Hector a zebra. Killies a lion.

HECTOR: No, man.

TY: The end, jack. The end!

HECTOR: That shit wrong, man.

TY: Where did you pick up this bullshit word 'wrong'? Lions and zebras, man.

HECTOR: No, man. No, man. Killies an animal. Hector a man. Hector down in the dust wif Killies' spear in his neck, right? And Killies say, If I was hungry, jack, I eat you raw. What's that shit, man? That a human being or an animal? That shit wrong.

TY: Why?

HECTOR: 'Cause it is!

TY: Buy why?

HECTOR: It wrong because it wrong!

TY: Yes! (*Pause.*) Yes, yes, yes.

HECTOR: Shut up, man. You never told me this shit can kill ya, know what I'm sayin'?

TY: No, tell me. What? Tell me.

HECTOR: We see this old suit go in the baffroom, right? Train station. So Tito watch for the cops. Me and King go vic the old suit. He in the stall, right? We wait till his pants down and we kick in the door. I pop him and he say, Please, please, and we hold his chest. We don't find nothin' in his pockets, right, so we grab his rings and watch, and his face turn blue, and he say, Please, please, call a doctor, and he fall down and die. Heart attack, right? I just wanted his cash, man. I didn't wanna smoke him, bro. Then Tito holler, Somebody comin', so we ran. What else could we do, man, know what I'm sayin'? Sometimes I wakes up in the middle of the night and see his face all blue and hear him screamin', Please, please . . . (*Enter Georgiane with a bundled blanket over her shoulder . . . She lays the bundle at Hector's feet.*)

TY: What's that?

GEORGIANE: Tell him, Hector . . . I've been waiting for the first snow so I could follow Hector's tracks and find out where he goes . . . And his tracks led me to a hunter's tree stand . . . This is your chance, Hector.

TY: Chance for what?

GEORGIANE: Tell Ty your little secret.

HECTOR: I ain't got no secret.

GEORGIANE: Tell Ty where you go and what you do.

HECTOR: Ty, we doin' our lesson today or what, bro?

GEORGIANE: Is that what you want? (*She writes on the blackboard "HECTOR IS A THIEF."*)

TY: What are you doing?

HECTOR: That's my name.

GEORGIANE: Very good.

HECTOR: Hector is a . . .

GEORGIANE: A what?

TY: What the hell are you doing?

HECTOR: Thhh . . . eeef.

GEORGIANE: You did it, didn't you? Say it. Say it.

HECTOR: Your woman crazy, Ty.

GEORGIANE: Show Ty. Open it. It's all yours.

HECTOR: That ain't mine.

GEORGIANE: I found it up your tree stand.

HECTOR: That ain't my shit, man.

TY: Open it. (*Ty begins to open it. Georgiane stops him.*)

GEORGIANE: No! You open it!

HECTOR: I ain't touchin' it. (*Ty opens the blanket. Inside are radios, liquor bottles, etc.*)

TY: What's this?

GEORGIANE: They're not your footprints from our kitchen door to

296 / *William Mastrosimone*

the tree stand?

HECTOR: Talk wif your woman, man.

GEORGIANE: You talk to me! You answer me!

HECTOR: You play chicken wif me, mama, you lose. See, man, you hate me right from the jump, man, right from the jump.

GEORGIANE: You tell it to the police.

HECTOR: I go to the big house, man, I ain't goin' alone. You dig that?

GEORGIANE: What do you mean?

HECTOR: I'm gonna have some company.

GEORGIANE: What company?

HECTOR: You keep bitchin', mama, and you gonna find out what company.

GEORGIANE: Ty? (*Pause.*) What's he mean?

HECTOR: You gonna run this farm by yourself. That's what I mean.

GEORGIANE: What's he saying?

HECTOR: She take somptin' from me, bro, I take somptin' from her.

GEORGIANE: Take what from me?

HECTOR: Your man . . . Catch this shit, mama . . . I just say Ty help me.

GEORGIANE: And who'd believe you?

HECTOR: Ty believe me, 'cause that the way it is, man.

GEORGIANE: What's he saying?

TY: I wanted to give him another chance.

HECTOR: Ty help me . . . You help a dude, it just like you did it too.

GEORGIANE: You knew?

TY: Yes.

GEORGIANE: You knew and you didn't tell me?

TY: I made him mail the money back.

GEORGIANE: It's always been me and you. Me and you. And you didn't tell me? You put our home . . . our home! . . . on the line for this thief?

TY: If he went up for this, he'd just keep going like Sam. (*Georgiane strikes Ty.*)

GEORGIANE: Sam's dead. Put him in the grave because he's starting to stink around here!

HECTOR: Man, this woman mess up your mind.

TY: Shut up!

HECTOR: You tell her to shut up, man.

GEORGIANE: Look, he's laughing in your face.

HECTOR: You tell this lady she want to be alone out here workin' this farm by herself, just keep mouthin' at me.

TY: How can you say that?

HECTOR: I ain't talkin' to you, man! I'm talkin' to her! (*Ty grabs Hector by his shirt and throws him around the room.*)

TY: How can you say that to me?

HECTOR: Don't make me pop you, bro.

TY: C'mon, pop me.

GEORGIANE: No, Ty, no.

HECTOR: Don't make me, Ty, man.

TY: C'mon, 'bortion! (*He slams Hector against the wall. Georgiane tries to stop him. Ty bounces him off the floor.*) Get away from me!

GEORGIANE: Ty!

TY: What's left for you now?

GEORGIANE: Don't!

TY: When you trash the people who care for you, what's left for you in the whole world? Who's your friend? What's left now? Where can you go? What can you do? Who can you call when you hurt?

HECTOR: Nobody, man! Nobody!

TY: I took you in! I fed you! Protected you! Gave you everything I had! How could you throw it all away for a mess of junk? (*Pause. Ty drops Hector.*)

HECTOR: What'd you 'spect from a streetdog, man? (*Pause. Exit Ty. Pause. Exit Georgiane. Lights down on Hector in the barn. Lights up on the kitchen. Enter Ty. Enter Georgiane. Enter Hector.*) Hey, Ty, man, let's go cut some cords of logs, man, 'case it gets cold out.

TY: Get your stuff and leave.

HECTOR: Bro?

TY: You heard me.

HECTOR: Like what do you mean?

TY: Get your things and go. Get out.

HECTOR: Where'my gonna go, man?

TY: I don't care.

HECTOR: The gang, man.

TY: I don't care.

HECTOR: The gang waitin' for me, man.

TY: Well, go with the gang and we'll read about you in the paper. Get gone.

HECTOR: Look me in the eye and say that, bro.

TY: Go! Get out! Now!

HECTOR: Some kid hang hisself at the Youf House, man, 'cause he 'scaped and they brough' him back. (*Ty grabs Hector by the shoulders and shoves him towards the door.*) I can't be no kine 'o person there, man, know what I'm sayin'?

TY: What kind of person are you here?

HECTOR: You gotta let me slide one more time, man.

TY: Forget it.

HECTOR: 'Cause they don't make no pie there, Georgiane. They don't make no good stuff like yours. I never sleeped in no bed wif clean sheets. I rather live in the woods, man, if I can't stay here.

TY: Maybe that's where you belong.

HECTOR: I'm gonna run wif the dogs, man.

TY: Good, get out.

HECTOR: That some cold shit, man.

TY: I'll tell you some cold shit, man. It's when you trash the people who care for you.

HECTOR: I ohways blow it, man, I ohways blow it. S'pose—

TY: No.

HECTOR: S'pose I change.

TY: Change?

HECTOR: I can change, man.

TY: Get your bullshit out this door.

HECTOR: Why, man? Why can't I learn my lesson now and change?

TY: Go change somewhere else.

HECTOR: I jus' never had the chance, man. I can do it, Georgiane.

GEORGIANE: Hector, I wish I could believe you but I don't. Nothing you can say will change my mind.

HECTOR: I'm gonna show yous, man! Someday you bowf gonna know yous was wrong.

GEORGIANE: We hope you do, but right now it's just all words, Hector, and we've heard it all before. You made fools of us.

HECTOR: But I'm sorry, Georgiane, man, I am, I am, I really really am.

GEORGIANE: We've heard that, too, Hector.

HECTOR: So you jus' think I'm some scumdog, right?

GEORGIANE: No.

HECTOR: Ain't no good, ain't never gonna be no good. Jus' born for the hard house, right, man? Born for a shiv 'tween my ribs, right? Born for a sawed-off to make a splatter on a wall somewheres, right? Well maybe you don't know me, man. Maybe you don't know me at all. (*Picks up the phone, dials 911.*) . . . Hey, what's happenin', man? Know all the farms ripped off? Well, guess what, man? I'm the dude, . . . Hector St. Vincent, and I ripped off another place you don't even know about, so yous better come get me . . . You know Ty and Georgiane Fletcher? . . . Yeah . . . they let me use their phone . . . And, oh yeah, you can call the Youf House in Trenton, man . . . My counsellor, Mr. Quackenboss . . . that fool can tell you all about me, man . . . Yeah, I be waitin' right here, man, right? (*He hangs up the phone. Pause. To himself.*) Ahh, man, why I go do that for? (*Seeing Ty and Georgiane stunned.*) Shit, yous don't even believe I called the chauffeurs, do ya? Well, you bowf gonna see how wrong you be when the chauffeurs pull up and smash my face on the hot hood of the bubblegum machine and make my wrist bleed wif the cuffs and hit my head when they shove me in the back seat. Don't be too proud, man, 'cause maybe I'm gonna run now. Shit, my homies are gonna come down hard on me for this shit. Nobody gonna truss me nohow. I'm worser than a snitch, man. I snitched on myself. Tito gonna whip my ass every damn day for this.

TY: You remember when Hector first saw Achilles?

HECTOR: Yeah.

TY: How did he feel?

HECTOR: Ascared.

TY: Why?

HECTOR: He knew he was gonna get wasted, man.

TY: And what'd he do?

HECTOR: Ran.

TY: Achilles chased him around Troy three times and then?

HECTOR: He turn and fight.

TY: Why?

HECTOR: Don't know.

TY: The poem tells why. (*Hands Hector the Iliad.*) Yours.

HECTOR: Your mother and father give you that, man.

TY: Now I'm giving it to you.

HECTOR: I can't hardly read it.

TY: You'll have a lot of time on your hands, I think, alone. (*After a long hesitation, Hector takes it, sits, flips aimlessly through the pages.*)

GEORGIANE: Do they allow visitors?

HECTOR: Sunday.

GEORGIANE: Pie?

HECTOR: Don't know.

GEORGIANE: I'll call and ask.

HECTOR: Can you make the pie different?

GEORGIANE: Yeah, sure, how different?

HECTOR: Can you be puttin' a hacksaw blade wit the apples?

GEORGIANE: I'll make that pie real special.

HECTOR: Don't even try
t'improve your pie.

GEORGIANE: But I'd like to try
to go sky high
to help you get by.

HECTOR: Now why would the FBI
want to go satisfy
a streetdog who dissed you and Ty?
None o' this you can deny.

GEORGIANE: True, we didn't see eye to eye.
Everyday your crap would multiply.
When you robbed neighbors on the sly
You stung my heart like a horsefly.

HECTOR: That ain't no lie!
So how do you justify
a beautiful apple pie?
I leff my room a pigsty.
I gave you the evil eye.

GEORGIANE: This is my reply:
When you made me cry
I could drop you in a deep-fry,
but after your call, by and by,
I saw another guy,
and it would gratify
both me and Ty
to see you flying high
and that is why
the FBI
just can't say goodbye . . .

Tamer of Horses / **301**

I really hate to be so crass

but I just kicked your poetic ass.

HECTOR: She all right, man! Your lady all right! (*Sound of a car coming up the gravel driveway. Ty looks out the window.*) My chauffeur here?

TY: Yeah.

GEORGIANE: Now you call us, okay?

HECTOR: 'Kay.

GEORGIANE: Ty, write our number down, please? And tell us what you need.

HECTOR: 'Kay. (*A loud authoritative knock on the door. Hector falls to pieces. Georgiane embraces him. Ty exits to answer the door. Georgiane rocks Hector in her arms. He cries like the day he was born. Enter Ty.*) I don't want you see me wit the cuffs, 'kay? So yous stay here. Don't be lookin' out the winda either, 'kay? Man, one day you be seein' an old man wit a cane come up your driveway. Jus' say, yo, Hector.

GEORGIANE: Take care, okay?

HECTOR: I knew a man

His name was Ty

He was cool

Not cool as I

He had a lady

She taught school

Believe me, jack,

the 'frigerator call her cool. (*He starts to go, stops, turns, points at Ty.*) Man, now you 'member all I taught you. (*Exit Hector. Ty sits. Beat. Georgiane sits next to him. We hear a car door slam shut and then the car fades away down the driveway. Ty and Georgiane face each other as the lights fade.*)

END

SUNSHINE

SUNSHINE was first produced in 1989 at the Circle Rep, New York City, NY. The play was directed by Marshall Mason with the following cast:

SUNSHINE .... Jennifer Jason Leigh
NELSON .... John Dossett
ROBBIE .... Jordon Mott

Characters

SUNSHINE
ROBBY
NELSON
JERRY

Setting

TIME: Now.
SET: *A private booth.* Sunshine's booth should be separated from the customer's booth with plexiglass. The only communication from one side to another is by a phone whose cord should be long enough to give her freedom of movement. Her side should have a rack with interesting changes of clothing. The booth should be angled so that in Scene One we see Sunshine from the customer's point of view. In Scene Three, we see the customer from Sunshine's point of view. Her side also has a door.
A street-level apartment. We should feel that Nelson hasn't accepted this place as his residence, that it's only a temporary hideaway. When he moved here, Nelson stacked all his possessions in one place, and as he needed things (dishes, pots, pans, clothes, etc.), he pulled them from cardboard boxes. So we see sealed boxes as well as open boxes, clothes hanging out when he needed something in a rush, or boxes with ripped corners or split sides when he was looking for something.

Somewhere we see a crisp, white uniform shirt with a paramedic patch on the pocket and sleeve, gold and blue, with a black pair of pants. The pants and shirt are sharp, well-tailored and durable.

There's a set of weights, a pile of laundry with the same kinds of pants and shirts, dark socks, underwear and t-shirts, and sheets. On one of the shirts we see a bit of blood. He obviously doesn't have company over or he wouldn't leave this mess so exposed.

SUNSHINE

Scene 1

A booth in a porn house. The scene opens in pitch blackness with a gradual rise of light. We see SUNSHINE from ROBBY's point of view.

SUNSHINE: Bet you have lots of girls.

ROBBY: Not really.

SUNSHINE: What's that smile? C'mon, cutie, how many girls you got?

ROBBY: One.

SUNSHINE: Can't fool me. You been in other booths?

ROBBY: Yeah, but it's a waste of time. And money.

SUNSHINE: What's amatter?

ROBBY: I don't know.

SUNSHINE: Raunchy?

ROBBY: Yeah. Awful.

SUNSHINE: Now you know where to come first, huh?

ROBBY: Yeah.

SUNSHINE: So what's your major?

ROBBY: Chemistry. How'd you know I'm in college?

SUNSHINE: I know everything about you, so be careful what you think. You have a smile that makes me wet, you know that? You blushin'?

ROBBY: No.

SUNSHINE: I'm gonna love this. You're sweet.

ROBBY: A lot of college guys come here?

SUNSHINE: Pretty lot, but not cute as you.

ROBBY: What do they do here?

SUNSHINE: Whatever they dream about. Far away from home?

ROBBY: North Dakota.

SUNSHINE: Farm boy?

ROBBY: Yeah.

SUNSHINE: Cow farm?

ROBBY: Hogs.

SUNSHINE: Ever go up in the hayloft and look at all that sweet-smellin' straw and wish you had a girl up there? I know you, don't I? S'pose you and me went up there ... What do you think would happen? Put some money in the slot, 'kay?

ROBBY: Okay.

SUNSHINE: How much did you put in?

ROBBY: Five.

SUNSHINE: Oh, babe, it's a dollar a minute. What'm I, a five-minute thing in your life?

ROBBY: That's all I have.

SUNSHINE: You're so cute when you lie.

ROBBY: Honest.

SUNSHINE: Pull out them pockets, you. (*He laughs, pulls out his pockets, pulls out some money.*) What's that green paper stuff, sweetie pie?

ROBBY: My supper money for the weekend.

SUNSHINE: Why don't you have me for supper? Put in ten. (*He laughs, puts in ten dollars.*) Should we get to know each other a little bit? What would you like to know about me?

ROBBY: I don't know.

SUNSHINE: I'll tell you anything you want to know before we lay down in the straw.

ROBBY: I don't know.

SUNSHINE: I'll tell you a secret if you tell me one, okay?

ROBBY: Okay.

SUNSHINE: I got a lover but he really doesn't know how to make me happy, that's why I work here. And I'm dyin'. Dyin' for love. There, I made a fool of myself.

ROBBY: No, no, no.

SUNSHINE: Now you tell me a secret.

ROBBY: I could say the same thing.

SUNSHINE: Really?

ROBBY: Yeah.

SUNSHINE: How can I make you happy, sweetie?

ROBBY: I don't know.

SUNSHINE: Anything you want. I'm here. Huh?

ROBBY: I don't know.

SUNSHINE: You wanna ride the mean train to Hogtown?

ROBBY: Yeah. (*Beat.*) What do you mean?

SUNSHINE: I mean it's just me and you, baby, and I'll do anything for you. Anything. You just ask me and I'll be happy to do what makes you happy. Any any anything. Where else can you get anything you want? Here. Only here. With me.

ROBBY: What time you get off work?

SUNSHINE: I wish I could, honey, but they'll fire me for that, and I need the job bad.

ROBBY: I won't tell.

SUNSHINE: I'm sorry, I'd love to, but we have to do it here. We have to do it now. You wanna see me?

ROBBY: Yeah.

SUNSHINE: What do you wanna see first?

ROBBY: I don't care.

SUNSHINE: You care. What?

ROBBY: I don't know.

SUNSHINE: You want me to put on something special for you? Bikini? Nightie? Jeans?

ROBBY: No.

SUNSHINE: Nothing?

ROBBY: Yeah.

SUNSHINE: You mind if I just open my robe? I get goose bumps in here. (*She opens bathrobe.*) See anything you like?

ROBBY: You're beautiful.

SUNSHINE: Undo your pants.

ROBBY: What for?

SUNSHINE: So I can see you.

ROBBY: What for?

SUNSHINE: I like it. Don't you wanna make me happy too?

ROBBY: Yeah.

SUNSHINE: I know you. I know all about you. Don't ask me how. I just do. I know how to love you. How to take care of you. All you have to do is let me. And I could make your puppy bark, you know.

ROBBY: What do you mean?

SUNSHINE: C'mon, undo those pants.

ROBBY: Is there a lock on this door?

SUNSHINE: Nobody comes in. You can turn the light off. See the switch? It's just us. (*ROBBY turns off the light in his booth.*) Whoa! What do you call that thing, killer? You have a terrific laugh, you know that? You're all ready, ain't ya? Me, too. Oh God, this is gonna be beautiful. The way you look at me, oh, stop, stop, or

I'm gonna come all over you … (*She sits, the flats of her feet on the glass between them. SUNSHINE is never exposed to the audience throughout this play.*) Is this good?

ROBBY: Yeah.

SUNSHINE: You tell me what you like, oh, please, please, you make me feel like a woman . . . Is this good?

ROBBY: Yeah.

SUNSHINE: You're good, you're so good . . . Don't stop, just don't stop, please, please, don't stop . . .

ROBBY: It's okay?

SUNSHINE: Yes.

ROBBY: It's okay in here?

SUNSHINE: Yes, yes.

ROBBY: Can I? Can I?

SUNSHINE: Yes, yes, yes … look at that … look at you . . . You're incredible . . . You're the kind of man I been lookin' for . . . Babe?

ROBBY: Yeah?

SUNSHINE: Would you mind cleanin' up before you go? Thank you, baby. You're such a good lover. Your girl tell you that?

ROBBY: No.

SUNSHINE: Oh, God, you're everything a man should be.

ROBBY: Thanks.

SUNSHINE: Don't say thanks. I'm just tellin' the truth. You know, you should let your hair grow.

ROBBY: Yeah?

SUNSHINE: I mean, you're perfect, but I like something to hang onto when I'm ridin' the mean train to Hogtown. (*He laughs.*) You gonna come back and see me?

ROBBY: Yeah.

SUNSHINE: Tomorrow?

ROBBY: I'm a little broke right now.

SUNSHINE: Was I okay?

ROBBY: You're beautiful.

SUNSHINE: You'll find the money.

ROBBY: Okay.

SUNSHINE: Can't wait.

ROBBY: I'll wait for you in the parking lot after work.

SUNSHINE: Sweetheart, I really wish I could. (*The red light begins to flash.*) See you tomorrow, okay?

ROBBY: Yeah.

SUNSHINE: Promise?

ROBBY: Yeah.

SUNSHINE: Me and you could have a beautiful thing.

ROBBY: Yeah.

SUNSHINE: You coulda had any girl you wanted in the whole place, beautiful girls, but you chose me.

ROBBY: You're beautiful.

SUNSHINE: I love you. I do. You made me so happy. (*The screen starts to come down. End Scene 1.*)

Scene 2

NELSON's studio apartment. It's raining on a cold November night. There are flashes of lighting without thunder. Blue-tinted street light comes through a sheet (used as a curtain) over a window. Otherwise it's quite dark in the small room. We see silhouettes of raindrops trickling down the window. NELSON, in his underwear, on his back on the couch, one leg over the armrest, one arm over his face, is asleep while the stereo murmurs a Frank Sinatra ballad. A sudden rumble of a garbage can startles NELSON. He springs up, sees an amorphous silhouette on the sheet curtain, turns off the music, goes to the window, pulls back the curtain and flicking on the outdoor light at the same time, sees the back of SUNSHINE's head. She turns, face to face with NELSON, and they talk through the glass.

SUNSHINE: Sir? Help me? Please? Sir?

NELSON: Move it! And don't leave your goddamn needles out there!

SUNSHINE: Somebody's after me! Turn out the light, please? (*Beat.*) Please! (*NELSON opens the door slightly, keeping the chain fastened. SUNSHINE slips her hand and foot in the space.*) Let me in?

NELSON: Hands out!

SUNSHINE: He's gonna hurt me! (*Sound of a van screeching wheels around a corner.*) Oh God! Don't let him hurt me, please? (*NELSON opens the door. She bolts in. He closes and locks it, turns off the outdoor light. Darkness once again. She hides, he peers through the sheet curtain.*)

NELSON: There's a van double parked.

SUNSHINE: Palm trees and sunset on the side?

NELSON: Yeah. You do something wrong? It's a cop.

SUNSHINE: Security guard.

NELSON: He's got a gun … Crossing the street.

SUNSHINE: Oh God.

NELSON: He picked up something from the sidewalk.

SUNSHINE: Glittery?

NELSON: Yeah.

SUNSHINE: My shoe heel.

NELSON: He's looking at this door.

SUNSHINE: Oh, shit.

NELSON: Here he comes. (*NELSON picks up something for a weapon.*)

SUNSHINE: You got a back door?

NELSON: No. He stopped.

SUNSHINE: What's that door?

NELSON: Bathroom. He's coming.

SUNSHINE: Oh, shit.

NELSON: Shh. (*The silhouette of JERRY appears at the door, backlit by the blue streetlight. He knocks. Beat. Knocks again, harder. Beat. SUNSHINE makes a sound. Beat. The silhouette tries to look in the door's window. Beat. The silhouette goes away. Beat.*)

SUNSHINE: Where is he?

NELSON: Looking in my mailbox. He's leaving. (*Sound of the van door opening and slamming shut, and sound of the van pulling away.*)

SUNSHINE: Can I use your bathroom? (*Exit SUNSHINE into the bathroom. She vomits. She's one of those people who sounds like she's dying. He puts on sweat pants and T-shirt. Beat.*)

NELSON: You all right?

SUNSHINE: (*Offstage.*) Oh, God. (*More vomiting. Beat.*)

NELSON: Excuse me?

SUNSHINE: (*Offstage.*) I hate this. (*More vomiting. Beat.*)

NELSON: Hello?

SUNSHINE: (*Offstage.*) There goes the pizza. (*More vomiting. Beat.*)

NELSON: You okay?

SUNSHINE: (*Offstage.*) I think it's over.

NELSON: Make sure. Want the light on?

SUNSHINE: (*Offstage.*) No! If I see it, I'll puke again.

NELSON: It's better you get it all out. (*He flicks on the bathroom light which makes her vomit violently.*) Cheap wine?

SUNSHINE: (*Offstage*) Don't remind me. I'm trying to think of nice things. Daisies. Puppies. Double dip chocolate ice cream. (*She flushes the toilet and re-enters patting herself with a towel.*) You got aspirins?

NELSON: Help yourself to a towel.

SUNSHINE: I did.

NELSON: Your knee's bleeding. (*He gets aspirins out of a doctor's bag.*)

SUNSHINE: I know. He's parked out there, down the street somewheres. I can feel it. (*He hands her a glass of water. She doesn't take it.*) You got a beer? (*She opens the refrigerator.*)

NELSON: No.

SUNSHINE: Yes you do. (*He takes the beer away from her and closes the fridge.*)

NELSON: Watch yourself. (*She opens the refrigerator again.*)

SUNSHINE: (*Beat.*) I'm sorry—I'm drunk. (*Beat.*) You got something rotten in your frig. (*Beat. He looks in, slams it shut. SUNSHINE sees a bottle of champagne with a pretty ribbon by NELSON's suitcase*) What's the occasion? I never had pink champagne.

NELSON: Hey, keep your hands off. You want a bandage?

SUNSHINE: No!

NELSON: Feet off the furniture.

SUNSHINE: Sorry.

NELSON: You do one more thing—

SUNSHINE: Please don't put me out there now. I'm sorry. I'll be good. (*Beat.*) You a doctor?

NELSON: Paramedic.

SUNSHINE: What's the difference?

NELSON: Two hundred thou. (*Beat.*) I drive an ambulance.

SUNSHINE: You can go through red lights and they can't give you a ticket?

NELSON: Yeah. Goodbye!

SUNSHINE: Fix me first.

NELSON: Sit there.

SUNSHINE: You have beautiful hands.

NELSON: Be still. You got cinders in there.

SUNSHINE: Hurts. (*He pulls them out with a tweezer. Beat.*) I was pronounced dead by an ambulance driver once.

NELSON: Was it ever confirmed?

SUNSHINE: What d'ya mean?

NELSON: Don't move.

SUNSHINE: Me and Jerry was in an accident and the van turned over and we was both in seat belts hangin' upside down

Sunshine / **311**

unconscious and the ambulance guy put his finger on my throat right here, and I could hear him even though I was blacked out, and he says to the other guy, "She's gone, work him." Then they pull me out, go through my wallet, see the back of my driver's license and says, "Hey, we got an organ donor over here," 'cause, you know, I believe in that, and I cough and they knew I was alive, and they gave me oxygen and couldn't do enough for me. I mean, who are you guys? God leave you in charge? That hurts!

NELSON: It's a minor cut, so shut up.

SUNSHINE: You talk to all you patients like that?

NELSON: Most of my patients are dead or unconscious.

SUNSHINE: Just your type, right?—I'm sorry.

NELSON: I said don't move.

SUNSHINE: I'm not used to men talking to me that way.

NELSON: Tough shit.

SUNSHINE: Give me that tweezer and I'll help you.

NELSON: Help me what?

SUNSHINE: Get that bug up your ass.

NELSON: How'd you get this?

SUNSHINE: Jumped out a van going a hundred miles an hour.

NELSON: Horseshit. You'd've broken both your legs, at least.

SUNSHINE: Well, it was going *fast*.

NELSON: Why'd you jump out?

SUNSHINE: He said he was going to crash into a brick wall and kill us both.

NELSON: Oh, we're talking about Mr. Wonderful here. Did he mean it?

SUNSHINE: You never know with Jerry. He's got problems.

NELSON: What's he, a regular customer?

SUNSHINE: Customer? I ain't no hooker!

NELSON: Oh.

SUNSHINE: Jesus!

NELSON: How do you know him?

SUNSHINE: I'm his wife.

NELSON: Sorry.

SUNSHINE: Oh, sure. After you besmirch somebody's reputation, you say "sorry"?

NELSON: What am I supposed to think?

SUNSHINE: You have to think the worst?

312 / *William Mastrosimone*

NELSON: What do you do?

SUNSHINE: Why don't you think the best?

NELSON: You work with Mother Teresa in the slums of Bombay.

SUNSHINE: You got a problem, you know that?

NELSON: You're a dancer.

SUNSHINE: Why do you say that?

NELSON: Wild guess.

SUNSHINE: Watch out for guesses, mister. They'll kill you every time. (*He dabs alcohol on cotton.*)

NELSON: This stings.

SUNSHINE: I don't feel nothing.

NELSON: Here goes.

SUNSHINE: Holy shit.

NELSON: Don't move.

SUNSHINE: Make it stop.

NELSON: It's not that bad.

SUNSHINE: Don't tell me. I feel it. Ever hear of Club Paradise?

NELSON: No. What is it?

SUNSHINE: It's a place where men can go to get what they can't get at home.

NELSON: What's it, a deli?

SUNSHINE: Men come to see me in a booth.

NELSON: A porn house?

SUNSHINE: You been there?

NELSON: No. I'm normal. Change the bandage every day.

SUNSHINE: I'm not a whore.

NELSON: You hear me?

SUNSHINE: You hear *me*?

NELSON: Yeah.

SUNSHINE: Men over there wanna get on their knees and adore me.

NELSON: I've been fighting the feeling.

SUNSHINE: Nobody touches me. There's a glass between me and my customers. Not for nothin' but my name's on the sign out front. Nobody else's. SUNSHINE THURSDAY, FRIDAY, SATURDAY NIGHTS. It's a big red neon on the highway. You never heard of me? Sunshine?

NELSON: Here's an extra bandage.

SUNSHINE: I'm famous.

NELSON: Famous to who? Creeps, loons, and jackoffs.

Sunshine / **313**

SUNSHINE: Most of my regulars got wives. Doctors and lawyers come see me. I got a professor who reads me poems. Businessmen. College kids.

NELSON: You're full of shit.

SUNSHINE: I never had an ambulance man. Come by sometime.

NELSON: I wouldn't be caught dead in that toilet.

SUNSHINE: They love me there. (*NELSON opens the door.*)

NELSON: Don't keep 'em waiting.

SUNSHINE: Thanks for saving my life.

NELSON: Anytime.

SUNSHINE: I owe you one.

NELSON: Right.

SUNSHINE: Take care of them beautiful hands.

NELSON: Yeah. (*Beat.*)

SUNSHINE: Wait.

NELSON: For what?

SUNSHINE: Can't you just wait a second? (*He closes the door slightly.*) How can you make me go? He's out there.

NELSON: I don't care, you understand?

SUNSHINE: He's gonna see me walkin' and roll down the window and say, "C'mon, get in," and we go home and have the same fight for the rest of our life.

NELSON: So don't get in.

SUNSHINE: How can I not when I hear his voice? He needs me so much. Oh, God, if I knew all my love for him was in my thumb, I'd bite it off and mail it to him. I even hate to talk about him. I feel like a cheater.

NELSON: You're all screwed up. Ever stop and think that maybe you make him crazy with that job of yours?

SUNSHINE: He got me the job. Can you think of a better job? Men say nice things, make me feel sexy, and pay me a lot. Bet I make more money than you.

NELSON: That's perfect for a screwed up world.

SUNSHINE: What can I say? Apply for a job. (*Beat.*) Can I stay here?

NELSON: Goodnight.

SUNSHINE: Just a little while till he goes?

NELSON: Don't even think about it.

SUNSHINE: I'm afraid to walk down the street now 'cause anybody could look at me and put me in their pocket. Do you know what I mean?

NELSON: No.

SUNSHINE: Can't you just believe me?

NELSON: You're drunk. Fresh air'll do you good.

SUNSHINE: Why's everybody so rotten? I hate this world. My soul hurts. You got anything for that, doc? Some day somebody's gonna look at me the wrong way and I'm not gonna say nothin' and I'm just gonna get on a train and change my name and cut my hair and when I see a little town, I'll get off and nobody'll know anything about me.

NELSON: You want a taxi?

SUNSHINE: And go where?

NELSON: I'm not a travel agent. Can I call somebody?

SUNSHINE: Who?

NELSON: You have a girlfriend?

SUNSHINE: No. Girls don't like me 'cause they're afraid I'll steal their men away.

NELSON: Okay, who?

SUNSHINE: My boss.

NELSON: What's his number?

SUNSHINE: No, I can't call Ara. She hates Jerry and I don't want her screaming at me tonight.

NELSON: Give me a number to call.

SUNSHINE: I can't think of one.

NELSON: What about your family?

SUNSHINE: My mother. I don't even know her number. I went to see her last Christmas.—Her trailer was gone. No forwarding address, no nothing—When I turned thirteen she said, "Girl, you're sitting on a gold mine." So you think I wanna call her?

NELSON: Well, do something because I'm busy.

SUNSHINE: Can I stay here?

NELSON: No.

SUNSHINE: All's I need's a little time to think. A little time to get my mind right.

NELSON: Not here.

SUNSHINE: Be a nice monster and let me take a nap?

NELSON: No. Off the bed.

SUNSHINE: Please, please, please, please, please? Don't make me go out there.

NELSON: Get lost.

SUNSHINE: A lotta men, you know, would love to have me stay in

Sunshine / 315

their apartment.

NELSON: Go find them. Move.

SUNSHINE: Let me just rest my eyes, babe?

NELSON: No.

SUNSHINE: Five minutes?

NELSON: Off.

SUNSHINE: I'm so sleepy from all that wine. Please, honey? (*She falls asleep.*)

NELSON: You can't sleep here. You have to go. Hey. Whoa. Hello? Jesus Christ. Hey! (*She doesn't move. He picks up the end of the bed and drops it. She springs up.*)

SUNSHINE: I just had the most amazing dream! I was in an airplane and we hit some turbulence and the wing caught fire and you were the pilot and I said, What now, Captain? And you said, We're gonna crash.

NELSON: You dreamt all that in two seconds? Hit the bricks.

SUNSHINE: How's it gonna hurt you if I sit here quiet?

NELSON: I'm expecting a phone call.

SUNSHINE: So.

NELSON: From my lady.

SUNSHINE: Your lady?

NELSON: Yeah.

SUNSHINE: Your lady.

NELSON: That's right.

SUNSHINE: That's beautiful.

NELSON: What?

SUNSHINE: You call her your lady.

NELSON: She's calling any minute now.

SUNSHINE: So if she hears a clit in the house, she might think the worst, huh?

NELSON: Maybe.

SUNSHINE: She don't trust you with another woman?

NELSON: It's a personal call.

SUNSHINE: When the phone rings, I leave, all right?

NELSON: No.

SUNSHINE: Don't make me go out there.

NELSON: Why don't you call the cops? Put the creep away.

SUNSHINE: He's my husband. We took vows. We said things to each other. Beautiful things. In a church. In front of people. I mean, why do we make those promises when we get married?

316 / *William Mastrosimone*

NELSON: So lawyers can eat.

SUNSHINE: You just don't understand.

NELSON: Use darker makeup. What you got don't hide the bruise he gave you.

SUNSHINE: You can't see nothing.

NELSON: Horseshit. I treat women like you all the time. I drive some of you right to the morgue with point-blank wounds. You lucky ones go to emergency where we try to put some of your teeth back in, splint your arms. And then Prince Charming shows up and you're back in love, until next time. I know 'em all by their first names now.

SUNSHINE: I leave and he'll die of heart attack.

NELSON: Horseshit.

SUNSHINE: Everything's horseshit to you.

NELSON: That's because most things in the world are horseshit.

SUNSHINE: Well, for your information, doc, his heart whispers.

NELSON: Whispers?

SUNSHINE: You're almost a doctor and don't know that?

NELSON: Whispers?

SUNSHINE: That's right.

NELSON: You mean murmurs.

SUNSHINE: Same thing, same thing.

NELSON: Nobody stays with anybody 'less they're gettin' something back.

SUNSHINE: Seventeenth of every month I fall apart, can't get out of bed, 'cause I get my period, hide under the covers, and Jerry's there feedin' me soup, spoon by spoon, holdin' me, sponge-bathin' me, holdin' me. I look forward to them five days.

NELSON: So for five good days a month you take twenty-five bad ones. Not too smart.

SUNSHINE: You just besmirched the whole meaning of what I mean.

NELSON: You're just as sick as he is.

SUNSHINE: You must've never been in love in your life, 'cause if you was you'd know if you had a choice between love and rotten fish you'd eat the rotten fish 'cause that can only make you vomit three days. But love, if it's real, stays and stays and stays. (*Beat. She goes to the door.*) My knee's killing me.

NELSON: Must be love.

SUNSHINE: Shut up.

NELSON: That means it's starting to heal.

SUNSHINE: Do I have to go? (*Beat.*)

NELSON: That phone rings, you are out that door by the second ring.

SUNSHINE: Thank you. (*Beat.*) Thank you very much. (*Beat.*) I really, really —

NELSON: Okay, okay.

SUNSHINE: So I'll just sit here and shut up. (*Beat.*) That phone rings, I'm gone. (*Beat.*) Could be any second now, huh?

NELSON: Yeah.

SUNSHINE: When was the last time you saw your lady?

NELSON: Five months ago.

SUNSHINE: What d'you do, tie it in a knot? (*Beat.*) What do you do for love and affection?

NELSON: Take a Valium.

SUNSHINE: She beautiful?

NELSON: What's beautiful?

SUNSHINE: If she's truly beautiful, you can't imagine her on the toilet. That her?

NELSON: No.

SUNSHINE: Liar. Skinny lips, but her face is, oh, so breathtaking. Now I know why you got that dyin' look on your face. You two serious? Of course you're serious, 'cause you're long distance. She make you scream?

NELSON: Scream?

SUNSHINE: You know. When you're *with* her.

NELSON: That's none of your business.

SUNSHINE: Sorry. (*Beat.*) Laundromat burn down? You're like me.

NELSON: Is that right?

SUNSHINE: You do your laundry when you're down to your last pair of underwear, right? (*Beat.*) I think I got cancer. I got a pain in my chest. (*Beat.*)

NELSON: Maybe it's just a pain in your chest. (*Beat.*)

SUNSHINE: Can I ask you a personal question?

NELSON: No.

SUNSHINE: Okay. (*Beat.*)

NELSON: What?

SUNSHINE: How come you can't look me in the eye?

NELSON: I look you in the eye.

SUNSHINE: For a second, then you look away. (*Beat.*) You have milk?

NELSON: Milk?

SUNSHINE: Regular milk.

NELSON: Yeah.

SUNSHINE: Can I have some?

NELSON: Help yourself.

SUNSHINE: Thank you.

NELSON: Glasses are in the thing.

SUNSHINE: I'd rather a bowl. (*She picks up the plastic bowl, makes a face, uses a kitchen towel to remove a smudge.*)

NELSON: What?

SUNSHINE: It's all right. You're a guy.

NELSON: I just washed that.

SUNSHINE: You missed a spot. Spoon?

NELSON: You want a tablecloth too? Drawer.

SUNSHINE: Everything you have's plastic. Spoons, forks. Paper plates.

NELSON: You like washing dishes?

SUNSHINE: Yeah.

NELSON: Well, I don't.

SUNSHINE: Food don't taste good on plastic. (*She puts the bowl on the table, takes a package of instant chocolate pudding from her purse, pours milk in the bowl, beats it with a spoon. NELSON watches.*)

NELSON: What's that, pudding?

SUNSHINE: I need it for when I get depressed. I bring it to work for my break. You think I look like Princess Diana?

NELSON: No.

SUNSHINE: Not a little?

NELSON: Not at all.

SUNSHINE: You think I should get my hair cut like her?

NELSON: What's her hair like?

SUNSHINE: Something like this and then it goes like this and then wham. She's something, don't you think?

NELSON: I wouldn't know.

SUNSHINE: You think I'm beautiful?

NELSON: I can't tell.

SUNSHINE: Well, look.

NELSON: I can't see underneath all that bullshit.

SUNSHINE: I only go to work like this. Ara says far as looks go I got nothing to look forward to. Once you get droopy eyelids you misewell marry the wolfman. I mean, some women blossom when they're fifteen and fall apart at twenty and that's it. And some are at their best at thirty-five. I work with this girl Barbara? You think I'm beautiful, you should see this piece of ass. But she don't have what I have. Men go to her once and never again. I got regulars who make appointments. But see, I gotta get out there and make it while I'm young 'cause my hair's my weakness. My lips could go any day now. My eyes are hanging in there. My bod's seen better days. But my hair was never there. (*Beat.*) You know, sometimes you're supposed to contradict people when they talk. You wanna lick the spoon?

NELSON: No thanks.

SUNSHINE: Yes you do!

NELSON: No I don't.

SUNSHINE: It's the best part.

NELSON: You.

SUNSHINE: You're a cutie.

NELSON: How long's this pudding take?

SUNSHINE: Five minutes.

NELSON: You used all my milk.

SUNSHINE: It says two cups. The carton wasn't even half full. You can't make it with less. It just lays in your stomach like a load of laundry.

NELSON: Now I got no milk for coffee and cereal in the morning.

SUNSHINE: You mad?

NELSON: What do you think?

SUNSHINE: Where's a store?

NELSON: Forget it. I'm leaving in the morning for a few days and I don't want things in the fridge.

SUNSHINE: Where ya going?

NELSON: Albuquerque.

SUNSHINE: What's there?

NELSON: It's halfway between us.

SUNSHINE: She's on the other coast?

NELSON: We'll meet in New Mexico for the weekend.

SUNSHINE: What's the occasion?

NELSON: Just to see each other.

SUNSHINE: I'm jealous! In a hotel?

NELSON: No, a garage. Of course a hotel.

SUNSHINE: With room service?

NELSON: Of course.

SUNSHINE: Where you can order anything you want and some cute boy brings it up on a silver tray?

NELSON: Yeah.

SUNSHINE: And when you come back to the room, you see somebody was there and turned down the covers and put a piece of chocolate on the pillow?

NELSON: The works.

SUNSHINE: That's really romantic.

NELSON: That's what the call's about.

SUNSHINE: That rat fuck.

NELSON: Who?

SUNSHINE: Jerry. He never did anything like that for me. (*Beat.*) And you got her favorite champagne, right?

NELSON: Yeah. Pudding's ready.

SUNSHINE: It's not five minutes yet.

NELSON: I'm busy here.

SUNSHINE: I can't go till I know where he is. Can I use your phone?

NELSON: Can't tie up the line.

SUNSHINE: Just to see if he's home?

NELSON: Quick.

SUNSHINE: You're a beautiful man. I wish I had a man with beautiful hands who called me his lady and looked like a lost puppy when he waited for me to call.

NELSON: Just make the call.

SUNSHINE: You mad again?

NELSON: Make the call.

SUNSHINE: Thank you. (*Dialing.*) I just hope he went home. (*To Jerry.*) It's me. I just called to say don't forget to feed Claws. Bye. I'm not telling you. Don't ask me where 'cause I'm not telling you. Jerry, you feed Claws right now. It *has to* eat twice a day. No. I'm not coming home till you change. No, I don't have your pills. I wouldn't take them. I'm positive. Absolutely sure. Wait. (*She looks in her purse, takes out a drugstore container of pills.*) Yeah. Well, I forgot! I took 'em to the drugstore and told the guy my husband takes these pills for his blood pressure, do they got side effects, and he said, "Definitely." (*She whispers.*) No, I didn't say your name. No, I tore the label off so nobody'd sees your name, thank you very much . . . Jerry? Jerry? Oh, God.

NELSON: What?

SUNSHINE: I think he's having a heart attack—Jerry?

NELSON: Give me that. (*NELSON takes the phone from her.*) Sir, I'm a paramedic . . . What're your symptoms? (*Apparently JERRY screams in NELSON's ear.*) Do you have a heart problem? (*JERRY screams again. NELSON hands the phone back to her.*) Creep.

SUNSHINE: (*On phone.*) I knew you wasn't dyin'! Some guy. Doctor. Yeah, I'm in the hospital. Where else would I find a doctor? He fixed my leg. I gotta go. The doctor wants to examine me. Seventy-five years old. Well, don't you trust me? Oh, that's nice. That's real nice.

NELSON: Don't tie up the phone.

SUNSHINE: Bye! (*She hangs up the phone. Beat.*) Can I call him back?

NELSON: No.

SUNSHINE: Quick?

NELSON: You are a real pain in my ass. Why do you want to call him again?

SUNSHINE: I shouldn't've teased him. He's delicate. He can't take it.

NELSON: He's a creep.

SUNSHINE: You don't know him. He's got some good points.

NELSON: I'm sure. He says he's sorry after he slugs you, right?

SUNSHINE: It only happened a couple times, and once I deserved it.

NELSON: Any man who hits a woman is a shit. And any woman who defends him is a bigger shit. What'd he do, starve your dog?

SUNSHINE: We ain't got no dog.

NELSON: Who's Claws?

SUNSHINE: My lobster.

NELSON: What's it, a pet?

SUNSHINE: Why else would I feed it?

NELSON: How dumb of me.

SUNSHINE: It's a living organism like anything else.

NELSON: It's an underwater roach that happens to taste good.

SUNSHINE: I can tell everything about a person by the way they treat an animal.

NELSON: I treat a lobster with lemon and butter. What's that say about me?

SUNSHINE: You're like everybody else.

322 / *William Mastrosimone*

NELSON: Must be tough being the only normal person in the world.

SUNSHINE: Jerry got two of 'em for our first anniversary supper but he stood me up and by the time he came home I got attached and gave 'em names and got an aquarium but Jerry forgot to feed 'em once and Claws ate Bug Eyes. You don't understand.

NELSON: No, I don't. (*The phone rings.*)

SUNSHINE: Albuquerque!

NELSON: Goodbye.

SUNSHINE: My pudding!

NELSON: Forget the pudding! (*Phone rings.*)

SUNSHINE: Good luck in Albuquerque!

NELSON: Thanks. Goodbye!

SUNSHINE: I'm jealous.

NELSON: Please? (*Phone rings.*)

SUNSHINE: Where's my purse?

NELSON: Where'd you put it?

SUNSHINE: If I knew that—

NELSON: Here! (*Phone rings.*)

SUNSHINE: What's your name?

NELSON: Why?

SUNSHINE: So I know what to call you when I remember you.

NELSON: Nelson.

SUNSHINE: Be happy, Nelson. (*He ushers her to the door. The phone stops ringing as he's about to pick it up. Beat.*) Oh shit. Oh shit. She's gonna call back. She thinks you was in the shower or something. Or she thinks she dialed the wrong number. I mean, she knows you're waiting. She's dialing right now. Right this very second. It's gonna ring any second. Here it goes. Here it comes.

NELSON: Yeah?

SUNSHINE: Here it comes.

NELSON: Yeah?

SUNSHINE: Right now. Please. Here it comes! Oh shit.

NELSON: Sonofabitch.

SUNSHINE: Oh, God, I rooned your life. Don't be mad.

NELSON: Son of a goddamn bitch. (*He gets a beer for himself. Beat.*)

SUNSHINE: Can I ask you a little favor?

NELSON: No, you can't have a beer!

SUNSHINE: My pudding?

NELSON: Go on.

SUNSHINE: Thank you. I can't eat it now.

NELSON: Why not?

SUNSHINE: You forgive me?

NELSON: Eat the goddamn pudding.

SUNSHINE: Oh, God, I besmirched our friendship.

NELSON: What's with you and besmirch?

SUNSHINE: That's today's word in my vocabulary builder. Hangs over the sink. When I brush my teeth I memorize the word of the day. Then you're supposed to work it into your conversation, so you retain it.

NELSON: Horseshit.

SUNSHINE: You always castigate me and make a brouhaha.

NELSON: Keep all your stuff together.

SUNSHINE: Don't worry. She's gonna call back. Why don't you call her?

NELSON: No.

SUNSHINE: You know she's there.

NELSON: It's up to her now.

SUNSHINE: How'd you meet her?

NELSON: Why?

SUNSHINE: I can tell if two people will stay together by when and where and how they met. I know, horseshit.

NELSON: Restaurant.

SUNSHINE: She a waitress?

NELSON: She was at the next table.

SUNSHINE: Check each other out?

NELSON: Gorgeous legs.

SUNSHINE: And you said something?

NELSON: No. She had a salad, goes to cut a cherry tomato with her fork, squirts right in my eye. Then she's in my face with her napkin, we laugh, we drink, three months later, we're married.

SUNSHINE: Oh, it's your wife. Separated?

NELSON: Yeah.

SUNSHINE: Her idea.

NELSON: Yeah.

SUNSHINE: So you're trying to patch things up.

NELSON: Yeah.

SUNSHINE: So why's she not calling back?

NELSON: Don't know.

SUNSHINE: What do you think?

NELSON: She puts things off to the last minute.

SUNSHINE: You reserved a room?

NELSON: I told you that.

SUNSHINE: One room.

NELSON: Yeah.

SUNSHINE: Same room? Big, big, big mistake. Big.

NELSON: She's my wife.

SUNSHINE: So no matter what happens, good or bad, that night you force her to get under the same sheets with you. Smart. Spring for another room. Not rooms next to each other neither. Rooms on different floors. You wanna blow her away? Different hotels. Then she gets the message—you're not there to get it wet. You're there to be with her. (*Beat.*)

NELSON: Not a bad idea. Where'd you read that, some woman's magazine?

SUNSHINE: No, I have a brain, thank you very much.

NELSON: Keep all your stuff together.

SUNSHINE: So what are you gonna say to her?

NELSON: Don't know.

SUNSHINE: You don't know. You don't know. What's that mean, you don't know?

NELSON: I thought I'd just play it by ear.

SUNSHINE: You gotta know what you're gonna say. Every second's gonna count.

NELSON: We got two days and a night.

SUNSHINE: In two days and a night you can't do a woman for the second time, 'cause she knows all your sneaky ways. S'pose this: S'pose she holds out till Sunday afternoon. S'pose it's time to take a taxi back to the airport and she still ain't said she'd come back. Now you're in the back seat of a taxi and the driver's listenin' and you see the airport ahead. You'll be makin' promises you can't keep just so you can tell your buddies you patched things up. You think you can just cough up for two tickets, rooms and champagne, and she's yours? That ain't enough! What are you gonna say, doc?

NELSON: Well, I have a general idea.

SUNSHINE: You're going to Albuquerque with a general idea? You wanna win her back or see America? She's a woman. You gotta say things. You have any idea what I'm talking about?

NELSON: No.

SUNSHINE: Most honest thing I ever heard you say.

NELSON: What do I say?

SUNSHINE: What do you love about her? (*Beat.*) You should know!

NELSON: I'm thinking.

SUNSHINE: You shouldn't have to think about it.

NELSON: What do you want, a grocery list?

SUNSHINE: You better take this more serious.

NELSON: I can't think what I'm gonna say until I'm there. On the spot. Then I know.

SUNSHINE: Okay. Okay. Okay. Picture this: You're holding hands, walking on the shores of New Mexico—sea gulls—waves breaking.

NELSON: The shores of what?

SUNSHINE: New Mexico.

NELSON: No ocean.

SUNSHINE: What's there?

NELSON: Desert. Cactuses. Snakes.

SUNSHINE: And you wonder why she don't call back?

NELSON: It's supposed to be beautiful.

SUNSHINE: You was never there? Is this a place where people go?

NELSON: It's halfway across the country. I didn't want to ask her to come back here, and I didn't want to go all the way there—

SUNSHINE: Yeah, yeah, you did one thing right. That's good.

NELSON: Don't torture me with all this shit now. Just tell me what to say.

SUNSHINE: First tell me what you was gonna say.

NELSON: That I miss her.

SUNSHINE: You can say that on the phone.

NELSON: I tried to see other women.

SUNSHINE: Good.

NELSON: But none of 'em worked out.

SUNSHINE: Fantastic.

NELSON: Except for this one nurse.

SUNSHINE: Excuse me. Don't say that.

NELSON: I worked double shifts to forget about her. If I can just get myself out the door, behind the wheel, I get lost for sixteen, eighteen, twenty hours. And not to come back here, I'd go to bars but I always meet the chick who's pissed off at some other guy. Finally I met a girl at Safeway while pickin' out a head of lettuce. We hit it off but she had a six-year-old kid who screamed for his daddy every time I went over. So that was that. So I just come home to sleep, but I can't sleep much, so, I don't know. Maybe I could have done better.

SUNSHINE: Done what better?

NELSON: You know.

SUNSHINE: No, I don't know.

NELSON: Okay. Maybe I could have loved Stephanie better.

SUNSHINE: Honest opinion?

NELSON: Please.

SUNSHINE: Horseshit.

NELSON: No matter what I said you were gonna say that.

SUNSHINE: You're right.

NELSON: Then why'd you let me go on?

SUNSHINE: To get it out of your system. (*Beat.*) I have listened to your diatribe and have given it a lot of cogitation. You want my advice?

NELSON: Yeah.

SUNSHINE: Don't say nothing.

NELSON: Nothing.

SUNSHINE: You know what nothing means? Nothing. You meet her, nothing comes out of your lips. You look at her. She says hello. Give her half a smile. You don't say nothing. Hug her. Tight. Make her tell you it's too tight. Nothing. In the taxi, you look at her. Her legs. Let her see you look at her legs. So how ya been? Good. How's work? Good. Up in the room. Nothing. When you make love to her, nothing. Nothing. (*Beat.*) But what's it matter, she didn't even call.

NELSON: She's playing her little games.

SUNSHINE: So you don't know if she's even gonna be on the jet.

NELSON: Right.

SUNSHINE: Why don't you just give her a call now.

NELSON: Her answering machine's on.

SUNSHINE: You left a message?

NELSON: Every day for two weeks. (*She makes a sound of surprise.*) What?

SUNSHINE: Two weeks. Fourteen messages. That's—disgusting.

NELSON: I know her. She'll call three o'clock this morning and say, "See you in Albuquerque."

SUNSHINE: But s'pose she don't call, you gonna get on the jet?

NELSON: Damn right.

SUNSHINE: I just got a very sickening feeling. Can I tell you something awful? She don't love you.

NELSON: Shut up. Just shut up.

SUNSHINE: I'm just saying it like a friend.

NELSON: You're not my friend, I don't want to be your friend, and I'm not interested in what you think. Got it? (*Beat.*) What makes you think that?

SUNSHINE: Fourteen messages. A sweet guy, Albuquerque, chocolate on the pillow, and she don't call back? This chick's hard, doc. Hard. And selfish. I hate selfish people.

NELSON: You don't even know her.

SUNSHINE: You was afraid she'd hear me in the room. Know why? She don't trust you with another woman alone. Know why? She don't give you the love you need, and she knows you're hungry for it, and if you're with another woman you might be tempted. See, I ain't jealous at all 'cause when I love a man, he has a hard time gettin' outta bed the next morning. I wring my man dry so he can't even think about another woman. 'M I right about her?

NELSON: Go on.

SUNSHINE: Am I?

NELSON: Go on.

SUNSHINE: I am.

NELSON: If you're so sure, why ask me?

SUNSHINE: 'Cause I love how your eyes shine when I ask ya. She ever tell ya 'bout your beautiful hands?

NELSON: No.

SUNSHINE: There she goes again.

NELSON: You're full of shit.

SUNSHINE: Know your problem?

NELSON: Yeah, I opened my door.

SUNSHINE: You think she's too good for you. Maybe she never took time to tell you what a man you are.

NELSON: You really think you know people.

SUNSHINE: At eyeballin' a man, I'm a Ph. fuckin' D.

NELSON: You're a good guesser, and that's it.

SUNSHINE: Sweetie, can I tell you something awful? It's over with her.

NELSON: Were you here before? The phone rang.

328 / *William Mastrosimone*

SUNSHINE: And it stopped. And it ain't ringin' now and it ain't gonna ring. It kills me to say this. (*Beat.*) She's got another guy.

NELSON: You're starting to piss me off.

SUNSHINE: I'm sorry.

NELSON: How do you know this?

SUNSHINE: 'Cause if she cared—

NELSON: Don't say "if"! How can you say she's got another guy?

SUNSHINE: 'Cause if she listened to her message machine, she'd hear the cry in your voice—

NELSON: —There's no cry in no voice—

SUNSHINE: —and if she heard that cry, she'd have to call you. Fact is—

NELSON: It's not a fact. It's a guess.

SUNSHINE: Fact is, she ain't been home in two weeks! The whore's been living over his house. And know something else? You don't love her.

NELSON: How do you know that?

SUNSHINE: You don't give a shit about that evil bitch.

NELSON: C'mon, c'mon, just shut up and tell me how you know this.

SUNSHINE: 'Cause when I call her names you don't defend her. (*Beat.*)

NELSON: Don't mean nothin'.

SUNSHINE: Oh no, no, no, sweetie. That's important. See, love, you just can't say it to yourself, so I'll say it for you. You don't love her. You're just lonely and need somebody.

NELSON: You're crazy. You know that?

SUNSHINE: Know what she is? She's a thing of cottage cheese in your life.

NELSON: *What?*

SUNSHINE: You know it's there in the back of the fridge for four months, and you're afraid to open it 'cause you know it's all pukey green with a smell that's gonna grab you by the throat. So you just leave it there and try and forget about it, and when it grows hair and starts to talk back to ya, ya gotta toss it. (*Beat.*)

NELSON: Toss it. Ever take your own advice? (*Beat.*)

SUNSHINE: First I try it on somebody else. Doc, this is my business. I see it every day. You can't never make somebody care. If they care, you know, and if they don't, you know. I think you know. (*Beat. Phone rings.*) Hey, Ph. fuckin' D. — hear that?

SUNSHINE: Shut up and have a good time. I'm jealous.

NELSON: Take care. (*Phone rings; SUNSHINE begins to leave.*)

SUNSHINE: I know I'll miss you.

NELSON: Yeah, yeah, yeah.

SUNSHINE: Don't forget me. (*Phone rings.*)

NELSON: Wait.

SUNSHINE: What?

NELSON: Have a seat. (*Phone rings.*)

SUNSHINE: Really?

NELSON: Quiet. (*Phone rings.*)

SUNSHINE: Wait! Play hard to get! Let it ring again! (*To telephone.*) Fry, baby, fry! (*To NELSON.*) Okay. Answer like you're mad.

NELSON: Shh! (*Answering.*) Yeah. Hey, was that you before? Shower. Where? Holy Jesus Christ. Mike, can't. Plane leaves seven-thirty in the morning. You try Al? Don? Sure, those folks don't answer their phones on their day off. Can't, can't. I'm not even packed yet. Don't give me no shit, Mike, I ain't been off for three months. Yeah, maybe I'll oversleep one day and the world'll fold up. (*Hangs up.*)

SUNSHINE: Bad problem?

NELSON: You know, a lot of people go through life thinking somebody owes 'em something, but they don't know who. They take one look at me and think *I'm* the fuckin' guy.

SUNSHINE: 'Least you know it wasn't her before.

NELSON: Goddammit.

SUNSHINE: How bad?

NELSON: Bad.

SUNSHINE: People die?

NELSON: Yeah.

SUNSHINE: How many?

NELSON: They don't know yet.

SUNSHINE: Car?

NELSON: Airplane.

SUNSHINE: Crashed?

NELSON: —Small plane tried to land in a parking lot. Rammed into a pizza joint.

SUNSHINE: God! Why're you just sitting here?

NELSON: It's my weekend off.

SUNSHINE: People are dying out there.

NELSON: Happens every day.

SUNSHINE: Don't you think you might save one person?

NELSON: I am saving one person. Me.

SUNSHINE: I can't believe you.

NELSON: It's a half-hour away. Most of 'em died on impact. It just took off from an airport, so it was full of fuel. Know what that means? Dental records won't help. It's a janitorial job.

SUNSHINE: I thought you was some kind of hero in a white suit who went around saving people.

NELSON: No more. After forty hours give me a paycheck and call me Mr. Nobody.

SUNSHINE: I think that's pretty disgusting.

NELSON: You in a booth with jerkoffs, don't tell me about disgusting.

SUNSHINE: No wonder the world's screwed up.

NELSON: Because of me. What happens when you're in the wrong mood and screw up at work? The creep don't get off? When I'm in the wrong mood people die. Tell you what: You worry about your conscience, I'll worry about mine, okay?

SUNSHINE: No, no, it don't work that way. That's your job. It's your job to go save people. You can't hack your job, quit.

NELSON: I quit every night and go back the next morning because it's all I know how to do. Know what I did today? I sutured lips back on a face. Delivered a baby. Plugged up a bullet hole with gauze. Taped a piece of skull on a kid who took a spill on his motorcycle. Pulled a little girl out of a swimming pool. And while on a bullshit call—a jerk with a splinter under her fingernail—we missed an old man who choked to death on a fish bone. That's what this job says to you every fucking day: "You think you handled yesterday? Wait till you see today." And I don't have any more to give today.

SUNSHINE: Little girl drown?

NELSON: No.

SUNSHINE: Why was she swimming alone?

NELSON: Her bicycle chain caught her jeans. Tumbles into the swimming pool. Bike dragged her right to the bottom. Never had a chance to cry out for Mommy. They always say the same thing: "I just went in the house for a second. We were gonna drain that pool next weekend." So you get there. You find signs of life. Evacuate the lungs. I.V. 'em. Throw the drug box at 'em. Every E.M.T. trick in the book and some you invented. You know how to save a life. You see a light flicker in the eyes and you work her hard and you keep working her hard even though you know she's been ten minutes without 02 and the brain damage is massive, massive, but you keep working her and working her because you are there to save a life and goddammit them young lungs snap back into action and you get a pulse and her eyes light up and she pukes and coughs and cries like the day she was born and people cheer and hug you and thank you ten million times. You're a hero. You saved a cabbage that looks something like a six-year-old girl who ain't never going to ride that bicycle again. Ain't ever going to run and play with her little playmates again. And her family's going broke for the rest of their lives to keep her lungs inflated. And when it's sunny, they'll strap her in a highchair on the front porch so she can watch other kids playing and she's there swinging her arms and drooling down her chin making sounds nobody understands. Or wants to. You've seen all this before. And no matter how many years you got on the job, none of it makes sense until it hits you one day you might do more good if, under pressure, you miscalculated the morphine dosage, put her in the back of the ambulance, let her mother hug her one last time, and make sure you catch every fucking red light from there to the emergency room so she's D.O.A. (*Beat.*) I was finished today when I had to pry her fingers off her doll. (*He gets a beer. Beat. He gets one for her. SUNSHINE hides her face, weeps mutely.*)

SUNSHINE: What was her name—the little girl?

NELSON: Why?

SUNSHINE: So I could light a candle for her.

NELSON: Don't remember. (*Beat.*) What's your real name?

SUNSHINE: Why?

NELSON: 'Cause nobody should have a name that's a weather report.

SUNSHINE: Well, Nelson, nobody should have a first name that's a last name. Chrys Ann.

NELSON: I never heard that before.

SUNSHINE: My real father ran away when he got my mother pregnant. When I was born, he sent her a letter on a Howard Johnson's napkin, "I love you, but I won't be a good father," and sent her a bouquet of chrysanthemums. So she called me Chrys Ann.

332 / *William Mastrosimone*

NELSON: Chrys Ann.

SUNSHINE: Yeah.

NELSON: Chrys—an—themum.

SUNSHINE: Yeah.

NELSON: How'd you get Sunshine?

SUNSHINE: Ara took one look at me and said, "Sunshine." She gives all the girls names. She's always there for us. If you get a crazy and ring the alarm, she don't just send the bouncers. She comes with 'em. She really cares. That's why I feel bad when I don't call and tell her I'm late.

NELSON: I have an idea. Why don't you use my phone?

SUNSHINE: I was afraid to ask. (Dials phone.) Ara? It's me. Phone booth. That's why I'm calling. I was wondering if I could take off tonight. No, I'm not drinking. You call him? He said that? (Cups phone, to NELSON.) She always figures it out. (To Ara.) Ara? Ara? Can I say something, please? I know you got a business to run, but can't my regulars see Sherry or Barbara? I know my name's on the sign—Ara—please listen? I would never do anything to hurt you either, but—Okay. Okay. Bye-bye. (Hangs up.) Everybody's asking for me. They all miss me.

NELSON: Creeps are people too.

SUNSHINE: We can't both go on strike. What'll all the needy people do? I'm like you. If I can get myself in the front door I'm okay, 'cause then the guys look and the music gets me, and I remember why I was put on this earth. I really appreciate—

NELSON: Yeah, yeah, yeah.

SUNSHINE: You take care of yourself.

NELSON: You, too.

SUNSHINE: Can I come visit you sometime?

NELSON: What for?

SUNSHINE: What for? "What for?" says the ambulance man. 'Cause I wanna know how you are. Won't you wonder whatever became of me?

NELSON: Yeah, I guess.

SUNSHINE: You guess. I'll be thinking of you.

NELSON: Okay.

SUNSHINE: Okay. You're funny, Can I call Jerry? I need a ride.

NELSON: I don't understand you.

SUNSHINE: He's five good days a month. How many good days you got a month? Talk me out of it.

NELSON: Talk yourself out of it.

SUNSHINE: Can't you talk nice before I go?

NELSON: Sure. Have a nice life with your creep.

SUNSHINE: He knows all my little bullshit ways. Anybody else would think I'm crazy. You know what I mean? (*Beat.*)

NELSON: No.

SUNSHINE: (*She dials; to JERRY.*) It's me. Phone booth . . . where I jumped out the van . . . I just called to say I'm goin' to work. Can you pick me up? . . . What do you have to do first? (*Beat.*) You can't cook. Boil water for what, spaghetti? Seafood? Jerry. Jerry. (*To NELSON.*) He's holding CLAWS over the boiling water. (*To JERRY.*) Jerry. Yes, that was really a doctor. I don't know what hospital. I just walked in. Why'd you call all the hospitals? Why can't you just believe me? Don't! Don't! Okay! I'll tell you the truth! I knocked on somebody's door and they let me use the phone . . . Did you really? Jerry, really? (*She hangs up calmly.*)

NELSON: Did he?

SUNSHINE: Yeah. And he thinks I'm gonna call back and ask him to pick me up ... But this time I don't care. He's just another person in the world.

NELSON: What can I do?

SUNSHINE: Call the police.

NELSON: What do I say?

SUNSHINE: He dropped my lobster in boiling hot water.

NELSON: That's not against the law.

SUNSHINE: Don't laugh at me.

NELSON: I'm not, honest, I'm not.

SUNSHINE: I loved that crustacean. Sometimes I couldn't sleep, and Claws is sleeping next the mermaid on the rock, and I'd press my face against the aquarium near the bubble maker and pretend I'm a lobster, smooshin' my lips on the glass like this, and Claws would see me and come towards me with his black antennas whipping around and his black eyes all happy and rolling back and forth, and he'd come and try and touch me, honest to God, through the glass, and I'd go around the other side and he'd come towards me there and keep trying to touch me with his big claws. (*Beat. She breaks down.*)

NELSON: There's a place down the street, Captain Jake's. You walk in the they got a big tank with a lot of, you know, lobsters. We could go over and pick one out.

SUNSHINE: You would do that?

NELSON: I think they're open till midnight.

SUNSHINE: You would really do that?

NELSON: Well, yeah. I know Jake. He'd give me a break on one.

SUNSHINE: It's not the same. Claws was my anniversary lobster. But thanks. (*Beat. She hides her face.*)

NELSON: Before you, Claws had a miserable life. Just another lobster crawling in the muck on the bottom of the vicious ocean. Eating sour seawead alone in a cold, dark, loveless life. One day when he was feeling lower than whale shit, he jumped in a lobster trap just to get the hell out of that cruel world. Ended up in a crueller one, with a thick red rubber band around his big claw in a grocery store. On ice. Behind glass. Human housewives strolled by. Hundreds of 'em. And Claws knew alls they wanted was to get into his shell. They didn't love him. They only loved him for his tail. Next thing he knew he was rolled up in butcher's paper with some other stiff, what's-his-name—

SUNSHINE: Bug Eyes.

NELSON: —tossed in a shopping cart, thrown on a conveyor belt, manhandled by a checkout girl, thrown into a bag with candles and a stick of butter and lemons. A lobster nightmare. They dumped him in a bathtub, forced him to listen to the sounds of forks and knives and plates set on the table. Next thing he knew, a pair of tongs reached in and plucked him and his pal out of the tub and he thought this was it. The end. But he got put in a tank, not a pot. Not boiling water. Nice water. Like the ocean. But better. Regular eats came out of nowhere. A mermaid blowin' bubbles day and night. The big time. And every now and then the only nice human he ever met would swoosh her lucious lips on the glass and he'd kiss her back. He finally found love in lobster heaven. Maybe the best life a lobster ever had.

SUNSHINE: You never had kids?

NELSON: No.

SUNSHINE: You should. And tell them stories.

NELSON: You have somewhere to go?

SUNSHINE: Ara's. She loves when I let her take care of me. She lives in a mansion.

NELSON: You can't be a guest forever.

SUNSHINE: I'll burn that bridge when I come to it. Can I ask a favor?

NELSON: Use the phone.

SUNSHINE: I'm all scuzzy and sweaty. Can I take a shower here? I always go in clean.

NELSON: Help yourself.

SUNSHINE: You're too sweet. (*She goes in the bathroom, flings her clothes in the doorway for NELSON to see. Everything. From offstage.*) Can I borrow something to wear?

NELSON: Like what?

SUNSHINE: (*Offstage.*) Sweats?

NELSON: Yeah.

SUNSHINE: (*Offstage.*) What about underwear?

NELSON: Mine?

SUNSHINE: (*Offstage.*) I don't mind, if you don't. I can't put old clothes back on after a shower.

NELSON: Boxers or classic briefs?

SUNSHINE: (*Offstage.*) I like briefs. More support (*Beat.*) If the open door makes you nervous, close it. (*Shower on.*) Ooooh.

NELSON: I forgot to tell you—that water could scald you.

SUNSHINE: (*Offstage.*) No, good shower . . . the water pounds you … hard.

NELSON: Best thing about this hole.

SUNSHINE: (*Offstage.*) Makes my skin all red . . . makes me feel so clean . . . I could stay in here for hours . . . If I had kids, I'd want 'em with a guy like you . . . And have dishes with flowers and forks and spoons that match . . . (*Shower off.*) . . . You got a towel?

NELSON: On the shelf?

SUNSHINE: (*Offstage.*) Where?

NELSON: There's only one shelf.

SUNSHINE: (*Offstage.*) I got soap in my eye. Show me?

NELSON: Where you got the other one.

SUNSHINE: (*Offstage.*) You're some kind of man.

NELSON: How's that?

SUNSHINE: (*Offstage.*) Most any other guy would've tried to pop me by now. Can I wear your robe?

NELSON: You're probably in it already. (*She appears suddenly, wet hair up in a towel.*)

SUNSHINE: I am!

NELSON: Who is this?

SUNSHINE: Me. Stop lookin' at me like that.

NELSON: You should be walkin' barefoot down a dusty road in Oklahoma.

SUNSHINE: Get out.

NELSON: Chewin' on a weed.

SUNSHINE: Don't look at me. My hair's straight, no makeup.

NELSON: You don't need all that crap.

SUNSHINE: Ara likes us to do it up big.

NELSON: Ara's full of shit. It hides you.

SUNSHINE: Men like it.

NELSON: Some men.

SUNSHINE: When I come visit I won't wear it. Good robe.

NELSON: Old.

SUNSHINE: That's what makes it good.

NELSON: I live in it.

SUNSHINE: She give it to you?

NELSON: For our first Christmas.

SUNSHINE: She probably got it on sale. Has a scent.

NELSON: Needs a wash.

SUNSHINE: No, a good scent. Yours. I like it. You got a comb? (*He gets a comb.*) Stop lookin' at me like that.

NELSON: Men look at you all night long. Why can't I?

SUNSHINE: You're a gentleman. (*Beat.*) You're welcome.

NELSON: I'm not—that.

SUNSHINE: You're a virgin, huh? Not like that, but you never had a real thing in your life.

NELSON: Another one of those things you just know about me?

SUNSHINE: No. Takes one to know one. (*She struggles with a tangle in her hair. NELSON takes the comb gently, tries to undo the tangle.*) Nobody ever did that 'cept my mother when we lived in a shack on the beach, and spiders came in the hole in the floor and crawled up the walls in my roon and I cried and she'd come in, take off her shoe, whack 'em all, and the wall was full of spider-smackin' stains, and she'd brush my hair till I wasn't afraid no more and I'd fall asleep. (*He goes to kiss her but she turns away and he misses. Beat.*)

NELSON: You're gonna be late to work.

SUNSHINE: You askin' me to go?

NELSON: No.

SUNSHINE: Then shut up. How can I leave you when it's rainin' and I know you're just gonna sit here playin' music that makes ya wanna jump outta window waitin' for her to call?

NELSON: Tell you the truth, I can't see myself get on that plane in the morning.

SUNSHINE: 'Cause of me?

NELSON: No, no, no.

SUNSHINE: 'Cause of me, 'cause of me, 'cause of me. I rooned your dream.

NELSON: If that's the way you want to rig it up, go on.

SUNSHINE: I just couldn't keep my mouth shut. I had to go diggin' and pokin'. Nelson, I don't wanna break nobody up.

NELSON: We're already broke up.

SUNSHINE: But you had a chance to be happy. Oh God, I am such a slut. I was almost out the door, but nooooooo, I had to hang onto you a few minutes more. And now look what I did.

NELSON: Is this where I'm supposed to contradict you?

SUNSHINE: No.

NELSON: Sorry to ruin your little tragedy, but you made me see things. Two weeks I'm waiting. Two weeks I'm dying here. Why the fuck don't she call? I take her shit like it's my job. Seven years I wake up next to her wondering what mood she's in so I could know what mood I'm supposed to be in. For one, two, three, four, five, six, seven years. And if I couldn't figure the right mood, I got two weeks of her silence for one, two, three, four, five, six, seven years.

SUNSHINE: You loved her.

NELSON: If that's what it is, give me rotten fish. (*The phone rings. He doesn't answer it.*)

SUNSHINE: It's her. (*Phone rings.*) Aren't you gonna answer it? (*Phone rings.*) Two weeks, Nelson. You only know me two minutes. (*Phone rings.*) Maybe she feels bad. (*Phone rings.*) Wants to make it all up to you. (*Phone rings.*) Give her a chance?

NELSON: I can't stand pink champagne. (*He takes her in his arms, kisses her til the phone stops ringing.*)

SUNSHINE: Shit.

NELSON: What?

SUNSHINE: Now I have to confess this.

NELSON: C'mere.

SUNSHINE: You know, Nelson, maybe you should get on the plane. I didn't count the rings but it was alot--that shows she's

338 / *William Mastrosimone*

got a conscious. You're a deep guy. You think alot. You save people. You go to Albuquerque. Maybe I'm just, you know, a five minute pudding, hello-goodbye. Be honest. What's that look in your eyes. Really be honest. Tell me.

NELSON: Let's take our clothes off.

SUNSHINE: I'm scared.

NELSON: Of what?

SUNSHINE: I'll never meet anybody like you again. I don't want it to be over when I leave.

NELSON: Remember the advice you gave me? Why don't we just say nothing. (*Beat. He takes her in his arms.*)

SUNSHINE: I wish I had a glass in between us like at work 'cause then I could be myself. (*Phone rings.*) She wants you back. (*Phone rings.*) And I don't blame her. (*Phone rings.*) Pick it up and tell her *something* before I go crazy! (*Phone rings.*)

NELSON: I don't have anything to say to her. (*Phone rings.*)

SUNSHINE: Then tell her that! (*Phone rings.*)

NELSON: I'm sick of caring about her. (*Phone rings.*)

SUNSHINE: Tell *her*! (*Phone rings.*) I'll wait outside. (*Phone rings.*)

NELSON: Stay. (*Phone rings. NELSON picks up.*) Yeah? ... No Sunshine here ... I think you've got the wrong number, pal ... Yeah, that's my number, but there's no Sunshine lives here .... Yeah, I'm sure ... (*Beat. He hangs up.*) The creep. He said, Well leave her a message. Get home.

SUNSHINE: Your number listed?

NELSON: Yeah.

SUNSHINE: Your name on the mailbox?

NELSON: Yeah.

SUNSHINE: He looked it up in the phone book.

NELSON: Would he come here?

SUNSHINE: No.

NELSON: Sure?

SUNSHINE: He's a coward.

NELSON: With a gun.

SUNSHINE: He can't shoot for shit.

NELSON: Now I feel better.

SUNSHINE: He goes for the police exam every January and fails. He's a joke. See his glasses? Cokebottles. He's legally blind. It's always somethin'. Now you're all torqued. Don't let him roon it for us. He won't come here. Let's just listen to the rain ... and the quiet between the drops. You think I'd stay if I thought he'd make trouble for you? Oh God, I'm losing you. Nelson? (*Beat.*) I'll tell you a secret if you tell me one. (*Beat.*) I ain't had love for over a year now. Jerry can't. I could have ten million men if I was like that, and Jerry wouldn't care if I went out and got satisfied. I mean he'd care but he expects me to. And I don't even when I'm dyin'. 'Cause I'm not a flooze. I'm not gonna be my mother livin' in a trailer eatin' Oreos and drinkin' beer and watchin' Wheel of Fortune alone. I wanna be in love with one man. And if there's a problem I wanna go to Albuquerque and make it all better. (*Beat.*) There, I made a fool out of myself.

NELSON: No, no.

SUNSHINE: I told you a secret; now you tell me one.

NELSON: I don't have one.

SUNSHINE: Be honest 'cause I know all about you. You know I do. I know how to love you. How to take care of you. All you have to do is let me. And I can make your puppy bark. (*He laughs.*) You have a beautiful smile. I'm gonna study you, find out what makes you happy so I can see you smile everyday. Tell me how I can make you happy now. (*Silence.*) Tell me. (Silence.) I know you've got some little secret … Tell me … (*Silence.*) I'm your … All yours. (*Silence. She opens the top of her robe to him, NOT TO AUDIENCE.*) See anything you like? (*Silence.*) You're a pretty tough customer.

NELSON: This what you do for customers?

SUNSHINE: It's make-a-b'lieve with them. Is it hot in here or is it me?

NELSON: Why don't you get dressed and go do this for your customers.

SUNSHINE: Oh, God, Nelson, I'm sorry.

NELSON: That's all. Goodbye.

SUNSHINE: Sweetie—

NELSON: I don't wanna hear it.

SUNSHINE: I'm really sorry. I say I love you to a hundred men a night. And when I go home and say it to him it don't mean nothin'. And in my dreams I wake up wet in the middle of the night and I'm happy 'cause I know it's all locked up inside of me. I'm savin' it for the right guy. You made me feel somethin' again.

NELSON: This part of your routine? I don't know. I can't tell. (*She*

goes to slap him. He takes her by the arm. Beat.)
SUNSHINE: Go 'head. I can take a punch (*He let her go. She breaks down, exits into the bathroom to dress.)*
NELSON: You okay? (*Beat.*) You wanna beer? (*Beat.*) I'm sorry this happened. (*SUNSHINE comes out dressed in his sweats. She puts on her coat and collects her things.*) You need a ride somewhere? (*She stops, her back to NELSON, starts to go.*) Here. Take this umbrella. (*SUNSHINE starts to break down again. She leaves without the umbrella. NELSON goes to the door, watches her walk away in the rain. Beat. He closes and locks the door, turns on Frank Sinatra, puts the bowl of pudding in the sink. Beat. He tastes it. Beat. He sits on the couch, finds her hair clip, looks at it as the lights fade to black.)*

Scene 3

This time we are in the booth seeing ROBBY from SUNSHINE's point of view. ROBBY's drawn face is pressed against the glass, his hand in his underwear. He's absolutely still, exhausted. Beat.

ROBBY: I can't.
SUNSHINE: Is it me?
ROBBY: Yes!
SUNSHINE: I'm sorry.
ROBBY: You're trying to make me hate you so I'll go in another booth. Don't tell me no.
SUNSHINE: C'mere.
ROBBY: Don't look at me!
SUNSHINE: I'm sorry.
ROBBY: You always stare at me!
SUNSHINE: Robby, love, you was here Thursday, Friday and twice tonight . . . Don't you think Killer needs a day off?
ROBBY: I want to — but I can't.
SUNSHINE: I know, I know.
ROBBY: No, you don't. You don't know.
SUNSHINE: Let's just talk.
ROBBY: No.
SUNSHINE: Touch heads.
ROBBY: No.
SUNSHINE: C'mere, baby. (*She presses her forehead against the glass. ROBBY touches his forehead to hers on the other side.*) I love you.

(*He hits the glass, startles her.*)

ROBBY: I don't want to hear that shit anymore. I'm dying over here and you just look at me. I'd go through this glass even if I knew it would cut me to pieces! (*He hits the glass.*)

SUNSHINE: Babe, don't do that, okay? (*The red flasher goes off.*)

ROBBY: Shit!

SUNSHINE: You staying, love? (*He puts money in the slot.*)

ROBBY: I'm overdrawn on my account. My old man wants to know why I spent two months' money in two weeks. On you. You. Now how do I eat for the rest of the month? Do you hear me?

SUNSHINE: Yeah, Robby, I do, I do. What can I do for you?

ROBBY: You know.

SUNSHINE: We have to do it here.

ROBBY: Sit. Cross your legs. Fix your hair. That's not how I like it. You must have me mixed up with somebody else.

SUNSHINE: No, honey—

ROBBY: Shut the fuck up. Stand up. Turn around. Sideways. Look at me. Don't smile! I didn't say smile! I don't want a smile when I'm dying! I never want to see a smile on your face again! (*Beat.*) You did that to make fun of me, didn't you? Don't say no. I wish I never met you. Can I have a picture of you?

SUNSHINE: I don't have any.

ROBBY: Can I take one of you?

SUNSHINE: Why, love? You can see me here anytime.

ROBBY: I need to have something . . . I told my friends I met the most beautiful girl in the world . . . That she loves me . . . That we have wild times . . . I didn't mention that there's this (*He hits the glass.*) between us . . . They think it's for real. I love you . . . I go all day thinking about you . . . Can't study, can't think of anything else . . . Flunked a chem exam . . . Knew the stuff cold …You could save me if you want to, but you don't want to . . . Just once . . . Just once without the glass between . . . I promise I won't do anything. (*She laughs. He hits the glass, striking at her.*) Don't laugh at me!

SUNSHINE: Don't do that. I wasn't laughing.

ROBBY: You laughed.

SUNSHINE: C'mere, you.

ROBBY: Please?

SUNSHINE: Let's try once more. (*She puts her feet against the glass.*) Make me happy. (*He takes out a flash camera, takes a picture.*) No!

ROBBY: I need something.

SUNSHINE: No!

ROBBY: A normal picture. Just stand there. Don't hide your face.

SUNSHINE: You listen to me, you little bastard! You open that camera right now and expose that film.

ROBBY: I need it.

SUNSHINE: Open that camera.

ROBBY: You'll meet me?

SUNSHINE: No. Open it.

ROBBY: Bye.

SUNSHINE: I push this alarm button, five bone-breakers'll meet you at the front door. Open that camera now.

ROBBY: It's just a picture.

SUNSHINE: No.

ROBBY: It's just for me.

SUNSHINE: You want me to push the alarm?

ROBBY: You'd do that?

SUNSHINE: You're lucky there's a glass between us, you loon, you creep, you jackoff. Take out the film!

ROBBY: I can't believe you'd do that.

SUNSHINE: Believe it. (*He opens the camera, pulls out the film, unravels it.*)

ROBBY: I really really love you.

SUNSHINE: No. You don't love me and I don't love you and it's all horseshit! Now get out of here and don't come back. (*Exit ROBBY. The screen comes down. She breaks down. SUNSHINE picks up the phone, presses a button. Beat.*) Ara? I have to go home ... I'm not gonna make it through the night. The screen goes up and I can't think of nothin' to say to my clients ... Ara, I can't stand to look at another man ... Can I at least take a break? (*The screen starts to go up.*) Wait, I have a customer ... I'll call you after this one. (*The slow screen reveals legs, chest, and then face of NELSON. He's in uniform and cap. Beat.*) Nobody called 911.

NELSON: How ya doin'?

SUNSHINE: Good.

NELSON: Good.

SUNSHINE: How you doin'?

NELSON: Good. What's this, a jackoff convention? So how's business?

SUNSHINE: Good.

NELSON: Good. You just sent a kid outta here crying.

SUNSHINE: Breaks my heart.

NELSON: We're on the way back from the hospital; saw your name on the sign out front. I was surprised you came back to work. (*Beat.*) Stinks in here.

SUNSHINE: Yeah, well, you know. Take any trips lately, doc?

NELSON: Just here.

SUNSHINE: Not Albuquerque?

NELSON: No.

SUNSHINE: Liar.

NELSON: Didn't go.

SUNSHINE: I thought you'd go and she'd be there and you fall in love again—

NELSON: Unhuh.

SUNSHINE: She call?

NELSON: Yeah. (*Beat.*) You were right . . . about all that. (*The red flasher goes off.*)

SUNSHINE: Oh shit.

NELSON: What's this? What I say wrong?

SUNSHINE: Put some money in the slot! Dollar a minute.

NELSON: We're good for five minutes. My partner's waiting in the ambulance outside; still on call. (*Beat.*) You got a break?

SUNSHINE: Not for a while.

NELSON: So how ya doin'?

SUNSHINE: Good.

NELSON: So you alright?

SUNSHINE: Me, yeah.

NELSON: How come I don't believe you?

SUNSHINE: I'm okay.

NELSON: Sure?

SUNSHINE: Yeah.

NELSON: That's good.

SUNSHINE: I'm good.

NELSON: No you're not.

SUNSHINE: I know.

NELSON: What are you, all besmirched from this place?

SUNSHINE: Shut up.

NELSON: Let's go outside and talk.

SUNSHINE: Talk here.

NELSON: Can't talk here. Feel like I'm buyin' a tropical fish.

Where's that door go?

SUNSHINE: Hallway.

NELSON: There's an exit door out back. Meet you outside that door.

SUNSHINE: There's an alarm on the door. Talk here.

NELSON: I can't talk to you with glass in between.

SUNSHINE: Works for other people.

NELSON: When you get off?

SUNSHINE: Four a.m.

NELSON: Jerry pick you up?

SUNSHINE: Jerry who?

NELSON: You at Ara's?

SUNSHINE: I live like a queen.

NELSON: But not a queen who can step out and talk to somebody when she wants. (*Let the actors overlap the following lines.*)

SUNSHINE: Don't upset me, okay?

NELSON: I didn't come here—

SUNSHINE: 'Cause I can't be—

NELSON: To upset you—

SUNSHINE: Upset when clients—

NELSON: All I said was—

SUNSHINE: Come in the booth—

NELSON: Can we talk somewheres else? (*End the overlap. Beat.*)

SUNSHINE: What can I do for you? (*Beat.*)

NELSON: What do I get for my money? (*Beat.*)

SUNSHINE: Anything you want. (*Beat.*)

NELSON: That a raincoat?

SUNSHINE: Yeah.

NELSON: Put that on. (*Beat. She puts on the raincoat.*)

SUNSHINE: I thought you came to see me.

NELSON: I did. Face the door.

SUNSHINE: I can't do this with you. Ever since I met you, everybody says you got the flu or something? 'Cause you rooned me. You're the only man in my whole life who wasn't all over me. I didn't want to leave 'cause I wanted to feel that way the rest of my life. I couldn't leave you 'cause I knew I would never feel that beautiful again. (*Beat.*)

NELSON: Face the door. (*Beat.*)

SUNSHINE: Sometimes I get real creatures from the deep come in here and gross me out, but you're the lowest creepy crawly most disgusting piece of shit that ever slimed up my booth ... name it bug ... My speciality's a bad girl you can push around. That make you feel like a man? I been workin' at it since I'm four and a half years old. I'm a trash bucket for everybody to dump their junk in. What's your disease, bug? I'm all yours. My body'll do anything you say. Ain't that a kick? Just don't ever ask me what I'm really thinkin' 'cause that could kill ya. That's mine. Name it bug.

NELSON: Open the door ... Meet me in the parking lot ... (*Beat.*)

SUNSHINE: And go where? Your house? For how long? The night or till you get sick of me?

NELSON: What about the train station? You said someday you're gonna just get on a train and go. If not you can stay in the booth till you're one of those played out zombies they stick in the back room dancing for dollars.

SUNSHINE: What's it to you?

NELSON: I'm here, ain't I?

SUNSHINE: And what do you want from me?

NELSON: A postcard.

SUNSHINE: Don't give me that shit. Nobody does nothin' 'less they get somethin' back.

NELSON: I need a lot of things in my life. A pain in the ass ain't one of 'em.

SUNSHINE: You sweet-talking bastard. (*The red flasher goes off.*) Your time's up.

NELSON: So's yours. I'll wait for you outside. I hope you come. But if you're not there in two minutes, have a nice life, Chrys Ann. (*NELSON touches the glass where her face is. Beat. the screen comes down and Nelson goes out of view. SUNSHINE sits in anguished silence. Beat. She hears another client enter the booth. She hears coins drop in the slot. Exit SUNSHINE, leaving the door open, as the screen rises and ROBBY presses his tear-streaked face against the glass.*)

ROBBY: Sunshine? Sunshine?

END